In addition to great archival assistance, I want to thank my secretary, Mary Lou Stephens, as well as Michelle Smithheart and Melissa Latham, for typing the seemingly endless stack of Annie Armstrong letters. In all, these women typed five file-crates full of letters. Mary Lou literally wore some of the letters off her keyboard. A mere thank-you cannot begin to express my gratitude for their commitment to this project. Additionally, I owe Josh Williams a special debt of gratitude. Josh wrote a special program that enabled me to search the letters by keywords. His help was invaluable. In a different vein, Jeff Ray offered much needed technical assistance with vital background material and my friends and colleagues, Dr. David Beck and Dr. Michael Travers tendered valuable assistance with proofreading. Thanks, guys.

Once Mercer University Press published *Send the Light: Lottie Moon's Letters and Other Writings*, it seemed only fitting to do a companion volume for Annie Armstrong's letters. Thus, this volume has allowed me the privilege of again working with Dr. Marc Jolley, Marsha Luttrell, and the staff at Mercer University Press. Thanks, Marc, for all you have done to bring these letters into print.

Finally, our son, David, helped Josh with the computerized aspects of this project. Having grown up in an historian's home, David will be the first to tell you that he would rather be a programmer. My wife, Johnnie, provided much needed assistance in the details necessary for making this manuscript publishable. As she proofread, organized, and re-organized material, she developed a deep appreciation for Armstrong's work for WMU. Thank you, sweetheart, for your labor of love with "Miss Annie" and many other things too numerous to mention.

Keith Harper
Wake Forest, North Carolina
1 August 2003

RESCUE THE PERISHING

Rescue the Perishing

Selected Correspondence of Annie Armstrong

Edited by

Keith Harper

Mercer University Press

Macon, Georgia

ISBN   0-86554-843-9 (hardback)   MUP/H603
        0-86554-870-6   MUP/P279

© 2004 Mercer University Press
1400 Coleman Avenue
Macon, Georgia 31207

First Edition.

Grateful acknowledgment is due the following for permission to use and quote from the letters contained herein:
    —Letters from the J. M. Frost Collection, the E. L. Compere Collection, and the Una Roberts Lawrence Collection are used by permission of the Southern Baptist Historical Library and Archives, Nashville, Tennessee, hereafter noted as SBHLA.
    —Letters from the H. A. Tupper Collection and R. J. Willingham Collection are used by permission of the International Mission Board of the Southern Baptist Convention, Richmond, Virginia, hereafter noted as IMB Archives.
    —Letters from the Annie Armstrong Collection and other WMU materials are used by permission of the Woman's Missionary Union, SBC, Birmingham, Alabama, hereafter noted as WMU Archives.
    —Letters for the E. Y. Mullins Collection are used by permission of the Archives of James P. Boyce Library, The Southern Baptist Theological Seminary, Louisville, Kentucky.

Library of Congress Cataloging-in-Publication Data

Armstrong, Annie.
[Correspondence. Selections]
 Rescue the perishing : selected correspondence of Annie Armstrong /
edited by Keith Harper.-- 1st ed.
    p. cm.
Includes bibliographical references and index.
 ISBN 0-86554-843-9 (hardcover : alk. paper)—ISBN 0-86554-870-6 (pbk. : alk. paper)
1. Armstrong, Annie--Correspondence. 2. Baptists—United States—
History. 3. Southern Baptist Convention—History. I. Harper, Keith, 1957-
II. Title.
BX6495.A67A4 2004
286'.1'092—dc22

                                                        2003026711

Dedicated to the memory of Annie Walker Armstrong

CONTENTS

Acknowledgments   viii

Introduction   1

Chapter 1   6

"I am not surprised that I occasionally become 'Kaflumexed'":

    The Annie Armstrong that Few People Know

Chapter 2   70

"Line upon line, precept upon precept":

    Annie Armstrong and the Work of WMU

Chapter 3   179

"If Miss Heck will not resign I *must*":

    Annie Armstrong and Controversy

Chapter 4   240

"I am standing for two principles":

    Annie Armstrong and The Training School for Women

    Missionaries

Chapter 5   308

"It is not my purpose to become an idler":

    Annie Armstrong's Life Beyond Southern Baptist Missions

Appendix 1   353

Appendix 2   357

Select Bibliography   363

Index   365

ACKNOWLEDGMENTS

If confession is good for the soul, it is time for me to confess. I had no idea how large this project would be when I first started it. As Corresponding Secretary of Woman's Missionary Union, Auxiliary to the Southern Baptist Convention from 1888 to 1906, Annie Armstrong wrote thousands of letters to a host of individuals. This volume is barely a sampling of the more than 2,500 letters I found in various Southern Baptist repositories.

I should also confess that I could not have completed this project alone. Happily, it is now my pleasure to recognize those individuals without whose assistance this project would never have been completed. First, I am deeply indebted to Bill Sumners at the Southern Baptist Historical Library and Archives, Nashville, Tennessee. Bill, along with Jean Forbis and Taffey Hall, cheerfully provided access to the J. M. Frost Papers, the E. L. Compere Papers and the Una Roberts Lawrence Papers. Likewise, Edie Jeter, archivist for the International Mission Board of the Southern Baptist Convention, Richmond, Virginia—and one of my favorite partners in crime—granted access to the H. A. Tupper Papers, and the R. J. Willingham Papers, while the International Mission Board granted permission to use the letters. Amy Cook, archivist for the Woman's Missionary Union, Auxiliary to the Southern Baptist Convention, Birmingham, Alabama, offered timely assistance with documents, pictures, and other unreasonable requests under difficult circumstances. She also made me laugh, which I greatly appreciate. Finally, I commend Dr. Sean Lucas, archivist for the James P. Boyce Library at the Southern Baptist Theological Seminary, Louisville, Kentucky. Unlike Amy, Sean did not make me laugh, but he did keep me apprised of the "skinny" on our favorite college basketball team, and he provided several interesting letters from Annie Armstrong to E. Y. Mullins. Closer to home, Dr. Shawn Madden, Librarian at Southeastern Baptist Theological Seminary, Wake Forest, North Carolina, provided access to whatever I needed to complete this project. Everything about each of these libraries and archives is first-rate. Southern Baptists have every reason to be proud of these facilities and the dedicated professionals who staff them. Thank you, all.

Annie Walker Armstrong,
corresponding secretary of the
Woman's Missionary Union
1888–1906. (Photo courtesy
of WMU archives,
Birmingham AL.)

Annie Armstrong at her desk. (Photo courtesy of WMU
archives, Birmingham AL.)

A "Brick Book," one of WMU's many fund raising promotions. (Photo courtesy of WMU archives, Birmingham AL.)

Delegates to WMU's organizational meeting. (Photo courtesy of WMU archives, Birmingham AL.)

The former site of Eutaw Place
Baptist Church, Baltimore MD.
(Photo courtesy of WMU archives,
Birmingham AL.)

I. T. Tichenor, corresponding
secreatary of the Home
Mission Board of the Southern
Baptist Convention,
1992–1899. ç

R. J. Willingham, corresponding secretary of the Foreign Mission Board of the Southern Baptist Convention, 1893–1914. (Photo courtesy of the Southern Baptist Historical Library and Archives, Nashville TN.)

T. P. Bell, editor of The Christian Index, 1896–1915. (Photo courtesy of the Southern Baptist Historical Library and Archives, Nashville TN.)

R. H. Boyd, founder of the first publishing board for the National Baptist Convention. (Photo courtesy of the Southern Baptist Historical Library and Archives, Nashville TN.)

Nannie Burroughs, first president of the Women's Auxiliary of the National Baptist Convention. (Photo courtesy of the Southern Baptist Historical Library and Archives, Nashville TN.)

Fannie E. S. Heck, president of
Woman's Missionary Union,
1892–94, 1895–99, and 1906–15.
(Photo courtesy of the Southern
Baptist Historical Library and
Archives, Nashville TN.)

J. M. Frost, secretary of the
Sunday School Board of the
Southern Baptist Convention,
1891–93, and 1896–1916.
(Photo courtesy of the Southern
Baptist Historical Library and
Archives, Nashville TN.)

INTRODUCTION

It is scarcely possible to imagine modern Southern Baptist life without the Woman's Missionary Union, Auxiliary to the Southern Baptist Convention, or, simply WMU. Since its inception in 1888, WMU has challenged Southern Baptists to give their hearts and resources to missionary projects in the United States and throughout the entire world.

Their far-reaching ministries and vision are in part a legacy of WMU's first corresponding secretary, Annie Walker Armstrong. Between 1888 and 1906 Armstrong almost single-handedly created a denominational consciousness among Southern Baptists by her innovative plans for promoting mission work at home and abroad, not to mention the torrent of letters that poured from her office. On the one hand, Armstrong created a unique "connectedness," a network of sorts, between dozens of missionaries and rank-in-file Southern Baptists through WMU. On the other hand, she helped connect the Home and Foreign Mission Boards with the Sunday School Board in the interest of missions.

By way of disclaimer, I have written neither a biography of Annie Armstrong nor a history of Woman's Missionary Union. Bobbie Sorrill's *Annie Armstrong: Dreamer in Action* and Catherine B. Allen's *A Century to Celebrate: History of Woman's Missionary Union* will supply interested readers with a wealth of information about this remarkable woman and the WMU.[1] Rather, I offer these letters and other writings with minimal editorial corrections, deletions and spelling changes because of the remarkable story that "Miss Annie" tells in her own words. Moreover, I chose *Rescue the Perishing* as a title for this volume because Fannie J. Crosby's classic hymn reminded me of Armstrong, particularly the first line of the last verse, "Rescue the perishing, duty demands it." No one can read Annie Armstrong's letters without gaining an appreciation for her intense missionary zeal and strong sense of Christian duty.

---

[1] See Bobbie Sorrill, *Annie Armstrong: Dreamer in Action* (Nashville: Broadman Press, 1984) and Catherine B. Allen, *A Century to Celebrate: History of Woman's Missionary Union* (Birmingham: Woman's Missionary Union, Auxiliary to the Southern Baptist Convention, 1987). See Appendix 2 for a brief chronology of WMU's accomplishments under Armstrong's leadership.

The letters in chapter 1, "I am not surprised that I occasionally become Kaflumexed," provide insight into Armstrong's personality. Combative. Kindhearted. Tenacious. Conscientious. Armstrong was all of these things, but there are aspects of her character that few people know. True, Miss Annie wore her heart on her sleeve, yet she was a self-sacrificing woman of principle who served her denomination without compensation. She worked hard as WMU's first corresponding secretary, and her letters suggest that she sometimes struggled to balance the demands of office and home.

Annie Armstrong understood her duties as corresponding secretary of WMU in broad terms. That is, as Auxiliary to the Southern Baptist Convention, she believed that WMU had a mandate to advance missionary work in whatever manner she deemed best as the letters in chapter 2, "Line upon line, precept upon precept," indicate.

At the most basic level, Armstrong masterfully built consensus between denominational leaders by using them as sounding boards and confidantes. She corresponded with men like I. T. Tichenor, R. J. Willingham, and J.M. Frost, corresponding secretaries for the Home Mission Board, the Foreign Mission Board, and the Sunday School Board, respectively. She also corresponded with various denominational workers, WMU leaders, and newspaper editors. She told them about every facet of her work and occasionally admitted that she probably wrote too many letters. Even so, her persistence allowed her to create a network between the various Southern Baptist boards as well as other denominational entities.[2]

Armstrong had many talents but she may have been at her best when it came to innovative ways to promote missions. She insisted that WMU create and distribute top quality literature. She advocated such things as mission fairs, mite boxes, star cards, and "box work," a sort of dry goods package that WMU sent to needy missionaries on the frontier. And, Annie Armstrong was among the first to see that Sunday School was an opportunity to promote mission work.

Armstrong advocated strong denominational ties among Southern Baptist churches. She drew sharp distinctions between "Northern work" and

---

[2] For information on Tichenor, Willingham, and Frost, as well as their respective boards consult the *Encyclopedia of Southern Baptists*, S.V. "Frost, James Marion," by James L. Sullivan; "Tichenor, Isaac Taylor," by Kimball Johnson; "Willingham, Robert Josiah," by E.C. Routh (Nashville: Broadman Press, 1958).

"Southern work." She also bristled when Gospel Missionism challenged the Foreign Mission Board's authority to manage the work in China.[3]

Given her strong will and determination, it was perhaps inevitable that Armstrong would clash with other Southern Baptist leaders. The letters in chapter 3, "If Miss Heck will not resign I *must*," illustrate her tenacity in the face of opposition, beginning with Miss Fannie E. S. Heck, President of WMU. Heck had served as WMU's president from 1892–1894 without serious incident. She was re-elected President in 1895 and in 1898 she and Armstrong became embroiled in a controversy over several issues, including how WMU best related to the Sunday School Board and the extent of Miss Heck's power as President of WMU. Their antagonism resulted in many bitter exchanges as both enlisted sympathy from Frost, Willingham, and Tichenor. Armstrong even sought Jonathan Haralson's legal opinion regarding WMU's constitution. An associate justice of the Alabama State Supreme Court, as well as president of the Southern Baptist Convention, Haralson sided with Armstrong but encouraged both women to lay their differences aside.[4]

Before the Heck-Armstrong Affair had completely settled, the *Christian Index*, a Baptist newspaper in Georgia, ran an article critical of certain WMU practices. Armstrong took the article as a personal affront. Doubtless, she would have confronted the author personally but she never discovered who wrote it. One final letter to I. T. Tichenor speaks volumes for Annie's combative spirit. She did not have the same rapport with Tichenor that she enjoyed with Willingham and Frost. Nevertheless, she had no trouble articulating her sentiments when compelled to do so.

The letters in chapter 4 "I am standing for two principles," indicate that the creation of a Training School for female missionaries marked a turning point for Annie Armstrong, WMU, and Southern Baptists in general. It began innocently enough when E. Z. Simmons suggested that Southern Baptists should begin a school for women missionaries. A veteran missionary to China, Simmons presented the concept to Southern Baptist leaders in 1900 while home on furlough. It seemed like a sterling idea. After all, Lottie Moon's work in China had inspired an increasing number of women to become missionaries, most of whom, Simmons believed, went to

---

[3] For a discussion of Gospel Missionism see Keith E. Eitel, *Paradigm Wars: The Southern Baptist International Mission Board Faces the Third Millennium* (Oxford: Regnum Books, 2000), pp. 31-85.

[4] Sorrill, *Annie Armstrong: Dreamer in Action*, 161–65. See also Appendix 1 for the Constitution and By-Laws of Woman's Missionary Union.

their fields ill-prepared for service. Moreover, many Southern Baptist women argued that America's urban areas needed a gospel witness and settlement houses afforded unprecedented opportunities for ministering to the urban masses. Most Southern Baptist leaders, including Armstrong, favored the idea even though she thought that Simmons should have mentioned it to her first.

All was quiet regarding the school until 1902–1903 when Southern Baptist Theological Seminary, Louisville, Kentucky, the soon-to-be home of the Training School, began admitting women missionaries to classes. Armstrong was furious. She had been studying other similar institutes, and she believed Southern Baptists were ill prepared to establish such a school. Moreover, she objected to women studying in the same classes as men because she believed the seminary was training women preachers. She also objected to the idea of WMU paying for a school it had received practically by fiat.

Unfortunately, Armstrong had made enemies during her tenure as corresponding secretary of WMU. Some used her opposition to the Training School as an opportunity to attack her loyalty to the Southern Baptist Convention in general. Stung by criticisms hurled her way, Annie Armstrong stepped down as WMU's corresponding secretary in 1906 and vowed never again to serve the denomination.

Having bid farewell to Southern Baptist missionary causes after eighteen years, Armstrong was ready for new challenges. She promised herself that she would not sit idle, and the letters in chapter 5 suggest that she had plenty of opportunities to keep her busy. According to her biographer, Armstrong managed Baltimore's Aged Men's and Aged Women's Homes for over twenty years and served Eutaw Place Baptist Church in various capacities, but true to her word, she never again served in a denominational capacity. Her old nemesis, Fannie Heck, was elected president of WMU in 1906, a position she held until 1915. Edith Campbell Crane succeeded Armstrong as WMU's corresponding secretary from 1907–1912, followed by Kathleen Mallory who served from 1912–1948. Both women were members of Eutaw Place Baptist Church, the same church where Annie Armstrong was a founding member and where she retained her membership until her death in 1938.[5]

Armstrong shunned all invitations to participate in denominational life beyond Eutaw Place until 1934 when WMU officials asked Armstrong if they could name the annual home mission offering in her honor. She

---

[5] Sorrill, *Annie Armstrong: Dreamer in Action*, 273–90.

reluctantly agreed, and in 1934, the WMU named the annual offering for home missions the Annie W. Armstrong Offering for Home Missions.[6]

In 1938, just months before she died, Annie responded to an invitation to send a message to WMU on its fiftieth anniversary. For the first time in thirty-two years, Annie Armstrong had a word for the WMU, a vibrant organization that she had molded in its earliest days. Her message read:

> My message for the Union in its fiftieth year is that I hope it may grow every year stronger and better. I would link with this thought the Scripture verse: "Speak unto the children of Israel that they go forward."
>
> For the young women in Y.W.A. my wish is that they "grow in grace and in the Knowledge of our Lord and Savior Jesus Christ."
>
> Do the Girls' Auxiliary members know the two verses most often read and committed to memory?—"For God so loved the world that he gave His only begotten Son that Whosoever believeth on Him should not perish but have eternal life.... . The Lord is my Shepherd."
>
> Tell the Royal Ambassadors to "be strong in the Lord and in the power of His might." I can say with emphasis that I have found this verse to be true.
>
> My message for the Sunbeams is the Shepherd Psalm.
>
> To encourage you in your special offerings for missions I would say: "Blessed are ye that sow beside the waters." Water suggests expansion and growth. After study of God's Word comes study of the fields. Then People pray. Then they give.[7]

On 20 December 1938, Annie Walker Armstrong, reconciled to her beloved WMU, left this world for her eternal reward. Her pastor, W. Clyde Atkins, eulogized her as a "dreamer in action," and so she was. These letters are a testimony to a remarkably energetic woman whose heart beat with a missionary pulse and whose soul continually searched for new ways to "rescue the perishing."

---

[6] The offering was renamed the Annie Armstrong Easter Offering in 1969.

[7] As quoted in Sorrill, *Annie Armstrong: Dreamer in Action*, 287–88.

CHAPTER 1

"I am not surprised that I occasionally become 'Kaflumexed'"

The Annie Armstrong that Few People Know

Perhaps not surprisingly, Annie Armstrong was a very busy woman who, even in her quiet moments, found it difficult to be still.

Sep. 29, 1897
Rev. A. J. Barton
Dear Brother:
I enclose a postal, which today's mail has brought from Mo. If it will not give you too much trouble, will you furnish Mrs. Snelling with the information she desires? It would require my going through Dr. Tupper's two books, and a number of scrapbooks, and it is out of the question my giving time to it, as my Stenographer is at present sick, with a severe attack of "chills," and I am obliged to attend a missionary meeting this afternoon. I am trying to dismiss the pile of letters that I brought home from the Mission Rooms before I have to leave—it does seem real strange to be writing with a pen.

What think you of the enclosed illustration which we have just had prepared for the S. Sch. Board? I do not like the arrangement of the young man's hair, and have ordered that changed. If I were at the Mission Rooms I would send another piece of work which I think very pretty, that we have had done for Dr. Frost. If I can think of it I will send it the next time I write.

Very truly,
Annie W. Armstrong
[IMB Archives]

September 27, 1899
Dr. J. M. Frost
Dear Brother:
Please find enclosed 50c., an annual subscription for *Kind Words* from Miss Mary H. Livermore, Red Springs, N. C. Let the subscription commence with October.

There is a number of quite important matters which I want to write about, and I hope I may be able to do so later in the day, but this is one of the days when my hands are more than full. Meetings, meetings, meetings are the order of the day. I knew that I had to attend one today, but I find it will be necessary for me this morning to go to the Annual Meeting of the Woman's Christian Temperance Union and make an appeal for workers for the Bayview (our City poorhouse) Mission. I did not know that I had to do this until on my way to the Mission Rooms this morning, so I shall have to go before that *august* body, trusting to make a very eloquent appeal without any preparation whatever. It has been my theory that no one had a right to make a public address without thorough preparation; but, of late, I have been forced to frequently trust to the inspiration of the moment, when making appeals, for I often have not time enough even to arrange my ideas.

I think you would have been amused at something that occurred yesterday. When I reached the Mission Rooms in the morning, after going to market, I found Dr. Barton awaiting me. He said that he had decided that he would go to Norfolk by the way of Baltimore, and so had come on to spend the day here. I was very glad indeed to see him, and after talking somewhat over mission affairs, I suggested, as he was not acquainted with Baltimore, I would show him a little of our City. As is frequently the case in desiring to have a stranger impressed with the beauties of one's native city, I proceeded to do something that I had never before done in my life, viz., to go up in the dome of our City Hall. When I reached the first landing, though, and saw before me a spiral staircase, I suggested that I would remain at that point, and for Dr. Barton and the guide to proceed to the top. This they did, and the effect was what I desired,—Dr. Barton is convinced that Baltimore is a pretty place.

Remembering that I had promised to open a meeting which was to be held at the Mission Rooms, by ladies from the different churches who would arrange for the lunch during the State Association, I had to leave the dinner table and rush down to the Rooms. When I had reached there, one of the clerks whom I had asked to select a passage of Scripture for me to read at this meeting, handed me just before I went into the room some notes which she had made, and I had to conduct this meeting,—the lady who was expected to take charge after I had opened the meeting was detained at home on account of the illness of her child—give a Bible reading, without one particle of preparation beforehand. I did manage, though to get things satisfactorily planned and get through before Dr. Barton came back.

There is excitement in this sort of life, but it certainly is not conducive to health to work under such high pressure. No one would think, though, from the way I have been rambling on, that I must try, if possible, to reply to two days' mail this morning.

More anon.

Annie W. Armstrong

[SBHLA, J. M. Frost Collection]

December 30, 1903

Dr. J. M. Frost

Dear Brother:

Your letter of December 28th received this A.M., and as these are holiday times it is enabling me, as the mail is comparatively light, to answer all letters promptly and to do a vast amount of work in other directions. I am really delighted at the amount I am accomplishing. Do you know that I am finding that I have sufficient physical strength to go to my desk an hour or an hour and a half before breakfast, and be at the Mission Rooms every morning by nine o'clock. I remain there until one, go home to lunch, get back a little after two, and stay at the Mission Rooms until six o'clock. After dinner I usually rest for a few moments and then work until half past ten or eleven. What think you of that for one who is in her fifty-fourth year? I thoroughly believe if God gives us a work to do He will supply physical as well as spiritual strength. I do though realize at times that He lays us aside in order that we may be better fitted to do His work.

I note you say, in speaking of letters to Superintendents from the Sunday School Board:

> "I think it would be better to have them sent out from Baltimore, and also that it would be better for them to bear the imprint of the W.M.U. rather than our own imprint."

No, no, no, while I am perfectly willing to do the work for the three Boards as I offered, I am by no means willing to make the appeal to the

Sunday Schools. I have already had to bear too much unkind criticism for me to be willing to do anything which I consider unnecessary and which persons could criticize. The money from the Sunday Schools will go direct to the Board, whose Secretary makes the appeal, through state channels, and the money will not be credited to the Woman's Missionary Union, so I see nothing whatever to be gained by having W.M.U. imprint on envelopes or material and I must decline to allow its being done. This is one of the many times when the Secretary of the Woman's Missionary Union proposes to help the general work and not let it be credited to the Woman's Missionary Union.

We have prepared for Dr. Willingham an order for a Sunday School Missionary service—I will send you one as soon as they are printed—to be enclosed in his letters. These will not have on them the W.M.U. imprint. The work of sending out the letters for Dr. Willingham will be done entirely at 233 N. Howard St., and the letters posted from Baltimore, but the only thing that will indicate that this is the case will be the Baltimore postmark attached at the post-office, and I do not suppose one person out of a thousand will notice this. This I consider the best way, and it is the only way in which the Secretary of the Woman's Missionary Union is willing to do this work.

Now as to the Sunday School Board appeal: If you desire to accept my offer to have letters from you, with whatever enclosures may be thought wise, sent to Superintendents the latter part of May, I would ask that you as soon as convenient have sent from Nashville 7,500 of your official envelopes. We cannot meet the prices you have given in Baltimore. As you order in such large quantities, you get the envelopes at cheaper rates than we could by having a small quantity printed. The additional price of sending these to Baltimore will not be as much as what will be saved in purchase of same at your usual rates. As I previously stated, I will be glad to have the envelopes as soon as they can be forwarded, for I wish to have them addressed in leisure moments. I could not undertake to do this work if it was to be done in May. It will have to be done by us during the winter and be held for mailing at the time appointed.

As to the program for Children's Day: From your previous letters I judge you wish a program prepared similar to those in previous years. If that is the case, I hope to send manuscript by the first of February. As in previous years it has been stated that the program has been prepared by the Woman's Missionary Union, I prefer to have same notice on that program. The programs will be printed, will they not, as formerly in Nashville, and sent out from the Sunday School Board office in such ways as you may deem wise? In your letter mailed from Baltimore we can send order blanks. When I send you the samples of Dr. Willingham's letter, with enclosures, I will have some other suggestions to make, but will defer doing so until I let you see the plan that he has adopted.

As near as I could hurriedly calculate, the list sent by Dr. Burrows has about 8,200 names. Over 1,200 of these are those of Superintendents in Missouri. Knowing of the Missouri plan, after consultation with Dr. Willingham, I wrote to Dr. Breaker. I send you copy of my letter and of his reply. From these you will see that as Dr. Breaker has declined to have Dr. Willingham make an appeal to the Sunday Schools in Missouri, I do not suppose, especially as the publications of the Publication Society are so generally taken in Missouri, that you could appeal to the Missouri Sunday Schools without causing friction. For that reason I have asked that you send 7,500 envelopes—I allowed a margin, thinking possibly the calculation may not be perfectly correct—instead of asking for 8,500 envelopes. If though you decide to disregard Dr. Breaker's wishes, send 8,500 envelopes.

I see no reason why there need be any public announcement in regard to the discontinuance of Missionary Day. We can for the present let it remain an open question as to how the Sunday Schools are to be asked to contribute to the Home and Foreign Mission Boards. As I previously stated, I have not taken up the subject with Dr. Gray in regard to details of the Home Board appealing to Sunday Schools. It is the idea though that the Home Board will make this appeal to the Sunday Schools next fall.

I am glad to have the information you have sent in regard to the Sunday School at Greenville discontinuing the use of the Blakeslee Series. This explains an amused look that I saw exchanged between two members of the church at Greenville, that were visiting Baltimore last Sunday when Mr. Millard made the announcement of the proposed change at Eutaw Place Sunday School. I had intended to ask these ladies what caused them to look as they did, but pressure of other matters caused me to forget to make the inquiry when they called at the Mission Rooms. I shall not hesitate to let it be known of the decision of the Greenville Sunday School, for I consider that Eutaw Place Sunday School has made a mistake and the sooner they rectify same the better.

By this mail I send you two new publications which the Woman's Missionary Union has just gotten out. I will be glad to have you glance over these and note the "ads." given to the periodicals of the Sunday School Board and the presentation of the work of that Board.

Well I have written you a volume, have I not? I shall stop right here and not let another matter be presented.

Very truly,

Annie W. Armstrong

[SBHLA, J. M. Frost Collection]

Annie Armstrong was a woman of principle and self-sacrifice.

April 14th, 1899

Dr. A. J. Barton

Dear Brother:

Your letter of April 13th just received. *Most certainly* you are at liberty to use the portion of Mrs. Pruitt's letter in the way that Dr. Willingham and the Assistant Corresponding Secretary of the Foreign Board deem wise. I trust it will prove a "center shot." I will today send to Mrs. Easterlin, Cor. Sec. Central Committee, of Georgia, the *portion* of Mrs. Pruitt's letter, which you returned. I will give the subject more careful consideration, and then decide whether or not it will be better to send copies of Mrs. Pruitt's letter to Central Committees as I first intended doing. I will though, not forward these at once, so you need have no fear of the portion of Mrs. Pruitt's letter, which you have retained getting into print before it appears in the *Foreign Mission Journal*.

A letter that has come to me this morning makes me feel that I have been almost guilty of sacrilege. You will recall I wrote in a joking way to you about a quilt that an old lady in South Carolina had made and wished me to dispose of. I did not at the time appreciate how much this quilt represented, and I only saw the comical side of this and other offerings of the same kind. I now am going to ask that you will kindly read two letters, which I enclose, one from the daughter of the old lady, Mrs. B. M. Foreman, and the other from the old lady herself, Mrs. R. L. Martin. After reading the latter, I am sure you will agree with me that that dear old saint must not be disappointed. I cannot dispose of the quilt for her, nor can I ask any one of our workers to do so, because after having the resolution passed which I did, I feel in honor bound not to in any way break through the rule which was made. It is *absolutely* necessary there should be such a rule, for if set aside it would be like opening a flood-gate. As you will see by Mrs. Foreman's letter, her mother's intention was to in this way make an offering to Foreign Missions. Should you or Dr. Willingham think it wise to present the matter to any one, or give publicity to it in the *Foreign Mission Journal*—not in the W.M.U. Department—I, of course, will turn the whole matter over to you. If this cannot be done I will purchase the quilt—ten dollars are not very plentiful with the Cor. Sec. W.M.U.—for I cannot feel that it would be right for that old lady to be disappointed. She evidently has taken it much to heart that she is not able to do as she planned—make a moneyed contribution to Foreign Missions. You will remember my suggestion to her was that she make a present of the quilt to a foreign missionary, but that does not seem to her to be the same thing as giving the money which it represents.

Very truly,

Annie W. Armstrong

P. S. No, I did not spend my early life in the country, so doubtless I am not a judge of the safety of those who perch on fences. I do recall a most ignominious sprawl that I had only several years ago when I attempted to climb over one. Perhaps you may be able to keep your commanding position, but still I advise you to descend.

P. S. #2. Kindly hand the enclosed letters from Mr. Maynard to Dr. Willingham. I have taken extracts from them.

[IMB Archives]

November 17th, 1902

Dr. E. E. Bomar

Dear Brother:

As I wrote you on Saturday, I thought the question which had lately caused me so much disquietude was settled, but some things have occurred since then, and really I am perfectly at a loss to know what I ought to do. Dr. H. H. Harris once said to me, "Miss Annie, I have learned to distrust my own judgment when my personal interests are involved," and I am having the same experience. I have prayed as earnestly as I know how for guidance and it seems as I look at the subject from one side that one course of action would be right, and then as I look at it from the other side, it would be wrong. I can and do appreciate that your hands are very full, but there is no one in Baltimore who I feel knows the bearings of the question, whom I could consult; and therefore I am going to beg that you will let me speak further to you on the subject, and that you will candidly give me your opinion. I had intended speaking to Mrs. Gwathmey when in Richmond, but had not the opportunity, so if you think wise to consult her before expressing an opinion I will be glad to have you do so.

Now as to what has occurred since I wrote on Saturday; yesterday I took the opportunity as we were dining at Mr. Levering's (Eugene) to show him the letters which I had received from Dr. Willingham. When I stated that I had decided to decline the salary which had been offered, he informed me that some moneys that for years Sister Alice and I had been receiving, would cease with this year: I had thought there was a possibility of this but had not known for a certainty that such would be the case until yesterday; this decrease added to losses previously experienced very materially lessens my income.

Eugene Levering insisted that I was not looking at things at all in the right light; that I had no scriptural grounds for the attitude which I had taken in regard to the woman's work, namely, no salaried officers. He said that the Bible plainly taught the workman is worthy of his hire and that those who preach the Gospel shall live by the Gospel. That the work that I am doing is parallel to the work of a missionary and that the Bible recognizes no difference between the man and the woman. He further stated that the principles that I had tried to inculcate were wrong and their tendency was to get people to think that even ministers should not be paid—Old School Baptist doctrine. I called his attention to the fact that Paul had worked at tent-making in order that he might not be chargeable to anyone on a missionary trip; he could not or would not see the force of this and said that was only an exceptional case. Mr. Levering further stated that I would be doing wrong not to let Sister Alice know of Dr. Willingham's letters. Feeling this might be the case I showed the letters to Sister Alice yesterday afternoon. I am thankful to say she did not take the same ground as Mr. Levering did, and told me that she wished me to feel perfectly free to decide as I thought wise.

So much for Mr. Levering's way of looking at things: Now for the other side of the question.

In the first place, as I mentioned to you previously, for nearly fifteen years I have tried to teach the principle of women giving their work without remuneration, and for me to accept a salary would be inconsistent with these teachings.

Secondly, it would open the door for State officers to expect payment for their services—already several ladies in different States do receive remuneration—thereby involving much expense.

Thirdly, it would probably be thought if the Secretary were to receive a salary, office expenses should decrease. I am now doing as much as is possible for me to do, even though I received a salary of five thousand dollars; I can do no more than I am now doing. I cannot reduce the number of clerks, unless the work is reduced; neither can I decrease traveling expenses, if it is thought wise for me to visit Societies, etc., etc. I have no way of securing passes on the railroads, and only on some roads can obtain clerical rates. When in Baltimore, Dr. McConnell stated publicly that his traveling expenses this Fall had only amounted to $10.00, - the advertisements in *Our Home Field* having secured for him the right to travel at this small expense. As Woman's Missionary Union does not issue a paper, I cannot have the same privilege. I call your attention to these facts, as I want you to recognize as I do that if a salary is paid the Secretary, expenses must necessarily increase, and should criticism arise there may be a falling off in receipts.

Now as to my course of action: I think I will make three suggestions along this line also.

1st. Decline the salary and announce the fact in the near future that at the close of the year I must give up the work, for owing to decrease in income it is necessary that I obtain some remunerative employment; but feeling as I do in regard to salaried officers of the Woman's Missionary Union, I have declined and must decline to accept a salary tendered by the Boards.

2nd. Keep on with the work, declining the salary, trusting that our Heavenly Father will in some way or other provide; I have not yet gotten to the point where I cannot meet all my expenses. In the prayer that we are told to offer, it is "Give us this day our daily bread;" we have no warrant in looking beyond today.

> "Build a little fence of trust around today,
> Fill it well with loving work and therein stay;
> Look not through the sheltering bars upon tomorrow,
> God will help thee bear whatever comes, of joy or sorrow."

3rd. Present Dr. Willingham's letters to the Executive Committee at a meeting to be held on Friday. Let them take what action they think wise. I am perfectly satisfied though, that they will insist that I accept the salary; if they do, request Mrs. J. H. Eager as Vice-President of W.M.U. for Maryland, to write to the other Vice-Presidents, telling of the offer and the reasons why it was made; ask that they will give their candid opinion as to whether it will be better for the work for me to accept the salary or resign as it has become necessary for me to obtain some remunerative employment.

You have no idea how bitter this whole thing is to me; it has been a great joy to me that I could feel that while I had not a large amount of money that I could give to the cause of missions, yet I was making an offering of my time. Then again, I know I am peculiarly sensitive to criticism and I have felt that as I was not a salaried officer, I was in a measure independent; all of this must be changed if I take this money; possibly, probably though, the feeling I have had in this direction has not been right; it may have been a wrong spirit.

Will you kindly let me hear from you before the meeting of the Executive Committee which is to be held Friday of this week? I fully recognize that I am asking of you something that you will not like to do, and I would not make the request but I do not know to whom else to turn. How I wish I could talk this matter over with Dr. Kerfoot!

Very truly,
Annie W. Armstrong
[IMB Archives]

December 13, 1902
Dr. R. J. Willingham
Secretary Foreign Mission Board, S.B.C.
Dear Brother:

I desire to acknowledge receipt of your two communications dated November 4th in the name of Foreign, Home and Sunday School Boards, one addressed to Executive Committee, W.M.U., and the other to its Secretary.

At a meeting held December 10, the Executive Committee carefully considered its letter and at my earnest solicitation took no action in the matter, though they cordially approved of the decision which I shall submit. Let me express my appreciation of the motive in offering $750.00 as "some compensation" for services rendered as Secretary W.M.U., but I cannot feel at liberty to accept any compensation until the whole question shall be presented to Woman's Missionary Union in Annual Session. The Cor. Sec. W.M.U. is their election and that body must decide if a paid officer is desirable. If affirmatively decided, whoever should then be elected to office, could be free to receive the salary which W.M.U. should attach to the office.

Copies of your two letters and of this one will be sent to Mrs. C. A. Stakely, Pres. W.M.U., and to each State Vice-President that all time and information at my command may be given. The President W.M.U. will be asked to present the matter to Woman's Missionary Union in Savannah, May 1903.

It will be my pleasure to continue to work as earnestly as in my power, to advance all the interests of the different Boards until the expiration of the year for which I accepted the office now held. I must however, be excused from attending the Annual Meeting in Savannah, as I desire this question to be entirely decided on its own merits and not biased by personal considerations.

May I ask that you will notify the Home and Sunday School Boards of my decision, and that you will recognize that I have earnestly sought to know what was best to be done for the work's sake?

Very truly,

Annie W. Armstrong

[IMB Archives]

Armstrong readily admitted that she could be single-minded, or as she put it, "extremely persistent."

July 10, 1893

Dr. T. P. Bell

Dear Brother:

Your letter of July 6th received, and I am very glad to know that the program for "Missionary Day" met with your approval. We were pleased to see that you had read it so carefully that alterations occurred to you, which we will gladly make as we earnestly desire that it shall be as helpful as possible, and the changes suggested by you, I think are improvements.

I had not noticed that the one who copied the program did not understand exactly the arrangement, and, in connection with "Questions and Answers on Foreign Missions" when the question was asked "How many preachers at this rate would your State have?" wrote your name in brackets, and so close that it seemed we were asking that you should give this information. I was a little annoyed at our seeming stupidity, and rather amused that you failed to appreciate that that arrangement was your own, being taken from *Foreign Mission Catechism*, and we were simply giving you due credit for it.

Today's mail brought the enclosed letter from Dr. Tichenor; will you kindly read same, and let me know what you think of his suggestion as to time for collecting Pyramid Mite Chests? It strikes me quite favorably to include Thanksgiving Day, for many persons seem to feel that at that time offerings ought to be made. The only thing that makes this doubtful, to my mind, is that it will undoubtedly prevent the Christmas Offering being as large as it otherwise would. At an Executive Committee session of the Woman's Missionary Union held in Nashville, the ladies desired that we prepare a Christmas program that could be used by Sunday Schools and bands as well as one for missionary societies, so that additional one must be prepared by the Executive Committee again this year. My own opinion is, however, that it will be better to make the one strong effort for "Missionary Day," and let the "Christmas Offering" take a secondary place. While the contributions are to be divided between the two Boards, according to the wishes of the donors, I believe the Foreign Board, even should it only receive 1/2, would, by extending the time to Thanksgiving Day, obtain more than if we do not accept Dr. Tichenor's suggestion. Please let me have your opinion on this point.

I have no doubt you think I am extremely persistent, but if I get hold of an idea which seems to me to be a good one, I some how do not feel comfortable until I see it carried out, or find that it is out of the question to do anything with it—this by way of explanation.

In a letter received from Dr. Frost today, he wrote as if he expected to make some changes next year in connection with the *Teacher*, so I want to again refer to the matter of illustrations, embodying the golden texts. You will recall in a letter you wrote me some time ago, you said you approved of the idea, and would speak to Dr. Frost about it as soon as he had sufficiently recovered to be at the office. You will remember at the time I spoke to you of the illustrations, I told you that I had a large number of copies of the *Watchword*, Dr. A. J. Gordon's paper, which contained many suitable illustrations, and these were at your disposal. If you will allow me I am going to speak right plainly on this point. I think you know sufficiently well how I regard our Southern work, to feel assured that what I say is not from a spirit of criticism, but from genuine interest; I do want the publications of our Sunday School Board to be taken by our Southern people because they are the *most helpful*, and not from *sentiment*. The Publication Society having almost unlimited means and many years experience, have secured some of the ablest, if not the ablest, writers in our denomination, so it will be extremely difficult for the Sunday School Board to compete with them if they provide only the same helps as adopted by the Publication Society. It seems to me it would be well to aim for variety, as well as to get the best writers at the command of the Sunday School Board for expositions on the lessons, etc. In order to see how this kind of help, namely: Illustrations, would strike one who is an earnest worker, I mentioned the matter to Rev. E. Y. Mullins this morning, he being at the Mission Rooms, and he seemed to think that it would prove most helpful. My own opinion being strengthened by what he said, I want to make an offer, which I will be very glad if you will accept. It is this; if Dr. Frost will arrange for such a department in the *Teacher*, and will put it in charge of Dr. T. P. Bell, I will, while in Asheville, cull from the copies of the *Watchword* that I have all illustrations that seem to me helpful, and place them in a scrapbook and send them to you. I think you could then, without taking a great deal of time, select a number that would be suitable and rearrange them a little so as to cover the ground wished. I have no doubt, that from the papers I now have in hand, I could send you from 100 to 150 telling illustrations. If such a department is opened, I will be on the lookout after that, and from time to time send what may come under my notice.

Should this strike you favorably please do not hesitate to accept my offer, as I assure you it will be a pleasure to arrange the scrapbook and forward same. You know, in this new arrangement that was entered upon, I was to be allowed to every now and then do some work for the Sunday School Board, which was to prevent the help being all on one side.

Please drop me a line as soon as convenient, giving your opinion as to Dr. Tichenor's suggestion. Address your letter care of Prof. W. F. Grabau, 34 Starnes Ave., Asheville, N. C.

Very truly,
Annie W. Armstrong
[SBHLA, J. M. Frost Collection]

Annie Armstrong worked long hours under difficult circumstances and paid a high price in health related issues. The following letters indicate that she suffered from neuralgia and recurrent dental problems.

October 23, 1902
Dr. E. E. Bomar
Dear Brother:
Your letter of October 22nd just received. I am sorry that I failed to make my meaning clear in the letter of October 20th, but under the circumstances, I am not surprised that I occasionally become "Kaflumexed"[8] as I am trying to do half a dozen things at one time—writing letters, getting out new literature, preparing for Annual Meeting, arranging to leave home for a trip to Virginia, making numerous addresses, visiting dress-maker, going to dentist, and, and, and, and etc. So much by way of explanation.

Now to business. The literature which is now on the way from Richmond—it has not yet been delivered—is intended for the Home Department. I desire 2,000 *additional*—I have 4,000 now in hand, but that is not a sufficient number—leaflets by Dr. Simmons to send out with the programs for the Christmas Offering. I will be obliged if you will let me have these as soon as convenient.

Kindly read the two letters which I enclose. Being still in a "muddled" state, I think it better to let Mrs. Tyler and Dr. McConnell speak for themselves. By this mail, I have written to Dr. McConnell inviting him to accept Mrs. Tyler's hospitality, thinking it would be mutually agreeable to you and Dr. McConnell.

I enclose samples of Christmas Literature. If you have time, I will be glad for you to critically examine programs and let me have your opinion of them. This year, we have made a new departure. We have decided to try and get the children and young people in the churches to join with the Woman's Mission Societies in the Christmas Offering. If this can be done, the receipts will be much larger. What think you of this?

Very truly,
Annie W. Armstrong
[IMB Archives]

March 11, 1905
Dr. R. J. Willingham
Dear Brother:
Your letter March 10th received. I cannot tell you how disturbed I feel in regard to mail going astray as it does. There must be something wrong but I cannot bring about any change. I have entered complaint at the Baltimore

---

[8] Armstrong's letter had this note: "See Webster's Unabridged."

Post Office in writing and also had one of the clerks whom I know employed at the Post Office, to interview the Asst. Postmaster, and they all tell me that nothing can be done except by the persons who send the letters. They can send out tracers. Not only are we losing letters that contain money but some important letters which are causing misunderstanding. If you can make any suggestion as to what I can do, I wish you would tell me.

As to the hospital to be built for Dr. Evans: I note your suggestion that I write to Dr. Evans and ask that he send a letter in regard to this, so it might be read at Annual Meeting. I will do this, but there is no certainty of our getting the letter in time so as you have kindly offered to write to Mrs. Barker, I would ask that you do so. The address is, Mrs. J. A. Barker, Clifton Forge, Virginia. Our plan is to ask some persons to present the object and so Mrs. Barker in inviting these persons will have to furnish them with data. So you will see we cannot wait for a possible letter from Dr. Evans. In writing to Mrs. Barker, kindly give whatever information you can in regard to the hospital.

I am glad to know that Dr. Bomar is better and hope it will not be long before he has regained his health. I realize, though, it is necessary that he should take a rest. I am sorry his breakdown has come at the time in the year when you need his help so much. Please be careful and do not over-tax your strength.

I have been suffering with neuralgia for some time but am now in the hands of the dentist and hope that through his help I may be relieved as possibly negligence in that direction is causing part of the trouble. I am under so much pressure all the time that I have not thought I could go to a dentist for several years, but I have been so miserable that I feared to start off on the trip which I am about to take (where I know I will have a good deal of exposure) in the condition I was, as possibly I would be laid aside. Dr. Bomar's breakdown I think shows that those of us who are trying to do this kind of work must be a little more careful.

Very truly,
Annie W. Armstrong
[IMB Archives]

In addition to her dental problems, Armstrong also suffered from frequent colds and stress related maladies, especially headaches.

November 18, 1896
Dr. J. M. Frost
Dear Brother:
Your letter of Nov. 18th received this A.M. I have shortly to attend an Executive Committee meeting, but before doing so, I want to write you a few lines. I note you say: "I will write you at length on my arriving home," and later: "I will write out my views fully when I get home." I am going to ask that you will let that letter, if possible, reach me by Monday morning, as there is a "Called Meeting" of the Mission Rooms Committee on that day, when this question will doubtless be decided. I do want to do what is right, and if I can see what that is, I am sure grace will be given me to do it. You have no idea how bitter this whole thing has been to me. The trouble coming from the source it has makes it peculiarly trying. How can Christians think that God would have them use in His work anything but honest and straightforward methods? I do thoroughly enjoy work and consider it a privilege if I can aid in the advancement of God's cause in any direction, but I am no fighter and I would be so thankful if I only could do the work without being put in prominent positions where, when persons want to make an attack on same, I have to be the target. I know some people are so constituted that they do not mind this sort of thing, but trouble of this nature always causes me to succumb physically. The recent attack of sickness which I have had—it has now lasted over two weeks—I am sure is entirely due to worry and anxiety. Dr. H. H. Harris some time ago said to me: "Miss Annie, worry is part of the work." Is it a necessary ingredient?

I enclose copy of an article which I forward by today's mail to *The Index.* I think you may like to have your attention called to it, so I enclose same. In sending it to Dr. Bell, I wrote as follows:

> Wishing to place before "our friends, the enemy," some plain truths, I suggested Sister Alice writing an article for *The Index.* She kindly consented to do so, clothing my ideas with words, and I now send you the article which I would ask that you let appear in the next edition of your paper, if it meets with your approval. We have not the slightest objection to Dr. Rowland's knowing from whence it emanates, so therefore have located the writer, but did not think it wise to give name. (I doubt if either Dr. Rowland or Dr. Flippo will be at a loss to supply same.) I suggested Sister Alice again using the nom de plume which she adopted when she wished, several months ago, to pay her respects to the "Society."

If you do not object, I would be glad to have your opinion of the article. If you consider its publication is not timely, send Dr. Bell a postal and ask him to withhold it.

Quite an important event has recently transpired of which I desire to speak, but will have to defer doing so until I can write again.

Hoping you reached home safely and not perfectly worn out with your round to the Conventions, I am,

Very truly,

Annie W. Armstrong

[SBHLA, J. M. Frost Collection]

Central Committee

Woman's Mission Societies

(Of Baptist General Association of Virginia)

Richmond, Va.

July 24th, 1897

Dear Miss Annie,

Your two letters of the 22nd were received yesterday. I am sorry to hear that you were disappointed in going to the Association, but under the circumstances, there was nothing else for you to do. I am also sorry that you still continue to feel so unwell, do try and spare yourself and take something to make you get well. Just think how much is dependent on you, and spare yourself for the dependent ones. My girls want to know when are you coming to see us for they want to know you. I have told them that I was very much afraid that you could not come as long as your Mother was so feeble. Anyhow I can assure you that just as soon as you can come there will be a warm welcome awaiting you. I have read carefully the article sent from Dr. Frost. I don't know how I failed to see that in my *Herald* last Dec. but I do not remember it. I am sure that is all that we could wish him to say, and now that I understand him if he will just make that change in his circular for our State to suit the Virginia plan, there will be no friction. I do not think it will be necessary for him to see the Cooperative Committee about that matter. I think I understand him. I am sorry to have missed seeing Mr. Clopton, please remember me to him. I was sure Dr. Frost would be pleased with that "present." I was at the Mission Rooms the other day, and called Mr.

Barton's attention to the picture, and he agreed…
(unsigned—Possibly from Mrs. A. M. Gwathmey, President)[9]
[SBHLA, J. M. Frost Collection]

April 12, 1899
Dr. J. M. Frost
Dear Brother:
Miss Buhlmaier has been in need of Polish and Bohemian Testaments for some little time. I told her, though, I could not secure a further supply until you were better. I now send you a letter which I received from her yesterday. If you can make a grant to the Immigrant Work, I hope you will do so in the near future, as we do not want to miss any more opportunities for placing in the hands of the incoming foreigners the Word of Life. Miss Buhlmaier found the Gospels very helpful.

Thinking it was only due the Sunday School Board that Miss Buhlmaier should make some acknowledgment of the help received by her from your Board, which could be used in your annual report should you wish to do so, I suggested to her writing a summary of her year's work. I now enclose the letter, which she has prepared. She has furnished a full report for the Home Board, and in it speaks of the help received from the Sunday School Board.

I hope you are feeling stronger. It is a trying experience, is it not, to be physically unable to do what one sees plainly ought to be done? I have for some little time past been far from well and today have been *enjoying* a very severe headache. We have just had an Executive Committee Meeting W.M.U., which usually uses me up, but commencing today with a headache, I am a little astonished that I am able, now the meeting is over, to do anything. How I wish we did not have Board meetings, or, in fact, any other kind of meetings. I can do office work for twice the length of time and not feel nearly so fatigued as I do after an Executive Committee session. But enough of this.

Very truly,
Annie W. Armstrong
[SBHLA, J. M. Frost Collection]

---

[9] Letter incomplete—only portion forwarded to Dr. Frost.

1901 (?)
Saturday Night [no date]
Dr. J. M. Frost
Dear Brother:

It is now quite late, and I have been suffering with a severe headache today, so under these circumstances I know you will excuse any seeming abruptness; so without any circumlocution I will state my reason for writing tonight.

It is to say, that if you have not made any arrangements for the program for Missionary Day, and still desire that I furnish it, I have decided to disregard the very earnest protest of some that I should not do so much work for the S. Sch. Board, as your Board was perfectly able to pay for having that work done by others, which I have been doing for years, and supply the manuscript as usual. If you desire to accept this offer please telegraph, also time (the latest) when manuscript can be in your hands. As I will have to be away a large part of the Summer, I would prefer that you do not request me to have plates of program made in Balto.

Another thing. I wish you would send such an advertisement as you desire printed on leaflets issued by "Mission Literature Department," when there are vacant pages.

It is at times interesting to see things from different standpoints. I enclose a letter from Mrs. J. B. Gambrell which gives a little different view of a subject now under discussion. Kindly return letter.

Thanks for copy of *The Professor*. I have not yet had time to read it but hope to do so shortly. I think it has been gotten out very attractively.

Hastily, but very truly,
Annie W. Armstrong
I hope Margaret is better.
[SBHLA, J. M. Frost Collection]

March 7, 1898
Dr. R. J. Willingham
Dear Brother:

It is with no little pleasure I send you a check for ten (10) dollars, contribution from the New Bethel Aid Society, Tyrola, Ind. Ter., to the Christmas Offering. Please send receipt for same to Miss Nancy Medley, Tyrola, Ind. Ter. If you were to see the letters I get from the missionaries at that point and in other sections of the Territory, you would appreciate, as I do, that contributions coming from that source do indeed represent self-denial. I cannot think, though, it is wrong to urge persons who have but little of this world's goods to contribute to the cause of missions, so I am trying as far as I have time and influence, to get the women in our frontier churches interested in missionary work.

May I now ask that you will kindly let me have as soon as possible the amount received by the *Foreign Mission Board* for the Christmas Offering since February 7th? I would request that you specify what was contributed in each State. We desire this data for insertion in W.M.U. Department in *Foreign Mission Journal* in April.

Hastily, but very truly,

Annie W. Armstrong

LATER. Your letter of March 7th received. We held this morning a prolonged session of the Executive Committee, W.M.U., and I find myself, as usual after such meetings, with a headache, so cannot reply to some questions you have asked in it. I hope, though, to write tomorrow, as there were several important matters which were considered this morning that must be referred to you.

I now forward check for two dollars and a half ($2.50), a club subscription to the *Foreign Mission Journal.* Please send ten (10) copies monthly to Mrs. Lottie Lainhart, 603 Scott Street, Baltimore, Md. She would like also to have the book, "How Christ Came to Church." This subscription comes from a Band, so they do not care to have the magazines sent separately. Let the subscription begin with the March number.

[IMB Archives]

January 24, 1901

Dr. J. M. Frost

Dear Brother:

Your letter of January 21st received. I, of course, appreciate from my own experience how impossible it is at times not to make mistakes when one is so pressed with work. The delay in having to return the check did not cause any inconvenience.

As to the question of the Mission Rooms. Dr. Kerfoot has been in Baltimore for several days, leaving early this morning. During his visit we discussed quite fully the future of the Rooms, etc., etc. I have thought it wise to leave the matter in his hands for the present, and you will hear from him on the subject. May I ask when he writes that you will reply promptly, as I desire there should be as little further delay in coming to some conclusion as possible.

We have greatly enjoyed Dr. Kerfoot's visit, and you can imagine it has been fruitful when I tell you that after presenting the cause of Home Missions at Eutaw Place Church last Sunday morning, one member of the church, Mr. S. G. B. Cook, who is engaged in business in London but still holds his membership in our church, and who is here on a visit, told Dr. Kerfoot that he would hereafter give $600.00 per annum to the work of the Home Board.

I am thankful to say Sister Alice is steadily improving. I have not thought it wise yet to give up the trained nurse, but hope in a few days she will be sufficiently convalescent to dispense with her services. I think just at present the family are looking for a breakdown of the Corresponding Secretary W.M.U. Grippe is very prevalent in Baltimore, and I have had not only a severe cold for some days past, but other symptoms. The nurse seems quite anxious to take me in charge, and to begin a series of ministrations, but I have no time for these, as the work at the Rooms is very, very heavy just now. I trust I will be able to weather it through this time as I have frequently before, without giving up. While I have not become a disciple of Christian Science, yet I have great faith in the influence of mind over matter.

Very truly,

Annie W. Armstrong

P. S. Will you kindly hand the enclosed envelope to Dr. Van Ness?

P. S. No. 2. I have just given order to the one who does our drawing, to make title page for Program for Children's Day. He promises to let me have the drawings for the title page and Mite Box next week. I will then have plates made and send them on to you with manuscript for Program, which is now underway.

[SBHLA, J. M. Frost Collection]

In spite of her infirmities, Armstrong was not one to take her doctor's advice.

June 18, 1900
Dr. I. T. Tichenor
Dear Brother:

The two Centennial manuscripts which you forwarded on Saturday, from Dr. J. B. Gambrell and Dr. E. Y. Mullins, received. I am sorry to have to write that I *cannot* attend to the printing of these or other Centennial leaflets which may be desired to be issued between now and the first of October.

For some months past I have been very far from well. Our family physician warned me more than a year ago, when I had an attack of grippe, that I must "rest" for six months; otherwise he seemed to think that the consequences might be quite serious. I felt that it was perfectly out of my power to do this, and so I have gone on in my usual way—getting to the Mission Rooms about nine o'clock each morning after attending to my housekeeping duties, and remaining there until six o'clock in the evening, then taking work home with me sufficient to keep me occupied almost every evening until I retire. In no other way have I been able to keep the work which seemed to devolve upon me from getting into arrears. My family have insisted that the way I was acting was suicidal, and I know I have largely lost their sympathy in the efforts which I am making to interest others in Missions, by persisting in the course which I felt was right.

Owing to Mother's feeble condition, I have not left the city for five years. Sister Alice, who is not strong, has insisted that she would not leave Baltimore this summer unless I do also. I have, therefore, felt that I must go. We close our house the eighth of July, and probably will not open it again until the first of October. During July and August the mail will be forwarded to me in Virginia, where we have taken board, and I shall at intervals come to the Mission Rooms. It will be in no sense a vacation, for it will really be harder for me to attend to the work in this way than if I could be at the Rooms; but I will have the change of air, and be relieved of housekeeping duties.

If I feel strong enough, during September I expect to go to the Indian Territory, stopping en route in different states so I may meet Central Committees.

Since receiving the manuscripts you last forwarded, I have seen our printer, who does our work at very low rates. He tells me that it will be impossible for him to print the two manuscripts which you have forwarded by the time I leave Baltimore. I cannot undertake to keep on getting out Centennial literature with my other duties, when not in Baltimore. I have tried to see if another printer who works for us at times, could print these leaflets; but his rates are much higher. I will, therefore, send the manuscripts by this mail to Dr. Frost, and ask that you send any others that come to you to him. As you know, the imprint of the Sunday School Board is on this literature, and being a publishing house, I think it is not asking too much of Dr. Frost—should he not be in the city, he could relegate it to Dr. Van Ness or to the business manager—to attend to the printing of same.

I hope soon to send you copies of the leaflet by Dr. Geo. B. Eager, also copies of those by Drs. Carroll and Felix, which are now in the printer's hands. The Annual Report W.M.U. has been printed, and I send copy by this mail. May I ask after glancing over it that you will hand same to Mrs. Barnes?

Hoping that you are feeling quite well, I am,

Very sincerely,

Annie W. Armstrong

[SBHLA, J. M. Frost Collection]

April 21st, 1899

Dr. J. M. Frost

Dear Brother:

Your letter of April 18th received. I hope in the near future to be able to send you full reports of what has been done by the Woman's Mission Societies for the Sunday School Board, classifying the boxes in the way you wish. It is extremely aggravating though, to find how thoroughly wanting in promptness many persons are. About three weeks ago I wrote to every Central Committee, asking them to be prepared to send in their reports by April 20th, and giving very minute directions how said reports should be prepared. This ground is covered by me *every* year. Mrs. Lowndes, treasurer, in sending blank for treasurer's report about two weeks ago wrote a parallel letter. Our books should close on the 20th. This morning, April 21st, I am about to send off four telegrams for four State Reports that have not yet come to hand. You will appreciate from this that it is not *always* possible for the Secretary of the Woman's Missionary Union to be as prompt as she desires. There are few things I dislike as much as I do dilatoriness and it does vex me when I find people so careless and giving so much unnecessary trouble. You may or may not be surprised when I tell you that one of the missing reports is North Carolina's.

I am glad to know that you now see daylight in regard to the Sunday School Board leaflet. We will be glad to have manuscript as soon as you can furnish same. It is the usual custom at the Mission Rooms for all manuscripts for leaflets used in the regular course of mission study to be submitted to two (gentlemen) members of the Committee. This takes a little time and I must give manuscript for the Sunday School Board leaflet to the printer, if not before we go to the Convention, directly after my return.

I appreciate your kind expression of interest in my health. I am sorry to say that I am really quite far from well. I have not seen a physician, nor am I willing to consult one, for I am perfectly well aware what his advice, if not orders, would be, and these I *cannot* follow. When I did at last consent to let the family send for a physician during the attack of grip I had last winter (I refused to see one until I felt I was largely over said attack, as I knew he would not let me keep on directing the work at the Mission Rooms and dictating letters while I was suffering so much with my head) he told me that I must during the course of the next six months take great care of myself, etc., etc. Sister Alice reminds me of this quite frequently, and I am sure if I were to let the family know how miserably I feel at times they would try and insist upon my making a change in some directions and that I cannot think would be right for me to do under existing circumstances. Mrs. Anson Nelson some years ago seemed to think I had adopted the same views that she held as to faith healing. I do not feel that it is wrong to use God-given remedies but sometimes one is placed in a position where she cannot avail herself of such and then I believe it is only right to trust ourselves entirely in God's hands. Work to me as you probably know is a perfect delight and I may not have had the sympathy that I should have with others who find it *hard* to do the Lord's business. I doubt if any of us fully appreciate that offerings are valuable in God's sight in proportion as they represent self denial. "Neither will I offer unto the Lord of that which doeth cost me nothing."

I am hoping after the meetings in Louisville are over that I shall have less worry and anxiety. These exhaust me far more than any amount of work. I am sure no one except my Heavenly Father knows how trying Miss Heck's actions have been to me during the past fifteen months. I sometimes question if I ought not to have persisted in carrying out the decision which I reached before going to Norfolk in August. It is worse than useless though, to think of the "might have beens" for it does not help to nerve us for present realities.

Hoping you are feeling quite strong again, I am,

Very truly,
Annie W. Armstrong
[SBHLA, J. M. Frost Collection]

Annie Armstrong was prone to a certain amount of vanity regarding her appearance. By her mid-40s she knew that she needed glasses but she really did not want them. Also, as her notoriety grew and WMU's various enterprises expanded, Armstrong received requests for her picture—and she refused nearly all such requests. The only known picture of Annie Armstrong is the one most often reproduced, and it was most likely made from a portrait of Armstrong when she was in her 20s. On the one occasion when she allowed her picture to be taken, she would not face the camera.

June 22, 1895
Dr. T. P. Bell
Dear Brother:

According to promise, I forward the manuscript for Missionary Day program so it will reach you some days before the time appointed by you—July 1st. I hope it will meet with your approval. Should, however, you consider any part of it not suitable, or changes desirable, you are at perfect liberty to alter, amend, or reject as you think wise. If there is time I will be glad to see proof of title page, but do not trouble to send proof of the other part of program. Please appreciate that the word "Light" on title page is not to be regarded as a model, but we simply desired to give the idea that the word was to be in large and fancy type. I hope you have decided to have a cut of the lighthouse on title page, as I think it would add much to the appearance. When you next write, I will be glad to have you tell me candidly what you think of the data for program. I consider that we have very thoroughly emphasized the idea, LIGHT, but do not think it contains quite as much information in regard to the mission fields as previous programs.

The packages of *Young People's Leader* and circular to Woman's Mission Societies received, for all of which please accept thanks. I am distributing these in directions where I hope they will tell.

By the way, I am quite sure you had no idea when you wrote the circular that it would be used in the way I find helpful today. I will give you the circumstance, for I think you cannot fail to be amused at the method I have adopted to let one of the officers of the Publication Society know, without the shadow of a doubt, where I stand. Be kind enough to read the enclosed letter which I received a few days since from Dr. C. R. Blackall, and then tell me if you see the connection between an article on Mexico and a picture of the Cor. Sec'y. W.M.U., who never has been to Mexico. I do not want to misjudge Dr. Blackall's motive in applying for this article, but the whole thing seems to me perfectly absurd. Could he have thought for one instant that I would accede to such a request? I recognize the fact *if he does not* that *Kind Words* is the paper that ought to be taken by Southern Baptist Sunday Schools, and those of us who are doing the work in the Southern States are to be introduced to our own young people through our own organs and not by outside ones. Do not think from this remark that I would have my picture in any paper. This letter of Dr. Blackall's recalls something that occurred in the long gone-by which really is rather an amusing coincidence. About 20 years or more ago, I had a picture taken, and, much to my astonishment and indignation, a minister, who is now one of the officers of the Publication Society, without my knowledge and before I had been furnished with copies, had a stereoptican slide made of said picture. The first knowledge I had of it was at an exhibition given by the reverend gentleman. You may imagine my indignation. From that time I determined that I would never have another picture taken and have strictly adhered to that resolution. This is certainly a queer, queer world and with some monstrous queer people in it.

I believe, though, I have failed to tell you what reply I made to Dr. Blackall. I of course declined and enclosed your circular in the letter, not making any allusion, however, to it. I send you one so you may see how thoroughly it covered the ground—of what I did not say. I could have replied to Dr. Blackall more concisely in these words: "Cor. Secretary W.M.U. is not for sale." Dr. Blackall's letter has decided me not to make the application which I thought of making to Dr. Rowland for writing for Miss Heck, for I do not suppose they would accept her contributions if she used a nom de plume.

Now for another item of business and then I must close. Miss Buhlmaier, German missionary, called to see me a day or two since and asked if you would be willing to furnish her with a further grant of 200 German Testaments with Psalms for distribution at the emigrant landing. She would also like to have copies of back numbers of *Kind Words* for distribution. She can make use of a number of these, as she has three sewing schools and would like to have the papers to give to the children; also an occasional paper in her house-to-house visiting—current numbers of papers are not necessary, but any old stock you may have on hand. Another request of hers was for picture rolls used in Infant Class teaching. Have you any old editions of these? If so, they could be utilized to advantage in her work. If you can make any or all of these grants to the German work, please forward them direct. Miss Buhlmaier's address is 835 N. Washington St., Baltimore.

When you have time, I will be glad to know what is your idea in regard to literature for young people referred to in your letter of June 15th. I doubt if it is necessary for me to say—I think you appreciate how much interested I am in the Southern young people being identified with our work—that you can count on any aid you desire from me in this direction if it is in my power to render same. When I can find a little leisure, I want to give you some ideas that have presented themselves to me in regard to ways of interesting the young people in our work, etc., etc.

Hoping you had a pleasant and profitable visit to Atlanta and have entirely recovered from your indisposition, I am,

Very truly,

Annie W. Armstrong

[Handwritten in margin] I am very thankful to be able to say that arrangements have been made so we will not have to move the Mission Rooms.

A postal received from Dr. Willingham this morning. He says "I am at office again, but very weak. My sickness the worst in twenty-five years. Mrs. Willingham writes: "Mr. Willingham has been quite sick, sicker than I have ever seen him. He is up again, and went to the office for awhile this morning but is still far from well."

[SBHLA, J. M. Frost Collection]

May 22, 1897

Dr. R. J. Willingham

Dear Brother:

Your letter of May 21st just received and noting that you desire an immediate reply, I have put other letters aside until I answer yours.

I am truly glad to know that Mr. Wm. Ellyson will accompany you to Mexico as you think it necessary to take the trip, for I can appreciate that it will be quite a relief to you to have a member of the Board with whom to consult while you are making the needed investigations. While the difficulties in that country seem to be of a serious nature, yet I think we have recently had such positive proof that our Heavenly Father has set His seal of approval on the work as done by Southern Baptists, that I trust when you reach Mexico you will find, as in the past, the "stone rolled away," even though it be "very great." I shall try, from the time you and Mr. Ellyson leave until you return, to daily ask that wisdom may be given both of you to know what God's will is and that He will have you specially in His own care and keeping while on this mission.

Now in regard to the request you have made. I think you appreciate that there are few things I would refuse to do if I thought they would be helpful to the cause which you and I both so dearly love. You have, however, asked one of the few things which I long ago decided I could not do, viz., have a picture of myself appear in a magazine or paper. You will probably be surprised when I tell you that I have not had a picture taken for over 20 years. I think you may be amused at a little incident which I will now mention (I know you will kindly not speak of this, but, in the light of recent events, the circumstance is rather entertaining). One of the present officers of the Publication Society is responsible for my reaching the conclusion which I did 20 years ago, that I would *never*, under any circumstances, have a picture taken again. The gentleman above referred to had very kindly offered his aid in connection with an institution which then very largely filled my time and thoughts, viz., the Home of the Friendless, which is a shelter for destitute children. I had arranged for a Christmas entertainment and asked for the assistance of this friend in giving a stereoptican exhibition. Not only were the children of the institution to witness the entertainment, but a thousand cards had been sent to children throughout the city in better circumstances, asking that they would attend said entertainment bringing with them Christmas offerings for the little ones under our charge. I had had a photograph taken a few days before that, but it had not been furnished me by the photographer, so you can imagine my surprise and, I must say, disgust when I saw my own picture appear on the canvass during the stereoptican exhibition. There were some circumstances connected with this that made some of my friends consider it a peculiarly amusing experience. I did not see it in the same light, and the effect it had was to lead me to assure my family that that was the *last* picture I should ever have taken, and I have strictly adhered to that determination.

Since I have been engaged in more public work, I have been extremely glad there was no picture of mine in existence which any one could use for a cut to appear in papers. I do not think such notoriety at all desirable for women. Numerous requests have come to me for pictures, and in some directions feeling has been shown when I declined to furnish them, but as I have never broken through the rule which I laid down for myself years ago, no one has a right to call in question my decision. Dr. Bell made the same request you have made only a few weeks ago in regard to the *Index*. I replied to him in the same way I have to you, so I know you will not misunderstand my refusing to do as you have asked. I will refer your request to Sister Alice, but I am sure she looks at the matter in the same light as I do. Miss Heck has refused to furnish her picture to the local papers where the Conventions have been held, but whether she will make an exception for the *Foreign Mission Journal*, I cannot say.

As to a "short history of the Woman's Work for the Woman's Department in July *Journal*." I have no doubt Sister Alice will be perfectly willing to prepare said history. I will, when I go home to dinner, ask that she write to you in regard to it.

There are several other matters of which I desire to speak, so I will take these up seriatim.

1. *Pictures for July Journal*. I note you are proposing to put in the *Journal* pictures of Drs. Carey and Judson, etc. During the Centennial Year, the Woman's Missionary Union got out a Centennial program for Children's Day. I enclose copy. You will see in it a number of pictures. These cuts we obtained from the Publication Society. I have the plates, and should you wish them and think there would be no objection to my furnishing you with them, they are at your command.

2. *Receipt for money handed you while in Wilmington*. Kindly let me have same—I do not recall the amount, but I have reference to the collection taken at W.M.U. meetings—as I desire to forward it to Miss Heck, so it may be included by the Central Committee of N. C. with their other vouchers.

3. *Check for Woman's Missionary Union expenses*. At a meeting of the Executive Committee of the Woman's Missionary Union, which was held yesterday, I was requested to write to the Foreign Board, asking that an appropriation of $300.00 would be made by that Board for W.M.U. expenses. The Annual Report is now being printed and several other publications which are necessary to be put into the hands of the Societies without delay, in order that the year's work may be started effectively. This necessitates our making quite large expenditures at the first of the year, so we will have to ask for check of the amount named.

4. *Collection for Foreign Board*. I think you will like to know how Eutaw Place Church is proposing to present the subject of the debt, so I enclose circular which was sent this week to the membership.

After you return home and have a little leisure, I want to ask you to help me to devise some way by which I can bring the cause of Foreign Missions more prominently before the Woman's Mission Societies and Bands. I am sure the Woman's Missionary Union is not doing all it should for the Foreign Board, and this year I do want that we shall raise every cent you have asked for us, viz., $30,000.00. It ought to be done, and I believe it can be done.

Very truly,
Annie W. Armstrong
[IMB Archives]

June 17, 1897
Rev. A. J. Barton
Dear Brother:
Your letter of June 16th received this A. M. In reply to your inquiry in regard to the tracts: "The Doom of the Heathen," by Dr. R. H. Graves, and "Go Ye, or Send a Substitute," by Rev. J. P. Green, I would say they were both printed some years ago by the Foreign Mission Board. I doubt if we have any copies of these leaflets at the Mission Rooms, but if they are needed for a special purpose and you cannot find any stray ones in your collection, I will make a search and see if I can come up with either.

The proof of Woman's Department in *Foreign Mission Journal* was received this morning. Sister Alice, who has not been at all strong for some months past, left home yesterday to pay a short visit to a relative a few miles from Baltimore—she would not consent to go any distance on account of Mother's feeble condition. Before leaving, however, she requested that I would mail the proof to her, as she preferred looking over same herself, so I forwarded it without delay and it will be returned, I am sure, promptly.

It is a pleasure to note that the work of the Sunday School Board has such a warm place in your heart. Ever since its organization, I have tried as far as was in my power to aid the Secretaries of this Board, as I consider there is no agency of the Convention that has in it greater possibilities.

In regard to the Bible Card and tract, I would say that the present issue is 15,000 copies of the leaflet and 10,000 of the card. Dr. Frost sent a few days ago between five and six thousand addressed envelopes to the Mission Rooms—I offered to have this work done for the Sunday School Board. In said envelopes samples of this literature will be sent to Superintendents. I think it quite probable that in the near future we will have a second edition of both card and leaflet, so I am going to ask that you will not hesitate to criticize as severely as you think wise the two publications, for I shall be only too glad to have all needed corrections made in the next issue. I fear we are attempting to do more at the Mission Rooms than can be done thoroughly, so mistakes sometimes are not noticed by us. I must acknowledge that proof reading is to me extremely disagreeable. I know I have gotten to the time when it would be advisable to use glasses, but those who have adopted same seem to find so much trouble from mislaying or breaking them, that I want to dispense with glasses as long as possible. I judge the close attention it requires to notice the mistakes in type setting is what causes the physical discomfort that I experience when I attempt to read proof, and so I relegate this part of the work to others perhaps more frequently than I ought. I really appreciate your calling my attention to the errors, which, however, I shall not attempt to discover until you let me know where they are to be found.

Very truly,

Annie W. Armstrong

P. S. Will you kindly see that the change in address is made in the Mission Rooms advertisement in the *Foreign Mission Journal*? It still gives 9 W. Lexington Street as the address for the Mission Rooms, instead of 304 N. Howard Street.

[IMB Archives]

August 17, 1897

Dr. J. M. Frost

Dear Brother:

I have just had a visit from Rev. J. O. Rust. We have had quite a spirited discussion in regard to the Whitsitt matter. I am under the impression that I was not quite as judicious as I should have been in expressing my opinion to a comparative stranger in regard to this knotty problem, so am feeling quite uncomfortable. I think after this I will be an interested *listener* when this subject is brought forward, but now to business.

Our Stenographer leaves for her holiday on Friday, so I am going to now reply to that part of your letter of Aug. 13th which needs to be referred to, as I shall, during the time of her absence, be a little more pressed with work. I note what you say in regard to furnishing a picture of myself to appear in the Convention Almanac. I can hardly think you are in earnest when you urge that I do this. As you seem, though, to be, I will give you my reasons for *positively* declining.

1. I do not consider that periodicals, newspapers, etc., are the places where ladies' photographs should appear. I appreciate, in holding the offices I do, that in a certain sense I am a public individual, but in another sense I am not, and I certainly do not feel willing to let myself be put before the public in any such light.

2. I have been perfectly surprised at the number of similar requests which have been made of me. Having repeatedly declined, should I break through the rule that I have made, it would of course subject me to criticism to which I object extremely. Not only have I been asked for pictures to appear in Baptist papers, but in others. It seems now to be a "fad" with Editors of papers to have appear in their publications pictures of those who are engaged in benevolent work. Then again, personal requests for photographs have been numerous. I now recall a perfect stranger asking to be allowed to *pay* for a "large picture" of the Cor. Sec. W.M.U. Being able to say, as I now can, I have not had a picture taken for over 20 years and *never* expect to have another, it makes it easier for me to decline these personal requests.

As you and I do not seem to see this matter in the same light, I want to ask if you would object to my suggesting to the Editors of the Norfolk daily papers, when they send to me as Cor. Sec. of the Woman's Missionary Union next spring for my picture (this now seems to be the regular order of things), that it would add interest to their papers for them to obtain the pictures of the wives of the Secretaries of the Boards, and, at the same time when they ask for Mrs. Frost's, for them to request one from Miss Margaret Frost, a talented young writer. It is probable that this illustrated edition will go into the lager-beer saloons in Norfolk, but it will also be in the hands of the delegates to the Southern Baptist Convention, and for that reason could you not ignore this fact? Possibly (probably), you will say this is not a parallel case. Perhaps not, but still, should there be cuts of the wives and daughters of the Secretaries of the Boards in the Convention Almanac, they would doubtless also be seen in the Convention edition of the Norfolk daily papers next year.

I sincerely hope you will not get offended at what I have said, but I do want you to appreciate how I regard this matter, and I know of no better way than to, as the children say, "turn the table." If I have not been able to convince you that I am right in the position which I have taken, I would be glad for you to state the case to Mrs. Frost, and I am sure she will for once disagree with her husband—try it and see.

Very truly,

Annie W. Armstrong

[SBHLA, J. M. Frost Collection]

June 1, 1898

Dr. J. M. Frost

Dear Brother:

Your letter of May 30th received and I do trust you carried out your intention to have forwarded to me the next day a package of programs, supplements and order blanks for Children's Day, as I have several orders from Central Committees waiting to be filled, and unless I can furnish this literature shortly, I fear it will be of very little service. I have some Bible cards on hand. I am hoping a large sum will be raised on Children's Day. In any case, though, I am sure this effort will very materially aid the Sunday School Board. I will send you extracts from a few letters in regard to Children's Day. Mrs. J. S. Dill, Va., says:

"I wrote you a postal that I thought best not to send out the literature for Children's Day. I have conferred since with Elizabeth Pollard (Cor. Sec.) and we have decided to have you send us 150 copies."

Mrs. John W. Starnes, Cor. Sec. of the Central Committee of Western North Carolina, writes:

"Your letter, with samples of literature for Children's Day, received. Please send me 100 copies of program, 100 supplements, 100 order blanks and 100 Bible cards. I find that sending these samples to the Woman's Mission Societies is the only way to get the country schools to observe these special days."

Miss M. L. Coker, President of Central Committee of S. C., writes:

"Since you have sent the programs, etc., we will send them out. Will try to get them off in a few days and hope they will stir up a greater interest. Our only reason for hesitation about sending them was the probability that specimen copies were already in the hands of Sunday School officers with whom our Societies were associated, and that it is already so near the time suggested. We are anxious to do all we can to increase interest in the work of the Sunday School Board, and especially in the Bible Fund."

Miss E. S. Broadus, President of Central Committee of Ky., says:

"Dr. Frost wrote me about the Sunday School Bible Day, and I asked him to send a supply of programs, etc., to Mrs. Woody. She was to write a letter, to be manifolded to be sent to each Society and Band in the State, asking them to help and to encourage the Superintendent to observe the Day and carry out the enclosed program when deemed best. I presume she has done this, but we could probably use more in the meeting above mentioned—an all-day meeting, to be held in Louisville." (Miss Broadus was writing from Charlottesville, Va.)

As this is the day for sending manuscripts to papers, I enclose monthly installment for the *Teacher*.

I forward two pictures of Dr. Fuller. I do not know that you will care for either of these. A photographer told me that good cuts can be secured from either. Dr. Fuller's grandson, Richard Kimbell, promised to send to the Mission Rooms another picture which he thought a better likeness than the small one enclosed. We have at home quite a good likeness of Dr. Fuller. You may have noticed it when at 1423 McCulloh Street, as it was in the room you occupied. It is a large picture, not half length, but taken a little above the waist, with hand in coat as in the one I send. It is considered a very good, as well as pleasing likeness. Should you wish me to do so, I could have a copy taken from it for you. If that is done, it might be well for you to give the size to which you would wish it reduced. Please do not let anything happen to the pictures which I now send, as they are not my property and are much valued by their owners.

You have no idea how many important matters there are which I must refer to you. These will have to be sent in installments, as the regular mail is accumulating to an alarming extent, so I cannot take time to refer to any of these today.

Who do you think was my last visitor? A photographer whom I have interviewed in order to carry out a request of Dr. Willingham, viz., to have pictures taken of the Mission Rooms (3), of which he desires to make use in the July edition of the *Journal*. That is to be a special edition, and he thinks if he can give a bird's eye view of the local habitation of the Woman's Missionary Union, it would interest some of the general readers. He further desires that the Secretary should be seated at her desk. This I have promised, but a position will undoubtedly be assumed which does not enable any one to recognize the occupant of the chair.

Very truly,

Annie W. Armstrong

P. S. I am just having one order filled for Children's Day literature from a Sunday School at Rockville, Md., which comes in response to the appeal which I made to the society at that point. Another order is waiting to be filled from the Seventh Church Sunday School, Baltimore, until the package reaches me from Nashville. If the money is sent direct to you from any Sunday Schools in Maryland, either from Children's Day or Missionary Day, please forward to me duplicate receipts. All money that comes to me from the Sunday Schools, either for Home, Foreign or Bible Work, will be forwarded to you, so I in turn ask that you send duplicate receipts to us for money that comes direct to you from the Sunday Schools in our State. Kindly give order to this effect to the one who is in the habit of sending receipts.

P. S. No. 2. I find I have not more than about 200 Bible cards left, so please follow up the programs with 1,000 Bible cards as soon as possible.

[SBHLA, J. M. Frost Collection]

June 6, 1898

Dr. J. M. Frost

Dear Brother:

It is near the close of a very fatiguing day and really I am hardly equal to writing any more letters, but as I have to leave home tomorrow to attend a District Association and be gone for two days, I must try and send you information in regard to several matters. Please excuse, though, all seeming abruptness, for I am quite worn out and far from well. Dr. Clopton takes tea with us tonight, or I should be tempted to play the part of an invalid, but now to business.

1. *Application from Miss Buhlmaier.* I enclose letter which will explain itself. Please note specially what she says in regard to her need for denominational literature. Shall Miss Buhlmaier, as heretofore, apply for

same to Dr. Gregory, who obtains it from the Publication Society? I would not be willing to make any application for supplies from that source, but as Dr. Gregory does not look at things in quite the same light, these tracts can be obtained through him, if it is not convenient for you to grant them. The general evangelistic tracts I secure for Miss Buhlmaier through the Secretary of the American Tract Society.

2. *Request from Rev. H. J. E. Williams*. Please note the request he makes for Bibles, books and tracts.

3. *Cards and papers from Bands*. I appreciate the point you make when you say: "I think your idea of getting the Bands to gather up these is very well, provided it could be worked with sufficient care, so that the missionaries would not think we were trying to palm old clothes off on them," and if the plan which I have suggested is approved by the Executive Committee, to whom I will submit it at the next meeting, I will write to Mr. Kuykendall and fully explain same before doing anything in the matter.

4. *Package of Children's Day literature*. It came duly to hand today and I partially distributed same.

5. *Pictures of the Mission Rooms*. Yes, these have been taken (one of each room) and having seen the proofs, I am prepared to say they are quite pleasing reproductions, but you are entirely mistaken in thinking there will be a recognizable likeness of the Secretary of same to appear in the *Foreign Mission Journal*. As Dr. Willingham asked that I would be seated at my desk, I am there, but no one could possibly say who it is. It is simply a figurehead and that is all. As I wrote you previously, I never expect to have another likeness taken.

LATER, June 7, 1898. I was not able to finish this letter last night, so will now add a few lines. I am writing, though, in much haste, as I must leave the Mission Rooms shortly to take the train. There are several matters, though of which I want to speak.

1. *Leaflets*. The printer has furnished a few copies of your leaflet. I enclose one. He promises to have the entire number ready for delivery the last of the week, when I will have shipped to you 10,000. I hope you will find the leaflet satisfactory. I do not think I ever read a leaflet as frequently as I have this one of yours. I noted, after you returned the proof, some mistakes that you had not corrected, so went over same again very carefully. Later an accident happened to the plates as they were being electrotyped, and so I again read the proof. I think I have read this leaflet three or four times, so shall be very much disappointed if there are any glaring mistakes

that I have overlooked. Proofreading to me is not a very pleasant occupation, so you can appreciate that I have paid a tribute to your leaflet which I do not as a general thing give to the numerous publications that we get out at the Mission Rooms.

2. *Packages of literature to be sent to pastors.* I will shortly be able to send you a sample package and hope to mail all of them before the close of the month. The appeal we changed somewhat and included in it a distinct paragraph for the Sunday School Board.

3. *Electrotype.* I return the one which you kindly forwarded a few days ago of the religions of the world. Please accept warm and hearty thanks for use of same.

I really must draw this letter to a close, but before doing so, want to refer to a paragraph which I find in your letter of June 3rd, viz., "My curiosity is somewhat up as to the 'news' which you have promised me, and leads me to make the remark: Be sure that nothing rash is done. It is so easy to do a rash thing that will bring much trouble." I have not sent you the news to which I referred in my previous letter for the reason that I have not had time to give you same, also that I was waiting for further developments. I judge, though, from the words of caution you have thought necessary to give, that you have some idea of what my news is. Will you pardon me for speaking plainly? As this trouble—which is to me very, very trying and I consider altogether unnecessary—has been caused by the desire on the part of the Secretary of the Woman's Missionary Union to carry out the plans of the Sunday School Board, I think I have a right to ask, not only for your support, but perfect openness. If information from any other source has reached you, I am going to ask that you let me know what it is. I of course do not expect that you will give your support, unless you think the Cor. Sec. W.M.U. is in the right. Of that, I am sure, though, any unprejudiced judge would decide in my favor. There are some things I am perfectly ready and willing to yield, but there are others that I cannot think I am called on to give up when it is simply a question of pleasing persons. If I am in the wrong, I trust grace will be given to cause me to make any acknowledgments, no matter how trying, but if in the right—and I thoroughly believe I am entirely in the right in this matter—I do not propose to yield one iota. When other persons do and say things that are wrong, if we condone them, it just makes them more determined to persevere in wrong doing, and so I feel that we ought to calmly and quietly continue in a certain course of action which leads them to appreciate just how we regard the matter.

My time is up, so I must close right here.

Very truly,

Annie W. Armstrong

P. S. This letter will have to be signed on the typewriter, as I cannot wait for it to be copied before I leave the Mission Rooms.

[SBHLA, J. M. Frost Collection]

June 7, 1898

Dr. R. J. Willingham

Dear Brother:

Your letter of June 6th received. I must leave in a few moments to take the train to attend a District Association near Washington. As I will have to be away for two days I must reply to your letter before I go. It will have to be written very hurriedly, so if I am not clear in my statement please excuse. Now to business.

1. *Dr. Dill's leaflet.* I have given order for 10,000 copies, to be printed and sent to Richmond.

2. *Pictures of Mission Rooms.* Yesterday the photographer submitted proofs and they were very pleasing. The execution is beautiful, and I think without doubt good cuts can be secured. Since receiving your letter, I have sent to the photographer and find prices for additional pictures will be as follows:

A single copy of any one of the three pictures, $1.00; one dozen copies from any one negative, $6.00; one dozen copies, four of each from three negatives, $9.00. The pictures will be mounted on large cardboard. I do not know what the size will be when completed. I hope to forward the three pictures to you on Friday, so they will reach you this week.

3. *Article on Baptist Mission Rooms.* I expect to return from the District Association Thursday afternoon. I have had to defer having carpets taken up at home on account of my absence, but have arranged for that necessary work to be done on Friday, so it is probable I cannot be at the Mission Rooms again until Friday afternoon. If possible, I will send you the article, which is now partly written, Friday evening. If not, certainly on Saturday. The title which I have thought of giving the article is: "A Need Supplied." Make any changes, though, you think desirable when it reaches you.

4. Notice of appeal for Missionary Concert of Prayer to pastors. If possible, I will send this on Saturday, reaching you Monday. I hope by that time also to forward samples of the different publications that will be sent in packages to pastors.

5. Electrotypes. Do you wish me to forward to Richmond the electrotypes which you selected for me to lay aside when in Baltimore? They are as follows: Japanese idol; Chinese punishment; African warrior.

No letter as yet from President of Woman's Missionary Union. As I have business with her as one in charge of work in North Carolina, I have written to her in regard to new publications and propose to ignore the total want of courtesy in acknowledging my former letter. I have not had time to write to Dr. Frost in regard to this new phase of trouble, but judge he has received information from some other source in regard to it from some words of warning which he seems to think it necessary to give me, but I must close right here if I am to get the train which I want to take.

Hastily,

Annie W. Armstrong

P. S. This letter will have to be signed on the typewriter, as I cannot wait for it to be copied before I leave the Mission Rooms.

[IMB Archives]

Annie Armstrong never married but she loved children and maintained a close relationship with her mother and sister, Alice.

March 25, 1895

Dr. R. J. Willingham

Dear Brother:

I expect you will think that I am deluging you with information in regard to the shelling of Tung Chow, but appreciating, as Secretary of the Foreign Board, that you like to be fully posted, when information comes into my hands which I think possibly you may not have, I feel better satisfied to send it on. This preamble will explain my reason for forwarding several printed articles, which came from China. After reading these, I would be glad to have them returned; that is, unless you have some immediate use for same. I know they will be welcomed by any of our State papers and I think it may be well to send to them one or two. If you agree with me in this, in returning them, let me know to which papers you would rather have them go. I have lately sent several original communications to

The Religious Herald, so think it may be better for forward these in other directions.

I am glad to know that both Mrs. Willingham and the little one are doing well. When I tell you that I have for nearly twenty-four years had charge of the Infant class at Eutaw Place Church, you will appreciate that I dearly love children. I used to periodically electrify our little family by telling them that I was going to adopt a child, but of late years the mission work has so completely occupied every moment, I have had to give up this pet idea. Please present my kind regards to Mrs. Willingham, and tell her if she were only in Baltimore I should certainly give myself the pleasure of calling to see the little new son.

I have received a letter from Mrs. Ginsburg, which I think you may like to see, as it tells of her plans, so enclose same.

Very truly,

Annie W. Armstrong

P. S. Please let me know when I shall forward bill for leaflets purchased from Mission Rooms by the Foreign Board.

[IMB Archives]

August 12, 1897

My dear Mrs. Stratton,

I am unable to be at the Mission Rooms today—Mother is not so well—but the mail is brought to 1423 McCulloh Street and the Stenographer is here, so I can dictate letters. I cannot delay writing, as there is an important matter which must be presented to you at once. It hardly seems possible, but the time has come when we must decide how we can most effectively carry out the Recommendation which was presented (and adopted by Woman's Missionary Union in Wilmington), not by one Board, but all three, in regard to Sunday School Missionary Day. You will note, by referring to the Recommendations which I enclose, that each one of the Boards has asked the Woman's Missionary Union to assist in making Sunday School Missionary Day effective. It is the only line of work in which all three Boards unite and for which they all ask our cooperation. * The Sunday School Board reaps no pecuniary benefit from the work they are doing in this direction, (it reports the money raised on S. S. Miss. Day) the contributions going to advance the work of the other two Boards, but through this means it is helping to educate the children along missionary lines, which is one of the primary objects of our Sunday School Board.

In presenting this matter to you, I think I will give you a quotation from a letter I received a short time ago from our President, Miss F. E. S. Heck. She writes:

"I was very much pleased with the X Rays program as you showed it to me in Wilmington. (In compliance with request, we furnished Sunday School Board with manuscript for program). I am of the opinion that if the Central Committees will send a copy to each of their societies at the proper time, and urge the women to use their influence to have them carried out in their churches, the number of churches observing the day will be much larger. This need not interfere with sending direct to Sunday School Superintendents, but will put an added force at work. Women *must* train the children for these exercises, and the women most likely to do it are in the Woman's Mission Societies. Why not, then, send copies and plans through the agency which has closest contact and most influence with these women? I am sure this would be a helpful thing in N. C., and I would be glad to send sample copy, etc., to all our societies, should you and the Sunday School Board think this best."

Dr. Frost does desire the assistance of the Central Committees and the aid of the societies, if possible to secure same, in getting Missionary Day generally observed. I now enclose samples of literature, and will be glad to furnish you with as many copies of each of the publications as you desire. In making order, please specify the number of each you wish.

There are other matters about which I would like to write, but I must finish dictating letters as soon as possible, so I can go to Mother.

Lovingly yours,

Annie W. Armstrong

[Handwritten insert at end of page] * I shall have to change this wording as I now see I have not been perfectly truthful in saying the S. S. Board receives no pecuniary benefit, as you report these contributions among your gifts.

[SBHLA, J. M. Frost Collection]

March 18, 1902
Dr. J. M. Frost
Dear Brother:

As you know, I left Baltimore February 24th, expecting to be absent four weeks, but when I reached De Land, Fla., last Saturday afternoon, on alighting from the cars I was handed several letters and a telegram. On opening the telegram which was from my sister, Mrs. Levering, I learned of Sister Alice's serious illness. I, of course, took the first train to Baltimore, and arrived here yesterday afternoon. You may imagine my distress when I found that the physician had thought it necessary to call in two trained nurses. This morning he tells me that Sister Alice has been very ill, but he hopes she is better. He evidently, though, does not consider she is out of danger.

I am now at the Mission Rooms, trying to get the work again in hand, but you can realize that I am not quite equal to considering important questions. I received your letter and am glad to know that you will make an address at the Annual Meeting of Woman's Missionary Union in Asheville—I will write of that later.

My reason for writing today is to send a list of boxes not previously reported, and to ask that you will at once let me have receipts for these. Those from Georgia are needed so that they may be included in this year's report to the Georgia Convention.

I was very sorry to learn from a letter received from Dr. Van Ness that you, too, have not been well. I hope your indisposition is not of a serious nature.

Very truly,
Annie W. Armstrong
[SBHLA, J. M. Frost Collection]

Armstrong had a sense of humor that sometimes appears in her letters unexpectedly.

August 18, 1897
Dr. R. J. Willingham
Dear Brother:

May I ask that you will kindly read the two letters of which I enclose, and then instruct me how to answer the inquiries these ladies have made on the following points.

1. Mrs. Gatewood, in regard to the disposition of jewelry. Lately I have had several letters from Mrs. Gatewood, who seems thoroughly interested in missions, her desire having been in the past to become a missionary, but circumstances prevented. It doubtless would be a pleasure to her to have this jewelry converted into money, but I appreciate the difficulty you experience in disposing of same. I am thankful to say that the Cor. Sec'y W.M.U., owing to resolution passed, is not at liberty to have committed to her such offerings.

2. Mrs. Starnes, Cor. Sec. of the Central Committee of Western North Carolina, as to the most effective leaflet to counteract Gospel Mission misstatements. Please let me know which you consider most effective, and if you have same for distribution, I will be glad if you will forward a number to 304 N. Howard Street.

I am now at the Mission Rooms, Mother being better, but as our Stenographer leaves tomorrow, I am quite busily engaged sending off letters, as I desire to have all now in hand answered before she goes—I am not a very rapid Typewriter, and so the daily mail will probably be all I can manage during her absence.

Very truly,

Annie W. Armstrong

P. S. Since writing the above, your letter of August 17th received. I will, when I have a little leisure, read Mrs. Maynard's article. Do you wish it returned to you for publication in *Journal*, or shall I make use of it otherwise?

I would be very, very glad to accept your kind invitation, but it is perfectly out of the question. I cannot leave home for a single day. Sister, Mrs. Levering, has been urging me all summer to come out and spend the day (if I will not stay longer) at her country home, but I really cannot be spared from the Mission Rooms, especially at this stage of things, even if Mother was well enough for me to go for a day's outing. My family and others enter a very strong protest against my being so closely confined, but I believe I am right, and daily strength will be given.

I do congratulate you on getting through with your housecleaning so early in the season. I think, if I had been in your place, I should have deferred same until the weather was a little cooler, or until Brother Barton had returned, so he might have a share in it. You can now sympathize with Mrs. Willingham in her semi-annual overturnings. I do thoroughly despise spring and fall cleanings. The results are very gratifying, but the means necessary to bring them about are not at all to my taste.

Yes, I agree with you that it is indeed "terrible how our Baptist Zion is stirred up." In what paper is Dr. Coleman's article? I have not seen it, nor did I know of any attack being made on the other members of the Seminary faculty. Yesterday I had a visit from Rev. J. O. Rust. We had quite a spirited discussion in regard to the Whitsitt matter. I am under the impression that I was not quite as judicious as I should have been in expressing my opinion to a comparative stranger in regard to this knotty problem, so am feeling quite uncomfortable. I think after this I will be an interested *listener* when this subject is brought forward. Mr. Rust is prepared to do valiant fighting for Dr. Whitsitt and seems to think, unless he is supported, that all organized work will come to naught in the near future. I certainly do not see things in this light. Mr. Rust told me, which I had not known previously (I do not see the *Biblical Recorder*), of the action taken in North Carolina against Dr. Whitsitt.

[IMB Archives]

December 23, 1898
Rev. A. J. Barton
Dear Brother:
Yes, your letters of Nov. 15th and Dec. 19th both received. The first one, I put aside, expecting to be able to answer it in person while in Richmond and was genuinely sorry not to do so. Since my return, I have been either too busy or too sick to give thought to anything that could be put aside. I suppose I have been indulging in a first class attack of Grip. Let it be what it may—the physician, whom I at last consented to call on, seemed so anxious to impress upon me that I must beware, take care, etc., etc., or else dreadful things would happen, that he did not announce his diagnosis of my present ailments—but if Grip it is, I would advise you steer clear of it. I have been for over ten days anchored at 1423 McCulloh St. In the meantime, though, I have had two visits a day from the clerks at the Mission Rooms, so have been able to keep the work from getting very much in arrears.

Now as to your "scheme." Do not imagine for one instant that you can equal Dr. Wharton. His latest is an effort to draw "young ones" to his store by fitting up the third floor with a toy machine shop, electric cars, stereoptican views and a magician. As you have asked for my opinion, I am going to give it without reservation. I think it a capital plan to interest the students in the various colleges in missions, but I pity both you and Dr.

Willingham if you will have to gaze on the wretched portraits which will be perpetrated by embryo artists. I consider it takes a very high order of talent not to make caricatures of persons when portraits are being made of them. Several years ago my brother-in-law, Eugene Levering, thought to gratify his wife by having an oil painting taken by one who was considered a first class artist. The picture impressed me as if it had been taken for Mr. Levering's own grandfather, who for the occasion was resurrected. I am reminded of a photograph album which I arranged in my girlhood days, when photography was not as successful as it is now. I amused myself with placing in this album some rather forlorn specimens and terming it the "gallery of frights." I would suggest that name, or "the Chamber of Horrors," for your office and Dr. Willingham's, after it has been decorated in the way you propose. It is your idea, is it not, to have pictures taken only of departed missionaries. If that is the case, probably good and only good will result from your "scheme," if you and Dr. Willingham can stand the ordeal. It has just occurred to me that I have at the Mission Rooms the picture of a missionary—one of our frontier friends—who seems to have made a study of attitudes. I think I will have it sent to you and would ask that you put it directly over your desk. I am sure it will be a good preparation for those to follow, but enough of this foolishness. I really am in earnest when I say I think the plan you have suggested will interest many students in our colleges in mission work.

Your allusion to Christmas has made me feel really a little heartsick. No, there can be little or no preparation in our home this year for Christmas cheer. Sister Alice has also had an attack of Grip, and so it will not be possible for us to make any festive preparations. I have long ago learned, though, that unless there are some "little folks" in a family, Xmas time is not a very bright season. Before the Mission Rooms absorbed so completely my time and attention, I used to try and make happy at this season of the year a large number of little ones in an institution of which I was a manager, but that had to be given up, much to my regret, soon after I became Secretary of the Woman's Missionary Union. I have often wished I could borrow some little ones at Xmas time, for I dearly love to see their pleasure and excitement over stockings, Christmas trees, etc., etc.

Hoping your little folks will thoroughly enjoy Christmas Day and that the father and mother will with them have a merry time, I am,

Very truly,

Annie W. Armstrong

P. S. You doubtless will recall that several months ago I asked that you let me have the names and ages of the children of the missionaries. You could not furnish these, but kindly offered to write and secure them for me. I did not care to put you to that trouble, and since then have secured not only the names, but slight sketches of a number. I now forward you copies of these, also of the letter that I have been sending to Central Committees, which will give you the use that I thought could be made of them. I send you a file of the letters, as I think possibly information they contain may prove of service.

Later. I have just received copies of the Convention Almanac for 1899. To emphasize what I have previously said in regard to pictures, kindly refer to Rev. W. B. Bagby on page 24.

[IMB Archives]

January 13, 1902
Dr. R. J. Willingham
Dear Brother:
Your letter of January 11th with report of Christmas offering received. The amounts are so trifling I hardly like to publish same, but as it is our custom to make report in February *Journal*, I expect I had better make the statement, and it will probably cause the treasurers to forward the money *instanter*.

Noting that you will have a Board Meeting on Tuesday, I now send bill for Christmas Offering expenses. Appreciating that your hands are very, very full preparing for the Board Meeting, I will not trouble you with several other matters, but I will write again either tomorrow or Wednesday.

I am glad to know that you are going to allow yourself a day off. I note, though, it is not a week day, but Sunday. Speaking of Sunday reminds me of a funny experience I had this morning. Mr. Millard yesterday gave us a remarkably, strong sermon, taking as his subject "The Tongue." This morning when he came to the Mission Rooms, he wished me to tell him why I could not work with Dr. Gregory. I declined giving him the information he desired, telling him I preferred to say nothing whatever on the subject. When he insisted upon knowing, I asked him if he did not recall the sermon which he had preached yesterday. He replied, "Oh yes, but sometimes for the good of the cause one is obliged to speak." It is a good deal easier to preach than to practice. Mr. Millard's curiosity got the better of him. I declined positively, though, to furnish the information which he desired.

I suppose it is nearly decided that Dr. Gregory will be elected as State Secretary for all his time. I am not a prophet, but if he gets the position, I think his term of office will be short. More anon.

Very truly,

Annie W. Armstrong

P. S. Our address is 233 N. Howard St. instead of 304. I think you will agree with me that we have made a good exchange when you next pay us a visit. We are on the third floor, and have no elevator, but to be lower down would cost more than I felt we ought to ask the Boards to pay for W.M.U. quarters.

P. S. No. 2. In addition to the bill for Christmas Offering expenses, I send another for literature ordered from Mission Literature Department S.B.C. in June, a part of it being sent to Richmond and the rest distributed by W.M.U., as per your order.

[IMB Archives]

January 28, 1903

Dr. R. J. Willingham

Dear Brother:

You astonished me a little that twice in speaking of the trip that I am about to take you advised that I should go to Tennessee. I did not at the time see the need for this, but I judge you had some idea of facts which have recently come to me.

In a letter written by Miss S. E. S. Shankland who for years has been "mainspring" of the work in that State, she says:

"I want to write at length but am tired, having just finished an article for *Baptist and Reflector* on Miss Havergal to accompany the motto Mrs. Wheeler selected for our Tuesday meeting, 'Another year is dawning.'

That was an interesting meeting. Brother Golden spoke very seriously of State needs, taking somewhat Dr. Kerfoot's view of base of supplies. Tennessee certainly is in straights, and I should not be surprised if our W.M.U. were influenced by the new State Secretary to devote particular attention to home duties. He finds a surprising amount of opposition to our organized work led by that man Hall. I do hope that wisdom will be granted us to walk as children of light. When dealing with a constituency so sadly in need of the little red school house, we can not expect immediate results and must not give offence. I really do not wonder at those plain, unlettered country folk resenting visits from well-clad city brethren and sisters, laying plans to get and handle their hard earned money. I believe I should be suspicious myself.

Brother Golden praised in highest terms the educational work of W.M.U. but said there was jealousy in some churches on account of our reports.

We have so much trouble to get reports, and to keep them straight, and we know even then that they are not correct that I heartily wish we might be altogether educational, and leave all reporting of funds to the churches, only of course it would be difficult to maintain connection with the Woman's organizations.

Well, well, Miss Annie will think I am talking treason when I am a loyal adherent but not one that can not bear a suggestion."

A day or two after the letter from Miss Shankland, I received the one which I enclose from Mrs. A. J. Wheeler, the President of the Woman's Missionary Union of Tennessee and Vice President of W.M.U. aux. S.B.C. You will see from Mrs. Wheeler's letter that she also is echoing Brother Golden's views.

The Corresponding Secretary of the Woman's Missionary Union of Tennessee is Mrs. A. C. S. Jackson who was a member of the church in Nashville of which Mr. Golden was pastor. Mrs. Golden was for several years Secretary of the woman's work in Tennessee and as is her custom, she is doubtless travelling with her husband. That is the state of things. Now, what ought to be done?

I can not go to Tennessee before the meeting of the Convention in May. The ladies in the other States are making arrangements for a trip which will take seven weeks instead of six. I will not, under these circumstances, be able to get back to Baltimore until about April 10th. I will need the time between that and the convention to close the year's accounts etc., etc.

I enclose a letter to Mrs. Wheeler which I purpose sending her if it meets with your approval. I think it will be wise for me to send copies of this letter to both Miss Shankland and Mrs. Jackson. I know I have not only the love of these three ladies but also their confidence, and I am sure if I enter my protest against the change suggested by Mr. Golden, they will be slow to move in the matter. The trouble though I anticipate comes largely from Mr. Golden and his wife, for they will have opportunities for ventilating their views as they travel over the State. Can you do anything? Would you be able to get Brother Golden to keep "hands off?" The impression I received in a call which the present Secretary of the Tennessee board made when I was last in Nashville, was that he thoroughly, entirely and fully believes in man's supremacy. His wife who is really a talented woman seems completely overshadowed and sat by almost as mum as an oyster. I do not want to offend the Tennessee magnate, so be kind enough to criticize the letter which I send to Mrs. Wheeler, making any corrections you deem wise in it. If you think it is better for me to say nothing whatever on the subject and let Brother Golden have the "right of way," I will pattern after Mrs. Golden—and be mum.

Very truly,

Annie W. Armstrong

P. S. Please return the letter for Mrs. Wheeler to me if you approve of it, and I will then mail it from Baltimore.

P. S. No. 2. It has been officially announced that Rev. Eldridge Hatcher has been appointed as Secretary of the Maryland State Board and has signified his willingness to accept if appointed. I have not the faintest idea that we can in Maryland offer a large enough field for Dr. Hatcher's son. My own idea is that it is to be a stepping stone to the office of a General Secretaryship. Where?????

[IMB Archives]

Even though she had a humorous side, Armstrong was a demanding taskmaster and had difficulty in keeping housekeepers and office assistants.

September 1, 1898

Dr. J. M. Frost

Dear Brother:

This is the day for sending data to papers, so it gives me pleasure to forward you the monthly installment of "Illustrations" for the *Teacher* and material for "Teachers' Exchange." I will today mail manuscripts and missionary items to 29 different persons, who I hope will have same printed in State religious papers and periodicals of the Boards. I do not want you to receive false impressions, so would say that to 25 go manifold matter. It is only to the organs of the Boards and one State paper that I send regularly special contributions.

I think you may like to know just what is the method we are adopting to get missionary information into State papers, so I will forward you copies of what was sent a month ago for insertion in September papers, when the Sunday School Board is the topic of study, to the 25 persons above alluded to, who we hope will see that it is printed, either in whole or part, in State organs. As in most of the State papers there is a Woman's Department, we can get information in regard to the subject to be studied inserted, even though the Editors of said papers may not be thoroughly in sympathy with the subject treated. I enclose clipping * taken from this week's edition of *The Baptist Courier* to exemplify what I have said on this point. Brother Thomas, having accorded to the Central Committee two columns each week in his paper, must print what is furnished him. I thoroughly believe, if this regular, systematic study of the lines of work, adopted by the Southern Baptist Convention and emphasized, not only through the organs of the Boards, but State religious papers and the literature gotten out by the Mission Rooms, continues, it will not be many years before Southern Baptists will be informed as to the work which devolves upon them, and larger contributions be secured.

As usual, there are several matters to refer to you, but before speaking of these I want to acknowledge your letter of Aug. 29th, which was thoroughly appreciated. I think you would be astonished if you were to know how often I have read portions of it, and I am sure it has helped me to see some things perhaps in a truer light. As you know, I have never heard you preach, but I think you have, in the letter you wrote Aug. 29th, sent a sermon which I trust will be productive of good. I believe I can say I am ready and willing to do the *right* thing, if I know what that is. Yesterday's mail brought a letter from Dr. Tichenor, in reply to the one I wrote him from which I sent you extract. I will later let you see it, but prefer to have your answer before forwarding it.

I appreciate the force of what you have said in regard to my taking a rest for the sake of the work, but it is perfectly out of my power to do so. Many and varied duties anchor me just where I am. Our domestic machinery is not running smoothly—I must change servants. Sister Alice cannot be over-taxed—if she over exerts herself in the slightest degree, she is completely prostrated. I feel almost as anxious about her as I do about Mother. No, no, no, this is one of the times when I must (humanly speaking) take risks. Last night after church, Mr. Millard was urging my attending a District Association with which our church is connected. As it would necessitate my being away from home over night, I had to tell him I could not go, but enough of this and now to business.

1. *Missionary Day literature.* I enclose order which comes from the member of the Central Committee in Missouri who distributes the literature in that State, Mrs. Will Firth. Will you kindly send to her at once the literature for which she asks? As she says 300 or more envelopes, I would suggest that you forward at least 500 envelopes. You will note I have added to the amount named by her 300 order blanks.

In sending this morning for Missionary Day literature,—I will fill this order—Mrs. A. J. Aven, President of the Central Committee of Miss., says:

"Missionary Day has never been observed in our State as I would like, owing to the fact that we cannot get the Superintendent interested. Dr. Frost was with us during the Convention and placed the matter so clearly before the ladies, that I hope we will do more this year."

Do you think it would be well for you to make a special effort to interest the Superintendents in Miss. in Missionary Day—an article in the *Record*?

2. *Writers for Young People's Scripture Union in Kind Words.* As you probably will remember, I have only secured promises from six (6) persons to do this work for 1899. On a separate sheet of paper I will send some names which you gave last year and to whom I did not find it necessary to apply. I would ask that you look over this list and let me know if it would be well to make the request of them this year, and if their addresses as given are now correct. In returning the list, let me have some additional names.

3. *Letters from Mrs. Kuykendall.* I am sure it is helpful for the officers of the Boards to know fully the condition of the work in different sections. The letters I receive are doubtless of a different nature from those that come to you, so I think it may be well for you to read the one which I now forward from Mrs. Kuykendall. She does not yet know of the effort that is being made to secure a camping outfit for herself and husband. I referred this matter to ladies in Kentucky, but have not yet heard whether they are prepared to respond. If they do not, I will turn in some other direction.

Very truly,

Annie W. Armstrong

P. S. Let me congratulate you on your new letter paper and also on the improved typewriting.

P. S. No. 2. Were you really in earnest in the desire you expressed to have some design for the Sunday School Board which could be used on letter paper, etc., and did you mean that you wanted me to see if we could offer any suggestions in regard to same? If so, let me have your idea as to said design. I find I cannot recall accurately what you said on this subject.

[Handwritten in margin] * I cannot find *The Courier* but you doubtless have copy so would call your attention to treatment of S. Sch. Board work in this week's edition.

[SBHLA, J. M. Frost Collection]

September 3, 1898
Rev. A. J. Barton
Dear Brother:

Please find enclosed subscription for *Foreign Mission Journal*. The letter which I forward will give you all needed information as to name and address.

We are having another intensely hot spell of weather in Baltimore. Perhaps I, with others, am feeling less able to endure it than those that came earlier in the season, but it is prostrating many. I judge, though, you would not think this was personally the case when I tell you how I occupied myself yesterday afternoon. Our domestic machinery has not of late been moving on smoothly—I have had to change servants—and one cause of the trouble seemed to be that the kitchen range did not work satisfactorily. Before installing another kitchen divinity, I determined I would remove all cause of trouble in this direction, so I had the stove men to come yesterday afternoon to make needed repairs. Appreciating that it is desirable for a housekeeper to know about the stoves even more than the cooks, I decided it was wise for me to forget for the time being I was a Secretary and to become thoroughly informed how to manage dampers, etc., etc. This did not of course require all the afternoon and so I concluded I would take the time to superintend the burning of an amount of paper, etc., which different cooks had allowed to accumulate. You have no idea what a magnificent bonfire we had. It is a great pity our family does not include some children, for I am sure they would have thought it was intensely amusing. Although it was *hot* work, yet I really quite enjoyed watching the flames in the open air. "Variety is the spice of life," so if you find your work at the office growing monotonous, I would recommend your having a bonfire.

Very truly,
Annie W. Armstrong
[IMB Archives]

January 24, 1899
Dr. R. J. Willingham
Dear Brother:

Your kind letter of Jan. 23rd received this A.M. I find there is a number of items of business which I must refer to you, so will reply to it at once. Before speaking of these, I will refer to several items in your letter.

I appreciate very highly the advice and information you have given in regard to my going to Missouri. As the audiences which I would be expected to address would include gentlemen, I do not think it would be wise for me to accept the invitation. Then again, as I considered the matter more fully, I realized that the time which they hold their meeting is just when we are the busiest closing the year's accounts, etc., etc. This cannot be done earlier, nor can I relegate it to any one else, so that also makes it impossible for me to accede to Mrs. Hatcher's request. I will decline on that ground.

As to Seminary affairs. I hope you appreciate if I had not felt, while not under a definite promise to Joshua, that I myself was rather bound not to give the information which is in my possession, I would not for one instant have asked a promise of you, for I have great confidence in the discretion of the Secretary of the Foreign Board. I do feel, though, that this trouble which is now pending is of such a serious nature that I think you ought to have the information, so the next time I see Joshua, I am going to ask permission of him to give you the facts and leave it with you to act as you may think wise. In the meantime, I want to call your attention to one or two points which you may, or may not, have noted.

It is quite plain to my mind that the Broadus family intends to support Dr. Whitsitt and if possible prevent his removal. I suppose your attention has been called to the article by Prof. A. T. Robertson, "The 1641 Date Proven," in *The Baptist Argus* of Jan. 19th. Miss Eliza Broadus yesterday sent me a marked copy of that paper. I had noted it before she called my attention to it.

Another thing. Did you notice that the leaflet which is now being circulated, written by Prof. Mitchell, "After Whitsitt, What," while he is in Chicago, was printed in Louisville, having on it the imprint of a Louisville printing establishment?

I am glad the leaflets are satisfactory. I do think very good work has been done. You will receive the balance of your order in the course of a few days. I will now proceed to refer to several other matters, taking them up seriatim.

1. *Unsigned receipts.* Your Stenographer enclosed receipts for check forwarded before you had signed them. I return same for signature.

2. *Check of thirteen dollars and seventy-five cents ($13.75).* I must acknowledge I am genuinely gratified to see how the women in Indian Territory are responding to the appeal which was made for the Christmas Offering. Kindly credit the Choate Prairie Society, Ind. Ter., with twelve dollars and seventy-five cents ($12.75)—Christmas Offering—and the Winfield Society, Ind. Ter., with one dollar ($1.00) and let me have the receipts. The Secretary who forwarded these amounts says: "There are others that have their money ready, but have not sent it in to me as yet."

3. *Letter from Miss Broadus.* May I ask that you will kindly read same, and then let me know whether you think it would be wise for us to adopt the suggestion she has made as to having the wife and children of Mr. Yohannon appear before the ladies at the Annual Meeting in Louisville? It would make quite a pleasant feature of our meeting, but if it is not probable that the Board will undertake this work, my own judgment is that it would be unwise to give prominence to that phase of missions, for doubtless many of the ladies would be anxious that we should have a mission at that point, if they became interested in Mrs. Yohannon. I would also ask that you note what Miss Broadus says as to Mrs. J. W. Low and let me know if she and her husband are expected to leave for China prior to the Convention.

I do not think I will trouble you with anything more today.

Very truly,

Annie W. Armstrong

[Handwritten at end of letter] Our Stenographer is to leave. I am sorry to have to make a change, but I do not think it would have been right to have increased her salary, on the ground which she wished to put it. If it had been done, the other clerks would, without doubt have also asked for an increase. We ought not, I am sure, allow W.M.U. expenses to increase very materially until the Boards receive larger contributions.

I of course realize that it will add quite materially to my labors to train another clerk—this one I have had for six years, and when she came to us it was on a salary of $2.00 a week—but I have done this several times and can do it again. We are now paying $8.00 a week and she wanted $10.00. I find I am indulging in tautology, but I am most too used up to have either ideas or words at command.

[IMB Archives]

August 28, 1899
Dr. A. J. Barton
Dear Brother:

Yours of August 26th received. Please accept warm and hearty thanks for examining manuscript for Christmas program. I have been so busy today that I have not had time to note suggested changes—will do so later.

By the way, I do think the printer to whom we give our "fancy" work has gotten out quite an attractive advertisement. I enclose one; thinking you may fail to discover its purpose, as several did to whom I handed specimens, I will inform you that it is a stamp book for pocket use. Should you wish to retain it, you are at liberty to do so, as the printer furnished me with a number.

A letter from Dr. Frost this morning tells how he regarded my suggestion as to the reprint of your article in State papers. I forward his letter.

Hastily, but very truly,
Annie W. Armstrong

P. S. I will be glad to deliver your message to Sister Alice.

Later. Since writing the above, your letter of August 28th has come to hand. I return letter with thanks for forwarding subscription. I readily appreciate how the mistake occurred, and am glad to know that you have a stenographer that *rarely* makes mistakes. I wish I had.

I am astonished that you do not see the extreme appropriateness of the "Text" used on the certificate. I thought you were more of a Columbus.

[IMB Archives]

Miss Annie knew that she had a temper—and so did her peers.

Monday Afternoon, 1899 (?)
Dr. A. J. Barton
Dear Brother:

"A fellow feeling make us wondrous kind." My own temper has been in quite an explosive state of late, and I have had so much difficulty in preventing others from discovering it, that I am prepared to remove all cause for such a catastrophe out of the way of the Assistant Secretary of the Foreign Board. I will assume the responsibility of extending the time for your manuscript being received in Balto. to *July 20th*. Be kind enough not to let anything prevent its coming by that date. I will ask the Committee to waive the rule as to the examination of manuscript—two of the ministers who compose committee usually read & endorse all manuscripts that are used in the regular course—but in this case that will not be necessary as we can trust the writer to send us a *first-class* leaflet.

Very truly,

Annie W. Armstrong

[IMB Archives]

October 8, 1900

Dr. J. M. Frost

Dear Brother:

Your letter of October 6th just received. May I trouble you to read copy of a letter which I have written to Dr. Van Ness?

In this connection permit me to say that as I previously have stated, a welcome awaits you at 1423 McCulloh St. whenever you see fit to come, but as I now know that you consider it is desirable to have opportunities "of establishing other centers of acquaintance, and in that way be more serviceable to the work" when you are in Baltimore, I shall *never* again embarrass you by extending an invitation to our home.

In a letter which I received from Dr. Kerfoot this morning, he says:

"If Willingham's statement is true as to the per cent of clerks who answer letters as compared with that of pastors, I very decidedly favor his idea of sending the documents to the pastors. It will also be a good thing to see how many pastors will be interested enough to help in this matter.

I agree, also, as to the advantage of a two-cent stamped envelope over a postal card."

In all matters of missionary policy, as well as in other directions, I believe the majority rules; so, as two Secretaries out of three think it wise to enclose a two-cent stamped envelope when writing to pastors, this will be done.

Very truly,

Annie W. Armstrong

[SBHLA, J. M. Frost Collection]

Apologies did not come easily for Annie Armstrong even when she knew that she was wrong.

1900 (Oct. 9?)
Tuesday Morning
Dear Dr. Frost:

I am writing this before breakfast; having been awake since a little after four o'clock. This time has been given to earnest thinking, re-reading your letter, etc., etc. While I cannot truthfully withdraw one thing that I said in the letter which I wrote yesterday, yet I now see that I ought to have had more regard to your and Dr. Van Ness' feelings, and not be so quick to resent what I considered was a breach of friendship. I can now ask that you will excuse me for writing as I did Oct. 8th.

I expect I have unduly magnified the teaching in Matt. 18:15, and in future I had better not attempt to straighten out difficulties, but leave them in God's hands, for having a quick temper I may not go about it in the right spirit, as was no doubt true in this case.

Hoping you will accept my apology, I am
Very truly,
Annie W. Armstrong

You are at perfect liberty to show this letter also to Dr. Van Ness—I believe I had rather you would.

[SBHLA, J. M. Frost Collection]

February 14, 1900
Dr. J. M. Frost
Dear Brother:

I enclose a letter received from Rev. J. Grimsley, of Oklahoma, whose name you forwarded last June as one whom the Sunday School Board desired should be aided in the way of clothing. His name was assigned by me, and as you will see, he has been aided by Societies in Alabama and Georgia in response to the appeals which I made for him. I think you will agree with me, under these circumstances, that it was a little peculiar for the Corresponding Secretary of the Sunday School Board of Oklahoma to say that reports of boxes received by Sunday School missionaries should not be rendered to me as the agent of Sunday School Board. Evidently it is desirable that those who have charge of the Sunday School work in

Oklahoma and Indian Territory be made to understand that assistance comes to the missionaries there *only* at the request of the Sunday School Board of the Southern Baptist Convention, and that the rules are made by that Board, and not by local Boards in Indian Territory and Oklahoma. I sincerely hope that you will take this matter in hand in both Indian Territory and Oklahoma, and see that it is put on the right footing; otherwise I must say that I do not think the Woman's Mission Societies should render this aid to Sunday School missionaries in these territories. As you are about to visit both Indian Territory and Oklahoma, will it not be possible for you to get the brethren there to understand matters and things,—also Sister Kuykendall? Rules must be observed, otherwise friction ensues. I return Mrs. Kuykendall's letter, so you can have it for reference.

It occurred to me as I read your letter of February 10th, which I now hold in my hand, that you felt a little hurt after receiving the one which I wrote you February 8th. I hope that this was not the case, but if it was and you deem an apology necessary, please consider that it is offered.

I, perhaps, do not weigh my words as carefully as I should when writing to the Secretaries of the Boards. I have an idea they know me well enough to appreciate that I would not say or do anything contrary to their wishes, unless I thought it absolutely necessary, and when this is the case, they will be kind enough to allow me to exercise the right of private judgment without getting annoyed; in order words, we agree to disagree at times.

As to your providing manuscript for leaflet: You are mistaken in thinking that *I* requested you to provide manuscript. I did not say anything to you on the subject. Mr. Wilbur was the one to make the request of you, so I read him that portion of the letter, and he will, if he has not already done so, write you on the subject in a few days.

Very truly,
Annie W. Armstrong
[SBHLA, J. M. Frost Collection]

Those who dealt with Armstrong regularly apparently expected her occasional outbursts.

Excerpt of a letter from T. P. Bell to J. M. Frost, December 23, 1897

As to the matter between Miss Annie and myself, I am in perfect ignorance of any cause of offense that she could have had against me. Last spring, at Wilmington, at her request I spent a whole afternoon revising the manuscript of my address on the WMU made at the Seminary in the Spring.

I yielded to all her requests, changing where she thought there ought to be some changes, even in some cases where I was uncertain about the wisdom of it. She has just simply cooled, quit writing to me and has taken Van Ness as her general advisor. I have nothing against her and have given her no offense so that she could have anything against me; I am not going to bother about the matter, but let it work itself out. She gets in those fits occasionally and then gets out of them.

[WMU Archives]

Armstrong was interested in and committed to missionary endeavors, but she feared international travel and struggled with foreign languages.

January 2, 1902
Dr. E. E. Bomar
Dear Brother:

Your letter of January 1st received this A.M., and I cannot tell you how thoroughly I appreciate your kind willingness to select texts and give study topics, etc., etc. for the Mission Card, 1902–1903. The fields and lines of work remain the same, but the order in which they are presented will be changed. It is not necessary, though, for me now to give the order, as I am going to ask that you will in treating each subject, do so on a separate sheet of paper. I will be glad to have you do as you did last year, prepare the material for six months, taking all of the foreign topics including the Foreign Mission Board. What think you of broadening your horizon, or possibly you would say narrowing it, and do the work for the entire year? I am sure if you will, Dr. McConnell and Dr. Frost will feel that they have cause to extend votes of thanks. If they do not, the Secretary of Woman's Missionary Union certainly will. I am not joking. I really think it would be very helpful, as well as extremely kind, if you would accede to this request.

Now for another small contribution. This comes from the wife of a frontier missionary in Texas, Mrs. C. R. Goodman, Theodore, Tex. Kindly return receipt to her, and let me have duplicate.

At this stage of things the men arrived who had been shaking carpets, and I have just been to our new building. I find much to my relief that I will be able to dispense with a large amount of rags, and still have carpet enough to cover two small offices, and have a suspicion of carpet in the workroom. The floor of the Room which will be occupied by the State Board and Ministers' Conference we purpose to leave bare. These gentlemen, being representative Maryland Baptists, can have the pleasure of skirmishing around and finding carpet for themselves. It is rather a funny state of things. When the Foreign Board declined to become joint owners of the Baptist Mission Rooms' assets, the other Boards, Home and Sunday School, were not unwilling to assume the responsibility of holding said property. That being the case, as the Woman's Missionary Union is—what shall I call it,—residuary legatee now that the time of division has come, leaves the Maryland representatives with nothing but one table, one armchair, and some of the most outrageously uncomfortable chairs, wooden seats, wooded backs with spokes in them, that you ever had the pleasure of sitting in. These aforesaid chairs keep in memory Dr. A. C. Dixon, now of Boston, who was the purchasing committee. Oh yes, I forgot, they do own a blackboard and some pictures of departed Maryland divines. I should feel a little uncomfortable about wafting off this property, but really the room which the Ministers' Conference will have, will be too small to allow for a very large amount of furniture, when all of the bronzes and blondes, who assemble Monday mornings, occupy their new quarters. But enough of foolishness. Please let me know when Dr. Willingham is expected home, as I wish to ask him to tell me where I ought to go and where I ought not to go when I start for Mexico. You know, I am a little scared at the thought of going to a foreign country. I was asking Sister Schimp just now who is to be my chaperone (as she was termed in Indian Territory) if she could speak Spanish. I suppose I should have asked her—you know she is a Swiss woman, and has voyaged around quite extensively—if she knew the Mexican language, but unfortunately she does not. She suggested, though, that we do as she did when she first came to America, provide ourselves with a dictionary. In my youthful days I never could pronounce French in anything but a thoroughly English way, and I am quite sure at this late day I would not be able even with the aid of a dictionary to make myself intelligible to the Mexicans we might meet. Sister Alice, I think, has taken a great deal of pleasure in the thought that it was utterly impossible for me to acquire a foreign language, and therefore I could not become a missionary. But really I must stop.

Very truly,

Annie W. Armstrong

[Handwritten at top of page] My stenographer returned today after an absence of several days caused by sickness. I think you will judge from this letter that she has not entirely recovered.

[IMB Archives]

July 5, 1902
Dr. R. J. Willingham
Dear Brother:

Your kind letter of July 3rd received and much appreciated. I find there are several matters that I want to refer to you today, but before taking these up, I would say I shall try and heed your words of warning as far as possible on this trip. As I have been to Indian Territory and Oklahoma in the summer when the thermometer was 108, I realize somewhat what is ahead of me, but I am not doing as much as we ask "our substitutes" to do, not only for a few days, but for weeks and months; so I do not think I have any right to refuse to take, what some persons call, "risks." I dearly love the work in which we are engaged, and I have no desire for my life to be shortened, as I would like to have the privilege of taking advantage of more of the opportunities which our Heavenly Father is giving Southern Baptists. How I wish that I had the ability to get our women to recognize fully what a glorious thing it is to be a co-worker with God in winning the world for Christ.

I know it would be wise to take a few days' rest before starting on a trip of three months, but it is out of the question for me to do so. I *must* get the work straight before I leave, and there are some things still to be done that will keep me occupied until I leave on Tuesday. * I expect, though, to be two days and two nights on the cars—will stop in St. Louis for a few hours—and I shall try and spend as much of that time a possible in sleep. Mrs. Schimp has seemed perfectly astonished at my power to sleep while on the cars. I am really trying to train myself to take advantage of these opportunities to "rest." But enough of personal matters, and now to business.

I am going to accept your kind offer and ask that you will take a little oversight of W.M.U. work during my absence. If you see or hear of anything wrong in Woman's Work in any of the States, will you not write to the President or Secretary of Central Committee—for names and addresses refer to State Literature Committees in *Foreign Mission Journal*.

I think in this connection I will send you extract from a letter which I have just written to Mrs. Stakely, as it refers to a point I expect we will have to guard. I have written as follows:

"I note in your letter of June 30th you say:

'Dr. Crumpton has been talking to me lately, and he is anxious that some arrangement be made whereby the large amount contributed by W.M.U. Societies to State Missions be include in our Annual Statement. I know that the Convention deals only with the Home and Foreign work, but he says he thinks we might properly include in our amount the large sums given each year through the State Boards. What do you think about it.'

Dr. Crumpton of course is not as familiar with the work of W.M.U. as is the Secretary of same. If so, he would not advocate the measure which he has suggested to you, in view of past history. When W.M.U. was organized in 1888, we had to take the work as it then was, and try to find some platform upon which we could unite. At that stage of things, the ladies were designating as mission funds money which was raised by them for all kinds of purposes, among them chandeliers and carpets for churches, pastors' salaries, etc., etc., anything, everything to which the women contributed. I recall in one state where the women claimed to have raised for Missions eighteen or nineteen thousand dollars, when we sifted out from this apparently large contribution, the money really given for Home and Foreign Missions, there had not been sent to the Boards $2,000.00, and yet the ladies in that state claimed that they were giving nearly $20,000.00 to Missions. Some of us recognized right away how thoroughly the ladies were deceiving themselves in making such reports, but we were starting a new organization, and we could not draw the lines too tight. We therefore had to let the ladies report what they would, but we ever kept before them that as Woman's Missionary Union was Auxiliary to the Southern Baptist Convention, and the expenses of Woman's Missionary Union were met by the Boards of the Convention, we could get out no literature for other objects. This, however, did not limit the Societies in any direction. They were at perfect liberty to work in each State as they deemed best. We have right along in our organization emphasized Baptist independence, but as Woman's Missionary Union is auxiliary to Southern Baptist Convention when we meet as a body, it is to consider the work entrusted to the Boards of the Convention, and leave other objects to be presented at other times by those authorized to do so. Gradually the ladies appreciated the wisdom of confining their reports to W.M.U. to the work as done by the Southern Baptist Convention, and leaving all other reports to be made at state meetings.

I cannot agree with Dr. Crumpton that it would be well to include State Missions in reports to Woman's Missionary Union, until State Missions are reported to the Southern Baptist Convention. If he thinks it is wise to report State Missions to Woman's Missionary Union, it certainly would be wise to report them to the Southern Baptist Convention. If the Convention does not consider that they should take cognizance of State Missions, neither do I think should Woman's Missionary Union. Woman's Missionary Union is simply an auxiliary of the Southern Baptist Convention, and I consider that the work of the Woman's Missionary Union should follow as closely as possible that of the Convention. Then again, perhaps Dr. Crumpton has not thought of this. In some of the states, the State Board has not only charge of State Missions, but also of orphanages, Ministerial Relief and Aged Ministers' Funds, etc., etc. Years ago, Dr. Warder of Kentucky interviewed the Secretary W.M.U., and offered his aid in our work if we would adopt as our line of work the seven objects that were in charge of the Kentucky State Board. I told him that that was not possible, as in some of the States they did not work for seven objects, while in others the number was larger than in Kentucky, which it was thought well to put in charge of State Board. I have given this subject during the years since W.M.U. was organized very earnest thought, and I have come very fully to the conclusion that we had better not do as Dr. Crumpton suggests in W.M.U. work, for the reasons given above, and others which I have not time to mention."

You will note from what I have said to Mrs. Stakely that I have come to the conclusion it would not be wise for W.M.U. as an organization to aid State Missions. If Dr. Kerfoot had lived and continued as Secretary of the Home Mission Board, I believe we could have done this without danger to the interests of Home and Foreign Missions, for he would have seen to it that State Secretaries did not monopolize Woman's Work; but as things now are, I am convinced it is better for us to simply present S.B.C. interests to Woman's Mission Societies, and leave all state interests to be pushed by those who have them in charge. Now as to several other matters:

1. *Foreign Mission Journals.* Kindly read letter from Mrs. M. J. Mitchell, and note what she says as to *Journals* being sent in bulk.

2. *Home for missionaries' children.* I will be very much obliged if you will speak of this and give the plan in the *Journal*. I suppose by the time I return to Baltimore letters will have come from different foreign missionaries, and we will know if there are any children for whom parents desire homes *at once*. If I find that the demand for homes for the children of foreign missionaries is not great, I think we will extend the offer to missionaries of the Home Board. Please read a letter which this morning's mail has brought from the wife of a missionary in Texas. She is replying the "Letter of Greeting" which was sent to all of the female missionaries on foreign fields, and the wives of frontier missionaries, from the Annual

Meeting W.M.U. in Asheville. I had not written to Mrs. Collins in regard to homes for missionaries' children. I have known, though, for years that the lack of educational advantages is keenly felt by the missionaries and their families who are occupying frontier fields.

My own idea is that if we can get this plan of work well inaugurated, it will result in great good. Not only will it aid individual missionaries, and give advantages of education to numbers of children, but it will cause Southern Baptists to come closer in touch with those who represent them on the different fields.

3. *Monthly missionary literature issued by Mission Literature Department.* I will be obliged if you will call attention to this in your notes in the *Journal.* The subscription list is increasing, but not as rapidly as I should like to see it. In this connection I would ask that you read letter which I found in this morning's mail from an active worker in Montgomery, Ala., and note the tribute she pays to the value of said literature.

4. *Places to be visited in Indian Territory and Oklahoma.* While I have not yet received a full list of the places that I am to visit in Oklahoma—that has not yet been sent by the Secretary, Rev. L. L. Smith, who is making arrangements for this part of my trip—I had a letter from Mrs. Kuykendall this morning, and also one from Rev. A. G. Washburn a day or two ago, of which I send you copies, as I would like you to know something of that part of my trip.

I find much to my surprise that it is after six o'clock, which is the time when we close the Mission Rooms, so I must stop right here. There were other things I wanted to say, so possibly you may have another letter from me on Monday.

Very truly,

Annie W. Armstrong

[Handwritten insert in margin] * Our force at the Mission Rooms will be two clerks less than we usually have during the Summer. One married in the Spring, and I did not fill her place, and I have notified the stenographer I would dispense with her services. She is so careless that I can not longer put up with her mistakes.

This decreases expenses while I am away, but it necessitated my getting a great deal of the regular work done before I left.

[IMB Archives]

CHAPTER 2

"Line upon line, precept upon precept"

Annie Armstrong and the Work of WMU

Armstrong wrote hundreds of letters to a variety of denominational leaders. The following letters represent how she skillfully built consensus between diverse interests.

Jan. 9, 1888 (?)
Dr. H. A. Tupper
Dear Sir,
Your letter of Jan. 5 received and while sorry you will not be able to write the leaflet yourself, we will be very glad if Mr. Bell would write it.

May we ask that you will urge Mr. Bell to accede to our request, which I write to him, to make by this mail. I am glad you think the Mission Room "is a good thing." The work there is steadily growing and we trust the information put in circulation, as to the needs & etc. of the various mission fields will arouse a greater interest, and will result in larger contributions to the Boards.

Very truly,
Annie Armstrong
I enclose a "prayer card" & also a program for monthly missionary meetings. I am not certain if I forwarded these to you before or not.
[IMB Archives]

June 16, 1891
Rev. T. P. Bell
Dear Brother:
I enclose *part* of one of the MSS. sent by Mr. Powell for you to publish in the *Foreign Mission Journal* if you desire to do so. The part that I enclose

is the commencement of the second leaflet, but I have reserved two pages of it which will make a short article for the state columns in papers during September.

Sister Alice expects to use part of the first article written "Cactus Land" in the W.M.U. department of *F. M. J.* in September. If you see fit to publish the enclosed, Mr. Powell will be very largely represented during September, as I have several short articles which I expect to send to be printed in state papers. As Mr. Powell is such a favorite, and we hold this material from him, I thought it might be as well to make use of it. Please return the MSS. which I enclose after you have made what use of it you desire, for it is probable we may at a later date make further use of it.

I send by express today the balance of the packages of prayer cards, etc. In this lot there are 4,840 which with the 3,800 sent last week, will make a total of 8,640. You will find in the box some additional copies of the circular and envelopes, as we had to order these by the thousand. I enclose bill for the prayer cards, etc. only charging you for the number used of the leaflet on Prayer and the Prayer Cards, as we of course will keep these in stock at the Mission Rooms. I enclose bill, but you need not have it paid immediately if it is not convenient. I have ordered the leaflets, and the printer has promised to have them ready to be sent to Richmond by Wednesday, June 24th.

On second thought, it occurs to me that perhaps it would be as well, if convenient, for you to pay the present bill and to allow the one for the leaflets to remain standing. I make it a point of always paying for all work done immediately, and as we have had some quite large calls on the treasury of the Mission Rooms; we may not have as large a surplus in bank as desirable; I simply mention this, having told you previously that the capital of the Mission Rooms was sufficiently large to allow bills to remain unpaid for some time—so it is, but the amount you are now ordering may go a little beyond what we can conveniently spare.

Will you be kind enough to return to the Mission Rooms the electrotype of the last map used in the *F. M. J.*?

Very truly,

Annie W. Armstrong

P. S. Last night was held the Baltimore Social Union, where I met Rev. E. Y. Mullins and Dr. F. M. Ellis; both of these gentlemen spoke of having received the circular, etc. so evidently it attracted their attention and was not thrown aside, so I hope that others will pay the same attention to your packages.

P. S. In packing the box of Prayer Cards, etc., we found, in order to get the number in, they had to be taken out of the boxes, so be kind enough to tell your clerk, in posting the packages, to be on the look-out for a package of blank envelopes—about 200 in number. They are tied together, so that when he finds one package that is all.

With regard to the leaflets you are now having printed—will you need all of them? or is the Foreign Board prepared to make a grant of some, to be distributed by the Woman's Missionary Union? I have had a letter from Miss Heck, in which she asked for a large variety of leaflets, for North Carolina, and I have but very few, that I can send her. The W.M.U. can only publish a few leaflets, and when it comes to dividing these among 14 States, they are very soon used up. As far as I can judge, the ladies are distributing the literature quite carefully. In the grants we make, we try to have one leaflet of each kind, do for a society. I do not think we can ask the ladies to be more economical than that, do you? The Prayer Cards, we are giving to individuals, as we are aiming to secure daily prayer for the suggested fields.

[IMB Archives]

March 2, 1892
Dr. T. P. Bell
Dear Brother:

I find there is another matter that I will have to refer to you, which today has brought.

Mrs. O. L. Hailey, of Knoxville, Tenn., has for several years been interesting the children of that section in Missions and has a department in the *Baptist and Reflector* which she calls the "Young South." About a year ago I suggested to Mrs. Hailey the use of the Cuban Brick Cards, and upon these she has collected (or rather the children have) about $800.00. Some weeks ago I asked her if she would not aid in the Centennial work; this she has consented to do, and proposes to put before the "Young South" as an aim the collecting of $1,000.00—$500.00 for Foreign Missions, and $500.00 for Home. When the Chapel Cards were submitted to her, she seemed to think that the amount needed ($5.00) to be collected on a Card was beyond what the little ones that she was working among could raise; so decided to change the plan somewhat but still use the Certificate idea. When she referred the matter to me I was very glad of this decision, as her work being a little outside had interfered somewhat with the Central Committee of Tennessee in presenting the Cuban Cards; so I think it will be better for her in a measure to have a plan of her own. You probably know Mrs. Hailey, she is a daughter of Dr. Graves and does not believe in Missionary Societies etc. I suggested to Mrs. Hailey, and she approves of the suggestions, that instead of using Chapel Cards she would use little wooden bells as Mite boxes and have a label across the base of them having twenty bricks on it, which will give the Chapel idea. These Mite bells have never been used in connection with our work, so she would have all the help that variety gives in this direction.

Now for the question I wish to ask: Can I be allowed to furnish Mrs. Hailey with Mite boxes instead of Chapel Cards for Centennial collection? They probably can be bought at $1.25 per hundred, with additional cost for labels. Another item of expenditure will be the sending of them out, which will be greater than the Cards. I believe, however, the money Mrs. Hailey will secure will justify the outlay; she seems to have interested quite a large number of children and they are looking to her for direction in missionary work.

Be kind enough to drop me a postal as soon as convenient, telling me what to do with regard to this matter.

Very truly,

Annie W. Armstrong

P. S. I have heard from the Home Board and we will send Centennial literature to Superintendents as soon as we can get packages mailed—I hope it will not be long before you will see some "returns."

[IMB Archives]

If this letter reaches you when you are occupied with other matters, please put it aside until you are at leisure, as I would like you to give the plan careful consideration which I desire to submit.

March 24, 1897

Dr. J. M. Frost

Dear Brother:

As you know, I have long felt that it would be most helpful if we could have more unity in S.B.C. work and methods, and have tried (but failed) to get inaugurated an educational work among the pastors by distributing literature regularly, presenting various phases of work as done by S.B.C. agencies, viz., Foreign Board, Home Board, Sunday School Board, Theological Seminary, Southern Young People's Union and Woman's Missionary Union. As it was not possible to secure the Foreign Board's cooperation in this effort—as you will remember, every other agency was glad to adopt this plan—it seemed wise to give it up, at least for the time being. I now want to make a suggestion which I think will in a measure accomplish the same end, and which can be undertaken by the Sunday School Board alone. It is for the Sunday School Board to issue a Convention Almanac. I enclose one gotten out by the American Board. While this in a measure gives you my idea, it only does so in part.

My thought is to have a brief sketch of each one of the six agencies. In addition to this, let the three Boards present the various lines of their work. If there is sufficient space, have a condensed account of each State organization (Board). While it would mean work to arrange such an Almanac, I believe it could be made a very valuable and interesting pamphlet. Illustrations would make it more attractive and they could doubtless be obtained.

Now as to the practicability of this. Of course, I appreciate, even if the plan is regarded by you favorably, two questions will immediately suggest themselves to you: First, how is the expense to be met: Second, who will do the work.

1. *As to the expense.* In order to accomplish the object I have in view, there would have to be a large number of Almanacs distributed free, viz., to pastors and possibly Sunday School Superintendents. As the Sunday School Board is prepared to make appropriations to the different States, would not this be as good an investment of a portion of the money which you propose to distribute as any other way?

It would place the Sunday School Board before the public in the way which I think it should be put—as a helper to *all* of our denominational enterprises.

It would also be a means of advertising the Sunday School Board very extensively.

Do you not think if copies of the Almanac were sent free to pastors and Superintendents, they would influence the sale of a sufficient number to pay the cost of the entire issue?

My idea is that it be gotten out in time for the copies to be presented to be sent, with a card of the Secretary of the Sunday School Board, as a Christmas remembrance.

2. *As to the work.* If you think I am capable of doing it, I will undertake, with the aid of a number on whom I should call for assistance, to arrange the needed data. I am trying to get the work somewhat ahead, so I think I could promise to engineer this matter, if you consider it would be

helpful and will give me your advice and let me use your name when needed to secure writers, etc., etc. Miss M. E. Wright, of August, Ga., for several years prepared a Missionary Calendar. She discontinued issuing same as the sale was not sufficiently large to cover expenses. It was an individual matter with her and not undertaken by the Boards or Woman's Missionary Union. I think without doubt I could have her help, and as she is a great favorite of Dr. Lansing Burrows, he probably would allow her to have access to the data which he collects for the Year Book.

I think I have now presented the subject to you as fully as is necessary. I will be glad to have you consider the question in all lights, and if it strikes you favorably, to let me know as soon as convenient, for if it is to be undertaken and I am the one to be responsible for manuscripts, I would like to have some little time to consider carefully just what is needed and on whom to call for assistance. If the plan can be fully decided upon prior to the Convention, it would be much easier to secure the cooperation of those on whom we propose to call if I could see them, than through writing.

Very truly,

Annie W. Armstrong

P. S. In addition to the Almanac published by the American Board of Missions, I am going to forward a Missionary Handbook, which was gotten out by the American Baptist Missionary Union, as that also is suggestive. Please return both books.

[SBHLA, J. M. Frost Collection]

February 2, 1898

Judge J. Haralson

Dear Brother:

As you have kindly offered your assistance in times past to the Woman's Missionary Union, I am going to avail myself of same and ask that you will allow me to present a matter to you and that you will let me have your opinion in regard to it. I shall have to tax your patience long enough to give a brief explanation before asking the question which I desire to have answered.

As you doubtless know, the work done by the Woman's Missionary Union is based upon Recommendations offered by the three Boards and adopted at Annual Meeting. They are then presented by the Cor. Sec. W.M.U. to State officers and by them to societies. Prior to the meeting in Wilmington, Dr. J. M. Frost, Secretary of the Sunday School Board, sent the

Recommendations of his Board as given on the printed larger slip which I enclose. At an Executive Committee meeting, held in Wilmington prior to the first session of the Annual Meeting of the Woman's Missionary Union, I found that there was a division of sentiment among the members of the Executive Committee in regard to the second Recommendation which reads:

> "Our Bible Work has grown immensely this year and we desire to see it still further increased. We earnestly wish that our Bible Fund could be enlarged and should be glad if Woman's Mission Societies would raise $1,000.00 for it."

When the Recommendations were presented to the delegates in annual session, there was considerable discussion and Mrs. I. C. Brown, of East Lake, Ala., who has since died, offered an amendment to the second Recommendation and it was passed as follows (see smaller slip):

> "Our Bible Work has grown immensely this year and we desire to see it still further increased. We earnestly wish that our Bible Fund could be enlarged and should be glad of the cooperation of Woman's Missionary Societies."

After the Resolution was adopted as amended, I requested that the "Chair" should construe the Recommendation, so, as Cor. Sec'y, I might understand what was intended by the wording. The President declined to do so, and on my insisting that I must have some definite instructions, the mover of the Resolution, Mrs. Brown, said substantially that her idea in offering the amendment was that no definite sum should be stated, but she hoped that larger sums would be contributed than the thousand dollars. As there was no further explanation offered or questions raised, I of course took this as the decision of the entire body. Later, at a meeting of the Executive Committee in Wilmington, a Resolution was offered and carried that hereafter no contributions should be reported which were made by Woman's Mission Societies in the different States at Annual Meetings, but those given to the three Boards, and the name of each Convention Board was mentioned.

Recently I was much astonished to learn that at least one person—and she is quite prominent in our work—thought I had not carried out the wishes of the ladies as expressed in Annual Meeting when I presented the work of the Sunday School Board to the societies, expecting that they would give moneyed contributions to the Bible Fund. When the charge was made by the person above referred to, I asked what the ladies meant by passing a resolution that the contributions to the Sunday School Board were to be reported, and she said that meant boxes of clothing, although no such distinction was made at any time in the course of the discussion, or afterwards at the Executive Committee meeting.

I have now given you the facts, so will you kindly answer the following questions:

1. Does not the wording of the Resolution as it now stands ("Our Bible Work has grown immensely this year and we desire to see it still further increased. We earnestly wish that our Bible Fund could be enlarged and should be glad of the cooperation of our Woman's Missionary Societies"), and construed by the one who offered the amendment, give ample authority to the Cor. Sec'y to send out literature, asking the societies to make moneyed contributions to the Sunday School Board and gather statistics of amount so contributed?

2. Has a presiding officer any right to decline to construe any Recommendation adopted by a body over which she is presiding? If, however, this is done, is not the explanation given by the mover of the amendment, and to which no opposition is made by any one, to be accepted as voicing the wishes of the body?

It has been intimated that others beside the one who spoke to me have not regarded the late action in the same light in which I do, so it is possible, at the approaching meeting in Norfolk, that the question may be further discussed. For that reason I have felt that it was only wise to be prepared to meet it, if my actions are called in question. I also feel that this is a matter of considerable importance, for if, through any misunderstandings or misconceptions, Resolutions should be passed adverse to the expressed wishes of the Sunday School Board, it would be harmful in many ways, hence my referring the matter to you, so that I may know just what ought to be done.

With kind regards to Mrs. Haralson, and asking that you will let me hear from you as soon as convenient, I am,

Very truly,
Annie W. Armstrong

[This is the *smaller* slip of paper referred to in the letter to Judge J. Haralson, from Annie W. Armstrong, dated February 2, 1898.]

SUNDAY SCHOOL BOARD

1. Woman's Mission Societies are among the most forceful agents for advancing our denominational interests. We earnestly desire to have their kindly consideration and cooperation in our work. They may help us by putting the Sunday School periodicals of the Southern Baptist Convention into all the schools, so far as possible, and emphasizing their missionary feature.

2. Our Bible work has grown immensely this year, and we desire to see it still further increased. We earnestly wish that our Bible fund could be enlarged, and should be glad of the cooperation of Woman's Mission Societies.

3. Missionary Day in the Sunday Schools, as observed last September, proved even a greater success than heretofore. We want the help of the Societies in this department also.

4. Some of the churches are beginning to introduce a Home Department of Sunday School work. We are earnestly hoping to have the cooperation of the Societies in still further extending this work and making it more effective.

5. We should like to have the Woman's Missionary Union consider the propriety of sending boxes of clothing to Sunday School missionaries. It seems to us to open an opportunity for great usefulness and for helping a very worthy class of workers.

[This is the *larger* slip of paper referred to in the letter to Judge J. Haralson, from Annie W. Armstrong, dated February 2, 1898.]

1. Woman's Mission Societies are among the most forceful agents for advancing our denominational interests. We earnestly desire to have their kindly consideration and cooperation in our work. They may help us by putting the Sunday School periodicals of the Southern Baptist Convention into all the schools, so far as possible, and emphasizing their missionary feature.

2. Our Bible work has grown immensely this year, and we desire to see it still further increased. We earnestly wish that our Bible fund could be enlarged, and should be glad if Woman's Mission Societies would raise $1,000.00 for it.

3. Missionary Day in the Sunday Schools, as observed last September, proved even a greater success than heretofore. We want the help of the Societies in this department also.

4. Some of the churches are beginning to introduce a Home Department of Sunday School work. We are earnestly hoping to have the cooperation of

the Societies in still further extending this work and making it more effective.

5. We should like to have the Woman's Missionary Union consider the propriety of sending boxes of clothing to Sunday School missionaries. It seems to us to open an opportunity for great usefulness and for helping a very worthy class of workers.

[IMB Archives]

July 1, 1901
Dr. J. M. Frost
Dear Brother:

I have been feeling so thoroughly unnerved for sometime past, that I do not believe I replied to your kind letter of June 20th as I should. I do want you to recognize that I *thoroughly* appreciated the full and cordial endorsement you gave to the work as done by Woman's Missionary Union for all three Boards S.B.C., and the way you spoke of the Corresponding Secretary's impartiality in the efforts she has made for the three Boards. I do believe in this request you did not say more than was correct, even though you did overrate her "ability," etc., etc. I do want to thank you for your hearty support.

Yesterday, on my return from Manassas, Va., where I had been attending a Missionary Conference which had been called by ladies at that point, I found awaiting me some resolutions which had been passed by the Executive Committee of the Woman's Baptist Missionary Union of Georgia. I enclose copy, as I think it well for you to see these. I also send letter which I received this morning from Mrs. J. D. Easterlin, Corresponding Secretary of the Georgia work. Kindly regard Mrs. Easterlin's letter as "confidential."

Possibly, probably, you may not know there is pending before the Home Board a resolution not to place a money value on boxes sent to Frontier missionaries. You will recognize that this is part of the result of Dr. Bell's antagonism to W.M.U. methods. I do not believe that the Board will pass the resolution to cease valuing the boxes, and even if they should, it will be a question that must be presented at an Annual Meeting before those who have charge of W.M.U. work could make changes in this direction. You will recognize, though, that should said change be made, it would probably also affect the interests which you represent. Oh, is not Satan busy?

Very truly,
Annie W. Armstrong

RESOLUTION
Whereas,

It has been charged in the columns of some of our denominational papers that the Corresponding Secretary has been exerting her influence upon the Womens' Missionary Societies throughout the South to contribute an undue proportion of their offerings to the Home Mission Board to the neglect of "that greatest of all causes" Foreign Missions, we, the Executive Committee of W. B. M. U. of the State of Georgia, call the attention of the denomination generally, and especially of the Baptist women of the South, to the following facts.

1. That it is the long established policy of the W.M.U. Auxiliary to the Southern Baptist Convention, to receive from the various Boards of the Convention at each of its annual sessions, requests as to the work, both as to its character and its amount that they desire the Union to do for them.

2. That the requests of these various Boards receive careful consideration in open session, previous to their adoption.

3. That these requests of the Boards as adopted at each annual meeting, are forwarded by the Executive Committee of the Union to each of the State Committees for their consideration and action, and that every Society in every State of the South is free to adopt, or modify, or reject, any, or all of these various recommendations. And, therefore, if there be any force in the statement that women of the South have been led to favor the Home rather than Foreign, the fault does not lie with the Corresponding Secretary, but with the Union itself, which adopted the recommendations proposed by the Boards. As matter of fact the records show that in no year since the organization of the Missionary Union have the requests of the Home Mission Board as adopted by the Union at its annual meeting been fully complied with. The amounts raised have always been less than asked by the Board, and recommended by the Union to the Societies.

The records show that every year the moneyed contributions to Foreign Missions have exceeded those raised for Home Missions, and only by adding the value of boxes sent to Frontier Missionaries which while of greatest assistance to these laborers, do not liquidate any obligation of the

Board to its Missionaries, can be made to appear that the contributions of the Home Missions Board have ever been equaled by those to the Foreign Mission Board. It is well known that when the indebtedness to the Foreign Mission Board amounting to $30,000.00 threatened to paralyze its work; that the Womens' Missionary Union in annual session "led by its Corresponding Secretary" voted to raise five thousand dollars for the extinguishment of this debt, and that no such special offering has ever been made to the work of the Home Mission Board.

Therefore, we the Executive Committee of the Baptist Womens' Missionary Union of Georgia, propose to accept in full our share of responsibility of the action complained of, and to rely upon our past record as all sufficient to vindicate us and our sisters of other States, from complaints made in some of our periodicals.

And, furthermore, we do not appreciate nor do we understand why, if at any time in our judgment we should consider it wise to make any extra effort for either of the Boards of our Southern Baptist Convention, it should be made the occasion of public censure by our denominational press.

RESOLUTION

Whereas,

There is now pending before the Home Mission Board of the Southern Baptist Convention, a Committee report which recommends that no valuation be put upon boxes sent by the Womens' Societies to Frontier Missionaries, and whereas,

The recommendations by the Home Board of the W.M.U. which met in New Orleans, have been adopted by the W.M.U. in annual session assembled, and which it is now impossible to change. Therefore,

We, the Executive Committee of the W. B. M. U. of Georgia, do most earnestly and respectfully request our brethren of the Home Board, that they allow the present method of sending boxes to Frontier Missionaries to continue without change.

[SBHLA, J. M. Frost Collection]

February 2, 1904
Dr. R. J. Willingham

Dear Brother:

As the mail is not so heavy on Tuesday as on other days, I have today been able to straighten out a number of matters. By express today—expressage prepaid—I send you a package containing envelopes, etc., etc. A few words of explanation in regard to the package.

In it you will find two boxes of unaddressed envelopes. The envelopes were purchased before the lists of superintendents came from Nashville, and as I was under the impression from Dr. Frost's statements that the lists would be about 10,000, I purchased that number, so I have sent you 1,000 envelopes that were not addressed.

The number of Sunday School Superintendents in Missouri is about 1,200 so you will find addressed envelopes in three boxes.

In three other boxes there are additional programs and letters sent from Richmond that were not used. Will it not be possible to send the programs to Missouri, even though they are not accompanied by letters in which an appeal is made for money?

I enclose bill for amount expended in sending letters to Superintendents. Permit me to call your attention to several items.

(a) You will recall I reported to you that Dr. Burrows expended thirty dollars in having lists prepared in Nashville. I sent check for that amount to him, and it was the understanding with you that one third of the amount should be charged to each Board. Since writing you on this point I have had several letters from Dr. Frost. It is quite evident that Dr. Frost is not pleased with the present plan of each Secretary making his own appeal to the Sunday Schools. When offering to have envelopes addressed for the Sunday School Board and to send letters from him, Dr. Frost requested that I would let the appeal for Children's Day go out in Woman's Missionary Union envelopes. I declined to allow this to be done and told him all that I was willing to do was the *work* and that I would not make the appeal to the Sunday Schools. He then stated that his force of clerks in Nashville was sufficient to do the work of sending letters out, and I assured him that I was glad to be relieved of that work. I have today sent to Dr. Frost the manuscript for program for Children's Day with electrotypes, and will have nothing further to do with Children's Day, leaving it entirely with Dr. Frost to present the matter as he thinks wise. Please do not get the idea from what I have said that Dr. Frost is *apparently* provoked. You know Dr. Frost. He is serene. Under these circumstances, as the lists now in Baltimore are not to be used by Dr. Frost, the price of copying in Nashville will have to be borne by the Home and Foreign Boards, so I have to charge each Board with $15.00.

(b) I was able to have the envelopes addressed by our regular force, so no charge is made for this. I could not though have programs and letters folded and packages put up, and really did not think it was wise to use the time of the clerks at the Rooms, to whom we were paying so much more, to do this work, so I hired young girls to put up the packages at fifty cents a day.

(c) 7,451 letters were sent out. Thinking you may like to know the number sent to each state, I will have the list given on a different piece of paper.

Do you think that there will be any way by which we can know how much will result from sending the letters direct to Superintendents? Dr. Bomar thinks that $10,000.00 would be a very small return. I certainly should feel very much gratified if that amount was secured.

Will you kindly let me know if the Foreign Board has regular times for meeting? If so, we will try and send for checks or present bills just prior to said meetings. Hereafter I am going to ask that the Treasurer, Mrs. W. C. Lowndes, will let you know when money for Woman's Missionary Union expenses is required.

Very truly,
Annie W. Armstrong
[IMB Archives]

Annie Armstrong understood that Sunday School offered a prime opportunity to advance missionary enterprises, as well as teach Bible lessons. Naturally, she stood willing to advance this cause.

July 13, 1896
Dr. J. M. Frost
Dear Brother:

I rather expect you have gotten to think that the Cor. Sec'y of the Woman's Missionary Union does not wait to consider very carefully any plan after it suggests itself to her, but proceeds to act at once. This is doubtless the case very frequently, but not always, as I am now going to submit a thought to you which came to me months ago. In fact, I discussed the subject with Dr. Bell in Chattanooga and then told him that if you did not want me to do this work for *The Teacher*, I would let him have for *The Index* the data which I would collect. He approved quite heartily of the plan which I outlined and will find space in *The Index* for the articles if you do not want them. Now for my thought.

Probably it is a sign of age, but in some directions I do not think we are making advance. In fact, some of the methods of Sunday School teaching when I was a child, I consider far superior to those that are adopted now, viz., memorizing the Scriptures and hymns. The latter, as far as my observation goes, has been done away with in Sunday Schools almost entirely, except in Infant Classes where children are not expected to be able to read. I think you will agree with me that this is a great loss to the rising generation, for I for one can testify that numbers and numbers of times a verse of hymn learned in childhood has in latter years brought to mind some blessed truth in times of need. It has occurred to me that it would be helpful to call attention to hymns in connection with the Sunday School Lessons. I will try and make my thought clear, but if I do not, please give me the opportunity of writing again on this subject, as I really believe the plan I want to suggest is a good one.

My idea is to suggest, in connection with each Sunday School Lesson, an appropriate hymn, printing perhaps not the whole of it, but two or three verses, and give if possible the circumstances under which the hymn was written and a little sketch of the writer. I mean to take the standard hymns, not just simply ordinary Sunday School tunes. Dr. Ellis, when he first came to Eutaw Place Church, delivered a lecture on "Hymns" and gave the histories of many. I think he made rather a study of the subject and often would, as he announced one, refer to the writer, etc., etc. I am sure if I asked him for this lecture, he would let me have it, or refer me to the sources from whence he obtained the data.

If you desire it, I will undertake for six months—say from January '97 to July '97—to carry out this plan in connection with *The Teacher*, using the space that is now given to "Illustrations." By the way, you never have told me what you thought of the "Illustrations." You will remember you declined to read same at the time I forwarded them, saying you would have to look over them when they were in type. I really would like to have your opinion of the illustrations. If you accept the offer I now make, please let me have *at once* the Scripture Selections for the Sunday School Lesson for the six months, viz., Jan. '97–July '97, as I must do this work during the summer if it is to be done.

Several days since I wrote to the gentlemen whose names you gave me in regard to furnishing comments or illustrations for the Young People's Scripture Union in *Kind Words* and *The Young People's Leader* for next year. As yet, I have had only one reply to these letters and that came this morning from Dr. Chas. Taylor, of Wake Forest College, who very kindly acceded to the request.

Hoping you enjoyed your vacation, I am,

Very truly,

Annie W. Armstrong

P. S. Something quite funny occurred a few days ago. Joshua Levering was taking tea with us—he is now living at his country place, so we occasionally have the pleasure of his being with us to a meal—and was giving an account of a late trip he had made in connection with his Presidential Canvass. As I have not time to read the daily papers very carefully, I did not thoroughly understand the platforms of the different political parties. He very kindly was explaining same and giving quite fully his views in regard to the Prohibition Party. I was intensely interested and did not notice, until Sister Alice called my attention to it later, how inconsistent Joshua was when he expressed the extreme disgust he did for the newspapers allowing the "liquor ring" to buy up their editorial columns. He said that even Mr. Childes, of Philadelphia, had not been able to withstand the pressure brought to bear upon him in this direction. This was an abominable thing when done against the Prohibition Party, but Joshua did not seem to feel the same disgust when it was told him some months before, that the Publication Society was using the same dishonorable methods. "Consistency, thou art a virtue."

[SBHLA, J. M. Frost Collection]

April 5, 1898

Dr. J. M. Frost

Dear Brother:

I know you must be quite busy, but there are several important matters which I desire to present to you and for which I am going to ask a careful consideration. As I have a number of other letters I must write this afternoon, I will dispense with all preliminaries and come right down to business.

1. *Home Department in the Sunday School.* Last Sunday our pastor, Rev. J. Millard, read the enclosed report of the Sunday School Home Department which Sister Alice, as Secretary, had furnished him. You will note she has given a summary of the year's work. I think you will agree with me, after examining same, that the Home Department in Eutaw Place School has proved to be a success. It was undertaken under quite trying circumstances. Some of our active workers did not see the need for it and thought it could not be worked successfully. I am sorry to say my brother-in-law, Eugene Levering, not only did not favor it, but attempted to prevent its being established by ridiculing the whole matter. I do not think he really appreciated what he was doing and simply wanted to worry Sister Alice, whom he is quite fond of teasing. There were several meetings held before it was inaugurated. At the last one Sister Alice let Eugene see that she really thought he was going too far, and that I suppose opened his eyes to the seriousness of the matter and he dropped any further seeming opposition to the plan. I mention this circumstance, so you can appreciate that we had difficulties in getting the Home Department inaugurated. Sister Alice and I, though, were both very anxious that it should be thoroughly tested at this point. I can assure you now, after a year's trial, that the pastor and officers of the school would not be willing that it should be discontinued. I want to call your attention to two or three points which perhaps have not been emphasized as strongly as I think they might be in advocating same. I of course will say nothing about the increased study of God's Word which is secured, or the sympathy it excites between parents who do not attend Sunday School and the children who go. This is apparent to all who understand the fundamental principles of the Home Department.

(a) The large amount of church visiting it secures. You will note there were 413 visits paid by the 15 visitors from Eutaw Place Sunday School. Quite a number of those who did this would never have called to see the persons to whom they took the Sunday School periodicals. I am sure, though, from remarks I heard made by those who did the visiting, when they became acquainted with the persons to whom they went, they really enjoyed their visits. I have learned, from being connected for years with a church where there is a large membership, that persons do not always welcome *church visitors*, if they have the idea that they are simply visited because it is regarded as a duty. This does away with any feeling of the kind. Those who go have a purpose in going, and those who receive them know that they have come on an errand. Thus the two meet on a pleasanter footing and we have found it is more fruitful. Good and much good, I consider, results from this phase of the Home Department work.

(b) The occasional visits it secures to the Sunday School from non attendants. You will see that during the year there were 94 visits made by members of the Home Department to the school. In addition to this, I would say that there was a special social given to the members of the Home Department, and while I was not able to go, I learned from those who were present that it was *thoroughly* enjoyed.

(c) You will note that the amount contributed by the members of the Home Department is quite sufficient to pay all expenses for carrying on same, if it was necessary to use their offerings for the purchase of literature. $66.37 were given by Eutaw Place members. As the church pays the expenses of the Sunday School, this offering will go for missions, with the school's offering.

When the canvass was made of the church, there were 104 persons who said they would become members of the Home Department. As the months went by, some of these failed to keep their promise to study the lessons and dropped out, but you will note there are constant additions being made to the roll, and probably those who join now are more thoroughly informed as to what is required, etc., etc., and will continue to do what they undertake. I have gone thus into particulars, thinking possibly you may not have seen the Home Department as fully at work as I have and that you may want to refer to same in your report. Should you wish, either in the *Teacher* or your report, to refer to this phase of work at Eutaw Place Church, I do not think there would be any objection to your doing so, for, as I previously mentioned, Mr. Millard read the report which I now send you from the pulpit.

Before leaving this matter, I want to offer a suggestion. If you consider it would be well to call special attention to this phase of the Sunday School Board work at the Convention and have not as many speakers as you desire, I think Mr. Millard could give a short talk on this subject which might be helpful.

2. *Letter from Mrs. F. T. Latham, of Medina, N. Y.* I send you this with a definite purpose in view, viz., that you may forward it to the Secretary of one of the Northern Boards if you think wise—Dr. Mabie, of the Missionary Union; Gen. Morgan, of the Home Mission Society, N. Y., or Dr. Rowland, of the Publication Society. You will note that Mrs. Latham desires to know whether we will furnish her mite boxes, if the pledge is made to use them

for our work. As the mite boxes have been gotten out by the Sunday School Board, I send the letter to you for the purpose named above. I think it well for the Secretaries of the Northern Societies to appreciate that we try to observe the Golden Rule, and in this way politely suggest to them that they observe the same by letting them see that we are perfectly willing to leave them their territory from which to glean. I could of course, and would, send this letter to one of the Northern Societies, but prefer to turn it over to you, so you might be able to say that you had declined, when occasion required, to accept contributions which should have passed through Northern channels. I have from time to time done this—not long ago I sent Gen. Morgan an application for the name of a frontier missionary, which came to me from a society at the North, and he seemed to very thoroughly appreciate the courtesy shown him—with very good results. There is, I am glad to say, very pleasant relationships existing between the Woman's Missionary Union and many of the missionary organizations of other denominations and the Northern Baptist Societies.

3. *Sunday School Institutes.* I suppose you are now arranging your policy for next year's work. If so, I do want to urge that you will *very carefully* consider the advisability of the Sunday School Board holding Sunday School Institutes. You will remember I presented this matter to you some time ago and you seemed to regard it at the time favorably, but nothing has been done in that direction. When Dr. Bell was Secretary, I also brought it to his attention. He outlined a plan of such magnitude—his idea was to get not only the Foreign and Home Boards to unite, but the State Board in the State where the Institute was to be held—that it simply was too ponderous to be worked. The more I think of this method for the Sunday School Board, the more thoroughly am I impressed that if rightly worked, it would be a power of great good. Will you permit me to put it before you in the light I see it and give you the reasons why it appeals to me?

(a) The large number of churches where there are no Sunday Schools in the Southern States prove conclusively that there is need for creating public sentiment in this direction.

(b) More efficient work could be done in Sunday Schools now in existence if there were better methods.

(c) The various phases of Sunday School Board work, which are now only touched on when the work is represented in State meetings, could be thoroughly explained and cooperation secured.

(d) If Sunday School Institutes were conducted under the auspices of the Sunday School Board, the periodicals issued by that Board could be presented and their adaptability shown in furthering the interests of the objects for which Southern Baptists are responsible.

(e) The Publication Society does not do this kind of work in the Southern States.

I of course appreciate that in some States there are State Sunday School Boards, but even where this is the case, I do not think there need be the slightest friction. There could be a union of effort in arranging for a Sunday School Institute. My idea is for the Sunday School Board to provide the speakers, or those who would be calculated to instruct in methods of work; that the Institute be held for one or two days. If the speakers, or at least some of them, are from another State, they would doubtless be more attractive. At first there might only be a local attendance, but if the Institutes prove helpful and are sufficiently advertised, in time there would be many who would be anxious to attend from different sections of the State where said Institute is held. I of course do not suppose you could in the course of the year hold one in each State, but I do trust a beginning will be made in this direction next year and something of the kind attempted. The Sunday School Board does make appropriations in one way or another to the States, and it seems to me you could make no better investment of the money which you propose to give to the States than by expending part of it in the way above indicated. Much is being said in favor of the cooperative work that is now being done among the colored people. My thought is for this same kind of work to be done by the Sunday School Board for Sunday School workers, and I believe it will be more fruitful in results than that being done among our colored brethren.

One other matter and then I must draw this long letter to a close. According to promise, I now forward copies of the correspondence which I have lately had with Dr. Rowland. It is probably better at times not to speak as strongly as one feels, but I must say it passes my comprehension how Dr. Rowland as a Christian man can justify himself in using the methods which he is adopting. I do sincerely wish it were possible for the Foreign Board to refuse to accept the money which the Publication Society gives to our work. Do you not agree with me that the explanation given by Dr. Rowland for having the Gospel Mission Department in the *Teacher* is puerile? I am astonished he could not make any better defense for his actions in this particular than he has.

You will note I accomplished one purpose I had in view in writing to Dr. Rowland, viz., I obliged him to acknowledge that the Publication Society has not made reprints of all the addresses that were made at their

Annual Meetings in the last twelve years. This being the fact, the prominence now being given to the address made by you in 1888 shows quite plainly that there was some ulterior motive for its circulation. I have sent you copies of Dr. Rowland's letters rather than the originals, for I thought possibly you might want to retain same. You are at perfect liberty to make use of them in any way you wish. I have also sent copies to Dr. Willingham. I told him that as Dr. Pitt seems to be ready and willing to defend the Publication Society, I should rather like him to see Dr. Rowland's letters, but for him to do in the matter as he thought wise.

Very truly,

Annie W. Armstrong

P. S. The mite boxes which you promised to forward have not yet arrived.

P. S. No. 2. I have seen the sketch for the title page of program for Missionary Day. It promises to be a very pretty piece of work. I expect it will be completed by the last of the month. I have concluded, though, that I want to take the program, with drawing, to Norfolk and let the ladies at an Executive Committee session see same—I think it will prove helpful in exciting their interest and securing their help in distributing it later on.

Please do not forget to let me see copies of the Children's Day program as soon as it is issued. I am quite curious to have a view of it.

P. S. No. 3. Since writing the above, I have had a visit from Dr. O. F. Gregory, who returned this morning from Norfolk where he has been in the interest of Convention arrangements. He told me something which I consider quite amusing. As you probably know, the day sessions of the Convention are to be held in the Freemason Street Church, but the Committee has secured some public building—I think he said it was the Music Hall—for the evening meetings. Our very modest and retiring Baltimore pastor, Dr. H. M. Wharton, has hired this building to preach in Sunday night, May 8th. He has not left it with the Committee on Religious Exercises to decide whether he is to have an opportunity to preach, or not. If you wish to have either the right or left-hand box reserved for you, let me know and I will use what influence I may possess with Dr. Wharton to assign same to you. Does not this inaugurate a new method in Convention proceedings?

[SBHLA, J. M. Frost Collection]

The WMU occasionally met opposition to organized "woman's work,"
but Armstrong deflected criticism against the organization by carefully
delineating specific roles for women in ministerial endeavors. She had no
patience for female preachers, and she made sure that everyone knew it.

May 25, 1895
Dr. R. J. Willingham
Dear Brother:
I have just received a letter which has personally given me a great deal
of pleasure, and I consider it means so much to the work that I want without
delay to send you a copy of it, for I think you will appreciate as I do that a
great advance has been made in this direction. I really would rather be able
to send you this letter than to forward a check for several thousand dollars,
as I think it will in the near future mean much more than that for Foreign
Missions. Before asking you to read the letter which I enclose, I will give a
few words of explanation.

Ever since the Woman's Missionary Union was organized, I have
appreciated that we could not make much headway unless the pastors were
in sympathy with the efforts we were making to interest the women and
children in missions, and if we could only secure the active cooperation of
the professors at the Seminary, we might then hope that large sums would
be raised, for as the students graduated and went to their charges, they
would then seek to have the women in their churches formed into
missionary societies. I soon learned that although Dr. Broadus did not
disapprove of Woman's Missionary Union—his daughter is President of the
Central Committee of Kentucky—yet he seemed to be a little fearful of the
outcome of this movement. I never heard him make an address on Woman's
Work or refer to it that I did not feel sorry he had touched on it at all, for
while he spoke as approving of it, he always ended with a warning that we
should not forget Paul's teaching—"let the women keep silence in the
churches," etc., etc. I could not help feeling that sufficient time has elapsed
to prove that Woman's Missionary Union could be trusted in this direction
as well as in some others, and always hoped that Dr. Broadus would give
our work his unqualified endorsement, but as far as I know, he never did,
and certainly in the Seminary our work was not spoken of—in proof of
which see statement made by Dr. Whitsitt.

Appreciating that we could not hope to have the assistance from Dr.
Broadus, I several years ago tried to get Dr. Kerfoot to lend his valuable aid

in this direction. I knew he thoroughly sympathized with us in our work, but as you probably know, Dr. Kerfoot is one who, if he is working along a certain line, throws his whole heart into that and forgets other things, so nothing resulted from that effort.

While in Washington, I had the opportunity of talking to Dr. Whitsitt and presenting to him some facts connected with Woman's Missionary Union work. Dr. Whitsitt, to my surprise, said that years ago, prior to the organization of the Woman's Missionary Union, he had advocated some advanced steps being taken in Woman's Work, so he was quite prepared to give earnest consideration to the matter. I will now ask that you read Dr. Whitsitt's letter. I of course will keep Dr. Whitsitt informed as to methods of Woman's Missionary Union, Plans of work, etc., etc., and furnish the students with literature if they are willing to try to organize societies. I cannot help thinking that what Dr. Whitsitt has done and proposes to do will bring into the treasuries of the Boards many thousands of dollars, for if the women largely in our Baptist churches throughout the South can be gotten to appreciate the need there is for them to aid, they can and will gather up "the littles." What a mighty host we have within the bounds of S.B.C. to enlist as workers.

There are other matters that I want to write about, but must defer doing so until next week.

Very truly,
Annie W. Armstrong
[IMB Archives]

July 24, 1896
Dr. J. M. Frost
Dear Brother:

Your letters of July 21st & 22nd both received. I replied to the first by telegram, but desire to offer an explanation of same now that I understand the reason which made you request that I send you additional plates of African Scene and Stone Dugout. I shall try to state the matter clearly, but if I fail, please excuse me, as I am far from well. In fact, I am dictating this while in bed, but am able to keep on with the work, as our Stenographer is here. Now to business.

1. *Plates for pictures.* As I think I previously mentioned, Sister Alice obtained cuts of the African Scene and Stone Dugout from *The Christian Herald*, 91–98 Bible House, New York, for use in *Kind Words*. Wanting

these pictures for the program, I prevailed on her to let me have them. The plate I sent you some days ago of the African Scene was the one we obtained from New York. I had a duplicate taken of that of the Stone Dugout in Baltimore, as the one sent us fitted in another plate which represented a Sod Dugout. As it had a piece cut out, I thought it better to send it in the shape needed for the program, so had plate made here. When your letter reached me, I supposed you thought we had the original plates of both pictures, hence my telegram. I am very sorry you are "a little fearful that the plate of the Stone Dugout is not going to print up very well, as it seems somewhat worn from use." By today's mail (registered package) I send you the plate which was forwarded to us from New York of the Stone Dugout. Should the printer think it might be well to use this one, I will have to ask that before cutting it he have a duplicate made as it now is, so Sister Alice can use in *Kind Words* the two together as she purposed. If you find neither of these plates will give good impressions and think it worthwhile to apply to *The Christian Herald* for other plates of the pictures, kindly do so without referring the matter to us.

2. *Cuts for title page of program and box.* As I previously wrote, the cause of delay in securing same is due to the artist employed by *The Christian Herald* being away on a vacation, and he turning our order over to the Photo. Electrotype Engraving Co., 232 William St., New York. It was not until yesterday that the drawing was submitted to us. They had made a little mistake in not appreciating that we wanted two sizes of the same picture, one for the box; the other for title page. The picture as submitted for box was entirely satisfactory and I suppose there will be no difficulty whatever in enlarging same, as doubtless the drawing had been diminished by photographer when sent to us. Sister Alice, who has conducted the correspondence, returned the picture at once with needed directions and asked that the plates be forwarded to us without delay. *Just as soon as they come to hand*, they will be sent to Nashville. If you think wise, please communicate with the Photo. Electrotype Engraving Co. and order the plates forwarded direct to you. I hesitate to do so, they having misunderstood the previous order, and think it may be best for us to see the plates first and order changes made if necessary, it requiring less time to send the plates from Baltimore to New York than from Nashville.

3. *Wording for mite box.* That has not yet been prepared and I do not feel quite equal to arranging same today. I am hoping, though, to be well enough to go down stairs a little while this evening to meet Rev. John Eager, who is to take tea with us. If so, I shall propose that Sister Alice and Mr.

Eager give a little thought to the matter and will forward you their suggestions without delay. I shall be glad to have this opportunity of interesting Mr. Eager in Missionary Day, and possibly (if I see that he becomes interested in this feature of the work) I may ask that he write an article for one of the State papers in regard to it.

While it is not *absolutely necessary* for me to refer to other points in your letter today, yet I think I will do so, as our Stenographer leaves tomorrow for a vacation of two weeks and if confined to the house, I may find it difficult to write soon again. As you have told me more than once that I may speak freely to you on any subject, I propose to avail myself of that liberty right now. Your letter was brought to me, with other mail, from the Mission Rooms this morning. I did not attempt to write any letters until this afternoon, so I have been able in the hours that intervened to think quite carefully over one or two matters to which you referred. What I shall say then is not on the spur of the moment, but after mature deliberation.

I appreciate that you are in a measure joking when you make use of such expressions as: "It seems to me that I do nothing but follow in the wake opened by others, especially by yourself," and "I am finding real delight and joy in my work and discovering such possibilities in it as I have not seen heretofore, nearly all of which I owe to you." I think, however, that you are in a slight degree in earnest, for you have spoken in this way once or twice before, so I am going to take up the subject seriously. I am quite sure you have forgotten in this connection what Paul said to the Corinthians, in the 12th chapter of first Cor., in regard to diversities of gifts. I could no more do the work you are doing than I could fly. God has given you a wonderful ability for leadership. You can and do, without friction, accomplish what many could never bring about. I do recognize than our Heavenly Father has given me quickness to see how to bring forces together. I am sure the success that has attended the Woman's Missionary Union (humanly speaking) is due to the fact that those who have been leading in this work have recognized that there are these diversities of gifts and we have not attempted to do work for which we were not fitted. I regard it as the sheerest nonsense for persons to claim that women can do men's work. We can go a certain distance and there we have to stop, and unless we have the support of our brethren, the work does not assume the proportions that it should. I am at this present moment an illustration of this fact. Within the last day or two I have had to meet some very trying things, and instead of being able to throw off the effects, I simply have had to succumb physically. No, no, no, there are limitations to the work that can be done by women. Our brethren are the God-appointed leaders.

Now I want to say to you in all seriousness: Please do not make use of such expressions as I have quoted, for they would be misunderstood and much harm would result if you were to speak in this way to others. I am truly glad and thankful for you to give me the opportunities of doing such work as I am capable of without assuming responsibility. If I had to appear before the public as the one who was responsible for some measures which I have suggested and the Boards have carried out, I would simply be made a target for criticism and I should long ago have been forced to give up the work, for I could not have borne it. On this point, I believe I am exercising some common sense. I in a measure know what I can do and what I *cannot*. The same mail that brought your letter also brought one from a prominent brother who undertook to tell me that he thought I was fitted for some work which I would be no more able to do than a kitten. "Them's my sentiments." Now to return to business.

4. *Home Department in the Sunday School.* As soon as I can, I will look up the publications that I now have in regard to the Home Department and obtain others. After looking these over, I will let you know if any suggestions occur to me. Do not feel worried at having mislaid the material I sent Dr. Bell. It is of no consequence.

5. *Attention being called to hymns with histories of same.* Since you consider the "Illustrations" helpful, perhaps it might be better for that department to continue as it is for at least the next six months. While I do believe in variety, yet on thinking the matter over more carefully (as I have done today), it seems to me that changing plans so quickly gives persons a little the feeling of uncertainty. Some may get into the habit of using these "Illustrations" and will feel disappointed if they do not find them in *The Teacher*, so, unless you think otherwise, I will now proceed to find illustrations for the first six months in 1897 and forward them to you in due time.

As to the hymns. What think you of this? Let me look around and see if I can find some interesting histories in regard to several well-known hymns, and furnish these to you to be used editorially. Two or three articles of that nature would draw attention to the subject, and later on the limited space which is now given to "Illustrations" might be sufficient when the subject is well understood, but I doubt if at first we could present the thought forcibly enough in a half page to be effective. Let me have your decision in regard to both of these matters, and if you accept the last suggestion, I will furnish, with as little delay as possible, the data to you on which you could base your articles. I do consider it is an important subject—memorizing hymns—to which attention ought to be called.

Have I not sent you a volume? I expect you will find it difficult to credit that I am feeling sick—women can talk under all circumstances.

Very truly,

Annie W. Armstrong

P. S. I have had this letter signed on the typewriter so that it may be forwarded without delay, as I want you to have the information about the plates as soon as possible.

[SBHLA, J. M. Frost Collection]

Cincinnati

Sep. 13 (1901 ?)

Dr. J. M. Frost

Dear Brother:

We leave Cincinnati by an early train tomorrow morning—I have remained a day longer than I expected to stay but it seemed necessary—so there is a good deal that I must do tonight. I do feel though I want to send you a few lines, as I appreciate how greatly you are interested in the work being done, and needed to be done among the colored people.

I cannot tell you how glad and thankful I feel, for I do believe our Heavenly Father has allowed me to accomplish even more than I anticipated when I accepted the invitation of the colored women to attend their annual meeting. They seemed to thoroughly appreciate my being at their sessions, and I am quite sure after this they will look to *Southern* Baptist women for aid and advice. In three different ways have they asked for our assistance, and at no point was any reference made to the work being done among them by Northern Baptists, with the exception of the Fireside Schools, and that is regarded as Miss Moore's work.

I had quite long conversations with both Dr. Boyd & Rev. L. G. Jordan today as to how we can help, etc. Dr. Boyd has authorized me to say to the Home Board, that his Board will pay one half of the salary of a woman missionary, if the Home Board will pay the other half, viz., $150.00. For this very small sum we will be able to very largely help the colored women, for they will then recognize that Southern white women are ready and willing to assist them through their own organizations.

Another way in which I think we can help them largely is—in establishing reading rooms in their churches, as was suggested by their President. At least, she did not state where the rooms were to be, but in talking the matter over with Dr. Boyd—it met with his approval—that was the thought.

No representative from the Northern Societies attended the women's meetings except Miss Moore, and she did not advocate any plans. I acted on your advice and did not attempt to connect our work with hers.

You will see from the program which I enclose, that the men were not present when I made the asked for address. I rather expected some of the women would have entered their protest to the exclusion of the brethren. But instead of doing so, they seemed to think it was very entertaining and Mrs. Schimp tells me it was very funny—I did not turn round, and as I was sitting in one of the front pews did not know what was going on—to see one woman go up in the gallery and take two men by the arms and escort them to the steps. This was after they had been repeatedly requested by the presiding officer to retire.

I expect to go to Cumberland, Md. tomorrow and from there to several other points in Md. but hope to be in Balto. by Sep. 18th. I had very pleasant visits to Springfield and to four places in Ky. after leaving Nashville. While this trip has been a long one, and at times quite fatiguing, yet I am not feeling at all broken down, and I do believe much good will result from it.

Hoping that Mrs. Frost has entirely recovered, I am

Very truly,

Annie W. Armstrong

Dr. Boyd told me today that Dr. McConnell has accepted the Secretaryship of the Home Board. Were you surprised at this? I am.

[SBHLA, J. M. Frost Collection]

Under Armstrong's leadership, the WMU engaged in far-reaching missionary endeavors.

June 23, 1893

Dr. J. M. Frost

Dear Brother:

Your letter of June 20th received this A. M., and as there are several things I wish to speak of I will reply to it without delay.

1. Fearing that complications may arise under existing circumstances, which may cause misunderstandings, I am going to offer a few words of

explanation as to the way I regard the Woman's Missionary Union's connection with the Boards, S.B.C., and how as Cor. Sec. W.M.U. I consider it to be my duty to act, as long as I hold the position I now do.

(a) I do not look upon the work of the W.M.U. as separate and distinct from that of the Boards.

(b) That W.M.U. is not only in name but in reality auxiliary to *all* of the Boards.

(c) That the Convention having decided to commit its work into the hands of *three* Boards, it is the duty of W.M.U. to aid as far as is their power *each* Board, and to so regulate their work that one interest shall not be advanced at the expense of another.

Now as to the practical working out of these definitions that I have given. I do not believe the most prejudiced opposer to W.M.U., if he would take the trouble to look into our methods of work during the past five years—the length of time since organization—but would acknowledge that there has not been the slightest effort by W.M.U. either to make any separation in the work, or to direct and control missionary operations, but quite the reverse. While the Convention only had two Boards, for several years after the organization of W.M.U., yet these two Boards were working on different lines, and yet I am quite sure neither Board can in justice say, that the officers of W.M.U. failed to represent the interest of their respective Board, (in their efforts to enlist the women and children in working for missions,) or allowed one cause to be pressed at the expense of the other.

Since we have had a third Board you know so well how W.M.U. has acted in connection with that branch of work that it is unnecessary for me to speak of that, so let me finish this subject with saying a few words as to the future. As long as I hold the Secretaryship of the Woman's Missionary Union, I propose to carry out the past policy and be loyal to all *three* of the Boards of the Convention, and not let the efforts of W.M.U. in one direction for one Board, militate against the interest of one of the others. In order that mistakes may not occur through ignorance, I do feel that I must be allowed the liberty to refer—as in the case of Dr. Harris' letter—any question to either of the other Boards, if it seems to me that conflict of interest might result. I think you will see that our work, looking at it in this light, is a little difficult, but if the Boards will *trust* us, knowing that if mistakes occur they are not made intentionally, I believe we can "go forward." Let me assure you of one thing, the present Secretary will offer her resignation if the pressure becomes too great, but she does not propose to deviate one particle from the position she has taken in this respect, for I believe it is what will best advance the cause.

2. I sometimes feel sorry that it is so, but I seem to be in a position where I hear and know of things that influence the work before they are made public. A piece of that sort of information came to me today, and as it affects the Sunday School work I will give it to you. Dr. O. F. Flippo formerly of Roanoke, Va. was at the Mission Rooms a day or two ago and also today. He told me that he had been offered the position of District Secretary of Penn. & Md. by the Publication Society, and that he would be at liberty to make his headquarters either in Phila., Hagerstown, Md. or Balto., but that he thought he would come to Balto. I have known Dr. Flippo for years, so I did not hesitate to talk very plainly and tell him in so many words that I wished he would not come to Md. but confine his labors to Penn. I do not think my eloquence had any effect, for I think he has decided to come. He said when he was in Phila. yesterday, they desired to give him his commission, but he preferred to wait until he had seen some persons in Balto. Dr. Flippo said the suggestion to locate in Balto. did not come from the officers of the Publication Society in Phila. I asked Dr. Flippo if he did not expect to include Va. in his parish, he laughed and said, "———— (I do not care to give name) said he was to be a rover." I told Dr. Flippo I was going to write and tell you of this so I feel free to give you the information.

As far as I know this is a newly created office of the Publication Society, and I am truly sorry that they have seen fit at this stage of things to pay us quite so much attention in Md. It is right hard at times is it not to realize that "all things work together for good."

3. While I have already written a longer letter than I ought to have taken time to write, yet there is another matter that I will have to speak to you about in the near future, if not now, so I think I will tax your patience a little longer, rather than to send another letter shortly.

It is with regard to the "Primary Mosaics." I think you know me well enough by this time to appreciate, that I do not hesitate to speak candidly in discussing a subject, and prefer to be treated in the same way. If I am not mistaken the arrangement with regard to that department in the *Teacher* dates with the year. Under ordinary circumstances it would of course be the right thing to wait for you to ask that we should continue doing that work should you desire it, but, as I mentioned to you last year, the only time I can give to such extra work is during the Summer, when I may either be away for a short time, or else under less pressure at home. The prospect is with the first of September I will have more to do than I have ever had, as I have undertaken some new work which will commence then, and will take several hours each day, or its equivalent during the week, so this added to what I now have in hand will not leave many spare moments. My part of the Mosaics has been to map them out, collect data, etc., and leave them in a rough state to be shaped up, altered and written out in full by Sister Alice, who at times improves them so that they are as new to me in many particulars as to others. This year's Mosaics—my part in them—were prepared while I was at the seashore last Summer, if that had not been the case, many months during the year I expect you would have received excuses instead of Mss., as it would have been impossible for me to have given the thought necessary to preparing them.

All this by way of explanation to the question which I am now about to ask.

Do you wish the "Primary Mosaics" to continue another year? Let me beg of you, as I am obliged to ask the question—for the reason given—that you will feel perfectly free to decide this question entirely in the light of what will best aid the Sunday School work, and that you will not consider those who have provided this material in the past. We have frequently urged that a very high standard ought to be aimed for in S. Sch. Convention publications, so if the "Mosaics" do not come up to that standard, I think it would not be doing justice to the cause for you to have them in the *Teacher* another year. Another thing also that it seems to me that you ought to consider is, that this kind of teaching having been given for two years, it might be well to introduce something else. For these and other reasons that will suggest themselves to you, I am going to ask that you will not hesitate to decide not to have the "Mosaics" another year should you think it best.

Hoping that you have entirely recovered from your late attack, I am with kind regards,

Very truly,

Annie W. Armstrong

P. S. While I have given you our policy both past and future in connection with the Boards, yet I failed to say definitely what we would do in this matter suggested by Dr. Harris. We will simply decline to act on suggestion for the reasons given above. I do not believe that Dr. Harris will press the point, when he sees that we regard things differently—as we have the work to do—but should he, I will then give him your letter and Dr. Bell's which puts it [handwritten in margin] out of power to act otherwise, as in the matter of S. School interests. The officers of the S. Sch. Board are the ones to whom the W.M.U. will look to for instructions, and certainly we will not adopt any plan that they oppose.

[SBHLA, J. M. Frost Collection]

April 11, 1894
Dr. T. P. Bell
Dear Brother:

Your letter of April 9th received, and I want to express my appreciation of your kindness in trying to obtain the information needed by the officers of the W.M.U. from the Secretaries of the other Boards during the late meeting at Macon. I think I can read clearly enough "between the lines" of your letter to know that it is not wise in the future for the Secretary of the W.M.U. to try and make her work easier by inviting others to assume responsibility that belongs to her office. As the children say, "If you will forgive me this time, I'll never do so no more." I cannot help thinking that the opinion I formed of the Secretary of the Foreign Board after that occurrence of several months ago—you recall his letters, which I forwarded to you—is correct. Dr. Frost has been so kind recently in trying to bring order out of confusion in connection with the Woman's Work in Tennessee, that I was almost prepared to "let by-gones be by-gones," but I do not believe he begins to appreciate how much harm he has done to the cause of Foreign Missions in bringing the pressure he did to bear upon the one who could and would, I believe, have put that branch of Southern Baptist work upon a solid basis. I know you do not like to hear this kind of talk so I will refrain, but you have no idea how bitterly disappointed I get in finding persons do not measure up to the standard that I think our leaders ought to reach.

I judge from what Dr. Gregory tells me that it is probable the different Secretaries, with the exception of Dr. Tichenor, are to be on the train we take for Dallas. If so, and the trip does not entirely use me up—for I cannot count on myself in travelling—I will try en route to Dallas to get from the Secretaries the information needed so that when the Executive Committee meets—Thursday, May 10th—in Dallas, I will know how to present matters.

I take it for granted from your letter you wish to consider what it would cost the Sunday School Board if the sample literature was sent out by them for Missionary Day. Of course, should such an offer be made by you, any part of the work can be relegated to Baltimore if the Ex. Com. is located here another year. The expense in sending out the sample literature beyond printing last year was as follows:

10,000 Letter Heads (printed)	$ 35.00
10,000 Envelopes (printed)	35.00
Typewriting 10,000 Letters	100.00
Addressing 10,000 Envelopes	20.00
Postage on letters with sample literature	400.00

This year, as I previously mentioned, I think a two-cent stamp will carry the sample literature with letter. We will certainly aim in getting it out to let it be so. If it is decided to have Missionary Day the first of October, it seems to me it would be well to send out the appeal and the sample literature not later than the first of August. I will be glad to have you let me know before going to Dallas, what part you think it wise for the S. S. Bd. to take in presenting Missionary Day to the Sunday Schools. As neither the Home or Foreign Boards suggested having such a day, nor have they done anything whatever toward making such a day effective—except after urgent, wearing-out efforts by the Secretary W.M.U. to bring them to a decision, etc., etc.—I am prepared to take rather high grounds in this matter and let the Secretaries of those Boards understand that in this particular they will have to agree to what some other persons think wise. I expect you think I am getting a little ferocious; perhaps I am.

Now for several other items upon which I desire your opinion, which will not be made public.

I enclose copy of a letter from Miss Moon forwarded to me by Miss McIntosh. This letter was read at an Ex. Com. Meeting held yesterday. I suggested to the ladies that it would be well to send Miss Moon's letter to Miss McIntosh, and the one previously received by me, speaking on the same subject, to Dr. R. J. Willingham and ask if he approved of these letters being read at an Ex. Com. session in Dallas. As the B. I. M. is proposing to make an effort to undermine the Woman's Work as conducted by the W.M.U., I think it would be well for the ladies to be posted with regard to this matter. In connection with this point, read a letter from Mr. Stout which Miss McIntosh also forwarded. I will be glad to know what you think of my suggestion.

Please also note, in reading Mr. Stout's letter, what he says about making the Christmas Offering more general. Do you think that would be wise? If it becomes a church offering, the appeal must come from the Foreign Board and I do not believe they will push this work; neither do I think they will be willing to antagonize the sentiment that is quite noisy in some directions with regard to "set days," etc., etc.

One other matter, and then I must close. Do you remember some time ago in writing, you referred to an article on "Suitable Reading for Young People" that appeared in *The Baltimore Baptist*, and asked that I would suggest to Mr. Barron that some one give a list of good books for young people? I delivered your message to Mr. Barron and he immediately turned and requested that I would write such an article. I declined doing so, but told him that I would secure the list of books from Mrs. A. J. Rowland, as I knew of no mother who was more careful in the training of a family of three boys than she was, and from Dr. Rowland's connection with the Publication Society, I was sure they could place in the hands of their boys the best reading matter. Mrs. Rowland very kindly acceded to my request and furnished me with the enclosed list which I send to you—to be retained should you desire it. Two of her boys were at the Mission Rooms some days ago and I went over the list with them, and they evidently had found much pleasure in reading a number of those named. A right strange thing has also occurred in this connection. In looking up some data at home a short time ago, I came across a pamphlet called "Books That Influenced Me." My attention having been called to this subject, I glanced over some of the chapters in the book and found they were written by prominent men, giving an account of the books that in early life had helped to mould their characters. This book is now out of print as I found by trying to obtain a copy to be sent to you. The one at home belongs to Sister Alice and she declined to let me have it, so while I forward it, be kind enough, when you have finished reading it, to return it to me.

Hoping your little people may find pleasure in reading some of the books suggested, I am

Very truly,

Annie W. Armstrong

P. S. Would the writer of the leaflet, "Giving to the Lord," care to know that said leaflet is now being used by two Presbyterian Boards? I had an order from the Woman's Board of the United Presbyterian Church the other day for several hundred copies, and Rev. S. H. Chester of Nashville also sent for copies. I do believe the time you took to write that leaflet was well expended and I expect in Eternity, you will find some sheaves have been gathered through its instrumentality.

[Handwritten in margin] Mrs. G. B. Eager declines to allow her name to be suggested for Pres. W.M.U. Mrs. T. A. Hamilton has been proposed—what think you of her? I fear Mrs. Gwathmey would not be willing, but am making inquiries in that direction.

[SBHLA, J. M. Frost Collection]

June 24, 1899
Dr. I. T. Tichenor
Dear Brother:

There are several important matters to which I desire to call your attention.

First. *Method to secure larger contributions from children and young people.* At the Annual Meeting, W.M.U., in Louisville, it was decided to issue Star Cards somewhat after the order of the one enclosed. I have had a very pretty design drawn, which I consider is quite an improvement on the one which I forward. The picture of a missionary will be framed in the star. Around it, in the points of the star, will be one hundred small stars, which will register gifts. On the back of the card will be a sketch of the missionary for whose support the money is contributed.

You, I am sure, appreciate that children and young people are much more willing to give to "special objects" than to contribute to the general cause of missions, not knowing, as they say, where or to whom their money goes. We have to be willing to do a little educational work along this line, and gradually lead them to appreciate that it is better to contribute to the work as a whole, than to a special missionary or field.

Dr. Willingham approves of this plan, and we are about to issue several cards for the Foreign Board, having on them the pictures of different missionaries—some States will try and raise the amount needed for the support of a missionary.

I think you know how anxious I am to have the work of the two Boards presented equally. If I am not mistaken, the plan which I have outlined will be popular. I now want to ask, if the plan meets with your approval, that you let me know if you deem it desirable to have Miss Buhlmaier and her work presented to the children in this way, and we try and raise the money needed for her support.

Second. *The appointment of a female missionary in the Indian Territory.* May I ask that you will consider the advisability of the Home Board's appointment Mrs. W. H. Kuykendall to work among the *white* women in Indian Territory? While in Louisville, I saw Mrs. Kuykendall several times, and was more and more impressed with her rare capabilities for doing this kind of work. Mrs. Kuykendall was an active worker in the W.M.U. of Texas, previous to her marriage, and although she has married a widower with children, I think it could be so arranged that she could leave home and travel with her husband, who is Secretary of the Sunday School and Colportage Boards in Indian Territory. Mrs. K. has a little property, and so would not require as large a salary as is paid to the female missionaries, that are employed in that locality by the Northern Home Mission Society, which is $400.00. I think Mrs. Kuykendall's services could be secured at $250.00 per annum. Mrs. K. made a most favorable impression on our workers, during the Annual Meeting, and should the Home Board think wise to make this appointment, I have no doubt but what the money required for her support would be more than contributed by the Woman Missionary Societies and Bands. Should this appointment be made, I would suggest that the Star Cards be used as a means of raising her salary. We must get these cards out in the near future, so, I will be glad to hear from you on this point as soon as convenient. I do not want to only have cards issued for the Foreign Board.

Third. *Check for Miss Buhlmaier's travelling expenses.* You will remember that the Home Board authorized the payment of Miss Buhlmaier's travelling expenses to Louisville, to attend the Annual Meeting. I now enclose bill for same, which amounts to $28.55. As this money has been advanced, I will be glad to have it returned as soon as convenient.

Fourth. *Packages of literature to be sent to pastors.* I enclose sample package and will be glad to have your opinion of the material. I hope to be able to mail the packages—there will be between six and seven thousand—next week. Certainly the educational work that is being done should result in greater interest being taken in missions, and larger receipts for the Boards.

Hoping the meetings of the State Secretaries and of Seminary Trustees, to be held in Atlanta next week, will be productive of great good, I am,

Very truly,
Annie W. Armstrong
[SBHLA, J. M. Frost Collection]

August 15, 1899

Dr. A. J. Barton

Dear Brother:

Tuesday's mail is always light, and as most of my correspondents do not write letters on Sunday, and a large proportion of them live too far away for the letters to reach me the day after they are written; hence, I am a little more at leisure than usual, and I am going to indulge myself in having a "chat" with the Assistant Corresponding Secretary of the Foreign Mission Board. I have gotten, though, so in the habit of classifying what I want to say under different headings, that I will still do this, although my purpose is not strictly to confine myself to business items.

At this stage of things I was interrupted by one of our Baltimore pastors, Rev. J. M. Wilbur, who paid quite a long visit; so part of the time I had expected to spend on this letter has been given to "chatting" with some one else. I will now proceed without further preliminaries to business.

1. *Picture of Rev. Peyton Stephens*. Will you kindly look over your photographs and see if you have one of Mr. Stephens and if so, let me have it *at once*? We are about to issue a series of "Star Cards," having on these the pictures of different missionaries. Our idea is in this way to stimulate collections among the children. I particularly want Mr. Stephens' picture, as he is the "Sunbeam Missionary." I wrote to our brother some little time ago and he sent me a picture. I thought I had things all straight, having secured the pictures of the other missionaries and material for sketches of their lives; but last night, when I was giving the order for "plates," the engraver told me that the picture I have of Mr. Stephens is a "half-tone" and that it could not be reproduced. I was extremely disappointed, as the "Cards" are already being called for, and I did not want to have any further delay. Should you not be able to send the picture, kindly direct and mail the letter which I enclose to Mr. Stephens, as I have not his present address.

2. *Date of the origin of Kind Words*. Our stenographer having recently been away on a vacation, and my having great antipathy to the blurred effect that is sometimes the result of taking copies of letters (my brother-in-law, Eugene Levering, has repeatedly informed me how wrong it is for me not to have copies of *all* the letters I write), I do not know just what I said in regard to this matter in the letter I wrote you August 8th. I must, though, retire from the position in which you have placed me, among "the learned doctors," and let you and Dr. Frost decide the important question as to the time when *Kind Words* did come into existence. If you will allow me, I would like to send your letter of August 14th to Dr. Frost, and let him see just the ground you

have for holding the opinion you do. While it is a small matter, yet I would like the dates and statistics in the "Hand Book" to be thoroughly accurate. Let me know if I may send your letter to Dr. Frost.

3. *Program for Missionary Day*. I enclose copy and would like to have your opinion of it. The Program was prepared by Miss Heck and the drawing for title page made in Nashville. I am very much afraid that, if this Program comes to the notice of Dr. Eaton, or rather Mrs. Peck, Dr. Frost will be called to account for Catholic tendencies, training the children theatrically, etc., etc. If I had seen the manuscript or drawing before the Program was printed, I certainly should have suggested "caution," but I only saw the Program for the first time yesterday.

I must reply to some letters, so will have to draw this one to a close. Before doing so, though, I would say that I was quite tempted last Saturday afternoon to send you some "news," as it bore on a topic which we discussed quite fully the day you spent in Baltimore; but I concluded, as the one who wrote me said that he had spoken only to one other person on this subject, that I was expected to regard what he said as confidential although it was not so stated. If you are good at guessing, you may let me have the benefit of your conjectures, and perhaps I may tell you whether you are right or wrong.

I am glad to be able to report that owing to there being fewer visitors at the Mission Rooms, and no meetings, I have our work quite well in hand, and some things done considerably ahead of time. I have two departments in *The Teacher*, and this work is completed for the year 1900, with the exception of a little copying. I am glad that this is the case, for I am sure when Dr. Kerfoot gets installed, he will find plenty of work for his subordinates. He knows how to "boss."

Hoping Mrs. Barton and the little ones are well and enjoying their country home, I am,

Very truly,

Annie W. Armstrong

Later. I have just been replying to a letter which Dr. Lansing Burrows referred to me from the Cor. Sec. of the Wisconsin Baptist State Convention. Thinking you may feel depressed as to the "slowness" of Southern Baptists to respond to the appeals made to them by the Secretaries of the Boards, it occurred to me that this letter might help to establish your equilibrium so I forward copy. "Distance lends enchantment to the view."

[IMB Archives]

September 7, 1899

My dear Mrs. Burnham:

Knowing of the willingness of the workers in Missouri to adopt any methods which may lead to more effective service, it gives me pleasure at this time, to direct your attention to three different plans of work for young people. These were all presented and discussed at the Annual Meeting and we are now prepared to submit them to the Central Committees in the various States, hoping that they may meet with hearty endorsement. They may be designated as follows:

Babies' Branch

Star Cards

Young People's Scripture Union.

The Babies' Branch is an effort to carry out from infancy the third special Recommendation of the Executive Committee which emphasizes the wisdom of a *graded system of Missionary Societies.*

The idea is, however, not to form Bands of babies, but simply to enroll them, giving to each a certificate of membership, which may be kept by the mother and in later years given the child who can treasure it until old age as an evidence of life-long association with mission work. It is appreciated that the mites of all the Baptist babies in our South-land may become a great factor in increasing moneyed receipts, but the main object is to interest the mothers in missions and in training their children to appreciate that one of the most important duties in life is to do their part in advancing Christ's kingdom.

The enrollment of the babies should be in charge of one earnest worker who is willing not only to enroll them, but to collect dues and as far as possible, keep the mothers in touch with the work. I think it would be well to have the Babies' Branch under the watch-care of a Woman's Society in each church, but if there be no such organization, any woman who loves Christ's cause and His "little ones" may undertake this work. Who can measure the influence that may result! Through the babies, the mothers may and we hope will become interested. Then, do you think it would be long before the Woman's Mission Society would be organized?

Mrs. Harris of Montgomery, Alabama, has written an article on the Babies' Branch, copy of which I send you with the request that you kindly have it printed in State papers, and also give information where the literature for this work can be obtained.

Star Cards are intended for use in the gathering of money for the support of special missionaries. They are, as you will see, very dainty and pretty. It is hoped that they will "take" with our young people proving helpful both in increasing contributions and interest by familiarizing them with the missionary for whom they are working.

For the use of the Societies and Bands *in general*, two sets of Cards have been issued, one for the support of Miss M. Buhlmaier who represents Home Mission work, the other in the interest of the Sunbeam Missionary and representative of Foreign work, Rev. Peyton Stephens. In addition to these, three special sets have been prepared on which are the picture and sketch of Mrs. N. Maynard, Miss Willie Kelly and Miss Claudia White. These will be used respectively by the "Young South" in charge of Mrs. L. D. Eakin and by workers in Alabama and Maryland.

The *Young People's Scripture Union* differs from the other two plans in that it is not a means of raising money, yet it is equally, possibly more important. As you probably know, the Young People's Scripture Union in connection with the Sunday School lesson, is a department in *Kind Words* of which I have had charge ever since its establishment. The aim is not only to make the young people more familiar with their Bibles by reading them daily but to increase interest in the Sunday School lesson and understanding of the bearing of one portion of Scripture upon another. Manuscripts for the Bible Readings are secured from some of the ablest ministers in the South. I am sure you will agree with me that our young people must be rooted and grounded in the knowledge of God's Word if they are to have a genuine appreciation of the plan of salvation, of their personal duty to God and responsibility for others.

During the past year, we were greatly encouraged by the number who signed the Membership Blank and a short time ago, we had the pleasure of welcoming to the Young People's Scripture Union, one whose home is in distant China. Enclosed you will find a copy of his letter in which I think you will be interested and also a specimen of one week's study from *Kind Words*.

May I ask that your Committee will give thoughtful consideration to this subject as well as to the two preceding ones and use their influence in securing as many members as possible from among the young people in Missouri. Perhaps in each church, may be found one who realizes the importance of Bible study and who would be willing to work for the success of this special department, securing names of those in the Sunday School and elsewhere, who desire to become members.

In addition to enclosures which I have mentioned, you will find samples of literature which have been prepared for the Babies' Branch (Do you not think it cute?) and Star Cards, also Order Blank which it will give me pleasure to fill as soon as returned by you.

Hoping that God's will may be done in all our work and that He will give guidance to us all, I am,

Yours, in Christian service,

Annie W. Armstrong

[IMB Archives]

December 19, 1902

Dr. R. J. Willingham

Dear Brother:

As you may or may not know, the Woman's Missionary Union requests the Societies to hold during the course of the year two weeks of special meetings, for prayer and study of mission fields. One the first week in January and the other the third week of March. The special offerings (Christmas Offering) taken up during the meetings in January go entirely to the Foreign Board. Those in March (Week of Self Denial) to the Home Board. While the moneyed offerings are definitely for each Board at the time named, yet, during these special meetings the work of both Boards is considered and programs so arranged.

I am now trying to formulate a plan for the "Week of Self Denial" and arranging to get out suitable literature. I therefore desire to submit to you a thought that has come to me in connection with the presentation of the work of the Foreign Board in March, during the Week of Prayer.

As you will remember, some years ago I had arranged a catechism for the work of all *three* Boards of the Southern Baptist Convention. This has never been printed, although the ladies have repeatedly called for same. It has occurred to me that it would be well to divide the catechism, getting out two; one for the Foreign Board and one for the Home Board, and furnish them to the ladies so they can be used for the first time during the meetings in March, and later letting it be permanent material for the work. The catechism for the Foreign Board will give foundation facts as to every line of work that the Foreign Board has undertaken, and I think it could form the basis of talks or papers at these meetings. So much for my first thought.

Now for the second. You will recall that the ladies have urged that we furnish sketches of missionaries. You did not think it wise to have autobiographical sketches of missionaries now on the fields and in that I perfectly agreed with you. I do think though it is not wrong after God has taken men and women to Himself for us to recognize that He has used them as instruments to accomplish His purposes, and I believe such teaching is helpful, for it stimulates one to recognize as Longfellow says:

"Lives of great men all remind us, we can make our lives sublime,
And departing, leave behind us, foot-prints on the sands of Time."

I enclose a number of short sketches of some of those whom God has used in His work in years gone by. My idea is to have these printed under one cover. I do not judge they will make more than an eight or twelve page leaflet. With the catechism and these sketches I think the ladies will have ample material for presenting the work of Foreign Missions during the Week of Prayer, in March, in a way that would be not only interesting, but stimulating. So much for the plan. Now for the necessary authority to carry it out.

Will the Foreign Board either print or pay for printing these two publications? It is perfectly immaterial to me whether they are printed in Richmond or in Baltimore. I would like though that the catechism should have on it a cover of stiffer paper, as I think it would pay to get it out in that shape, for we want, if possible, to get the Bands, if not Woman's Mission Societies, to make a study of the catechism. I should like to have 15,000 of the catechisms for distribution in W.M.U. work and 10,000 of the sketches.

I submit this material now and would ask that you examine same as soon as convenient, and let me have your decision, for we want to get to work on the program, and cannot do this until I know what character of material we will furnish the ladies. If you approve of the plan please do not hesitate to make any corrections you may think wise in manuscripts before returning them to me. If you have not time to do this will you kindly ask Dr. Bomar to make a critical examination of same?

Very truly,
Annie W. Armstrong
[IMB Archives]

November 10, 1903

Dr. R. J. Willingham

Dear Brother:

I reached Baltimore this morning and am again at my post hard at work. As usual I find a large number of letters that had to be put aside until I could attend to them, but I hope in a few days to get things again in hand and ready to inaugurate new plans, etc., etc. I find there are several matters that I want to refer to you.

(1) *List of Sunday Schools.* When you meet Dr. Frost in Staunton will you kindly explain to him the plan that I suggested to you in regard to sending letters quarterly from the Secretaries of the three Boards to the Sunday Schools, and asking their cooperation and contributions in any line of work that the Secretary of the Board making the appeal may deem wise. Please also state to him that this plan, if adopted, carries with it the idea that we will not make the effort previously suggested with the Baptist Young People's Unions. I would also ask that you request him to furnish me without delay a list of the Superintendents, or Sunday School officers, with their addresses, that he has in *all of the states*. I think that Dr. Frost has stated that the Sunday School Board furnishes between nine and ten thousand Sunday Schools with literature, so if that is the case, the list that we are now asking for will consist of nine or ten thousand names. If Dr. Frost cannot have the entire list sent to me without delay, please ask that he have it forwarded in divisions, as I will commence to have envelopes addressed as soon as the list comes to hand.

(2) *Envelopes for Letters to Sunday Schools.* It is, of course, the idea that the appeal from you to the Sunday Schools will be enclosed in your official envelope. Please let me know what you would have to pay for ten thousand envelopes in Richmond, so that I may know if it will be cheaper to have the envelopes printed in Richmond and forwarded to Baltimore, or to have them printed here.

(3) *Dr. Bryan's Address.* I am correct, am I not, in thinking that Dr. Bryan was the missionary that you thought it wise to write the letter to the Sunday Schools, which will accompany yours, making a plea for "better equipment" in the way of houses, etc., on foreign fields.

(4) *Letter from Corresponding Secretary Foreign Mission Board.* Appreciating that you are very busy and remembering that you stated that you would be more at leisure in December, I think we can wait until December for your letter. I would like to be able to mail the letters about the first week in January.

(5) *List of Societies in Indian Territory.* Will you kindly have the *Foreign Mission Journal* sent for one year to the ladies whose names I enclose on a separate sheet of paper?

(6) *Support of Schools.* At the last session of the Annual Meeting of the Woman's Missionary Union in Norfolk I told the ladies of the aim of the Sunbeam Band of Free Mason St. Church to raise during the next fifteen months the $375.00 needed to provide a building for the school in charge of Miss Moon, and also that the Woman's Missionary Union would now try to secure the money needed for the support of *all* the schools in Foreign countries. As I previously mentioned to you Mrs. Williams, the Band Superintendent in Virginia, will try to get the Bands in Virginia to raise the money—$500.00 or more—for the support of a school at Canton. The ladies seemed much interested and pleased and several afterwards spoke of it as a good thing. I am quite sure the plan will work well and I hope to be able to get the $14,000.00 needed for the school work largely from sources that heretofore gave very little, if anything, to Foreign Missions. I will as soon as possible write to all of the missionaries where there are schools and ask for the definite information needed to bring this work to the attention of W.M.U. workers.

Hoping that the session of the General Association of Virginia will be as harmonious and profitable as was the Annual Meeting of the Woman's Missionary Union of Virginia—the ladies certainly had a good meeting—I am,

Very truly,
Annie W. Armstrong
P. S. The enclosed check for $6.45 is from the Woman's Missionary Society of the West Washington Church, Washington, D. C. Please send receipt for same to Mrs. Annie R. Hunter, 1211—34th St., N. W., Washington, D. C.
[IMB Archives]

Annie Armstrong insisted that WMU distribute high-quality literature on all facets of Southern Baptist missionary work.

July 30, 1891
Mr. F. L. Butler
Dear Brother:
Your letter of July 29th just at hand, and I am extremely sorry to learn that *all* of the leaflets were not at that date at the Foreign Mission Rooms.

You were correct in thinking that Mr. Bell had ordered *eleven* different varieties of leaflets. The order was as follows:

Japan	5,000
Japan as a Mission Field	5,000
Land of the Southern Cross	5,000
Evangelical Italy	5,000
Some Reasons for Supporting etc.	5,000
Africa	5,000
Africa, Opportunities, etc.	5,000
China for Christ	5,000
China, The World's Great Mission Field	5,000
Mexico	5,000
God's Call, etc.	3,000

In giving the order, Mr. Bell granted 500 copies of each of the leaflets to the Woman's Missionary Union, to be distributed to the Woman's Missionary Societies; these were not forwarded to Richmond, but will be sent direct to the societies from Baltimore.

Since receiving your letter, I sent to the printer (as he had shipped the leaflets) to know how he had sent them. He replied that all *eleven* leaflets that were printed had been shipped at the same time to Richmond in *two* boxes.

Will you be kind enough to make inquiry with regard to the second box, and let me know at once if the Steamboat Co. has not delivered it? I would also ask if you find the numbers sent to correspond with the order, minus the 500 copies of each, which have been reserved.

Please address your letter to Mountain Lake Park, Garrett Co. Maryland, as I leave Baltimore tomorrow for a short time. I will, however, have the mail forwarded from the Mission Rooms and attend to the work as far as possible while away, so send any orders for barrels, etc. during that time that may be needed.

I am sorry that the mistake which you call my attention to with regard to the *Foreign Mission Journal* has occurred. It is, of course, an error of the printer, which was not noticed. I hope persons will see from the previous statement that it is a mistake, and in ordering papers will not seek to take advantage of the error.

Very truly,
Annie W. Armstrong

P. S. May I ask that you will send a postal if the leaflets are received or not as I shall feel quite anxious until I shall hear from them.

[IMB Archives]

September 18, 1897
Dr. J. M. Frost
Dear Brother:

You, or rather Margaret Reynolds, have given me proof this morning that it is well to regard Paul's admonition to the Corinthians: "Let him that thinketh he standeth take heed lest he fall." I must acknowledge I had come to the Mission Rooms feeling rather "toploftical," as I was highly delighted with the success of some recent efforts I had made. When I opened your envelope, however, and found that that midget of 10 years, to whom I had sent the leaflet, "Our Bible," with Bible Card, urging that she would interest some of her young friends in the Bible Fund of the Sunday School Board, had discovered a mistake in the publication which I had not noticed,—whether made in copying or otherwise, I cannot tell, but will try and find out—the change in my feelings was somewhat rapid. If the comical side of the question had not struck me, I should be in the depths. As it is, though, I am prepared to say that I am extremely sorry the mistake should have occurred, and will try in future to exercise more care and have Scripture references verified. As there are only two verses in the 117th Psalm, persons of larger growth than Margaret would class it under the head of a printer's error and so the Sunday School Board will not, I hope, be very severely censured. Woe betide us, though, if "Senex" has her attention called to it. In that case, you will simply have to say that the manuscript for the leaflet was furnished by the Secretary of the Woman's Missionary Union. I have been repeatedly warned that after the would-be Reformers have gotten matters adjusted to suit them in regard to the Seminary, they will turn their attention to the Woman's Missionary Union. I am not "scared," but I am anxious that we should exercise all due care so as not to give ground for *just criticism* at this stage of things in the management of W.M.U. affairs. Having attended to a number of your commissions, I will now proceed to report on same.

1. *Plate for title page of Teacher.* I forward same by express today and enclose proof. You will note it is made just the size that was submitted to you and which you sanctioned. I return marked copy of the title page of the *Teacher* previously sent. I also forward samples of paper. Primrose would

be my choice. The fine lines on the new cover would, I think, show up better on the light paper rather than on darker shades.

2. *Illustrations for W.M.U. department in Convention Almanac.* I enclose two which we have had prepared and send plates in package. I have forwarded manuscript, with pictures in position desired, to Dr. Burrows by today's mail. When it reaches you, I am going to ask that you carefully read same and let me know if there is anything in it to which exception could be taken. For the reason given above, I am more than usually anxious to exercise caution.

3. *Picture for Sunday School Board calendar page of Convention Almanac.* I now submit to you drawing for same. It is in right proportions to be reduced. I hope it will strike you as favorably as it has those to whom I have shown it in Baltimore. The original sketch was made by Miss Shankland, so if you approve of the design, I am going to ask, before you return same,—that is, if you wish plate made in Baltimore—that you will let Miss Shankland see the sketch and then let me have any suggestions as to changes that either of you deem wise. There are two alterations which Sister Alice and I both think ought to be made, viz., a little shading, so as to give the effect that *two* books are being held by the young man. As you will note, we already have had a change made in that, as the first time the drawing was submitted, a mistake had been made in wording. Then again, we desire that the young man's face should indicate a little more strength. Both of these alterations can readily be made, but I thought it better to send it to you for criticism before having anything further done.

Appreciating that you are always busy, I will by this mail write to Miss Shankland and ask that she call at your office to see the picture.

4. *Sunday School missionaries to be aided.* I am glad to receive the names you forwarded and will write to the three Texas missionaries today. Let us have additional names, either from Texas or other States, if you deem wise. I can without doubt secure aid for them. This phase of work is quite popular, and, except in very few States, the ladies will, I have no doubt, be as willing to aid Sunday School Board missionaries as Home Board missionaries, and I think it will prove helpful in many ways for you to have this line of work as an adjunct to the Sunday School Board.

5. *Bible Fund of the Sunday School Board.* I enclose [a] note received from Miss Buhlmaier, which I am sure you will read with interest. I also send copy of a letter which I will today mail to officers of State Central Committees. I felt that Miss Buhlmaier's letter and the one from Dr. Eager gave me an opportunity of bringing the Bible Fund indirectly, but forcibly,

before our workers. I have learned that it must be "line upon line and precept upon precept," if we would get persons thoroughly interested in any direction.

6. *Annual Meeting of the Woman's Baptist Home Mission Society of Maryland.* This you know will be held the first day of the State Association—Tuesday, October 26th. At an Executive Committee meeting, which occurred last Thursday, the ladies left the arrangement of program to the President. That being the case, I am prepared to extend an invitation, which I now do, officially. Before doing so, though, I will give you in brief what my idea is for that meeting. As yet, I have not called the attention of our workers in Maryland to the Bible Fund. As there is almost an entire cessation of effort in Baltimore during the summer months, I thought it better to let the matter rest until the fall. I now want at the Annual Meeting to bring that before the ladies in as forcible a way as possible. It has occurred to me that if I let Miss Buhlmaier first give an account, in the graphic way that she can, of the distribution of Bibles and Testaments at the Immigrant Pier, and then you follow her in an address of 20 or 30 minutes, the subject would be very strongly and favorably impressed upon the ladies. I would have to ask, though—for if this is done, we can have no special speech on Home Missions—that you will speak quite fully of the frontier work. I can supply you with all needed data. I would be glad if you would also refer to the importance of the work among the colored people. In fact, I want in your speech for you to make a double plea for the work of the Sunday School Board and also the Home Board. Please let me know as soon as possible whether you will accede to the request which I now make in the name of the Home Mission Society of Maryland.

As I said last year, I do hope we may have the pleasure of having you as our guest during your stay in Baltimore. This is my desire, but Mother is steadily failing, and it may be so that we will find at that time she is not well enough for us to entertain. Will you not, though, consider yourself as engaged to stay with us and so decline other invitations until I can see whether we will be able to have the pleasure of a visit from you, to which I have looked forward for some time.

7. *Sunday School Missionary Day literature.* The 1,500 mite boxes you sent came to hand yesterday. More than half of these have already been given out. The Maryland schools are calling for them in larger numbers than I expected, so I am going to ask that you will send *at once* 1,000 more mite boxes and 500 additional programs. I have enough supplements.

8. *Conference to have been in Nashville.* I was really astonished to hear you say that you knew nothing of the proposed conference until just before it was decided not to have it. I had supposed you were one of the prime movers in same. I heartily agree with you in wishing "that somebody would do something, if only it would be the wise and proper thing." Dr. Barron is here from N. C.—he takes tea with us this evening, so I will learn more definitely the condition of things in that State—and he told me that Mr. White, State Secretary, says every interest is suffering there on account of this excitement.

There are other items which I would like to give you, but must not make this letter any longer, so will close right here.

Very truly,

Annie W. Armstrong

[SBHLA, J. M. Frost Collection]

December 12, 1902

Dr. E. E. Bomar

Dear Brother:

I do not know whether you met, while in Oklahoma, Rev. J. W. Solomon, Reed, Oklahoma. He is a man that you would recall if you ever saw him, as he is of gigantic proportions. He was formerly a missionary in the employ of the Home Board, and one for whom we secured assistance in the way of boxes of clothing. He is not now on the list of those aided by the Woman's Missionary Union. He is in charge of a colporteur wagon in Greer County. As I understand it the wagon was given by the churches of that county, but the books etc. are furnished by the Publication Society. Mr. Solomon is a member, or was, of the Oklahoma Board.

While in Oklahoma last summer I became so indignant at the trend of things—inequality in contributions being sent North and South with equality in amounts given by Northern and Southern Baptists for the development of Oklahoma and Indian territory—that I could not refrain, before leaving the Territory, from giving vent to my feelings when talking to some of the ministers in whom I had confidence. Mr. Solomon was one of these. He had not realized just what was being done, and when I gave him the facts, he promised me to help correct same. I asked if he would be willing to take missionary literature in his wagon that had been issued by the Home and Foreign Boards and distribute this as he had opportunity. He told me he would. He also promised that he would try and help our Woman's Work and let me have names of women in various churches to whom I could write and get them to organize societies.

I had fully intended speaking to you or Dr. Willingham of Mr. Solomon, but amid the pressure of other things I forgot to do so. I though have just been replying to a letter from our Brother, in which he sent me the name of a lady in a church to whom he wanted me to write. This has brought the whole matter to memory, and I now want to ask that you will write to Mr. Solomon and offer to furnish him with Foreign Mission leaflets, and get him, if possible, to secure subscribers to the *Foreign Mission Journal*. I think he can do this and I believe with a little effort on our part we can get Mr. Solomon to become thoroughly interested in mission work, not only in Oklahoma, but elsewhere.

I am making very, very, strong efforts to get the Woman's Work in Indian Territory, Oklahoma and District of Columbia on a better basis, as far as S.B.C. interests are concerned. I think you may like to see a letter which this morning's mail has brought from one of the frontier missionaries in Arkansas. A few days ago I sent a letter—I enclose copy—to every frontier missionary that we are aiding with boxes of clothing. I also forward copies of letters which I sent to every Society that I knew of in Indian Territory and Oklahoma, and also letters which I sent to one lady in each of the churches in the District of Columbia and to subscribers of the *Foreign Mission Journal* and *Our Home Field* in the District. I shall certainly be greatly disappointed if we do not, this year, have quite a good Christmas Offering from frontier sections and District of Columbia. Indian Territory, Oklahoma and the District of Columbia I now feel are under my special care, and I will look after the work in these sections personally.

I will be glad to have you read these form letters, which I send, and then let me know if anything suggests itself to you by which you think I can aid the work in those sections. I, of course, recognize that I must not be *too* pressing or I will defeat the object we have in view.

There are other matters, but I will not tax your patience more at this time.

Very truly,

Annie W. Armstrong

P. S. I have already sent out over 90,000 envelopes for the Christmas Offering and we still have nearly two weeks in which to receive orders. This is a much larger number than we have distributed in any previous year. Dr. Willingham has asked for $8,000.00. I put the mark at $10,000.00 and hope for $12,000.00. This year we are calling on the children and young people, as well as the women, to make an offering at Christmas to the work in China.

P. S. No. 2. Several days since Dr. Willingham sent me a letter from Miss Claudia White. In sending letter she failed to give her address in San Francisco, so may I ask that you will kindly supply the needed directions on the letter, which I enclose to Miss White, and mail same?

[IMB Archives]

January 15, 1903
Rev. R. M. Inlow
Dear Brother:

Your letter of January 7th received and read with much interested and pleasure.

Let me assure you that I am not only willing but glad to help you as Field Secretary of the Sunday School Board in any way I can. And I believe I can be of service to you, especially in the work you are about to do in Indian Territory and Oklahoma.

As you may, or may not know, the Woman's Missionary Union has for more than ten years been sending, at the request of the Home Board and later the Sunday School Board, boxes of clothing to missionaries in these Territories, and so a large number of the missionaries who supply the church in these sections have been assisted and are being assisted by Woman's Missionary Union. This branch of the work has required my being in constant correspondence with the missionaries. I was surprised at one telling me last summer, when I was in the Territories, that he had one hundred letters from me. At first I thought that this was an exaggeration, but later, when I remembered how many years I had been writing to him I appreciated that it was a fact.

As I mentioned to Dr. Willingham, when talking about the work in Indian Territory and Oklahoma a few days ago, I believe if I have influence at any point it is in the Territories, and I am glad to be able to place this at your disposal. You can count on me to assist you in any way that you may indicate.

I now send you list of missionaries in Indian Territory and Oklahoma that the Home Board has asked that we assist during the present Conventional year with boxes of clothing. I thought if you had these names you would know on whose assistance you could count in presenting the work of the Sunday School Board. These gentlemen, as I previously mentioned, I am in constant correspondence with, and should you think wise to write to them and care to mention that I suggested your doing so, you are at perfect liberty to use my name.

As you have suggested that we be mutually helpful to each other, I am now going to ask two favors:

(1) As you visit churches in Indian Territory and Oklahoma that you will try to organize Woman's Mission Societies, and when this is done that you will let me have names and addresses of the officers. I enclose a little pamphlet "Suggestions to Woman's Mission Societies," which contains a constitution and many helpful hints. I also send one or two leaflets, which will give you some idea of the work of Woman's Missionary Union, as will also the Annual Report which I forward by this mail. I enclose copy of a letter which I am sending to every Society in Indian Territory and Oklahoma, as it shows the basis upon which we desire the ladies to work.

(2) If you do not think it possible or feasible to organize Societies that you will obtain for me the name of an active woman worker in each church that you visit, and I will then write to her and see if I cannot, in time, secure her cooperation and eventually the formation of a Society.

I have no doubt you will think I am making large requests of you, but as you have offered your help, I feel at liberty to do so. I can promise you if a similar draft is made by you, on me, it will be honored.

An extract from a letter which I received a few days ago will, I am sure, give you pleasure. It is from Mrs. J. J. Farmer, whose husband is pastor of the church at Tecumseh, Oklahoma, which I visited last summer. Mrs. Farmer writes, "Our Juniors are now taking 20 copies of *Kind Words* instead of the Junior Union."

Hoping that you will find much pleasure in the work, in which you are now engaged, and that it will grow rapidly in your hands, I am,

Very sincerely,
Annie W. Armstrong
[IMB Archives]

June 24, 1904
Dr. E. E. Bomar
Dear Brother:

I returned to Baltimore last Tuesday after an absence of ten days spent attending the Conference of the Young Women's Christian Associations at

Asheville, North Carolina, meeting Societies in that section and visiting several of the mountain schools. I had a very pleasant and I think profitable trip, although driving for three consecutive days over rough mountain roads did use me up and I had to spend last Sunday in bed. Like Mother Hubbard's dog though I very soon revived, and on reaching Baltimore Tuesday morning after travelling all night, I went immediately to the Mission Rooms, as I knew there was a large amount of work awaiting me. I notified my family that I had arrived safely and that they would see me later in the day. Since then I have been packing literature, mailing boxes, etc., etc. This is the time in the year when we are providing State officers with new publications to inaugurate the year's work. I am thankful to say I have gotten off the literature to every state except Texas and Oklahoma and can now turn my attention to some other matters.

I find that there are several that I would like to refer to you.

1. *Pictures*. Before leaving Baltimore I ordered half tone cuts made of three pictures taken from the scrap books which I showed you. I enclose the proofs of the three pictures. What think you of them? I consider they are fine and really they are clearer than some of the pictures in the scrap books. The photo-engraver was here this morning and he told me that they are using a new kind of electric light which enables them to get the pictures without retouching plates. I am to pay for the three cuts $5.87. Can Richmond do better than that?

I do not know if that is the regular price, but it is the price for which I can get the work done. The young man who does the work has worked for us for years and he seems thoroughly interested. He tells me that he does the very best for us. I am sure this is the case in every particular.

2. *Topics for study in October, "Medical and Educational Work in Foreign Lands."* Thinking it would be a little difficult to secure manuscript for leaflets presenting just what it seemed to me would be wise, as we have never had leaflets on these topics, I thought it better not to apply to any one for said manuscripts but to have them prepared at the Mission Rooms. I now send you the one on "Medical Work." Will you kindly read same very critically and suggest any changes you deem wise. Do not hesitate to make alterations in copy. As I have to leave Baltimore July 7th and will be away for three weeks, I will have to have a large amount of printing done in the next two weeks, so I will be obliged if you will return manuscript immediately.

I hope to be able to write to Dr. Willingham today. I may though not be able to do so until tomorrow, as there is a number of things I must attend to. If Dr. Willingham is in the office, please tell him that I will send him a "budget" shortly.

Very truly,

Annie W. Armstrong

P. S. Kindly return pictures. How about "China for Juniors?"

[IMB Archives]

Missionary boxes rank among WMU's more unique missionary enterprises at the turn of the century.

Nov. 18th, 1890

Rev. E. L. Compere

Dear Brother:

Your letter of Nov. 7th received, and it is a great pleasure to know that I had not in any way offended you. I knew that I had not *intentionally* done so, but I feared from your silence that in some way I, perhaps, had done something that you did not approve. I know your time is so completely occupied and there are so many things pressing upon you, that I do not wonder that you have not time for letter writing, but not having heard from you since meeting in Texas, I thought possibly in the work we are now engaged in—sending boxes to missionaries—we might have done something that you did not quite approve. Let me ask you never to hesitate to let us know, if we at any time fail to work in a way you consider wise. I can say, for myself personally, and I think also for all the other ladies, that our desire is to do the most good and to the greatest number, but from not being on the spot, we may at times fail in accomplishing what we desire, so we will consider it a kindness, if at any time you will offer any suggestion that you think needful.

There is a little mistake that has been made in the appendix to the Minutes of the "Baptist General Association of Western Arkansas and Indian Territory." In speaking of the work of the Woman's Missionary Union the Report says: "The ladies of the Woman's Missionary Union etc. * * * Express a willingness to aid all they can by collecting money, boxes of clothing for families, books etc." The mistake I refer to is in saying we propose to collect *money*. All money raised by the Woman's Missionary Societies for Home Missions is sent to the Home Board at Atlanta, Ga. The Board has expressly asked that in undertaking this new line of work namely—sending boxes to missionaries—that *no money* shall be forwarded to missionaries. I think you will see the wisdom of this. Where are the salaries to come from if the churches and societies send direct to the missionaries? The salaries are meagre now, but if the Board does not receive the money; how can they pay even the very small salaries that are now paid. The thought was the clothing could frequently be obtained where money could not, and the missionaries could be aided in this way, and so supplement their salaries.

I know you will be pleased to hear that the ladies in the various States are entering upon this line of work—sending boxes to missionaries—so enthusiastically, that we have been able to get Societies to aid all the missionaries that we have had letters from, and now desire more names. Are there any more missionaries in Western Arkansas or the Ind. Ter. that you think need assistance, if so please let me have their names and addresses, and I will try and see what can be done for them. I will send you a list of those you, previously gave, as you may not remember whose names you have not given. I will also mention those we have heard from and to whom boxes have been or will be sent.

Missionary	Heard From	Box to be sent
Rev. J. W. Black	"	"
Rev. H. H. Monser	"	"
Rev. I. Napier	"	"
Rev. Jos. Barnes	"	"
Rev. John W. Miller	"	"
Rev. E. B. Harlan	"	"
Rev. C. L. Alexander	"	"
Rev. J. H. York	"	"
Rev. V. M. Thrasher	"	"
Rev. W. M. Morris	"	"
Rev. I. N. Briggs	"	"
Rev. J. B. York	"	"
Rev. L. F. Patterson	"	"
Rev. W. B. Herndon	"	"
Rev. T. N. Watkins	"	"
Rev. A. A. Spiller	"	"
Rev. R. P. Claborn	"	"
Rev. G. W. Bazter	"	"

Rev. H. C. Ridling I received a postal from, and he promised to write, but I have not yet heard from him whether he desires assistance or not. If there are other missionaries that you think it would be well for us to aid, please let me know as soon as possible, as there are some societies willing to send boxes and I have not names to give them.

With kind regards and wishing you much success in the arduous work you are engaged in, I am

Very truly,

Annie W. Armstrong

[SBHLA, E. L. Compere Collection]

February 5, 1894

Rev. E. L. Compere

Dear Brother:

Your letter of January 25th received, and while I know that you and the missionaries in Indian Territory very much overestimate my part in the work, yet I am truly thankful that our Heavenly Father has used me as an instrument to help in securing aid for some of our frontier missionaries who are having to endure so many privations and hardships. What I would value even more than any personal expressions of appreciation, would be that the missionaries earnestly pray that our Heavenly Father will bless the efforts made by the Woman's Mission Societies to advance the cause of Christ and that the women all over our Southland come up as a great host to the "help of the Lord against the mighty." Our numerical strength is very great and yet our offerings are comparatively very small; in God's sight, I know this is not pleasing to Him, and until we do as a people "bring the tithes into the store-house" of the Lord, we cannot expect that the "windows of Heaven" will be opened and we will receive the full blessing that is promised. As women we have a large work before us in trying to train the children to know about and love missions, so I do believe that much of the future of this work under God depends upon how the women of this generation act. If we are going to "stand all the day idle," the missionary seed will not be sown in the hearts of the children and the harvest will be meagre. Let me beg of you my brother, to pray earnestly for the Woman's Work, for I am sure there is just at this point much need for prayer. Something has been done toward arousing our women, but how few comparatively speaking are at work.

I note what you say about Rev. J. B. Barnes of Bengal, Choctaw Nation, Indian Territory, and will write to him for particulars about his family; after obtaining these, I will try and see if I can secure assistance for him.

I have no doubt you are correct in the conclusion you have reached, from the facts that have come to your knowledge, with regard to Mr. Sellars. In any case we will not attempt to secure help for him unless you forward his name, as it is not now in our list.

It gives me pleasure to send you a list of the missionaries whose names you forwarded to us during the present conventional year, and for whom we have either obtained assistance or hope to secure same. I dislike very much not to accede to any request you make, but having several years ago written to the Home Board when you made a similar request, asking if they desired that I would furnish you with the amount of help given to the different missionaries through the boxes of clothing sent to them, the Board decided that it was better not to send you the valuation of boxes. This help is so very uncertain, that in no case does the Home Board wish that it should influence salaries. I believe the ladies try to be conscientious in estimating their gifts, but while they may represent the amount of money that is placed upon them, yet of course the missionaries, if they had have had that amount of money put in their hands, would have spent it very differently. Another reason why I feel that it would not be well to grant your request is that while I may report to you that a missionary has had no help today, tomorrow a box may have gone to him, and yet I may have no report of that box being sent for a month, six weeks, or maybe two months after it goes. It is quite difficult to get the societies to understand the need for promptly reporting. I hope you will appreciate the reason that exists for declining to accede to your request.

Wishing you and all your loved ones the blessing of God which "maketh rich," I am

Very truly,

Annie W. Armstrong

[SBHLA, E. L. Compere Collection]

Dallas, Texas

Sept. 8, 1898

My dear Miss Armstrong:

I am quite ashamed to forward you the constantly recurring request from societies: "Please send me the name of a missionary with small children" but I've had three of the letters sent out returned to me with this request and two contained this piece of advice (?): "You ought not to ask any society to send anything to *large* children, let *such* go to *work* and earn their own clothes." Alas, alas, what a crop of tares has sprung up all over Texas as a result of *one* selfish, vicious man's sowing. Truly they are all among the wheat and one must be very patient and careful "lest we root up the wheat also." So far as the personal abuse heaped on my husband and the innuendos against myself, they trouble me not at all. Our Father will shield us from any real harm; but, the work, the cause of missions seems retarded by this constant misrepresentation of the workers. No one outside of Texas can comprehend the intricacy of our difficulties. To give you an idea let me tell you one instance of misrepresentation. I had succeeded in getting the Societies in three of the Baptist Churches in this city to begin preparing boxes for the frontier. This Baptist (?) Cataline (I beg Cataline's pardon for the insult) sent his emissaries to tell the societies "*not to send those boxes* for if boxes were sent the State and Home Boards deducted the amount of valuation from the salaries of the missionaries and appropriated the sum to their own private use." The sisters came directly to me telling the whole story and giving the name of their informant. If you can do so please send me three letters from missionaries having small children. I will try to get the "returned letters" taken by some of our city churches. I fear I've taxed your patience. God bless you.

    Lovingly,
    Mary T. Gambrell
    [IMB Archives]

November 2, 1899
Dr. J. M. Frost
Dear Brother:

I know you will be pleased to hear that the interest in the Box Work is so great—we have made no effort to draw attention to this phase of our work this year through the distribution of special literature—that I now have in hand a number of applications for the names of missionaries that I cannot fill. I have been going carefully over the Registry this morning, therefore, and find that there is one missionary whose name was given to us by you, as in need of assistance, who has not replied to the letter I wrote him. Possibly, probably, the correct address was not furnished. I will write to this missionary again today, but think it wise, as the Societies whose applications I hold are quite anxious to engage in this line of work—almost every mail brings additional requests—to refer the name of this missionary to you, who has not yet replied to my letter. The name is as follows: Rev. J. R. Hodges, Ardmore, Indian Territory. Will you kindly look into the matter and see if the proper address was given to me?

The Box Work no longer needs any further effort to emphasize or to popularize it. It now has sufficient momentum to secure all the assistance that is required in this line for the missionaries. The only thing necessary to be done in this direction is that wise and judicious methods be adopted in carrying it on.

Here is a pleasant item. As I previously told you, I am now making a special effort to secure the cooperation of the ladies for the Young People's Scripture Union in *Kind Words*. This morning I had a letter from Miss Alice A. Leake of Madison, Ga., in which she writes:

> "I have tried to engage the attention of the young people in the Scripture Union, and enclose ten names. Two others have promised to sign, and I think others will follow. They are expecting to hear from you that they have been admitted to the Scripture Union. Will try to get more names tomorrow."

The Blanks that have been filled out are by persons ranging in age from 11 to 23 years. I will be genuinely glad if we can have a large number to promise to daily study their Bibles, but do you not think we have gotten ourselves into quite a large business, having to send a personal letter to each member. If it grows too burdensome, I will have some mimeographed letters struck off.

Very truly,

Annie W. Armstrong

[Handwritten at end of letter] Since writing the above a letter has been received from Mr. Miller. I enclose same. Our brother seems hardly to realize what great inconvenience he might have caused if the Secretary of the S. Sch. Board had not been able to help in this emergency. I do not know if we can trust him to send ms. later—you note he has offered to take another month. Please let me know the name of the place in Ala. where Mrs. Ledbetter lives as I cannot make it out.

[SBHLA, J. M. Frost Collection]

Hico, Texas
Jan. 11, 1900
Miss Annie W. Armstrong
My dear Sister:
Your kind letter of 6th inst. to hand. As this is the first letter of its kind, it has been my pleasure to read, I am somewhat at a loss to know just what to say in reply. If I had it, God knows I would rather send you ten dollars than to receive one from you. I do not know that I deserve a single favor at your hands, and yet, as God seems to be pointing in that direction, we shall very gratefully receive anything He may direct His loved ones to give us. I, therefore, take great pleasure in complying with your request. At present, I am working in six counties, one of which last year, sent more prisoners to our State penitentiary than any other county in Texas. Let me tell you something of just two of the hundreds of homes which I have visited and found without Bibles. One was the home of a wicked man, so said his wife confidentially, who for ten years had been promising to buy his wife a Bible. The husband was away from home, while the wife was sick in bed. There were three beautiful little girls in this home; the eldest 8 or 9 yrs. old. They did not have a Bible, book or paper of any description in this home. So said the wife and mother, and also that they did not have a cent of money. Of course, I gave her a Bible, and the children some cards and papers and left them happy.

During Christmas week, I visited a home of nine members, and, when I had induced the husband to buy a small Bible and three little Testaments, all at absolute cost, for the larger children, the mother made the following statement: "We have been married seventeen years, and this is the first Bible we have ever owned." In a single day in the country, I found ten families without Bibles in their homes. I have found boys and girls 12 to 15 years old who could not tell me what a Testament was, who Jesus was, & c. Others from 15 to 20 years old, who had never visited a Sunday School. I have found men with families, who did not know what Psalms meant in connection with the New Testament. A wife and husband with grown children told me they had two Bibles; one was a 25 ct. primer, the other Hitchcox's Analysis of the Bible. Of course, I left them the Bible. While on this field I have had stolen from me, gloves, whips, hitch rains, shirts and Bibles. All of which are my personal loss. But with all these facts before you, you must not decide that all the people in this section are bad people. We have many of as good people as the world affords. Our motto is a Sunday School in every church and community where Baptists live; a Bible in every home; and every child taught the way of life. May God speed the day when this is true in Texas.

Your Brother in Christian love and work,

M. L. Davis

S. S. & Col. Missionary

MEASUREMENTS

Rev. M. L. Davis, aged 43—bust $38^{1/2}$—waist 34—length of back, neck to waist 21—sleeve, inside seam $21^{1/2}$—pants, inside seam 36—neck $16^{1/2}$—shoe $8^{1/2}$.

Mrs. Nannie L. Davis, aged 37—bust 36—waist $28^{1/2}$—length of back, neck to waist 16—sleeve, inside seam $18^{1/2}$—skirt 44—neck 14—shoe $5^{1/2}$.

Unus H. Davis (boy), aged 12—bust 33—waist 31—length of back, neck to waist 14—sleeve, inside seam 17—pants, inside seam 14—size of head 21—neck $14^{1/2}$—shoe $4^{1/2}$.

Willie Lee (girl), aged 9—bust 27—waist 25—length of back, neck to waist $11^{1/2}$—sleeve, inside seam $15^{1/2}$—length of skirt 21—neck 12—shoe 2.

Dora Bell (girl), aged 7—bust 25--waist $23^{1/2}$—length of back, neck to waist 10—sleeve, inside seam 12—skirt $17^{1/2}$—neck $10^{1/2}$—shoe 11.

Artie May (girl), aged 4—bust 24—waist 23—length of back, neck to waist $9^{1/2}$—sleeve, inside seam 12—skirt $16^{1/2}$—neck 11—shoe 9.

POST OFFICE AND FREIGHT ADDRESS: HICO, TEXAS

SPECIAL NEEDS: What we desire mostly is some sacred verses, cards, tracts, Testaments and little books to give to poor children. We very earnestly desire an interest in your prayers. May the God of all grace lead us by His gentle and unerring Spirit.

P. S. My dear Sister Armstrong: It would amuse you to have seen the children as mama called them one at a time to take their measurements.

They suggested all sorts of things. The measuring of their heads seemed to puzzle them worse than anything else.

The thought in your letter that impresses us, parents, most deeply is suggested by the following words: "Our substitutes on the frontier, & c." Yes, we represent God, and thousands of His followers who are interested in this *hard* and yet delightful work. While I am not receiving half as much salary as I have received for school teaching, yet, we are living, and have no fears but that He will in His own way provide for all our *needs*.

With most grateful hearts do we thank you and all in any wise connected with the Union for your expressed sympathy and deep interest for our welfare, and the work in which we are engaged. May heaven's blessings smile upon you all.

Your Bro.,

M. L. D.

[SBHLA, J. M. Frost Collection]

January 2, 1900

Dr. R. J. Willingham

Dear Brother:

I received two small contributions for Foreign Missions, which I enclose.

$1.25 is a Christmas Offering from the Panola Hill Baptist Church. Send receipt for same to Rev. W. B. Toney, Kennady, Ind. Territory.

25 cents is an offering from five little boys for the work in China. Kindly return receipt for this to Rev. S. W. Fuson, Cushing, Oklahoma.

Your letter of December 30th received. I am glad to know that it will be possible for you to arrange to come to Baltimore so as to preach on Sunday, January 14th. For several reasons I think it will be better for that to be the Sunday that you will be with us. I will see Mr. Millard tomorrow, and after letting him decide at which service he would rather have you to preach, I will then see one of the other pastors. As soon as arrangements are made, I will let you know.

I received a letter from Miss White this morning, in which she suggested the bringing of a Chinaman to Baltimore. Her idea is that this Chinaman that has come with her from China, may be employed to work among the Chinese here. I do not know whether this is feasible or not, but I think it premature letting the Chinaman come just now, so I have written to her, suggesting that she would meet, while in Baltimore, the ladies interested in that branch of work, and if they thought it desirable the Chinaman could come later on. I really did not feel quite equal to entertaining a Chinaman.

Thanks for enlightening me as to the meaning of "M.G." It really had never occurred to me that the brother was using that means to inform me that he was a "minister of the Gospel." I do not know whether it is helpful or not to see the ridiculous side of things. I must acknowledge some letters that I get do amuse me intensely. I had one from a brother the other day in Indian Territory, who had been quite generously helped. After expressing gratitude for the assistance that had been secured for him, he goes on to say:

> "But the part that makes me feel sorry is they did not send me a suit of clothes that will do to wear to the Convention in May, and to the General Association, nor any Association where they meet in towns of any size. They sent me two very nice $10.00 suits, but they are little short, bob-tail fellows that are not in style for ministers at all. Of course, they will do to wear about home, preach in the country or in small towns, but they will not do for the larger towns, such as get all our important meetings. I can't afford to miss these meetings, neither can I afford to have remarks made about my appearance in the pulpit, especially by the missionaries of other evangelical churches, and this they are ever ready to do if a man looks odd in his manners and his clothes, especially the latter."

The brother goes on to request with much earnestness that I try to secure for him "a Prince Albert" suit. At times it is simply impossible for me to personally reply to all of the letters that come, so occasionally, I hand over to one of the clerks letters which do not require that I shall dictate the answers, and judging this was one of that nature, I gave it to her, letting her understand that I did not purpose to do as the brother had requested. Her reply, I thought, was simply killing. It has not yet been posted, so I will send you an extract from it. She writes:

> "I am extremely sorry, but I cannot promise to help you to secure a Prince Albert suit. On referring to our books, I find that both boxes previously received are extremely valuable. Not many of the missionaries receive as much assistance. It would be impossible, under the circumstances, for me to make effort to secure a greater supply, or make any special requests. Could you be present at the

Ministers' Conference, which is held at the Mission Rooms every Monday morning, I think you would be surprised by the cut of some of the garments which are seen here at times. Brethren from the surrounding country come to the City Conference, and I think a $10.00 suit, though not a Prince Albert, would be quite an addition to some wardrobes. I do appreciate your desire to appear well in the eyes of those of other denominations, but as Robert Burns has said
'The rank is but the guinea's stamp,
A man's a man, for a' that and a' that.'
Good clothes are most desirable, but if yours are comfortable, I do not think it wise to worry about the cut. Character will assert itself, and exert an influence for God under all circumstances."

I, of course, signed this letter, so making myself responsible for it, but I do not think it would ever have occurred to me to quote poetry under these circumstances. I think, though, our clerk talked common sense, don't you? But enough of foolishness.

Yes, we too are having intensely cold weather. I hope though it will not be long before it moderates.

Very truly,

Annie W. Armstrong

P. S. I enclose the two clerical tickets which you kindly secured for me. If it will not give you much trouble, may I ask that you will have them renewed for this year?

[IMB Archives]

Letters like the one from M. L. Davis and the unnamed missionary in the Indian Territory may have inspired this circular letter to missionaries in 1901, not to mention her closing remarks to E. E. Bomar in a letter dated 9 March 1901.

CIRCULAR TO MISSIONARIES.

(1901)

At request of Home and Sunday School Boards, Woman's Mission Societies have for several years been sending boxes of supplies to our substitutes on the frontier whose salaries are inadequate to the support of themselves and families. Since the knowledge of the facts has been brought to notice, much interest in this branch of work has been created. We earnestly desire that nothing shall dampen the enthusiasm for this needed work. Therefore a little explanation to recipients of boxes, and a cordial co-operation on their part may prevent some mistakes which have been made.

1. Boxes inevitably differ greatly in value. The Executive Committee should not be considered responsible for this variation, nor yet should the difference be allowed to excite jealousy. Strong and weak societies send their gifts, the latter frequently representing great self-denial. If the missionary will recognize that the box is additional to, and in no wise detracting from, his salary, he will better appreciate the aid. If some of the contents are not available for his family, let him give them to needy members of the congregation. If unfit for use—we greatly regret that such should ever be sent, societies being asked to make the Golden Rule a gauge for gifts—let them be destroyed.

2. In replying to letter of inquiry, please be *prompt* and give full particulars of *measurements, ages* and *special needs* of each member of family. Also give *Railroad* address as well as *Post Office* address, and some particulars of field. If the societies are to be interested, something of interest must be communicated to them. Even should the information have been previously given, be kind enough to repeat it, as a fresh distribution of names is made each year; and each society needs the information.

3. When the box is received, will the missionary *promptly* acknowledge this receipt, and expatiate somewhat on the pleasure derived. When this fails to be done, the society's interest flags and it is difficult to secure the service another year.

4. Boxes will probably not be received at *earliest* until three months after letter of inquiry has been answered. Should a missionary not hear from a society by this time, let him notify the Secretary of the fact.

5. While effort is made by Woman's Missionary Union to have a box sent to every missionary reported to them by Home and Sunday School Boards, or State officers at request of said Boards, a *promise* to send such aid is not made. Therefore we hope disappointment will be cheerfully borne, expecting better results another year.

ANNIE W. ARMSTRONG
Corresponding Secretary, W.M.U.
304 North Howard Street
Baltimore, Md.
NOTE.—Items of Personal Information required regarding each member of the family. Fill blank and return.
[SBHLA, J. M. Frost Collection]

March 9, 1901
Dr. E. E. Bomar
Dear Brother:

I find there are several matters which I must refer to you this morning, and these I will speak of before taking up different points in your letter of March 8th, just received.

1. *Subscriptions to the Foreign Mission Journal.* I enclose letter from Mr. C. G. Dilworth and 50c. in stamps. Our brother seems to have overlooked the fact that the price of the *Journal* is 35c. except in clubs. I will leave you to decide whether to furnish the *Journal* at the price, or notify the one who sends subscriptions that he has made a mistake.

2. *Leaflet, "The Things That Remain."* I have a request from Mrs. A. E. Jennings, Water Valley, Mississippi for 50 copies of that leaflet. Will you kindly forward same direct to her, and send a number—500 or a thousand will do for present use, if you prefer to send package by mail—to the Mission Rooms, 304 N. Howard Street?

Now as to various points in your letter:

(a) *Subscription to Monthly Literature for Mrs. A. J. Lane, Tenn.* I return receipt with thanks.

(b) *Suggestions from the Fourth Interdenominational Conference of Woman's Boards.* I appreciate your careful reading of same. I will now hand the paper over to Sister Alice, and let her know what your judgment is in regard to printing parts of it in the *Journal.*

(c) *Meager reports of Christmas Offering.* This is one of the provoking things in our work; for instance, Missouri is credited on your books with having given $3.15. In a letter which I received this morning from Mrs. Manly J. Breaker, Cor. Sec. of Central Committee of Missouri, she says:

"You will be glad to know that the Christmas Offering was somewhat over $300.00 this year, while last year it was but $225.00."

And so it goes. The explanation is that, while Treasurers of State Boards request, and in some instances insist, upon the contributions of Woman's Mission Societies passing through their hands, they will not designate the contributions when sent to the Boards. It is one of perplexing problems how to bring about a change in this direction. Before the Conventional Year closes, I will ask that the Central Committees give me accurate reports of the amounts contributed by Woman's Mission Societies for the Christmas Offering, and these will be published in the May *Journal,* making the Central Committees responsible for the figures. I think when you see that report, you will be not quite as disappointed as you now are, at the results of the effort. The experience of years shows me that this is the explanation of the small return that the Foreign Board is able to report.

(d) *New Plan for increasing Missionary Information in Sunday Schools.* I will now state same and ask your opinion of it. I have not time to refer to the gentlemen whose names you sent—thanks for forwarding them—and anyway, I hardly feel at liberty to do so until I have presented the matter to Dr. Frost. With the Secretaries of the Boards it is different. The work is so thoroughly one, that what affects one phase of it, affects all; therefore, I am at liberty to ask for "opinions" from them, even before plans have been decided upon, which must be carried out by another Board. This, of course, only refers to suggestions which *I* desire to make. Now for the question in point.

In writing a short time ago, Mrs. T. C. Carleton of St. Louis said:

> "I hope you have seen Manual and cards just issued by Missionary Union for Sunday School Work. Cannot we have something similar for our work, home and foreign? I believe Missions in the Sunday School is the keynote to the situation. Have insisted on this for years. (Mrs. Carleton is, as you probably know, the wife of one of the pastors in St. Louis). Have always appreciated *Kind Words* so much on that account, but I think that does not quite meet the demand. We need a Manual and cards, if possible; or something your fertile brain may plan better."

I had not seen the Manual and cards gotten out by the Missionary Union, but immediately sent for these. It does seem right strange that about two years or eighteen months ago the thought came to me that it was desirable, if not necessary, that we should have a Handbook of Southern Baptist Missions, as it was difficult for new workers to obtain definite information on *all* phases of the work. It could be found where those who knew where to search for it, but foundation facts on all fields and phases of S.B.C Missions were not in any one publication. I proceeded to carry out this idea, and as there was leisure, had manuscript prepared for said Handbook. It was in due time presented to Drs. Willingham, Kerfoot, and Frost. After examining it, each one most kindly, and in some instances, enthusiastically endorsed same.

On getting printers' estimates, I found it would require quite an outlay to have it printed, if the Handbook was to be distributed free. The Boards and Woman's Missionary Union furnished workers with so much free literature, that they are unwilling to purchase same; so we could hardly expect to sell a sufficient number of copies of the Handbook to pay for the edition. Many persons would also be disappointed if they could not obtain this compendium of missionary information without paying for it. If the Sunday School Board sees fit to adopt a similar plan to that just being put into operation by the Missionary Union, the material with the exception of illustrations, is all ready. We can probably change a little the methods, so as not to seem to be copying; but the fact remains that parallel material to that prepared by the Missionary Union was arranged for all three Boards, S.B.C. long before the Missionary Union put into operation their plan. It seems a little strange that the character of material which is now reposing in the safe at 304 N. Howard St. is very much after the same order as that printed in the Manual which the Missionary Union have gotten out. They, however, only treat six different fields, while ours is for both Home and Foreign Missions, and gives information on the work of the Sunday School Board.

By this mail I send copies of the Manual and cards gotten out by the Missionary Union. Will you kindly glance over these and let me know what you think of our trying to get the Sunday School Board to adopt some similar method for further training the young people in the S.B.C. Sunday Schools along missionary lines?

I will have to ask that you return the printed matter which I send, as I have no other copies. Dr. Kerfoot and Dr. Frost will be in Baltimore either the last of the week or the first of the next week, so if it does not tax you, I would like your opinion upon this point in the near future.

One other matter and then I must close. *No, no, no*. Please do not imagine for one instant that I failed to recognize the magnitude of the work that devolves upon you and Dr. Willingham. I would not be willing, no, not for a day, xxxx to *permanently* "swap" places with you. To have to be responsible for securing and expending the money for our foreign work, selecting the missionaries, deciding all knotty problems that come up on the different fields, etc., etc., would drive me wild. As it is, the *wardrobes* of the Frontier missionaries are just about as much as I want to be responsible for. Do you know many of the missionaries seem to feel that, in some way, I am accountable, if the needed clothing does not arrive just at the time it is wanted, and if each individual garment does not fit. I have sometimes said that it seems that many of them have an idea that the Mission Rooms are a great department store, and they simply have to announce when they need watches, saddles, bridles, buggies, musical instruments, artists' supplies, as well as suits of clothing, etc., etc., etc., etc., and that these will be sent instantly.

Very truly,

Annie W. Armstrong

P. S. Mr. and Mrs. Chambers will take tea at 1423 McCulloh Street this evening. They are both making a very favorable impression in Baltimore. Mrs. Chambers was at the Mission Rooms this morning on her way to see a Chinese woman, with a teacher from the Chinese school. I have entered my protest to their being overtaxed. Mr. Chambers told me, I think, that he had five invitations to preach tomorrow. He was at Eutaw Place Church last Sunday, and again on Wednesday night.

[IMB Archives]

Beyond consensus building among Southern Baptists entities, Armstrong tried to create a genuine denominational awareness among Southern Baptists. She staunchly advocated regional missions and drew distinctions between Baptist work in the North and South when she could.

August 8, 1894

Dr. R. J. Willingham

Dear Brother:

As it is uncertain about your visit to Asheville and as my business with you is pressing, I write instead of waiting upon that uncertainty. I am sorry to be obliged to write (1) because the need exists for presenting the matter; in my judgment, a vitally important one. (2) The correspondence involves the necessity of speaking to the discredit of Mrs. Stainback Wilson, Sec. Central Committee of Ga. (3) The letters submitted are regarded by writers as confidential; though, to me, where subjects concern the interests of W.M.U. and the Boards, which are identical, I cannot feel at liberty to retain them from the knowledge of the officers of the Boards.

Statement of the case.—I have known for some time that sympathy existed with the Gospel Mission. I had hoped it was largely limited to North Carolina and would gradually die out, ceasing to affect W.M.U. work. Presenting the letters of Miss Moon and others, contradicting the injurious statements of "G.M." to the leaders of our work at Dallas, was hoped to stop this disaffection. This is not the case as shown by enclosed letters and quotations.

I will now give quotations from letters or refer to ones enclosed and would ask that you read these in the order named.

1. In a letter from Miss Heck of July 28th, she says: "Miss Leslie Pleasants writes me from Asheville that on account of a possible tendency to consumption she has given up going to join Mr. Herring's party this fall. She had, however, become thoroughly identified with this movement, and one of our best Societies, Wilmington Young People, had withdrawn from us and taken her as their missionary."

2. Read Mrs. Wilson's letter to me marked "1."

3. Read letter marked "2."

4. I received a letter from Miss M. E. Wright of August, Ga. Vice Pres. W.M.U. written Aug. 3, in which she says: "Mrs. Wilson has written me a letter, the full import of which, I do not feel sure of. I begin to feel nervous when I see her handwriting on an envelope and when I finish reading it, I am divided between indignation and intense anxiety. Especially the part relating to the "G.M." I want you to note. I am going to send it for you to read and return. I will not make any comments but leave you to form an unbiased opinion. My sister and I have been surprised to find a knowledge of and sympathy with the "G.M." where we least expected it and we have been growing more and more anxious. They are evidently leaving no stone unturned, and it seems to me that the Board position will have to be put before the people plainly through the papers."

5. I have taken extracts from the letter written by Mrs. Wilson to Miss Wright and you will find it with the others marked "3."

Regretting deeply to say it, with the growth of years, I have had a growing lack of confidence in Mrs. Wilson and her methods of work. Do you not judge from her enclosed letters that she is not only becoming alienated from the Boards but is ready to advocate Gospel Mission? From her prominence in Ga. work for many years, also from active part taken in the general organization, which has given her a wider notoriety, do you not think her influence could be used very detrimentally by "G.M?" By reference to Mrs. W's letter to Miss Wright, you will see Mrs. Wilson is thoroughly posted not only by "G.M." but is familiar with their operations in other States. If remaining with us as a supposed friend to the Board, she could more certainly use her influence for harm than if openly known to espouse the cause of "G.M."

Mrs. Wilson is a most difficult and dangerous (because of her methods) subject to handle; yet an imperative need exists, in my opinion, for action of some kind. Can the facts to make her position untenable be given to the public? If so, how?

I write of this whole matter, distasteful as it is to me personally, because I feel sure Mrs. Wilson's disaffection will be largely used to the injury of the Board's work. I have had two letters on this subject from Mrs. W. (the ones enclosed) but have answered neither. I need your advice before doing so and am unwilling to take a step without the backing of your instructions.

Hoping and praying that you may be guided at all times to know what is the right thing to do when difficulties arise in connection with the work, which has been committed into your hands, I am

Very truly,

Annie W. Armstrong

P. S. Be kind enough to return the letters sent.

Since writing the above, I have had a letter from Mrs. A. M. Gwathmey, Pres. W.M.U., who as you probably know has been for some months in South Carolina. Mrs. Gwathmey writes:

> "My brother Dr. Chas. Manly, is travelling through this state attending the different Associations, and he says that the ladies are working very hard on the debt. There is a great tendency in this State as well as N.C. to go over to the Gospel Mission, and one of the arguments that they use is, that they require no Board to handle their money, and hence have no trouble about their being any debt. This is a very serious question I think."

How I would like to ask the persons who talk in this way, to consider how long a time the Gospel Mission has been in existence. I am not a prophet, but should that Mission last for nearly 50 years and meet some years of general financial depression, I think its supporters will have a debt to meet. Do you not find it difficult to preserve your equilibrium when you have to deal with such unfairness?

[IMB Archives]

September 26, 1894

Dr. R. J. Willingham

Dear Brother:

I expect if I have to send you many more letters of the same character as this and one or two that I have written you recently, you will begin to dread to see a letter bearing the stamp of the Woman's Missionary Union, knowing that some perplexing question is to be presented to you. I do feel, though, when questions of such magnitude arise, unwilling to act without the advice of the Secretaries, but, rest assured, I will not trouble you with any minor matters than can be arranged by me without said advice, as I appreciate how much you are taxed. I will now present two subjects for your consideration.

1. *Rev. Z. C. Taylor and children.* Be kind enough to read the enclosed letter which I received yesterday from Rev. Z. C. Taylor, and note especially what he says in regard to being perfectly at a loss to know what to do with his four children. From conversation I had with Mrs. W. B. Bagby when in this country, I appreciate the condition of things is such in Brazil, that it would be altogether wrong to leave children there without the constant watch care of a parent. Mr. Taylor of course cannot go on with his work if he has to remain at home to look after his little ones, so some provision ought to be made for the children. You will see that he says there are no members of his family who could take the children.

To me this question assumes a decidedly serious and personal aspect, for Mr. Taylor told me when in this country three years ago, directly after the operation Mrs. Taylor had gone through with that he had purposed if she had died to bring the children on to me in Baltimore. As Mrs. Taylor was then recovering, I did not think it was necessary to tell him how completely out of my power it was for me to assume the charge of his little family. Knowing that Mr. Taylor, though a magnificent missionary, is one whose judgment is not very good in every day affairs, I think it more than probable that in the near future these children will be sent to America and possibly consigned to my care. For many reasons—my mother's feeble health, every moment of my time being more than needed for the varied duties which now devolve upon me, etc., etc.—it is perfectly out of my power to consider for an instant my taking these children to care for.

Now what can be done with them? Several years ago it was very seriously considered, and could then have been arranged without much trouble, the wisdom of starting a home for missionaries' children like the Northern Baptists have at Newton Centre. One of our most earnest workers had offered a house for this purpose and was then prepared to do much in this line. On due inquiry, though, we found that at that time there were comparatively few children in the families of the missionaries who needed such a home. Too few to make it advisable to start such an institution. Things have now changed very completely and I am quite sure the lady who made this offer would not now be prepared to do anything in this direction—later I will speak more definitely on this point should you wish it. As there is no one specially interested in the starting of such a home, and the money being so much needed to carry on the work, I do not consider it would be feasible for us to try in this way to arrange for Mr. Taylor's children, but must make some special provision for them alone. The thought has occurred to me that it might be well to get them into the Virginia Orphanage if the character of the children who are there aided is such that it would be right for us to advise Mr. Taylor sending them there, and admission could be obtained for them. I know very little of the Va. Orphanage and for this reason write to you for information. I think the Taylor children are from 3 to 8 or 9 years of age, the oldest being a boy. We have, as you doubtless know, a small Baptist orphanage in Baltimore, started by Rev. H. M. Wharton and largely carried on by him. I judge that the children who are received there are, as a general thing, of very plain parentage and I hardly think it would be right, even if permission could be obtained, to place Mr. Taylor's children with that class of little ones. Is not Dr. Hatcher President of the Va. Orphanage and would it be possible for you to see him and find out what the prospects are in this direction, etc., etc.?

If such an arrangement could not be made, or if it is not advisable to have it made, do you think it would be possible to find some Baptist who would take the little ones and provide for them for the amount that the Board allows for the children of missionaries? Am I not right in thinking that $100.00 a year is given for each child? These are the only two ways which have presented themselves to me by which we might hope to have these children taken care of. Even if Mr. Taylor does not propose himself sending the children either to the care of the Foreign Board, or to me as Secretary of the Woman's Missionary Union, I think it is very evident that if we want him to continue to do effective missionary work in Brazil, some provision must be made for them. If it would not tax Mrs. Willingham too much, will you not talk over this matter with her and see if she can offer any suggestions? I of course am ready and willing to make any arrangements for them, if I know in what direction it might be well to make an effort.

2. *Gospel Mission and Woman's Missionary Union's work.* This morning's mail brought a letter from Mrs. Stainback Wilson, enclosing what seems to be some pages of *Our Missionary Helper*—the paper circulated among Georgia societies. I send these to you as I desire you to see the character of the articles, etc., etc. You will note that it is designated "Gospel Mission Department, conducted by Mrs. C. E. Kerr." *Our Missionary Helper* has been issued for perhaps a year or more. The work done in that

paper has been of a very poor character, except re-prints, and I am quite persuaded that the editorial matter in this division of the paper has not been done by Mrs. Kerr. Another point. The printing and paper used has been of the most indifferent kind. This is of a very different order, so evidently a special arrangement has been made and more money is being used to print this department than has ever been used before. The question naturally arises, from whence does this money come? Another question suggests itself to me. Why are these pages printed separately unless it is intended to use them much more widely than the paper as a whole? I think it is very probable that these pages will be sent, not only throughout Ga., but in the other States. From Mrs. Wilson's long connection with the Woman's Missionary Union, she knows, either personally or by name, many of the earnest workers and I very much fear, unless some active steps are taken to counteract the influence which is being exerted, much trouble will arise in this direction. As you doubtless know, through our way of working, we have learned *how* to distribute literature so it will reach many. I cannot tell you how anxious I am to prevent the Woman's Mission Societies from being alienated from the Boards and I think, unless some vigorous measures are inaugurated, through ignorance, many societies may accept the plausible statements of the Gospel Mission and send their funds in that direction. Will you allow me to offer a suggestion to you?

While Mrs. Wilson's disaffection is more against the Foreign Board than the Home Board, yet in statements she has made, you can see that her feeling of opposition is to all Boards and her interest is in the Gospel Mission. The Home Board being located in Ga. could bring local influence to bear which the Foreign Board could not do alone—on this point I am going to speak very freely, for I am sure you will regard what I say as confidential, only to be used where in your judgment it is absolutely necessary and where it will not cause needless friction. Nearly two years ago I had a long conversation with Dr. Tichenor in regard to Mrs. Wilson and her methods, which for years I have felt were harmful. Dr. Tichenor then told me that he perfectly appreciated the state of things as did also Dr. Gibson, the State Secretary, and that Dr. Gibson had then some one in view to take Mrs. Wilson's place. I had hoped at the Ga. State Convention of '93 such a change would be made, but nothing was done. Now for the suggestion. It is that on your way to the Texas Convention, which I suppose you purpose attending about the 10th of Oct., that you arrange to meet Dr. Tichenor and Dr. Gibson in Atlanta and talk over these matters with them. Dr. Gibson, as I have been told, is a bold, strong and fearless man and would probably deal with a matter of the kind wisely and fearlessly. He could inform the pastors as to what is being done and doubtless secure the removal of Mrs. Wilson on the ground that the *Missionary Helper*, the organ of the Woman's Societies in Ga., without the knowledge or consent of the ladies, is now an organ of the Gospel Mission, Mrs. Wilson and her sister, Mrs. Kerr, being joint editors of the paper—if requested to do so by the two Boards.

I have tried to give you all the facts in regard to this trouble in my possession. I know, though, how difficult it is in writing to make one's self clearly understood, and appreciating that this may be a crisis in our work, I would say that, if you consider it *absolutely necessary* for other members of the Foreign Board as well as yourself to have me answer questions before this Board can decide what steps to take, and this can only be done satisfactorily by my coming to Richmond, I will try to take time and come. I would ask, however, that you do not write me to come unless you consider it essential, as I now have to act as house-keeper at home, owing to my mother's feeble health, and there is also a great pressure just now in our work, but as I previously mentioned, my anxiety is so great to prevent the alienating of our Woman's Societies from the Boards, that I would make any sacrifices in my power to help to counteract the influences which are being exerted to undermine our work. Should you tell me to come, please state what day would be most convenient and also let me know how long it would require me to remain. Would it be possible for me to come to Richmond, attend to what was needed and return to Baltimore the same day? While there, though, I would like to have time to see Mrs. Gwathmey and Miss Juliet Pollard. For that reason I would prefer your appointing a day subsequent to Mrs. Gwathmey's return to Richmond, which I think will be about Oct. 1st, but perhaps you know better than I do the date when she will be home. In making the offer I now do to come to Richmond, please appreciate that I will be willing to meet as many of the members of the Foreign Board as you care to call together for this purpose, but would ask if you make the number large, that either Mrs. Gwathmey or Miss Pollard will also be invited to be present as I would prefer to have some other lady with me.

Very truly,

Annie W. Armstrong

P. S. If the suggestion I have made in regard to your seeing Drs. Tichenor and Gibson and consulting with them how best to get matters arranged in Ga. should meet with your approval, do you not think it would be wiser for me not to send the letter to Mrs. Wilson—even should you have decided that it covers the ground in a satisfactory way—which I referred to you, but for me to leave the whole question just as it is to be decided by the Secretaries?

[IMB Archives]

BOYS' AND GIRLS' DEPARTMENT
THE BAPTIST WATCHMAN
Mrs. Stainback Wilson, Editor
Atlanta, Ga.
April 20, 1895
My dear Sister:

It has been a long while since we had any communication. Having been so intimately associated with you in the W.M.U. work since its organization, I can but feel a deep interest in a work in which I feel I was so unjustly severed. I will not complain however, as I believe the All-wise hand which makes no mistakes is guiding me, and has brought me safely thus far through great sorrow and tribulation, and I doubt not has work yet for me to do in other lines. This persecution (for that is its name) has opened my eyes to many things in which they were blind before. It has been a wonder to me, yet a great grief that Christian women, Christian men, members of our C. C., and of the Boards *especially* the Corresponding Secretary of the Home Board *could* treat one as they have me, who had for 16 years served them faithfully as I did. My writings in *Index* all these years, my editorial department in *Baptist Basket* for 5 years, and in *Our Missionary Helper* for 2 1/2 years, all bear me out in asserting that I observed the strictest allegiance to all the Boards, never for one moment questioning the wisdom of their plans, but always rallying the women of my State to the support of their recommendations. It is a source of untold gratification to me, that I have through all this great trial, had the love and confidence of all my co-workers from every section of the State, as an immense pile of letters will show. But then the trial came, the persecution began and led by Miss Wright as V. P. of W.M.U., and became so full of strife and dissension, I with nearly all the older members of the C. C. withdrew, and organize as you were advised, and still proposed to continue work for the Boards, as we were, as we always had been loyal to them. Right here is where work was instituted of which I am ashamed, and it has opened my eyes to the extreme measure, the terrible whirlpool of centralization into which our Boards and their allies of woman's work are drifting. The C. C. as I before said led by Miss Wright in her official capacity assailed me and my co-workers, and the Boards took it up in a lengthy dissertation of my actions (written by Dr. Tichenor); I am misrepresented in almost every paragraph, my motives impugned, and even my letter of resignation to the C. C. which was written in a loving Christian spirit seeking nothing but peace, was garbled in such a manner as to give it an entirely different meaning from what was intended. This *cruel* treatment well nigh prostrated me, for it came as a clap of thunder in a clear sky, all being done without my knowledge in the beginning, and without a hearing before the Boards in which I could have explained matters. But I cast the burden on the Lord, and true to His promise he sustained me, and I bore it all in silence, making no attempt to defend myself against their unjust attack, which was not only heralded through the *Index*, but in the most sensational of our city papers! I pursued this course for the good, as I hoped, of the cause which was so dear to my heart, not entering a continued controversy, and presenting such ridiculous appearance as that of Christians fighting each other.

This step of Miss W. and the C. C. has proven as I told them it would, a most disastrous one to our work as it has been conducted all these years. Many have quietly withdrawn and make no reports, and it is not known just what they are doing. It has been a great ad. to the Gospel Mission movement. Many inquiries have come to Mrs. Kerr from Societies, pastors and people as to what it is, and many converts to their methods have been made. To my mind a greater impetus has been given the movement by the unwise boycotting *Our Missionary Helper* by the C. C. than it would have attained in 10 years with the little G. M. Dept. it had conducted on the most conservative plan, with a department for 16 pages *exclusively* in the interest of the Boards. The result has been a great awakening to these methods in Georgia, the rallying of G. M. forces from other States which carries the *Helper* into many localities where its influence was never felt before. Boycotting is not to be commended anywhere, and especially among Baptists who should be the freest people on earth. I learn that the Virginia Central Committee led by their President, who is also President of W.M.U. is boycotting that dear little *Baptist Basket*, which has been a most valuable coadjutor of the Boards, because it has published letters from the Gospel missionaries! Think you such measures will be blest by our Master who rebukes his beloved disciple in these words for just such a spirit? I have from the beginning planted myself firmly on this platform, Acts 5-38 & 39, whatever Miss Wright may say to the contrary. But the Lord has graciously sustained me through what has been next to my great bereavement in the loss of my husband, the sorest trial of my life. May it not be that He has another work for me to do? I have not felt that it was in the line of the Gospel Mission methods, therefore when the *Helper* was converted into a G. M. organ, I withdrew as editor; but I cannot say this will not be His leading into this field of labor. I have long since dedicated my life to His service, and am willing to be led by my Father's unerring hand. He has given me moral and Christian courage to do pioneer work,—service which may call down the criticisms of the brethren and sisters, yet if it be His leading I can bear such reproaches, and like Paul "Glory in tribulation."

And my dear sister, I must tell you how I was shocked, and my eyes opened to the Baptist Board *"ring"* into which we are drifting, something which had never before occurred to me, when the Executive Committee refused to let our Executive Committee which had organized for the work of the Boards, have the free literature published in their interest. I asked myself, who pays for this literature? Does not my church, my W.M.S. and all those over our Southland pay for it? Then what right has the Executive Committee W.M.U., or even the Boards which claim to be "The servants of the churches" to withhold it from any missionary Baptist man, woman, or organization who wish to use it in raising contributions for missions as represented by the Boards? My sister, the arbitrary manner in which our Boards are conducting their work is bringing among our people a state of things which they will not tolerate. Indeed much *real indignation* now exists in many places, as we instance in their treatment of Miss Divers of Mo. I presume you know all about it. The great falling off in contributions to the Boards and apparent lethargy of the churches mean more than the stringency of the money market. It behooves them and their supporters to stop the unwise measure of boycotting and ostracizing those who even "sympathize" with other methods, and to make prayerful and solemn enquiry "what have our methods to do with the present disastrous condition of things?" The above paper is the organ of the South Georgia Convention which represents a very large territory in our State. I accepted the editorship of one department, not knowing that there was any sympathy on the part of the chief editor with G. M. methods. See what he says in last issue:

> *"The Missionary Helper*, published and edited by Mrs. C. E. Kerr, of Atlanta, has been enlarged and improved. Each of its state departments is edited by men who advocate the Gospel Mission plan, of each church being directly responsible to the missionary. If the

churches of Georgia could be brought to this Bible plan what an impetus would be given to missions."

I have severed my connection with the W. B. M. U. on 18th Dec. just 12 days before the close of the 3rd quarter of our State Conventional year, and was pained to see no report for Georgia in the *F. M. J.* with the other States. Cannot say why the new Secretary did not give it. I could have given it if asked for. I enclose the work as rendered me by the societies for the time I served as Corresponding Secretary. I do not know that it will be of use to you, or that you will be allowed to use it, not "coming through the regular channel," but I send it, regretting that in the providence of God it is the last I shall ever render you. O, how sweet have been our relations these seven years—what precious friendships and loving friends have grown out of this service! And how cruel seems the persecution that has severed this connection! But our greatest sorrows and disappointments are often the very blessings in disguise sent for our good, and we are reminded that "*All things shall work together for good etc.*" When dear old Jacob cried out in the agony of his soul, "*All these things are against me,*" he little knew the blessings of peace and plenty with a restored household that was obscured by the great sorrow that threatened his peace, his *very life.* So I feel that what is to me as great a sorrow, will ere long bring sweet comfort in just that line of work which *He* shall give me to do. With many kind remembrances and good wishes, I am yours in loving service.

Mrs. Stainback Wilson

Have you seen Mrs. S. R. Ford's appeal to the sisterhood in April issue of Ford's C. *Repository* in behalf of Mrs. Cranford & the G. M.? This letter is not intended for others than yourself, though it contains nothing more than I would say to any dear friend.

Report of service rendered W. B. M. U. of Georgia as Corresponding Secretary & Treasurer, for 8 months and 18 days of Conventional year, 1894-95.

As Cor. Sec'y Letters Received		768
Letters written		1049
Postals received		109
Postals written		484
W.M.S. organized	28	
Y. L. S. "	3	
C. M. B.	17	
Total	48	

Several hundred packages literature distributed, including that for Missionary Day and Christmas Offering.

Treasurer's Report

140 Societies, representing 39 Associations, contributed to

Foreign Missions	1718.05
Home Missions	2243.89
State Missions	840.75
Other Objects	<u>3679.86</u>
	$8482.55

Affectionately submitted,
Mrs. Stainback Wilson
Former Cor. Sec'y & Treasurer W. B. M. U.
Atlanta, Ga.
[IMB Archives]

May 4, 1895
Dr. R. J. Willingham
Dear Brother:

I have just received confirmation of what I feared. Different ones in Georgia have assured me that they thought Mrs. Wilson would not go to Washington, as she had no following and her influence was a thing of the past. I could not agree with them, although I hoped they were right and I was wrong. The information that has just come is from Mrs. J. D. Easterlin, Atlanta, who writes:

"I received a telephone message from Mrs. Wilson yesterday, asking who were the ladies going to the S.B.C. from Atlanta and intimated she would go. I hope the Lord will give you strength to meet any trouble she may try to give in the right spirit, and give you all wisdom to do just the right thing for His glory."

Ever since Mrs. Wilson took the stand she did, I have appreciated that she was being used by others, and have thought that an effort would be made to organize a Woman's Department for the Gospel Mission and Mrs. Wilson be put at the head of it. If that was to be done, the time and place to inaugurate such a movement would doubtless be in Washington. As you probably know, *Our Missionary Helper*, Mrs. Kerr's paper, now has four

State Department Editors, viz., Mrs. C. E. Kerr, Atlanta, Ga.; Rev. Ben M. Bogard, Fulton, Ky.; Rev. M. P. Matheny, Gastonia, N. C.; and Prof. H. T. Cook, Greenville, S. C. I think you will judge from this, as I do, that Mrs. Kerr and Mrs. Wilson are not working single-handed, but they are united with others who are in the forefront of this Gospel Mission Movement.

It appears to me that an effort will be made to get the Woman's Missionary Union to recognize the Gospel Mission, and if that is not successful, then Mrs. Wilson and others will try to cause a division in our work—not only in Ga., but in the other States.

I have given you this information, for I wanted to ask an interest in your prayers that God will so take control of matters, that nothing can be done but what will best advance His cause. I also felt that I would like to have you think a little over the subject and be prepared to advise us what ought to be done, if the steps I have suggested are taken by Mrs. Wilson and others who sympathize with her—one great difficulty is that we do not know who are supporters of the Gospel Mission and who are not. I am thankful, though, to be able to say that, as far as I know, there are none of the ladies in the different States who have any but the kindliest feeling toward the Cor. Sec. W.M.U., and I believe I will be able to get the delegates to weigh carefully the facts which we may present, and not allow prejudiced statements to unduly influence them.

I would again ask that you bring with you to Washington the letters from Miss Moon, Dr. Hartwell, and others, which give the strongest proof that those who are now engaged in this movement did not in the past work wisely and well, and other facts of a similar character.

Very truly,

Annie W. Armstrong

P. S. Is it not true that the unexpected is what always happens? I had thought that I would have the remaining few days to quietly finish up the odds and ends previous to our meeting, write a number of letters that still remain unanswered, etc., etc., and now I must take the time to try and be prepared to show the ladies, if necessary, what was the cause of the troubles in Ga.

P. S. No. 2. We have, according to your request, gotten out a catalogue of the Mission Rooms of a size that can be enclosed in letters. I send one. I am very sorry to note that the printer has made a very stupid mistake in regard to the advertisement for the *Foreign Mission Journal.* You will note that he gives as address, "*Home Mission Journal*, Richmond, Va." I was so pressed with work at the time the proof was sent to me that I did not carefully examine same. I hope, though, persons who desire to subscribe for the paper will appreciate that it is a printer's mistake. We are proposing to distribute copies of the catalogue at the Convention, hence the reason for haste in getting it out.

[Handwritten in margin] We received today from the printer the tabulated statement of W.M.U. contributions since organization in 1888—I enclose one thinking you may like to glance over it.

[IMB Archives]

April 14, 1898
Dr. Lansing Burrows
Dear Brother:
Your letter of April 13th received. You are entirely mistaken in thinking that I am not interested in the "personal details" which you give in regard to the Year Book. I am so interested in them, that I am going to ask to be allowed to make use of the information you have given and present same to the Secretary of the Publication Society, if his attention has not already been called to the glaring mistakes made by the one who this year compiled the Year Book. I had not noticed these, so think it only right to get your permission before appearing to be a Columbus. I of course will not mention to Dr. Rowland who attracted my attention to these mistakes. Dr. and Mrs. Rowland, while in Baltimore, were warm personal friends, but I so thoroughly disapprove of the methods adopted by Dr. Rowland since he has become Secretary of the Publication Society, that I am not at all unwilling to let him appreciate just where I stand on the questions which he seems desirous to put before our Southern people in such false lights.

Another point to which I wish to call your attention. In writing to Dr. Willingham a short time ago, I sent him copies of Dr. Rowland's letters, so he might see how Dr. Rowland sought to excuse himself in granting a department in the *Teacher* to the Gospel Mission. I wrote him as follows:

It is probably better at times not to speak as strongly as one feels, but I must say it passes my comprehension how Dr. Rowland as a Christian man can justify himself in using the methods which he is adopting. I do sincerely wish it were possible for the Foreign Board to refuse to accept the money which the Publication Society gives to our work, etc., etc.

Dr. Willingham replied:

"I have read your correspondence with Dr. Rowland with interest. The Publication Society has not given us much this year. They have gradually been going down until this year they sent us $250.00. The explanation they give as to the Gospel Mission Department may be satisfactory to them, but certainly is not to many people in the South who know of its movements."

After hearing from Dr. Willingham of the gradual decrease in the appropriations made by the Publication Society to the Foreign Board, I thought I would like to see when the decrease began. I have looked through the file of Convention Minutes since 1889 and find the following:

CONTRIBUTIONS OF THE AM. BAP. PUB. SOCIETY
TO THE
FOREIGN MISSION BOARD, S.B.C.

1889	$ 1,000	1894	$1,000
1890	2,000	1895	500
1891	1,000	1896	300
1892	1,000	1897	450
1893	-----	1898	250

Do you not consider it quite a significant fact, that the decrease in the appropriations from that source to our organized Southern work has been since the Gospel Mission has been in existence? If we are to credit the statements made by those who are in charge of the Publication Society, their ability has increased, and so it does not seem necessary, if their interest were as great as in former years, that they should cut down the appropriations to the Foreign Mission Board. As those in charge of the Gospel Mission make no annual report of money received, at least as far as I know, it is possible that the Publication Society officers, in their desire to be "broad," may be helping to provide the needed funds to carry on that work. Any way I do think it would be wise for attention to be called publicly to the fact that the Publication Society has decreased their appropriations to the Foreign Board. I do not propose giving my publicity to this until after the books of the Foreign Board are closed, for if Dr. Rowland appreciated that he would be asked to explain his reasons for the decrease, he might send on to Richmond sufficient money to equalize the amount given this year to that appropriated in former years, and I for one do not want money coming from that source for our work. When in Norfolk, I shall probably give the facts to which I now call your attention to the Editors of the *Index* and see if they wish to ventilate this matter in the columns of their paper. Should you prefer to do the same in regard to the errors which you have found in the Year Book, do not hesitate to say so, and I will of course not refer the matter to Dr. Rowland.

Very truly,

Annie W. Armstrong

P. S. I shall earnestly try to send you the table for W.M.U. work at the time given, April 25th.

[SBHLA, J. M. Frost Collection]

April 5, 1905

My dear Mrs. Leake:

I returned to Baltimore yesterday evening, having had an unusually interesting and profitable trip. I am perfectly delighted at what is being accomplished in the way of Christian development through our Mountain Schools, and feel that we cannot over-estimate the importance of this branch of work. Much has already been accomplished but if the needed funds can be secured and the schools better equipped, much more will be done in the future. The equipment in many places is totally inadequate and I was thoroughly astonished to know of the high grade of work being done with the accessories so poor. We cannot too highly honor the men and women who are giving their lives to the Mountain School work. I think it should be put on the same plane as all other missionary work, for it takes just as much real devotion to endure the privations and hardships in these Mountain Schools as on a mission field. I hope to be able to give an account of this trip in the May editions of *Our Home Field* and *The Foreign Mission Journal*, also some pictures of the Schools.

I am thankful to say while the trip was necessarily trying in some particulars, yet I returned home feeling better than when I left Baltimore. I did, though, have to spend a large part of the first Sunday after leaving home in bed, but was able to keep every engagement that had been made for me. In addition to visiting ten Mountain Schools, I met the ladies at a number of places. In the nineteen days that I was away, I travelled 2,124 miles, visited sixteen places and made twenty-seven talks. Eighty miles were travelled in carriages or buggies, as some of the Schools are off the railroad. One day I drove twenty-nine miles. Some of the roads were simply dreadful. I was told by way of consolation that it was made much easier travelling when there was mud. The bouncing over roads made one feel quite ready to retire as soon as an opportunity offered. Very unexpectedly, though, at this season of the year, the weather was simply charming. We had rains several times but they never interrupted travel. I was with Rev. A. E. Brown, Supt. of the Mountain Work most of the time, and I cannot speak too highly of him and his work. Certainly the Home Board has "the right man in the right place."

I enclose sample program for Children's Day with Mite Box. Will you kindly fill out order blank and send to Dr. J. M. Frost, Nashville, Tenn., for the number of programs, etc., you can use to advantage in your state? I know you appreciate the importance of the Bible Fund, so it is not necessary for me to speak of this. I hope the Sunday School Board will have your hearty cooperation in the effort it is making to place the Bible in the hands of those who are without.

Very sincerely,
Annie W. Armstrong
[IMB Archives]

April 18, 1905
Dr. R. J. Willingham
Dear Brother:
Your letter April 17th received. I return receipt for the thirty cents forwarded and have sent literature to Mrs. Wills.

I know it will be a relief for you to have your son and his wife with you and hope that it will not be long before Mrs. Willingham will be entirely restored. I have just been writing to different ones in Indian Territory and Oklahoma offering Mrs. Pollard's services as Organizer in one or the other of the Territories. Thinking possibly you may be amused to see how I have covered the ground with Miss Burdette, I send you copy of my letter. Miss Burdette and the Corresponding Secretary of the Woman's Missionary Union have in years past been very good friends. I remember when I introduced Miss Burdette at a meeting in Indian Territory, prior to the unification, Miss Burdette said: "If you love each other as Miss Armstrong and I do there will be no trouble." At the last meetings, though, in Indian Territory and Oklahoma Miss Burdette and I crossed swords quite frequently. I doubt if the women who did not understand the real condition of things appreciated this, but I certainly knew every time Miss Burdette made a thrust. She repeatedly claimed independence and could not understand the necessity of matters being referred to others. So much for

Northern ways of working. The more I come in contact with said methods, the less of cooperation do I want between Northern and Southern Baptists.

Now, for a piece of news: Notice was given at our church according to constitution last Sunday that there would be a meeting Wednesday week when the name of one for pastor would be presented. While the Committee on pastor for Eutaw Place Church has been entirely noncommittal, yet it is quite well understood that the one to be suggested is a Mr. Dodd—I am a little uncertain about his name, I have had so many things of late to think about—from Newark, N. J. He preached for us Sunday week. He is about forty and unmarried. His sermons were unusually interesting and forcible. He is represented as an all round man. I am extremely sorry that we are not to have a Southern man at Eutaw Place Church, but am so relieved that we are not going to experiment with a young man that it almost reconciles me to have a Northern preacher. I hope if Mr. Dodd? is going to be our pastor he will throw himself heartily into Southern work. The Committee appointed to suggest a pastor has done rapid work, do you not think? Mr. Millard only left Baltimore March 16th. The church is to be repaired this summer, so possibly even if Mr. Dodd (I really do not believe that is his name, it sounds a trifle unfamiliar; possibly you may know who it is, he succeeded Dr. Fish at the church in Newark, I rather think the name is Dobbs) is elected and accepts, we may be sampling ministers until next fall.

Very truly,
Annie W. Armstrong
[IMB Archives]

October 31, 1896
Dr. J. M. Frost
Dear Brother:
There will be a meeting of the Mission Rooms Committee on Monday, after which I will write you fully as to the action taken. I was not present on Wednesday at the evening session of the Association, but learned there was quite a heated discussion in regard to the payment of rent of the Mission Rooms by the State Board. I do not want to do anything that will militate against the advancement of the work, but I do feel truly indignant. After 10 years labor in this direction, that there were none of our pastors we could (or would) place before the newcomers the work we are doing in this particular in its true light.

I think you will be interested in some circumstances in connection with the meetings on Thursday, so I will forward you a report. Dr. Rowland made a spread-eagle address on Thursday morning. Told what the Publication Society had done and how they were prepared to act the part of general benefactor; stated that they were about to publish a Young People's paper (weekly) of 16 pages for the phenomenally small sum of 50 cents per annum (he was asked if this was to take the place of *The Baptist Union* and said: "No, as it would not embrace the Culture Courses, but was to provide the Young People with general information"); the Society was about to publish Bibles at very *cheap* rates, also books; their periodicals were to be greatly reduced in price; that the Society desires to place a Sunday School missionary in each Southern State—it has one in almost every Northern State—said missionary to teach methods, etc., etc.; that the Society was prepared to strike hands with the Southern people in taking advantage of the immense industrial development of the South and the large increase in population which was bound to follow; intimated, in connection with the suggestions about State Sunday School missionaries, that the Society was prevented from carrying out these plans.

Dr. Rowland was obliged to leave before the close of the session, for which I was very glad, as I did not want to meet him. I did, though, have quite an encounter with a minor officer of the Society, Dr. O. F. Flippo. In years gone by I have known Dr. Flippo quite well and he was aware of the way I regarded the organization which he represents. Dr. Flippo, after greeting me, proceeded to speak of a late edition of one of their publications which he termed a "Southern number," and referred to a poem that he seemed to admire, written by Sister Alice. I knew that Sister Alice had not written any article for the Publication Society and told him so. He acknowledged that it was a re-print. When I went home and told Sister Alice of this, she was perfectly indignant. The poem had been furnished by her to a New York paper. It certainly was a mean thing for the Editor of the Publication Society periodical, knowing the position Sister Alice occupied in the Southern work and our feelings in regard to their methods, to print anything to which her name was attached. I did feel so provoked at this and other actions of the officers of the Publication Society, that I did not hesitate to express my opinion of same in very plain language. I told Dr. Flippo that there were some persons whom the Publication Society *could not buy*. This remark of course called forth a protest and some counter charges in regard to Southern methods. I found Dr. Flippo, although prepared to laud the Publication Society to the skies, was really quite disturbed at the defection in his own territory, viz., Va., in favor of the Board at Nashville. He also said that recently there had been a delegation of colored men to visit Philadelphia, and that the Colored People had cut loose from the Publication Society and accepted overtures made by the Nashville Board. (You *probably* know of this action, so I will not give later information which was furnished me on this point the next day by one of the leading colored pastors in Maryland). Dr. Flippo wished me to think that their loss in this direction would not prove our gain.

When I expressed the disgust—I did not hesitate to speak plainly—I felt for the methods adopted by the Publication Society, Dr. Flippo wanted to give me proof that those of our own Board were not at all what they should be and desired that I should see letters that were in Philadelphia—I am sure he was largely referring to those which led to the proposition made by Dr. Rowland prior to the Convention in Chattanooga. I assured him I would not be willing to read them. He said this correspondence would have to be published. It does seem strange, if the Publication Society is in such a flourishing condition and the growth is as rapid as the officers of that Society depict, that they are not willing to have the Sunday School Board to do the work in its own way. That, however, does not seem to be the policy of the American Baptist Publication Society. As I told Dr. Flippo, it is with them the desire to monopolize and crush out and then act the part of benefactor—the same methods adopted by the Standard Oil Company. Dr. Flippo predicted that the day would come when there would be only one Baptist Publication Society. I told him that time alone could decide this question. Our conversation was interrupted, but later Dr. Flippo met me again and his parting salutation was: "Well Miss Annie, I will leave and so the air will be clearer." My reply to this was: "I do trust you will change your methods."

Hoping you reached home safely and enjoyed your visit to Baltimore as much as we did having you with us, I am,

Very truly,
Annie W. Armstrong
[SBHLA, J. M. Frost Collection]

June 4, 1897
Dr. J. M. Frost
Dear Brother:

Owing to my having to attend the District Association this week, I am a little late in forwarding data to papers—I like to send it the first day in the month. I now enclose "Illustrations" for *The Teacher* and "Cullings" for *The Teachers' Exchange*. As I previously wrote you, I have sketches of twelve well known hymns written, which I purposed forwarding to you monthly, but noting that the two I sent have not yet appeared in *The Teacher*—please do not think I have any feeling in regard to their not being printed—I suppose you have not room for these, so I will not forward others. I will hold them for a short time subject to your order, but if you have not space for them, I will make use of said hymns in other directions.

The printer has not yet been able to furnish copies of the Bible Card. I hope to send samples of these to you in a few days.

I want to give you an incident that occurred at the District Association, but before doing so, will refer to you several items of business.

1. *Writers for Young People's Scripture Union during the year 1898.* Today's mail has brought from Dr. Boykin a list of the daily Bible Readings for next year. Will you now kindly send me the names and addresses of 15 or 18 gentlemen whom you think it would be well to invite to furnish manuscripts for this department in *Kind Words* next year? My acquaintance with Southern Baptist writers is very limited, so I will have to ask you to furnish names. I ask for a larger number of names than manuscripts needed, as doubtless some will decline.

2. *Grant of Bibles and Testaments for the Immigrant Mission.* I have just received a letter from Miss Buhlmaier in which she says:

> "I called at the Mission Rooms the other day on my way home from the landing. My intention was to tell you that I am out of Testaments, having given away about 75 of them within a week. Will you be kind enough to write Dr. Frost to send another supply? I would be obliged if I could have German, Polish and Bohemian. If not the latter, certainly the two first mentioned. It does my heart good to see how eagerly God's Word is sought after by these people."

Will you kindly furnish Miss Buhlmaier with Testaments and Bibles. Her address is: Miss Marie Buhlmaier, 835 N. Washington St., Baltimore, Md.

Now for my incident and then I must close. The District Association which I attended this week was held in Rockville, a small town in Maryland not far from Washington. I was quite surprised one evening, as I was about to enter the church, to see Dr. O. F. Flippo, District Secretary of the Publication Society, standing on the sidewalk. Having had several quite *plain* talks with Dr. Flippo in regard to the methods of the Society with which he is now connected, and in view of the late episode of Dr. Brown at Pittsburgh, I did not feel specially anxious to meet him, so I entered the church at once, though the friend I was with said: "Miss Annie, there is a gentleman who wanted to speak to you."

The first report that was presented that evening was on Sunday Schools. After the reading of it, the Moderator invited Dr. Flippo to speak. After Dr. Flippo expressed his pleasure at being at the Association, etc., etc., he took up the subject of Denominational Literature; told how necessary it was that we should avail ourselves of what was so amply provided for our use by the Publication Society and the Sunday School Board. In referring to the last named publications, he termed them: "excellent." In no way, shape or form did he draw any invidious comparison. The publications of Cook in Chicago were condemned and an effort made to prove, although they were cheap, they were not suitable for Baptist schools. No claim was made that the Publication Society furnished Sunday School supplies cheaper than the Board at Nashville. In referring, though, to the Publication Society, Dr. Flippo termed it: "The Southern Society," which was organized only a few miles from the town of Rockville.

I could not help being intensely amused at this complete change· of methods in the representative of the Publication Society. Do you think Dr. Rowland has learned the lesson and has now notified his subordinates that the wiser policy is for them to cease to anathematize the Sunday School Board, or do you think the change was simply one of Dr. Flippo's own making? As he left the pulpit and passed down the aisle, he stopped and gave me a very warm grasp of the hand. If I had had an opportunity I think I should have told him that I congratulated him on the change of methods. As he had to catch the train, however, before the close of the meeting, I had no opportunity for conversation.

Very truly,

Annie W. Armstrong

P. S. Since writing the above, the printer has sent samples of the Bible Card before it is died out, so I now have the pleasure of sending you one and also copy of the leaflet. I hope they will meet with your approbation. I consider the card a very pretty piece of work. When finished, it will of course have the printing on back.

P. S. No. 2 (June 5). I was not able to get this letter off yesterday, so since then yours of June 3rd has been received. The leaflet: "Our Bible," has been printed, the entire 15,000, with the wording, "Published by," on same. I appreciate the point you have made and of course something must be done to prevent the criticism to which these very usual words might give rise. Now what can we do? I never consider trouble in a question of this kind. We must make things *right* if possible. I have been to the printer to see what he would suggest. He tells me as the leaflets are bound and printed, it would be very difficult to put an ornament over the words: "Published by," and so block them out, as after the leaflets are folded and cut, the margins vary somewhat and the ornament might not strike the words exactly. It would require very careful work and would cost $1.25 per thousand to do it. His suggestion is that we change the wording of title page in one of the six ways indicated in package I forward. To add this wording to title page would cost $1.00 per thousand. If you consider this the best way to remedy the evil, the $15.00 will not be charged to the Sunday School Board account, but I will see that it is paid otherwise.

There are three other ways by which these offensive words can be removed.

1. Erase same with typewriting rubber (this would be a slow and very laborious process).

2. Mark the words through with black ink by pen.

3. Mark the words through with red ink by pen.

I now enclose samples of all these varied forms and would ask that you consider the matter carefully and let me know what you think we had best do. Let me have your decision if possibly by return mail, and I will have the correction made in the way you think best. None of the leaflets will be sent out until corrected.

Manuscripts for program for Missionary Day. I will forward manuscripts on Monday, and then you can carefully consider same and see if they are in the shape you desire. If I can find time tomorrow, I will re-read said manuscripts and write in regard to them on Monday.

We are now at work on the ten points ("Questions") which you asked that we would furnish for the circular that you propose to send out in regard to the various agencies, S.B.C. I hope to be able to forward these in the course of a few days.

You have no idea how much there is I want to tell you, but I am sure neither you nor I have the time for any longer communication. I will say, though, there are some new developments in regard to work among the colored people about which I must write you in the course of a few days. I am expecting next week to have a visit from Miss M. G. Burdette, Cor. Sec'y of the Woman's Home Mission Society of the North, Headquarters Chicago. How glad I would be if I could see you previous to this conference.

In a certain sense I agree with Brother Jasper that "the world do move." Yesterday I wrote quite a long letter to Dr. Burrows and the next one to this to be dictated is to him. In it I propose suggesting that he defer having his conference with you—if it was arranged to be in the course of a few days—until I can furnish him with some information that he seems not to have been able to secure, which I hope to forward to him some time next week. Please return the leaflet which is altered in the way you decide would be best.

[SBHLA, J. M. Frost Collection]

January 15, 1898
Rev. A. J. Barton
Dear Brother:
Your letter of January 14th, enclosing 34 cents, received. It gives us pleasure to send leaflets to that amount to Mr. Bankston and I now enclose receipt for same.

As I purpose sending Dr. Flippo's letter to Dr. Frost today, I have had copy made of it and now forward same, also extracts from Dr. Frost's address to which Dr. Flippo refers and which he enclosed in his letter. Please hand the extracts of address to Dr. Willingham after you have read them, and at the same time ask him not to show them to any one else until we see what Dr. Frost intends to do. I have very little doubt but that Dr. Rowland, or some advocate of the Publication Society, will use portions of Dr. Frost's address in the reply that will be made to the Editorial in *The Index*. It is certainly a funny position in which Dr. Frost is now placed and possibly he may be a little sensitive in regard to the matter, so I would prefer that you make no mention of the circumstance until we see if any publicity is given to it.

If your curiosity is excited in regard to "another departure" about to be made by the Publication Society of which Dr. Flippo speaks, you can ask Dr. Willingham to what it is probable he has reference. I am not perfectly certain, but I shall be quite surprised if I am wrong in my conjecture. As I told Dr. Willingham yesterday, I propose to reply somewhat at length to Dr. Flippo, making some suggestions to him as an officer of the Publication Society, by which that Society can furnish more information as to Baptist work and workers than they now do, for they certainly have been remiss in ignoring some phases of work if they pretend to do as Dr. Flippo says: "The American Baptist Publication Society, through its Periodical Department, have always tried to give information to Baptists about Baptists throughout the world." I had hoped to write that letter today, but a very large amount of mail that ought not to be laid aside will prevent. I have also just had a letter from Miss Heck, President of the Woman's Missionary Union, telling me that she will come to Baltimore next Thursday to spend a week, so I shall be under a great deal of pressure trying to get the work into shape, in order that during her stay I may give her as much of my time as she desires. Do you often wish that the days, instead of being twelve hours, were twenty-four hours long?

We did enjoy Dr. Willingham's visit extremely.

Very truly,

Annie W. Armstrong

P. S. Please find enclosed 35 cents, annual subscription for *Foreign Mission Journal* to be sent to Mrs. Wood Herron, Dadeville, Tallapoosa Co., Alabama. Mrs. Herron desires subscription to commence with January.

Another item. Today's mail has brought a letter from the President of the Woman's Mission Society in the church of which Dr. Hall has charge in Norfolk. Mrs. Thorne writes:

> "Missionary matters are improving somewhat with us, thanks to the earnest and persistent efforts of our pastor's wife, Mrs. Hall. We are about to assume the support of a missionary in the foreign field. We sent a few days ago a box of provisions, valued at $45.00, to Rev. Colwell, Ind. Ter. Our Christmas Offering for China will be small—I fear not over $10.00—but as it is more than it was last year, we must not complain. We have a good sister working at subscriptions for the *Foreign Mission Journal* and also for the *Home Field*. I am in hopes we may get 50 copies of the latter and as many of the former. We took about as many copies of the *Journal* last year as come to Norfolk altogether the year before, but last year there were but a few over 100 that came to Norfolk. What do you suppose our Baptist churches are doing?"

I send this extract, thinking that possibly some influence might be brought to bear upon the other churches in Norfolk to get them to subscribe more largely for the *Journal*.

[IMB Archives]

January 18, 1898
Dr. O. F. Flippo
Dear Brother:
Your letter of January 12th received and read with much interest. I appreciate your kindness in letting me see how a Southern man who has crossed the border looks at things from the standpoint he now occupies. As they appear to me somewhat different, although much pressed with work, I must take time to give you my impressions of them and then let you be the judge as to who has the most correct view of the matter. Permit me to say, though, before I go any further, that I sincerely hope you will not have the idea that your letter annoyed me in the slightest. I really must acknowledge I was intensely amused at some portions of it, for I consider you were so altogether mistaken in the conclusions you had reached, that I found them quite entertaining. Possibly (probably) you may, after reading this letter which I now propose to write, regard me as a person so thoroughly blinded by prejudice, that I cannot see things in a correct light. Well, if that is the case, you and I will "agree to disagree," but I will have the happy consciousness of having given you *facts* that ought to open your eyes and lead you to appreciate that the officers of the Publication Society have made at least one blunder. I will now take up different points in your letter seriatim.

1. *Convention Almanac.* I am glad to know the Almanacs you ordered have been received and I hope, after a critical examination of same, the little pamphlet met with your approval. I failed to see the press notices to which you refer, but said Almanac was not expected to take the place of the Year Book. It covers entirely different ground. I find it of much service.

2. *Gospel Mission Department in American Baptist Publication Society Teacher.* Permit me in this connection to quote quite largely from your letter, grouping what I desire to say differently from the order in which you have it. You write:

"Why does not *The Index* man turn his guns on those Southern Baptist papers that have reported the work of the Gospel Mission people, and time and again opened their columns to them for correspondence?"

Do you make no distinction between the official organ of a denominational Board or Society and a religious newspaper, which is the property of a private individual? I regard them entirely in a different light. The one is responsible to the denomination that supports it; the other is free to do as the owner thinks wise.

Then again, you say:

> "But, Miss Annie, why rail out against the American Baptist Publication Society for giving a little bit of information about a body of Baptists who are as true to Baptist doctrines and as true to Christ as any other Baptists, but who happen (wisely or unwisely) to differ from the larger organization in methods of work?"

In reply, I would say that if those who do advocate the Gospel Mission would simply confine themselves to giving information in regard to the work done by them, no one, I am sure, either North or South, would feel disposed to say ought against the Publication Society granting them just as much space in the *Teacher* as the Editors might deem wise, but you certainly must know that such is not the method adopted by those who have the Gospel Mission in charge. They do so misrepresent facts, that they give altogether erroneous impressions. A little circumstance that came under my own observation is a sample of the methods they adopt. Some time ago I received a copy of their official organ and noticed an article in it headed: "Chinese Market." I glanced over it and was very much surprised at the small prices quoted for different articles of food. Mrs. R. H. Graves, of Canton, China, was at the Mission Rooms at the time. I handed her the paper and asked if those were the prices she paid for different articles in Canton. After reading it, she said: "Why no, Miss Annie." I then requested her to write opposite to each article quoted the prices that she paid. I will now give you some of these prices.

PRICES AS GIVEN IN PAPER	PRICES GIVEN BY MRS. GRAVES
Eggs, per doz., 4 to 6 cents	10 to 12 cents
Chickens, a piece, 5 to 6 cents	25 cents and up
Beef, 5 to 6 cents	$7\frac{1}{2}$ cents
Mutton, 5 to 6 cents	15 cents

If the writer of the article had said that these were the prices in the interior of North China, which was doubtless the case, he would have been speaking the whole truth, but when he headed his article: "Chinese Market," he was giving a false impression. You appreciate, I am sure, that half truths are the most pernicious stories that can be told. One of the points made by the Gospel Mission is that the salaries paid to missionaries heretofore have been too large, and the money of the people is being wasted by the Board. If $450.00 is the amount needed by those who are doing the work in charge of the Gospel Mission for their support, a missionary in Canton ought to receive two or three times as much, if prices in other directions are parallel. No, no, no, those who are advocating the Gospel Mission are not so much trying to interest persons who have hitherto taken no part in missionary work, but are aiming to sow seeds of distrust in the minds of those who have heretofore supported the organized work. There is no difficulty in securing any amount of proof that such is the case. I have numbers of letters in my possession which substantiate all I have said on this point.

Noting you say: "The Am. B.P. Soc., through its Periodical Department, has always tried to give information to Baptists about Baptists throughout the world," I desire to call your attention to some facts which prove that just at this time you are not doing what you claim. There are various Baptist organizations in the United States of which no mention is made in the *Teacher*, which are doing a much larger work than is being done by the Gospel Mission. Permit me to call your attention to these.

(a) The American Baptist Education Society, which last year raised $19,120.75.

(b) The Baptist Young People's Union of America. I am sorry, but I cannot at present give its constituency.

(c) The Woman's Baptist Foreign Mission Society of the West. Receipts, $49,159.32.

(d) The Woman's Baptist Home Mission Society. Receipts, $66,275.13.

(e) Woman's American Baptist Home Mission Society. Receipts, $34,113.31.

(f) The German Baptist Conferences, etc., etc.

Another point to which I desire to call your attention. Is not the *Teacher* making sectional distinctions, when it gives to the societies of our Northern Baptists three times as much space to report their work as is given to the Southern Baptist Convention, which has a constituency of 1,529,191, nearly twice as great as that represented by the Northern Societies?

I have already taxed your patience too much, but before closing, I would say that I had a letter yesterday from the Secretary of the Foreign Mission Board of the National Baptist Convention, which gives the needed explanation in regard to that portion of your letter where you are a little mysterious, viz., where you say:

> "He (referring to your Periodical Editor) will have another 'Departure' soon from which the *Index* man and some other Baptist Editors will gather material for another brutum fulmen against the Society."

I will not, therefore, have to ask for further light on this point.

Hoping your Editorial Editor will act on the suggestion which I now offer, viz., accord to the different organizations which I have named space in the *Teacher*, so those of us who desire to have information as to what Baptists are doing throughout the United States (if not the world) may find it by referring to the Publication Society *Teacher*, I am,

Very truly,

Annie W. Armstrong

P. S. Please present my kindest regards to Mrs. Flippo, and say to her that if I can at any time aid her in the work she is doing for missions, I hope she will not hesitate to call on me.

[IMB Archives]

American Baptist Publication Society
Philadelphia
January 28, 1898
Miss Annie Armstrong
Dear Sister:

I am really sincere when I say that I most thoroughly enjoyed your letter. It is good to have a friendly interchange of views, now and then, so that we may help each other to a better understanding of questions that divide us. I can assure you, Miss Annie, that I have imbibed no new views on any of the questions at issue since I "crossed the line" and came to Philadelphia to work in the interests of the American Baptist Publication Society. I held the same views I now entertain in Va., and advocate them in all my pastorates. And let me add, that there are many brethren in the South (who have not crossed the line) who hold the same views—men who are loyal to the South, and love the S.B.C. ten fold more than the narrow, exclusive, sectional Baptist leaders, or rather, drivers, whose policy is so divisive, and so detrimental to the best interests of our Southern Baptist Zion. And some of these true spirits will be heard from in the course of human events.

It was hardly necessary, Miss Annie, to "sincerely hope that you (I) will not have the idea that your (my) letter had annoyed me (you) in the slightest." I really did not write to "annoy" you. Truth does not annoy you. Nor did I "after reading your letter, regard you as a person so thoroughly blinded by prejudice, that you cannot see things in a correct light."

After this disclaimer I will now turn my attention to those "facts that ought to open your (my) eyes, and lead you (me) to appreciate that the officers of the Publication Society," &c, &c.

1. I am more than ever convinced that the partisan and bitter attacks of the *Index* against the A.B.P. Society for giving a few items of news of the doings of the Gospel Mission People, are unjust and wholly indefensible. The attack is perfectly understood at the Rooms, and Dr. Rowland is well satisfied with the vindication the Soc. is receiving from some true spirits at the South—men who are not in harmony with the Gospel Mission Method, but who believe and know that it is not wise to try to club them into measures. Why cannot the *Index* man, and two or three other papers, see that they are only gaining friends for the G. M. People and the A.B.P. Society? Why do they not turn their guns on the *Western Recorder* for publishing Bostick's letter last week? It is said that the "Organs of the Society are responsible to the denomination." &c.

That is true, Miss Annie, and the Society is all the while conscious of that fact, and is ever striving to give the Baptist denomination what it needs. The Society has a large constituency, North, South, East, West, and it is honestly trying to serve that constituency by keeping it posted as to what Baptists are doing in all parts of the world. I do not say that the Society is giving satisfaction—perfect satisfaction—but it comes nearer to it than anything else that bears our name, and holds our faith. It is simply amusing to read the fulminations against the G.M.P., and the A.B.P.S., in the *Index* because the *Teacher* happened to give a little space in its columns—forty-eight lines—for these people to tell their brethren what they are doing in the name of the Lord. The Society will never allow the G.M.P. to attack the organized work, nor shall the organized work attack the G.M.P. in the columns of the *Teacher*. This is just what some of the Southern Baptist papers have resolved to do—papers whose editors showed themselves men of better spirit than to take the whip and the club to the Society (notwithstanding they were written to do so)—and we stand with them. The G. M. People, or some of their supporters, have been very much concerned over the late tirade against them and the Publication Society, and in a kind spirit have asked Dr. Rowland to decline to report their work, if by doing so the Soc. should be compromised in any way. But the reports will be continued. Dr. Rowland is a man hard to intimidate. He doesn't scare worth a cent.

I have carefully read your strictures on the "Chinese Market" incident but, indeed, Miss Annie, I cannot see how you make out such a serious charge of falsehood and deception against that people from the market report. Markets and prices are fluctuating. I could go through this city and find great differences in prices and modes of living. Articles of food are in the comparative degree—good, better, best. I may be satisfied with the "good," while some one else may buy the "better" and other some the "best." We may quote the markets according to the prices we pay, and still be on the road to Heaven.

There is one thing we must all admit—namely—that the G.M.P. have some earnest consecrated men and women among them. They are irregular in work and methods, but they love Christ and have been redeemed by Him. They are not at work for fun. Now, then, how would it do for the *Index* man, and some other "calling-fire-down-devouress," to read Phil 1st. 15-18, also Mark 9th. 38-39?

2. In conclusion permit me to note your exceptions to my statement that the "Publication Society through its Editorial Department, has always tried to give information *to* Baptists *about* Baptists throughout the world." This remark did not apply to the *Teacher* alone, but to *all* of our periodicals, of which we have nearly a score.

(a) You arraign the Society for neglecting to report the work of the "American Baptist Education Society." Suffer me to remind you that this Society is not an active body. The Society reports every thing the "Education Society" does. See our Year Book.

(b) You arraign the Society for neglecting to mention the work of The Baptist Young People of America. Pardon me for calling your attention to *Our Young People*, which periodical has a good report, from all over the country, every week. In the same excellent periodical is found every week a report of the Y.P.S.C.E., and "The King's Daughters and Sons."

(c) You arraign the Society for neglecting to report the activities of the "Woman's Baptist Foreign Mission Society of the West:" for neglecting to report work of the "Woman's Baptist Home Mission Society;" for neglecting to report the work of the "Woman's American Baptist Home Mission Society;" also "The German Baptist Conferences, etc., etc."

Now this is a terrible arraignment. But as a matter of fact we have never heard any complaint from these Bodies, for they know that space has been offered them in our periodicals, and the "Colporter" from time to time is giving reports of their work; and in addition, the Society is sending the workers grants of Bibles, tracts and other literature as the needs of the workers prompt the appeals. Besides, in our Year Book ample space is given these Bodies, and full information is found in the Society's Year Book, which the average Baptist can procure no where else.

3. As to the charge of "sectional distinctions" in giving to the Northern Societies "three times as much space to report their work as is given to the Southern Baptist Convention," I have this to say in reply: The Society publishes *all* the matter our Southern compiler sends. The elect Southern lady who gathers the facts for us is not restricted. See Dr. Rowland's letter in this week's *Index*. Then again, let me ask you to note the receipts of the Northern Societies, and the number of workers in the different fields, as compared with the activities of the S.B.C., and you will see how natural it is to give more space where so much more is required.

And now, Miss Annie, what else? I wish we could see eye to eye. Candidly, the A.B.P. Society is the friend of the South, and of the S. B. Convention.

I have read the S.B.C. Almanac through. It is good as far as it goes, but why so narrow and exclusive. The most complete Year Book that Baptists ever saw will soon be in their hands. Every Southern State is represented, as well as Baptist interests in all the World. And this volume is published for Baptists at great loss, each year, to the Society.

Pardon this long epistle. There was much in your long and interesting communication that deserved attention, and this is the explanation of the great length of this letter.

Wishing you great prosperity in your work, I am,

Yours very truly,

O. F. Flippo

Later. I note that the *Index* this week has washed off its war paint. Its heart is better than its pen. I long to see peace in our Southern Baptist Zion.

[IMB Archives]

January 29, 1898
Dr. R. J. Willingham
Dear Brother:

I have no doubt you think I have been remiss in not sending the leaflets which you ordered more promptly, or explain why this was not done. Permit me now to make the needed explanation. I had hoped every day while Miss Heck was here—she left last night—to be able to write, but, as you can imagine, during her limited stay in Baltimore I had to give her much of my time and be with her at a number of meetings, also pay some attention to social claims which I usually disregard, so I was only able to write letters which could not be put aside. I have been in a perfect rush during the last week and am now feeling somewhat used up. I hope, though, in the course of a few days to get everything in the usual order. It passes my comprehension how you are able to entertain the no. of missionaries and others you do, and still look after the work at the office.

In regard to the leaflets, I found that of those you ordered we had not in stock as large a number of any one as you desired. I preferred to send those that you had selected rather than others, so at once gave order to the printer. He promises that one-half will be ready to ship to you on Monday and the others in the course of a few days. I will, as desired, send literature by boat.

Now in regard to two other matters. First, it gives me pleasure to enclose check for seven dollars and twenty-five cents ($7.25) and letter from an earnest worker in Indian Territory, which will explain from whence it comes, etc., etc. I do feel truly gratified to find that the efforts which I have been making for some little time past are beginning to bear fruit, and that there are now quite a number of societies in our frontier churches. Please return receipt to Mrs. N. F. Coleman, McAlister, Indian Territory, for the amount, dividing it in the way she requests.

Second, this morning's mail has brought a reply to my recent letter to Dr. O. F. Flippo. Noting that you express some curiosity as to how he would answer the one I sent him, I think you may like to see said reply, so I forward copy to you. I am not at all convinced by Dr. Flippo's logic, but I am at present feeling most too worn out to decide whether I shall call his attention to some further inaccuracies, etc., etc. I suppose you have noted Dr. Rowland's article in the *Index* of this week. If not, please look it up and see if you do not agree with me that the Secretary of the Publication Society is following in the footsteps of the brethren of the Gospel Mission in misrepresenting facts. As this letter of Dr. Flippo probably outlines the future policy of the Publication Society in regard to various matters connected with our Southern work, I think Mr. Barton may like to see it, so will you kindly hand it to him. I have not the slightest idea that Dr. Flippo expected that I would regard his letter as a personal communication, so you are at perfect liberty to give any of the facts it contains to any one to whom you wish to mention the subject.

Before closing, I want to tell you of something that I consider extremely amusing. Yesterday I had a letter from Mrs. J. D. Easterlin, Corresponding Secretary of the Central Committee of Georgia, who is a warm personal friend of Miss M. E. Wright. In it she says:

> "I understand from good authority that Mrs. (Stainback) Wilson is preparing an article to be published in the *Index,* if Dr. Bell will use it, attacking Miss Mary E. Wright because of her connection with the B.P. Soc., they having given space in their *Teacher* to the Gospel Mission Work. I hope it will not be published."

You will remember how some of us tried to prevent Miss Wright accepting the position which she now holds in connection with the Publication Society, and I judge it must be extremely annoying to her to be associated, as she now is, with Mrs. Kerr, but for Mrs. Wilson to take this opportunity to express her enmity to Miss Wright by reason of her connection with the Publication Society is supremely ridiculous. Miss Wright has not as yet written to me on the subject.

There are other matters of which I would like to speak, but time will not permit.

Very truly,
Annie W. Armstrong
[IMB Archives]

February 5, 1898
Dr. O. F. Flippo
Dear Brother:
Your long and interesting letter of January 28th came duly to hand. I had about decided, owing to extreme pressure of work that I would be impolite enough not to reply to same, but it seems to me that would hardly be courteous, after your taking so much pains to enlighten me on various phases of the subject which we have been discussing. Let me say, though, as

this will cancel my obligation and as I appreciate that you, too, are very much occupied, I will not consider it at all discourteous if you make no reply to this letter.

Now in regard to the subject upon which you have written. It appears to me that you are occupying a position so close to the luminous orb which fills your horizon—the Publication Society—that you do not see some of the fantastic (do I dare say, ridiculous) shadows that are being cast. A number of these shadows extend Southward. Permit me to introduce some of these curious figures to you by name.

1. *Phenomenal Growth.* In the Publication Society *Teacher* of January 1898, under the heading of the department: "Baptist Gospel Missions," is the following statement, made by one who supposedly knows whereof she speaks, Mrs. C. E. Kerr, Editor of *Our Missionary Helper,* "the general medium of communication between the home and the field Gospel Mission workers." She says, "The seventeen church missionaries in China—also called Gospel missionaries—are at work in Interior China."

In a communication which appears in the *Religious Herald* of February 3rd, 1898, from Dr. A. J. Rowland is the following statement:

> "Considering the fact that these people are Baptist people, and they have from twenty to twenty-five missionaries on the foreign field preaching Baptist views," etc., etc.

2. *Different light in which the Cor. Sec'y of the Publication Society, Dr. A. J. Rowland, and the District Secretary of said Society, Dr. O. F. Flippo, regard the same matter.* You will remember I suggested, in my previous letter, that the Publication Society was not reporting all the work done by Baptists in the *Teacher*, and as they were taking no notice of much older and stronger missionary organizations than the Gospel Mission, it appeared to me quite unnecessary that a department should be accorded to those who were regarded by many as doing harm rather than good. You replied as follows:

> "Permit me to note your exceptions to my statement that 'the Publication Society, through its editorial department, has always tried to give information *to* Baptists *about* Baptists throughout the world.' This remark did not apply to the *Teacher* alone, but to *all* our periodicals, of which we have nearly a score."

Dr. Rowland—I quote again from the article in this week's *Religious Herald*—says:

"We were trying to get all branches of missionary work done by Baptists reported in the *Teacher*."

3. *Fluctuations in the market.* It is clear to see that Mrs. Flippo does not relegate to you the duty of purchasing table supplies, for if that was the case, I am sure you would not have come to the conclusion you have, as stated in your letter. Permit me to quote from same.

"I have carefully read your strictures on the Chinese Market incident, but indeed, Miss Annie, I cannot see how you make out such a serious charge of falsehood and deception against that people from the market report. Markets and prices are fluctuating. I could go through this city and find great differences in prices and modes of living. Articles of food are in the comparative degree—good, better, best. I may be satisfied with the 'good,' while some one else may buy the 'better' and some the 'best.' We may quote the markets according to the prices we pay and still be on the road to heaven."

If Philadelphia prices double and triple when going from "good" to "best," we do not in Baltimore know anything of said fluctuations. If you were to reverse things and give prices on the following: sound, specked, spoiled, I could understand that there might be such changes, but we certainly do not desire our missionaries to purchase supplies of the last named variety.

This letter is already too long, but before closing, I am going to ask, should you be in Norfolk in May in attendance on the Southern Baptist Convention, that you will introduce me to those brethren to whom you refer as "sectional Baptists, or rather drivers." I had thought I was quite well acquainted—if not personally, certainly by reputation—with those who are leading our Southern Baptist host, but I have never come across any "driver" among the number and I should like to have him pointed out to me, for perhaps it would be helpful to get him (or rather, they, as you speak as if there was a number) to turn his attention to the Woman's Missionary Union. We might make more rapid progress, if there are those who possess this talent.

With kind regards to Mrs. Flippo, I am,
Very truly,
Annie W. Armstrong
[IMB Archives]

February 10, 1898
Dr. R. J. Willingham
Dear Brother:

I have not yet been able to find time to write you in regard to the Recommendations of the Foreign Board. I doubt if I have ever been under greater pressure that I am at present—we are getting out literature, etc., etc. for the Week of Self Denial, which is to be observed for the Home Board in March—so, I am forced to allow everything to wait that does not demand immediate attention. I hope to write in regard to these shortly.

My special reason for sending this letter is to ask if there is any probability of the Foreign Board making any appointment of female missionaries in the near future. There is a young lady whom I could recommend most highly that has just graduated from the Johns Hopkins Training School for Nurses. She desires to go out as a foreign missionary. While not a member of our church, she has attended there and we know of her capabilities, etc., etc. I did not want to speak to her on this subject, unless there was some possibility of the Board making new appointments before long. I am sure she would be an efficient missionary and will probably make other arrangements in the near future, hence I would ask that you let me hear from you on this point as soon as convenient.

The printer promises to have the balance of the leaflets ordered ready to send to Richmond the last of the week, so I hope to forward box in the course of the next few days.

I expect you will think I am exaggerating when I tell you my hands are more than full, and yet I have taken time to reply to Dr. Flippo's last communication. I really could not resist the temptation to call his attention to the different ways in which he and Dr. Rowland had regarded various matters. I enclose copy of my letter to Dr. Flippo, as I think possibly it may amuse you to read it. Please appreciate that Dr. Flippo is a friend of long standing and one who rather enjoys plain talking. As I told Dr. Flippo, I do not propose to continue this correspondence, for really I must not waste further in this direction.

I was truly sorry to learn that Mrs. Willingham is so far from well. I do hope you will relegate to Mr. Barton all duties that will prevent your giving the needed time to being with Mrs. Willingham until she is quite strong again. Is it not possible to get her to go with you on a little *pleasure trip*? A complete change of air and scene would, no doubt, do her an untold amount of good. Do as Mr. and Mrs. Levering did summer a year ago—take a second wedding trip.

Very truly,
Annie W. Armstrong
[IMB Archives]

As Armstrong saw it, the WMU played a vital role in assisting every facet of denominational life. Under the heading "In Union There is Strength," note Armstrong's comparison of the WMU to a hand.

1900 (?)

WOMAN'S MISSIONARY UNION
THE GENERAL ORGANIZATION OF
SOUTHERN BAPTIST WOMEN.

Annie W. Armstrong
An Auxiliary to the Southern Baptist Convention.

"Not to be ministered unto, but to minister." The central figure of the world, the greatest man, the King of Kings, our Lord and Master came not to be ministered unto, but to minister. In His incarnation, by the emptying of self, He grasped not at divine sovereignty, but service. "I am among you as one that serveth" was His testimony of Himself and as a helper of men, He went about doing good, practicing true humility and true greatness, the exemplification of His own teaching "Whosoever will be great among you, let Him be your minister and whosoever will be chief among you, let Him be your servant."

Southern Baptist women as the servants of Christ and a part of the working force of the churches, have recognized the beauty and power of serving others. That spirit which controlled the Master's life prompted them to form a General Organization for the purpose of helping the various agencies of the Southern Baptist Convention. The object of Woman's Missionary Union and that of the Boards S.B.C. is one, namely, the promotion of evangelical and educational missions. Yet, Woman's Missionary Union has chosen to occupy the position of an AUXILIARY, and has scrupulously maintained it. From the Boards, Recommendations are received each year, which after being adopted at the Annual Meeting, become the basis of effort. W.M.U. has at no time claimed or sought to exercise any rights and privileges as an independent missionary body.

Its Origin and Beginning.

For years before the formation of the General Organization, Southern Baptist women were active in Mission Work, had banded together in local Societies, and in some instances, State organizations had been brought into existence. But being very conservative in their ideas, it was not until 1887 that a general meeting was held, at Louisville, Kentucky, for the purpose of considering the formation of an organization which should embrace the whole South. As those present were not delegated by their respective States, it was finally decided that the different State Committees should be asked to appoint delegates to another meeting which should convene the next year at Richmond, Virginia. As a result, in May 1888 (during the meeting of the Southern Baptist Convention) thirty two delegates from twelve States assembled together with power to take such action as might be deemed advisable after full consultation. The representatives of ten States heartily endorsed the formation of a General Organization. Those from the other two, Virginia and Mississippi, preferred awaiting further action by their respective State Committees. In 1889, however, these two States fell into line, and by 1891, the fourteen States had become a part of the general organization. Eighteen States, including Territories and the District of Columbia, now cooperate with Woman's Missionary Union in efforts to "stimulate a missionary spirit and the grace of giving among the women and children of the churches, and aid in collecting funds for missionary purposes to be disbursed by the Boards of the Southern Baptist Convention." (Preamble to Constitution.)

In Union There Is Strength.

The hand, a beautiful place of God's mechanism, admirably constructed and adjusted to varied uses, its divisions, acting separately, yet most efficiently when harmoniously converged, is an excellent illustration of the Southern Baptist Convention in its diversified branches of Christian activities. The divisions of the right hand, beginning with the first finger, may be designated as Foreign Board, Home Board, Sunday School Board, Theological Seminary. The Foreign Board is the agent of the Convention to which is committed its work in Foreign lands. The Home Board stands in the same relation to the Convention, with our own country and Cuba as its field of operation. The Sunday School Board aids Sunday School interests, especially in providing a literature which inculcates the spirit of missions, and supplies information regarding the work as conducted by the Foreign and Home Boards, S.B.C.—separate fingers, yet most harmoniously coming to the aid of one another. The Theological Seminary in Louisville is an adjunct of the Convention by educating a ministry which will advance interest in the Convention missions. Woman's Missionary Union is placed in the thumb to express, by location, its facility beyond that of the other divisions to reach each and all of the fingers. Receiving Recommendations from the three Boards, it carries them out, advancing interests of each Board in methods best suited to its own abilities. To these three Boards, all missionary collections are forwarded by the States, as directed by the donors. This *sending of all contributions to the Boards*, the employment of no missionaries, and the payment of no salaries to officers, are the special features which differentiate Woman's Missionary Union from the other Boards S.B.C. and from many Woman's Mission Boards.

The work of Woman's Missionary Union, being also a five-fold force, may be represented by the left hand. The divisions, beginning with the thumb, being (1) an Executive Committee, located in Baltimore with marked facilities for reaching the other forces through letter, suggestions and literature; (2) State Central Committees, the general State forces guiding State affairs; (3) Woman's Mission Societies, the local organizations where suggestions from the Executive and Central Committees are carried out; (4) Bands, in which young people are trained for future usefulness, and (5) Literature, standing for information widely distributed through leaflets, magazines, weekly papers, etc.

The most cordial relationship exists between Woman's Missionary Union and the Convention Boards, one evidence of which is that its printing, postage, expressage and clerks are paid by them.

Four beneficial results have followed the plan adopted of carrying out Recommendations from the Boards: It has proven to doubters that woman's work as promoted by Southern Baptist women does not conflict with that of the churches, since it is in perfect harmony with their recognized agencies. It has been the means of raising a large amount of additional money from women and children toward the work of the Home, Foreign and Sunday School Boards. It has exerted a stimulating influence on the churches, thus increasing general contributions. It has caused W.M.U. to become a power in the educational training of young people.

Special Lines of Work.

Continued effort is made to carry out all Recommendations from the Boards, yet the special objects of work are: Christmas Offering, Frontier Boxes, Week of Self Denial, Missionary Day, and Children's Day.

Co-extensive with the existence of W.M.U. is the Christmas Offering made in behalf of the Foreign Board. In 1891 the sending of boxes of supplies to needy missionaries was begun. In 1895 the Week of Self Denial was instituted as a means of increasing moneyed contributions to the Home Board. Missionary Day was inaugurated in 1894 for the purpose of training young people in sympathy with Southern Baptist Convention work, and of increasing collections to the Foreign and Home Boards. 1898 marks the introduction of Children's Day in June, the object being to increase the Bible Fund of the Sunday School Board.

Financial Results.

The close of the first year of organized effort showed an increase in contributions of nearly ten thousand dollars over the preceding year. During a short history of twelve years from 1888 (date of organization) to 1900, Woman's Missionary Union has given towards the work of the three S.B.C. Boards ($616,238.00) six hundred and sixteen thousand, two hundred and thirty eight dollars which amount includes box valuation. Total contributions for the Conventional Year 1899 to May 1900, amounted to eighty-three thousand, two hundred and sixty-six dollars ($83,266.00) an increase of $19,154.00 over any preceding year.

The recent inauguration through W.M.U. instrumentality of an "Annuity Fund" by the Home, Foreign and Sunday School Boards is a cause of special thanksgiving.

Another Cause for Thanksgiving.

Succeeding years but increase the number of thoughtful people who appreciating the wisdom of the position taken and the good results which have followed, are now giving their support. The short life of W.M.U. may well be described in the beautiful language of Scripture which portrays the path of the just as that "which shineth more and more unto the perfect day."

[SBHLA, J. M. Frost Collection]

CHAPTER 3

"If Miss Heck will not resign I must"

Annie Armstrong and Controversy

In the late 1890s, Annie Armstrong and Fannie Heck waged a bitter battle over who controlled WMU.

Raleigh, N. C.
May 13th, 1898
My Dear Miss Armstrong:
After all our plans to the contrary, my mother and I reached home before you did. On leaving you Tuesday afternoon we went directly to Virginia Beach, but had not finished registering before a telegram calling us home on account of the sickness of our little motherless baby was handed us. Fortunately we were able to catch the first train home and were here by three the same night. The baby is better, but my own little sister, nine years old, has since our return been taken quite sick. This is we hope nothing serious.

I would like to be able to think of you as somewhat rested after the fatigues of the Union, for I remember how completely you were exhausted when I came to Baltimore after the meeting in Washington.

For myself, I was feeling so very unwell most of the time that I could hardly keep up at all. A rest, however, has set me up again.

Ever since, after great indecision, I determined to again take the office of President of the Union, if such should be the wish of the ladies, I have been thinking very much of the New Year's work.

As you know, it is impossible for me to be in Baltimore frequently, or to attend in person the meetings of the Executive Committee. To obviate in some measure the disadvantage this absence places me under in counseling with the Committee as in my office I should, I am this year going to ask you to send me, at least a week before each Executive Committee meeting, a detailed statement of all matters to be brought up at the meeting. I can thus have a day or two to think all these matters over and give my opinion in regard to each in a letter to the Executive Committee. This cannot, of course, wholly take the place of my being with you in your councils as it would be my pleasure to be, but it is the nearest substitute for it that can be made, and I shall look forward with deep interest to these monthly statements of matters to be considered by the Executive Committee, and give them prompt and earnest consideration.

Most earnestly trusting that this year may see great, very great advance in the Union's gifts and may it be the best in all of our history, I am,

Yours very truly,

Fannie E. S. Heck

Our town is literally in mourning today over the death of the first officer killed in the war—Lt. Bagley, second in command on the Winslow. His family is one of our prominent ones and he was himself an admirable young man. This, with the streets full of the State guards who are mobilizing here, bring the war very near home—nearer than even the view of the cruisers. Besides this we have a first cousin in command of one of the ships now before Havana, Captain Chadwick of the New York.

[SBHLA, J. M. Frost Collection]

May 20, 1898

My dear Miss Heck,

I have been under extreme pressure of work ever since my return from Norfolk and have now only a few moments in which to write this letter, so will ask that you excuse all seeming abruptness in immediately referring to several points in letters recently received from you and dispensing with all preliminaries. In your letter of May 13th you write:

> "As you know, it is impossible for me to be in Baltimore frequently, or to attend in person the meetings of the Executive Committee. To obviate in some measure the disadvantage this absence places me under in counseling with the Committee as in my office I should, I am this year going to ask you to send me, at least a week before each Executive Committee meeting, a detailed statement of all matters to be brought up in the meeting. I can thus have a day or two to think all these matters over and give my opinion

in regard to each in a letter to the Executive Committee. This cannot of course wholly take the place of my being with you in your councils, as it would be my pleasure to be, but it is the nearest substitute for it that can be made and I shall look forward with deep interest to these monthly statements of matters to be considered by the Executive Committee, and give them prompt and earnest consideration."

I would say, in reply to the request, that several reasons influence me in declining, which I will not take your time to state, feeling that the ground is covered in the first By-law of the Constitution, which refers to the duties of the President, last clause. It is as follows:

"In her absence, the Vice President from the State where the Committee may be located shall take her place."

As the work of the Executive Committee is to carry out the Recommendations of the Boards adopted at Annual Meeting, at any time that you desire to submit your views upon any of these lines of work, a letter from you before the monthly meeting—these are held the second Tuesday in each month, with the exception of the months of July and August—will be presented and duly considered.

I also desire to forward at this time a transcript of a portion of the Minutes of the Executive Committee meeting held May 17th—a complete copy of the Minutes will be sent later (Miss Martien has not yet furnished this)—as it is an answer to your letter of May 14th. It is as follows:

"Letter read from Miss Heck concerning preparation of programs. On motion of Miss Alice Armstrong, decided as there are four programs prepared during the year, two for Children's Work and two for Woman's Work, that Miss Heck be requested to prepare one of each kind, the Cor. Sec. to prepare the remaining two. Carried, Mrs. Lowndes dissenting.

"On motion of Mrs. Cox, the program and appeal of Woman's Work to alternate from order of last year, leaving it optional with Miss Heck in regard to which program she selects for Children's Work."

It may be well for me to mention that during the present Conventional year it will be necessary for two Children's Programs to be prepared. The one for Children's Day is printed prior to the Convention and partially distributed. The other for Missionary Day, Dr. Frost desires manuscript to be in his hands, if not before the meeting of the Convention, very soon afterwards, so you will appreciate that the preparation of the Children's Programs must come in this Conventional year, although they will not be used until next year. I will be glad to have you decide as soon as convenient, so I may know which of the Children's Programs I am to prepare.

The time which I could give to this letter is exhausted, so I must close, but not before expressing a hope that the little ones in your family have been restored to their accustomed health.

Very truly,

Annie W. Armstrong

P. S. I enclose check for ten (10) dollars for postage. Will you kindly return receipt for same, as Mrs. Lowndes has to have vouchers for all monies paid out by her, so at the last of the year, when the accounts are audited, the receipts are on file.

[SBHLA, J. M. Frost Collection]

Between 5 April and 27 May 1898, Heck wrote three letters to R. J. Willingham explaining her understanding of the role that the President of WMU played in shaping Union policy. Unfortunately for Fannie Heck, she was neither as persuasive nor as prolific as her adversary, Annie Armstrong.

Raleigh, North Carolina

April 5, 1898

Dear Dr. Willingham:

For some time I have wanted to write you in reference to the matter of which you spoke in Richmond, the difference of opinion between Miss Armstrong and myself as to the proper interpretation of the wishes of the Union in regard to making the annual contributions to the Sunday School Board. If you remember I told you I had spoken of the matter only to Mrs. Lowndes, Treasurer of the Union, who not having been at the meeting in Wilmington when the matter was discussed asked to be allowed to write of it to Mrs. W. J. Brown, vice-president of Maryland. Mrs. Brown is a relative of Miss Armstrong I think. At least a life long friend who had from the first been associated with the Executive Committee. Last year she roomed with

Miss Armstrong at Wilmington. Knew from one of my opposition to the recommendations to be brought in by the Sunday School Board and endeavored to change my opinion before the matter was brought up in the meeting. Went there prepared to oppose anything which would prevent the Union committing itself to giving a definite sum to the Sunday School Board and spoke once or twice strongly on that side, bringing out arguments of her own and supporting Miss Armstrong. I tell you this to show you how intimately she was connected with Miss Armstrong in this that you may better appreciate what she says. She wrote me after receiving Mrs. Lowndes' letter which evidently gave her a very clouded idea of the situation. I replied stating that the matter between Miss Armstrong and myself was not whether it was well to contribute to the Board or not, but whether the Union did not in the action taken mean to say that they did not wish to so contribute. My letter was a statement of what occurred at the meeting in full. Given because as I told Mrs. Brown I would value her opinion more on this matter than that of anyone else, and adding that if I was wrong I will be so glad to be set right. Mrs. Brown replied: "I agree with you in your interpretation of Mrs. Brown's letter, Mrs. J. C. Brown of Alabama since dead. Both from the impressions made on one at the time and from the wording of her motion it was evidently offered and passed from a conviction that it was unwise for the Sunday School Board to ask for money at that time, or for the ladies to endorse this request." This certainly seems very conclusive evidence that my interpretation of the wishes of the Union were correct and Miss Armstrong's were certainly not. Miss Armstrong could certainly not have said anything to Mrs. Brown at the time to lead her to think she held a different opinion. But for the future the Sunday School Board work is a recommendation on this point cautiously this year. It says: "We wish to have the Woman's Mission Societies to continue their cooperation in the advancement of our Bible work and the enlargement of our Bible fund. This work is opening beautifully and is full of possibilities. The collections from the children's day services in the second Sunday in June will be used for the distribution of the scriptures. The ladies can help us greatly in this."

In view of all the facts and interpretation put on cooperation this year it takes little insight to see that if this recommendation passes this year unchallenged it will open the door wide for unlimited urging of our limited funds next year. Already the Sunday School Board is advertising the Bible Day exercises prepared by the W. M. Union.

Dr. Frost soon after my return from Baltimore and evidently after hearing from Miss Armstrong writes of the Bible work as follows: "Our Bible work is making great advance. The requests that come to us are many. The women have been very serviceable to us in this matter and while they did not undertake to raise a sum for which I asked, yet they have carried out the spirit and even the letter of the resolution which they passed. I do not believe they have set their hands to a nobler work or one more far-reaching for the advancement of a cause and I believe as the work grows stronger through the years the future will fully justify all they have done in our behalf. I never think of this work without being grateful to them and to the Master. They have every where without hesitation taken hold of the work with real energy and helpfulness."

I do not know of course just how Dr. Frost interpreted the spirit and letter of the resolution, nor what he means by "they have everywhere taken up the work with energy." He can hardly mean the societies contributed money or that the Central Committees have urged this upon them for outside of Maryland I do not suppose that $50.00 has been contributed by the societies to this Sunday School Board. The items under this head in the quarterly reports in the *Foreign Journal* are boxes to Sunday School missionaries in almost every case I think. But I am writing too fully what I wish to say is this of the report of state secretaries to be rendered to the Union Miss Armstrong says under the heading "What Shall be Reported" and (?) "For Sunday School Board money contributed to the Bible Fund and valuable boxes sent to Sunday School missionary." This letter is a copy of one to be sent to all the state treasurers if I am not mistaken. By it I consider Miss Armstrong has relieved me of all further responsibility of bringing this matter to the attention of the ladies. She has clearly stated her belief that the Union was to give to the Bible fund. These ladies are well posted on the work of the Union. I have no wish to impose my views on them against their own will. It seems to me clear that my course is to let the matter rest here. If the position Miss Armstrong has taken is challenged be ready to say it was not mine, but if the lady is willing with this clear light before them to let matters stand as they are I have no right to suppose as their presiding officer that they do not know what they are about. Have I? This is as it seems to me after much earnest thought. Do you think I am right or wrong?

I am sorry to have trespassed so long on your time.

Yours very truly,

Fannie E. S. Heck.

I am sure Mrs. Brown would state her opinion if asked for it, but would not like to have her letter to me quoted.
[SBHLA, Una Roberts Lawrence Collection]

Raleigh, North Carolina
May 25, 1898
Dear Dr. Willingham:
I am sorry to be forced to write you again real soon of Union matters but the enclosed letters will explain the necessity. You will remember that in Norfolk I told you I should ask Miss Armstrong to send me each month a week or more before the Executive Committee Meeting a statement of the matters to be brought up there that I might think the matters over and send a letter to the Committee giving my opinion on the matters to be discussed. My position as president of the Union it was my privilege to do. As you have always expressed your belief that the office of president of the Union was analogous to that of the president of the Foreign Mission Board you will be more than astonished at Miss Armstrong's reply to this request. Will you kindly lay this aside now and read first my letter and then her astonishing reply. Having read these letters you will naturally ask, what course of action I will pursue. Two courses are open to me, one wrong and the other right.

The former which I cannot doubt is the one which Miss Armstrong wishes me to pursue is to resign as President of the Union, without stating reasons leaving work entirely under her control.

The right course and the one I shall pursue is to have decided once and for all what is the position of the president of the Woman's Missionary Union. This is my unquestionable duty not only to myself and the one less than three weeks pledged to fill this office for a year to the Union and to those who in all future times shall hold the office I am now so unfortunate to occupy.

If the necessity of this decision shall lead to discussion of an unpleasant nature none will regret it more than I, but the call for such decision has been brought on by no fault of mine but by the simple discharge of what I know to be the right and duty of the office given me. Of course I shall not for a moment entertain the interpretation put upon the constitution by Miss Armstrong, namely that during my absence from Baltimore the President of the Union is not the president though elected to that office by the entire body, but that the vice-president of Maryland nominated by the Maryland delegation for that office is president. That while I stand before the world as president and am responsible for the act of the Executive Committee of the body I am and have become for eleven months of the year (having as typical met the Executive Committee once a year) only as private member of the Union having no privilege greater than any one of them to write to the Executive Committee on lines of work already adopted, or have my letters read there. But copies of the minutes of the Executive Committee are sent to me only by the courtesy of that body by way of information of acts passed of which I have no previous right to be informed that that committee not only controls all matters under the direction of the Corresponding Secretary but also virtually names the chief officer of the Union, the one who shall be the vice-president from Maryland being decided in the committee before each annual meeting of the Union. Such an interpretation would I know shock beyond measure the sense of the Union, but even were they to acquiesce in it I would not for a moment fill so false a position having the name of president of a body when having absolutely no voice in its favor. To leave matters in its present shape would be an injury to the Union, for it would be to decide for all future time that all power and management and control of all Union matters resided in the Executive Committee located in Baltimore. A Committee self-perpetuating virtually and also electing the chief officer of the Union. Being president this year I have used the personal pronoun, but only as a representative of the office held. The question effects years long after these few months I shall hold the position, if indeed I hold it more than a few weeks. But having arisen it must be settled now.

What I intend to do is this. I shall write to each member of the Executive Committee stating the question that has arisen between Miss Armstrong and myself and ask the vice-president Mrs. Graves who I am persuaded has not the slightest thought of such a meaning attaching to her office to bring the matter up for final discussion in the Executive Committee meeting of June, Tuesday 14.

If the majority of the committee then decides that Miss Armstrong is right in her interpretation of the constitution or in other words that the president is to know and has no right to know of the proposed action of the committee the governing body of the Union except through the courtesy of the Corresponding Secretary, or in still other words if they shall not request Miss Armstrong to send me the statement asked for with the view of receiving and considering my opinion at the time of action I shall at once resign my nominal position stating to all who have a right to know the Central Committee that I resign thus speedily after my acceptance of election because it is impossible for me to hold the position of president in a body where by action of the Executive Committee my absence from the seat of action makes this office one in name only.

I cannot express to you the pain this necessity for such action causes, but such is my deliberate decision. Though this step on Miss Armstrong's part is but the culmination of a long, long course of disregard for the views of the president. I shall bring in no harshness to the discussion. The question must be decided on its merit. So you can understand that the chances for a fair hearing of my side are small when all the ladies to decide are almost strangers to me and will be unable thus under the immediate influence of Miss Armstrong and her sister at the time of decision. I am aware that you may say that only the Union in full session has the right to decide the duties of its own officers. To refer to them the question in its present personal bearing would create such a division and so cripple the work that I would much rather take the unfair hearing before the Executive Committee and bear the consequence,—the consequent misrepresentation before the workers at large.

You may say also write to Miss Armstrong of the course you will pursue. If she persists in her refusal. Do you think, knowing her as you do, that this would have any effect other than to cause her to overawe the committee with a threat to resign and the care of the whole work if her will is disputed, a threat she has used in time past on one or more occasion. I doubt not the same threat will be used now and will in the end accomplish the end she wishes, but I shall still use my rights to appeal to the committee. Only their decision can give me a legitimate reason in the eyes of the Union, which has just elected me, to resign and leave them without the highest officer as they suppose for the year.

Though I of course understand that you would prefer to having nothing to say in Union matters if for the sake of the Union work you have any counsel to give me I shall be most happy to receive it. I must however be frank to say that I can see but one course to pursue—to delay or dally with the issue I hold now would be false and cowardly. It would lead Miss Armstrong to see the false position she has taken and to retreat the interpretation put upon the constitution and her consequent refusal I shall be glad to have the matter go no further, but I know of no friend who will undertake this and nothing short of the definition of the president's office such as the agreement to send the statement asked for by me will be accepted.

I shall wait a few days to hear from you before writing members of the Executive Committee. With sincere desire for your counsel I am

Yours very truly,

Fannie E. S. Heck

Will you kindly send me list of missionaries children that this work may be gotten under way?

[SBHLA, Una Roberts Lawrence Collection]

Raleigh, N. C.

May 27, 1898

Dear Dr. Willingham:

You letter of the 26th has been received and I will write you of the matter under discussion later.

For the present I only wish to say that I would not wish Miss Armstrong to know the contents of my letter to you for the present or indeed anything further of my position in the matter then that I have written you in reference to it.

There is one question I would be very glad to have you answer if you can do so consistently with the course you deem best. Did Miss Armstrong tell you of her letter to me before or after it had been mailed? Your presence in Baltimore and this letter are so nearly so coincident that I cannot tell. Believe me.

Yours very sincerely,

Fannie E. S. Heck

[SBHLA, Una Roberts Lawrence Collection]

EXTRACTS FROM MINUTES OF EXECUTIVE COMMITTEE
MEETING OF WOMAN'S MISSIONARY UNION, HELD
JUNE 14, 1898

On motion of Miss A. W. Armstrong the regular order of business was set aside, to consider the question brought up by Miss Heck.

Cor. Sec. read portion of correspondence between Miss Heck and herself of May 13th & 20th.

Miss Armstrong gave her reasons for declining to grant Miss Heck's request, and read 1st By-law of Constitution.

Letter from Miss Heck to Mrs. Graves read by Rec. Sec.

Miss A. W. Armstrong gave her reasons for considering a resignation at last Annual Meeting, and read the correspondence between herself and

Judge Haralson. She also gave some items in connection with the framing of the Constitution.

Prayer by Mrs. Graves.

Mrs. Nimmo made the following motion:

As a difference of opinion had arisen between the President and Corresponding Secretary W.M.U. concerning the last clause of Art. 1, By-laws of Constitution W.M.U., I offer as a motion that the matter be referred back to W.M.U. to be considered at next Annual Session; they having adopted the Constitution can better interpret its meaning and spirit.

Motion seconded.

As a substitute for this Miss Alice Armstrong offered the following, which was carried after discussion:

That in view of difference of opinion between the Pres. and Cor. Sec. in construing the Constitution, the Executive Committee is unwilling to come to any conclusion until an expert decision shall be rendered by Judge Haralson.

RESOLVED that the whole matter lie on the table till September, at which time it is hoped that the Committee will be in the city and the decision duly considered.

[SBHLA, J. M. Frost Collection]

June 30, 1898

Judge J. Haralson

Dear Brother:

Again I am going to trespass on your friendly interest in Woman's Missionary Union to ask your legal opinion on a point in question. I will be as brief as possible, though I am forced to give the facts for a clear understanding of the case.

The matter I submitted to you last spring on the proper construction of Dr. Frost's recommendation to W.M.U. in reference to his call for moneyed assistance for Bible work was an issue made by Miss F. E. S. Heck, Pres. W.M.U. I did not state the name at the time, though I am now forced to do so. Her direct charge against me was that of enforcing my wishes about the recommendation against the decision of the body. That this was entirely erroneous was proved (1) by moneyed contributions having been made for the Bible Fund; (2) by no objection being raised at the Annual Meeting; and (3) by a recommendation of precisely the same wording being passed at the meeting in Norfolk. In the face of these confirmations of error on Miss

Heck's part, she has failed to make the slightest reparation to me of what she knew I regarded as a fundamental thrust at my trust-worthiness to be Secretary. Of necessity this conduct has strained relations between us.

Directly after her return to Raleigh from Norfolk, May 13, I received the following letter from her, (copy A) the gist of which is that she requests me to send her "at least a week before each Executive Committee meeting, a *detailed statement of all matters to be brought up at the meeting.*" (Italics mine).

This unprecedented request in ten years' history—probably unprecedented in any history of similar organization—and in view of existing relations, together with (1) the enormous work entailed in complying; (2) the impossibility of keeping things up to date by closing business "a week before each meeting;" (3) the possible unwisdom of opinions formulated under such disadvantages; (4) the confusion resulting in the meetings from deference to advice thus formulated; and finally and covering all, (5) that the constitution neither required it of the Secretary, nor sustained the President in the request. For all of the above reasons I declined May 30, advancing only the last (no. 5). See copy B.

To June 13, I received no further communication. On that day, the day preceding the monthly Board meeting, I received a notice from Miss Heck (see copy C) that she had referred the question at issue to the Executive Committee at its next session. I enclose her communication, with Constitution and By-laws. (See copy D).

This communication was read before the Executive Committee, June 14, *each member, save myself, having already received a copy* from Miss Heck. In order to a proper understanding of the present relations, I then, *for the first time*, except to my sister and the Vice President, made known to the ladies the charge brought against my stewardship by Miss Heck, last winter. The *whole* question was thus open for consideration.

My refusal of Miss Heck's astonishing request for "a detailed statement, etc.," was based upon *my* construction of the last clause of By-law 1. This construction is the basis of Miss Heck's eleven rejoinders in her communication to the Ex. Com., whom she asks to decide the case, and if adversely, she will throw the discussion of the matter into the annual meeting.

The Ex. Com. was unwilling to decide—in fact was unable to decide intelligently—until an expert opinion of the proper construction of By-law 1, last clause, could be had. They referred the matter to you, laying Miss Heck's communication on the table till your decision could be had.

May I summarize the points upon which we would be glad to have your decision:

1. The last clause of By-law 1: "In her absence, the Vice President from the State where the Committee may be located shall take her place"—Does this not mean that duties, responsibilities and prerogatives of absent President pertain to said Vice President in other ways than *presiding* at monthly and annual meetings?

2. Does the Constitution sustain an absent President in making the request for a detailed statement of all matters to be brought up at an Ex. Com. meeting, at least a week in advance?

3. Does the Constitution require this service of a Cor. Secretary?

4. Through whom does custom, courtesy and parliamentary law require an official communication to be sent to an Executive body?

5. Is it customary, proper, or fair to send a copy of charges against a fellow officer, to every member of a body, omitting that officer, asking the members to sit in judgment upon the charges?

We have reached a delicate and dangerous place. We need your wisdom and experience; we need Divine aid.

Asking that you will let me hear from you as soon as convenient, I am,

Very truly,

Annie W. Armstrong

Cor. Sec. W.M.U.

P. S. Permit me to call your attention to the fact that when Miss Heck forwarded her communication to the different members of the Executive Committee, and at the same time included copy of the letter she wrote to the Cor. Sec'y May 13 and reply to same, while she gave her letter in full, she only sent a portion of my reply, written May 20. In submitting documentary evidence, is that permissible? For full text of my letter, see copy B. I forward copy of Constitution and By-laws.

[SBHLA, J. M. Frost Collection]

Montgomery, Ala.
July 5th, 1898

Miss Annie W. Armstrong
Cor. Sec. W.M.U.
Dear Sister:

This is in reply to your letter of the 30th ult., communicating to me the resolution of the Executive Committee of the W.M.U., adopted at the meeting of the 14th of June, 1898, calling for my construction of the last clause of Art. 1 of the By-laws of the Association, which reads:

> "In her (the president's) absence the Vice President from the State where the Committee may be located, shall take her place."

This question seems to me to be easy reply. Art. 1 of By-laws defines the duties of the president of the Association to be:

1. To preside "at annual meeting of the Woman's Missionary Union."

2. To preside at "all meetings of the Executive Committee."

3. To appoint "all committees not otherwise provided for" (This would include committees appointed at the annual meetings, as well as at the meetings of the Executive Committee, if any should be needed to be appointed.)

4. To be and act as a member of all standing committees "of the Union," appointed at the annual meetings. The Executive Committee, I take it, has no standing committees. The president is a member of such committees, *ex officio*, and acts as any other member, with same rights and privileges, and no more. Her duties as president of the Union, do not accompany her into a standing committee meeting. Membership of such committees is alone conferred on her, by virtue of her office as president.

5. To call, "through the Recording Secretary," meetings of The Executive Committee, when in her judgment needful, or, at the request of five members of the Executive Committee."

These enumerations comprehend all the presented duties of the president. It will be seen that the By-laws alone define the duties of the president. The Constitution, Art. III, creates the office of president, and the other offices of the Union, but does not prescribe their duties.

If the By-laws had not prescribed those duties, the president would have been endowed with the discharge of such duties as generally appertain to the office of president of such bodies, under general parliamentary law, and these would have been to preside at the meetings of the Union, preserve order and govern the body according to accepted parliamentary rules.

But the By-laws of the Union define the duties of president, and these are the ones, therefore, she is to perform.

The office of a vice president from each State, is created by Art. III of the Constitution, and the duties of these officers are prescribed in Arts. 1 and 2 of the By-laws. By Art. 1 it is provided, that in the absence of the president, "the vice president from the State where the Committee may be located shall take her place;" and by Art. 2, that "the vice presidents shall be considered as an advisory board of the Executive Committee, who are entitled, when present, to vote at its sessions."

If the president of the union is absent, at the annual meeting, it would not be seriously contended, that a vice president would not be the proper party to call to the chair, to organize the meeting; and this would come from general parliamentary practice, and not because the Constitution in terms so declares. But in the absence of the president, at an Executive Committee meeting, the Constitution declares who shall preside. It is the vice president from the State where the Committee may be located. If she were also absent, then, if another vice president were present, I would say, from implication and propriety, that she ought to preside; and if no vice president should be present, then the Committee should select one of their own number to do so.

The term, "shall take her place," as employed in the closing sentence of Art. 1 by By-laws, means, take the place of the president, *for the time*, to do any and all things the president as such might or could do, if present. As president *pro tem*, she would preside with the same powers and duties attaching to her temporary incumbency, as if she were president, and would be entitled, under Art. 2 of By-laws, to vote notwithstanding she presided. In all this there is no unauthorized displacement of, or interference with the presidential office, or with the responsibilities and prerogatives of the absent president. In other words, there is no official antagonism thus created. It comes about as matter necessity and propriety.

If the president of the S.B. Convention were absent at any annual meeting, a vice president takes his place, to perform such duties as the president would perform, if present.

The duties of the Corresponding Secretary are prescribed by Art. 3, of By-laws. Unless some duties were prescribed for her, it would be uncertain, at least, what duties she should perform. Her duties having been definitely prescribed by law, except such as are prescribed.

I find nothing in the Constitution or By-laws which would make it incumbent on the Corresponding Secretary to furnish the President, a week, or at any other time beforehand a detailed statement of all matters to be brought up at an Executive Committee meeting. She might not know all that would be brought up; and if she did, as stated, her prescribed duties do not embrace such a duty. If she complies with a request of this kind from the president, it would be by the way of courtesy, and should be accepted as such.

Let me add, that from the correspondence submitted to me, it is evident that relations between the president and corresponding secretary have become strained and embarrassing, and that, not about "the weightier matter of the law." I beg to suggest, if allowed, that all else except these weightier matters should be passed over, for the good and glory of the great cause for which they both are so zealously and effectively devoting their valuable lives. May the Spirit of Christ rule in their minds and hearts, to the end, that a spirit of love, forbearance and accommodation may prevail, and all else pushed aside, that the good work may go along, even more prosperously than heretofore.

Faithfully,

Jon' Haralson

As Miss Heck has written to me about these same matters, to which I replied substantially, in construction of the duties of the president, as above, I deem it respectful to her, to send her a copy of the above letter to you, which I do by this day's mail.

[SBHLA, J. M. Frost Collection]

In spite of Judge Haralson's admonition that both parties should settle their differences amicably, Armstrong freely expressed her sentiments about Fannie Heck to Southern Baptist agency leaders like I. T. Tichenor, J. M. Frost, and R. J. Willingham. As the following letters suggest, Armstrong was a worthy adversary who selected her allies carefully.

Armstrong did not correspond with Tichenor as frequently as Frost and Willingham regarding Fannie Heck. Nevertheless, her letter dated 8 April 1899 scarcely concealed her annoyance with Heck's leadership of WMU.

April 8th, 1899

Dr. I. T. Tichenor

Dear Brother:

Appreciating that your hands are very, very full, I dislike extremely adding to your work in any direction, but I really do not know what to do, so am going to ask that you will kindly allow me to state what is now disturbing me, and that you will then suggest what I ought to do under the circumstances.

In January I wrote to Miss Heck, as President of the Woman's Missionary Union, prior to any arrangements being made in regard to the Annual Meeting, to know if she desired to make any suggestions as to program, etc., etc. She made no reply whatever to that letter. Each month, after the Executive Committee meeting, I have sent Miss Heck a copy of the "Minutes," so in this way she knows exactly what has been done by the Executive Committee. Not once during the course of the year has Miss Heck made the slightest acknowledgement of receiving the "Minutes," or expressed an opinion of any action taken by the Executive Committee.

In the paper which the Secretaries of the Boards presented to Miss Heck and myself, and which we both signed, is the following:

"We also agree with Judge Haralson's position what when a Vice-President acts for the President in her absence is only for the time and occasion. She does not continue to act as President after adjournment of the meeting at which she presides for and in place of the President."

Although Miss Heck has acted in the discourteous way she has, I was determined that I would, for her remaining term of office, accord to Miss Heck every iota that was due her in the position she holds, so I wrote her March 28th, the letter, of which I enclose copy. Miss Heck has not seen fit to make any reply to this communication.

I now want to ask what should be done in regard to calling the Executive Committee session. In previous years I sent the notices out to the members, as I was doing all the corresponding that was required for the Annual Meeting. It was not thought for one instant, as far as I knew, that I was infringing on the President's prerogative, as the Executive Committee session prior to the Annual Meeting, seemed necessary, in order to make final arrangements for said meeting. The first by-law of the constitution reads:

"The President shall preside at the annual meeting of the Woman's Missionary Union and all meetings of the Executive

Committee; shall appoint all committees not otherwise provided for; shall organize new societies; and shall be, ex-officio, member of all standing committees. She may, through the Recording Secretary, call special meetings of the Executive Committee, when in her judgment needful, or at the request of five members of the Executive Committee. In her absence, the Vice-President from the State where the committee may be located shall take her place."

If Miss Heck continues silent in regard to the Executive Committee meeting, do you think it would be better for me to refer this matter to the Vice-President from Maryland, and ask her to call the Executive Committee meeting, or shall I go forward, as in previous years, sending out notices, or, would it be better to omit the meeting altogether? The latter course would cause much comment and retard business very materially during our Annual Meeting. Kindly let me hear from you on this point as soon as convenient.

Very truly,
Annie W. Armstrong
[IMB Archives]

Armstrong may have seen R. J. Willingham as her closest ally in her battle against Fannie Heck.

June 22, 1898
Dr. R. J. Willingham
Dear Brother:
By express today, expressage prepaid, I send you the balance of the leaflets ordered, "Christ and Mexico." You will recall you ordered 3,000. 1,000 copies were sent to Richmond with Dr. Dill's leaflet. In package you will find 1,250—the balance (750 or one-fourth of the entire order) I have reserved for distribution through Woman's Missionary Societies.

As you did not seem anxious to accede to the proposition which I made to represent Woman's Missionary Union at the Conference in New York, I have, after consultation with Mrs. Wm. Graves, Vice President, decided to notify the Committee that we must decline to appoint speakers at said Conference. As the Woman's Missionary Union does not hold mixed meetings and as we learn this is the custom of the Conference, we cannot invite any of our workers to do this service. I of course will try to word my letter as courteously as possible, but I think it better to give our real reason for declining.

I will be obliged if you will send me a number of copies of the leaflet, "Plain Questions Answered as to the Foreign Mission Work," also any others you may have for distribution. I have been trying to furnish the different Central Committees with literature and find that our old stock now needs replenishing.

Now for two or three items of news.

1. My brother-in-law, Eugene Levering, informed me several days ago that he had had a visit from Rev. W. D. Powell and wanted to know if I had seen him. I told him he had not called at the Mission Rooms. Mr. Levering seemed a little curious to know how far I was posted as to the recent troubles in Mexico and Cuba. I appreciated that nothing would be gained by discussion of these, so, much to his surprise, I told him I preferred not to say anything on the subject. This prevented my obtaining any information from Mr. Levering as to the way Mr. Powell explained matters. Eugene stated that Mr. Powell was on his way to the Publication Society, the mecca of all—I do not recall the word he used, so can only give you the impression I have—disappointed Baptists, and that he had been offered several positions by said Society. I am sorry to find that the troubles in Mexico seem to be known in Baltimore, for on Monday two of the ministers referred to them in conversations I had with them. I suppose, though, we have to expect this, as Mr. McCormick has relatives in Baltimore.

2. It is probable Dr. Tichenor will be in Baltimore in the course of a few days. Miss Heck has been acting in such a strange way—calculated to do so much harm—that I must have the benefit of someone's advice and counsel on whose judgment I can rely. As I told you when in Baltimore, I was unwilling to let others know how badly (I consider) Miss Heck acted last year and of her late unreasonable request. Miss Heck, however, since then has made it impossible for me to keep silent. As the work of the Woman's Missionary Union is so intimately connected with that of the Boards, I am sure it is better for me to turn to one of the Secretaries of the Boards for this counsel than to anyone else. This I purpose doing. I thought it wiser to see Dr. Tichenor, rather than to write to him on the subject, so he has very kindly acceded to the request which I made for him to come to Baltimore. I am ready and willing to give you now, or at any time, any information you desire in regard to this matter, but I do not purpose forcing it upon you. If you wish to be posted as to what has occurred, let me know and I will send you the needed information, also any later developments. The whole subject to me is intensely disagreeable and I can appreciate how others may prefer not to know of it, so I shall understand, if you do not refer

to this matter in your next letter, that it is your preference not to know anything more of it.

I am glad to say we are getting on satisfactorily with the work of sending packages to pastors. As there are nine different publications in each package, it takes some time to handle these, but we have already put up over 4,000 and I think there is no question but that the entire number will be mailed before the close of the week. I am anxious to get these off as soon as possible, as there is other work I want to take up.

Very truly,
Annie W. Armstrong
[IMB Archives]

July 22, 1898
Dr. R. J. Willingham
Dear Brother:

The letter written July 8th from Montgomery, Ala., signed by the Secretaries of the three Boards, S.B.C., came duly to hand. It would have had a more prompt reply, but I was informed of your continued absence from Richmond, and as the request was made for replies to be mailed to you, I delayed sending this letter until your return to Richmond.

In compliance with the expressed wish of the Secretaries of the three Boards, S.B.C., after referring the matter to Judge Haralson, President of the Convention, who signified his approval, I would say that I accede to the request to meet Miss F. E. S. Heck, President of the Woman's Missionary Union, with the Secretaries of the three Boards and Judge Haralson ("if his engagements will permit"), in order that the "differences that have arisen" between the President and Secretary of Woman's Missionary Union may be duly considered.

I would respectfully suggest that Washington, D.C., be the place appointed for the meeting and the date named be as early as possible. I appreciate that a more central point for place of meeting will be desired by the majority of those who will attend the Conference, but, under existing circumstances, my mother's feeble health, I have to make this request which I do, for if my presence at the Conference is thought to be necessary, I will have to ask that it be held at some point near Baltimore, so I may be able to reach home in a short time if I am there required.

Very truly,
Annie W. Armstrong

Cor. Sec'y W.M.U.

ADDITIONAL. In notifying you of my willingness to attend the Conference which the Secretaries of the Boards have thought wise to call, I must be allowed to make a request. It is that during said Conference all complimentary expressions, or words of appreciation, in regard to the work that may have been done by either the President or Secretary of the Woman's Missionary Union will be dispensed with by those who have called this conference. What is involved is of so grave a nature, that I am sure it ought to be met without any effort on the part of any one present to make persons feel elated. If God has used any of us as instruments to accomplish anything in the advancement of His cause, to Him be the honor and not to the one He has used. Then again, you have not the slightest idea how much trouble Miss Heck's actions have already caused in Baltimore. Two members of the Executive Committee were at the Rooms several days since and told me that it had meant to them many sleepless nights. I am sure the question ought to be considered in a most serious way. *I* am not prepared to regard it in any other light.

Dr. Frost writes: "I think the Lord is guiding in the matter and we must keep ourselves open and subject to Him." I think I do see God's hand in the way He is showing some of us what ought to be done under existing circumstances, but I fail entirely to see any sign of God's hand in what has occurred. I trust He will overrule it for good, but it seems to me the thing itself has been prompted and directed solely by Satan. I would say before closing that Sister Alice advised that I would not consent to be at the Conference which is proposed to be held; that I had placed in the hands of Judge Haralson and the Secretaries of the Boards the facts, and so I was not called on to undergo any further physical strain in this direction. I appreciate, though, there may be some points made by Miss Heck which have not already been covered, and also I feel in a measure obligated to do as Dr. Tichenor and the other Secretaries ask, having put the matter in Dr. Tichenor's hands, so that reason, unless providentially prevented, I will be at the Conference which I sincerely hope will be held as soon as possible, for I do want to have things settled.

A. W. A.

[IMB Archives]

Feb. 6th, 1899 [It is possible that this letter could be dated March 6th, 1899 and not February 6th. The Nashville Collection contains a typescript of the same letter that is dated March 6th, 1899 but the letter is obviously incomplete and was not reproduced on W.M.U. letterhead.]

Dr. R. J. Willingham

Dear Brother:

I have a most unpleasant duty to perform; but as it appears to me to be a duty, I will perform it.

While not included in the written agreement signed by Miss Heck and myself in Norfolk, it was verbally stated by Miss Heck that she would decline re-election to the presidency of W.M.U. and let her determination be known by March 1. She has not fulfilled her promise.

By today's mail a letter from her informs me that she intends going to Louisville. Here is the statement: "I do not know of any one from the State, beside myself, who expects to be present." This announcement in connection with Miss Heck's unfilled promise and all the history lying back of it has led to make a decision. I do not intend to go to Louisville. Under the very strained relations existing between us, I am unwilling to be thrown with her during an annual meeting, as my office requires. Nor do I feel it prudent to tax my nervous energies in this association.

As the President's election precedes the Secretary's, I will have a letter in the hands of some trusted agent in Louisville declining re-election as Secretary if Miss Heck accepts election as President.

I have plainly stated my ultimatum because I wish you, Dr. Tichenor and Dr. Frost to know my purpose beforehand. As you have been the channel of correspondence with Miss Heck in these matters, you are entirely at liberty to communicate my decision to her so that, as presiding officer, she may make arrangements accordingly. If she does not learn my intention at this time, I shall let her know later. At the W.M.U. Ex. Com. meeting on next Tuesday I will inform the ladies of my purpose.

Of course, all arrangements for the meeting at Louisville will be made by me with the usual care, that the work may not suffer loss. Every thing will be in readiness to hand over to my successor.

Very truly,

Annie W. Armstrong

Additional.

Executive Committee Recommendations for 1899. It occurred to me that it would prove helpful if this year, after the recommendations of each Board were presented and adopted, we would in recommendations from the Executive Committee show the ladies *how* the work could be done. I now send you those that have been prepared in connection with the ones that the

Foreign Board have offered. May I ask that you will read these quite critically and let me have your opinion of them, returning the copy which I now send? They have not yet been submitted to the Executive Committee, so changes can readily be made.

Before closing I want to say I sincerely trust you will not misunderstand my motive in taking the position which I have in regard to attending the Annual Meeting in Louisville, etc., etc. As I see things this seems to me to be the best way to prevent trouble in the future.

A. W. A.

[IMB Archives]

February 7, 1899
Dr. R. J. Willingham
Dear Brother:

Your letter of Feb. 6th received this A. M. I have been under so much pressure today—two meetings, one of the Foreign Mission Society this morning, and this afternoon, an Executive Committee meeting of the Woman's Interdenominational Missionary Union of Maryland—that I have not been able to write the letter I wished to send you before you left for your Southern trip. In a few moments we must close the Mission Rooms, so I can only send a few lines.

As you are going from point to point, I desire to furnish you with facts concerning the aggressiveness of the Mormons which have lately so impressed me. In order that you may know just what we have recently done, I send you copy of a letter (the one to Miss Coker) which I have mailed to the officers of the Central Committees, another to pastors in Maryland, with resolutions passed at a Quarterly Meeting of the Woman's Baptist Home Mission Society of Maryland, and a third to one of the Congressmen-elect from Maryland. I also send a printed document gotten out by the Presbyterian Board of Home Missions. These various papers will give you largely the facts. May I ask for them a careful reading, and when you have opportunity that you will aid in the effort we are making to get the ladies to appreciate how Mormonism is spreading.

You did not mention in your letter when you expected to return to Richmond. I sincerely hope you will be back by the first of March. You will remember that is the time appointed by Miss Heck when she was to make her decision public. As yet, she has said nothing whatever to me on the subject. In a recent communication from her that was published in a South

Carolina paper, she spoke as if her purpose was to go to Louisville in May. You will remember you told me that if I heard nothing from Miss Heck, after allowing five or six days to elapse beyond the time appointed by her, if I would notify you, you would write to her. It is *absolutely* necessary that our workers in the different States have due notice given of any proposed changes,* so that is the reason I feel anxious to know whether you will be in Richmond the first of March.

Hoping you will have a pleasant and successful trip South, I am,

Very truly,

Annie W. Armstrong

P. S. I wish I had time to give you some encouraging items that have recently come to me. The Christmas Offering in one church in Louisiana was one hundred (100) dollars.

[Handwritten insert]

*If Miss Heck will not resign I *must*.

[IMB Archives]

July 27, 1899

Dr. R. J. Willingham

Dear Brother:

Sometimes one feels too keenly in regard to a matter to trust one's judgment; so, I am going to ask that you will kindly advise me what to do under existing circumstances. This morning's mail has brought a letter from Mrs. Stakely, and one that she enclosed from Miss Heck. Kindly read said letters.

As to Miss Heck's sending letters to state papers from missionaries in previous years: This was altogether superfluous, for, as Corresponding Secretary, I *always* have in hand more letters from missionaries than can be utilized in this way, and, as you will appreciate, it is the duty of the Corresponding Secretary, (What would you think of Prof. Winston's taking this part of your work on himself?) and not of the President, to do this kind of work. I, however, during Miss Heck's term of office, allowed her in this instance, as well as in many others, to ignore the rights of the Corresponding Secretary. I think you will agree with me that it is quite a strange piece of business for Miss Heck, who is now simply a State Vice-President, to have had copies made of these letters for distribution before consulting either President or the Corresponding Secretary whether this was desired. As I wrote you yesterday, I am now having a tremendous piece of work done in this line, having copies made of *six* letters to send to District Vice-Presidents in all of the States to be used at District Associational Meetings, when Central Committees desire them. I have not in any way, shape or form intimated to Mrs. Stakely that there was any trouble between Miss Heck and myself, but I really do think that Miss Heck is going beyond proper bounds in this instance, and I expect this is only a beginning. I sincerely trust I may never have to meet any one else who so perfectly disregards the rights of others as does Miss Heck.

This morning's mail has brought a letter from some one else who is not feeling very tranquil. Thinking perhaps you may be able to pour oil on the troubled waters in that direction also, I will ask you to read the letter which I forward from Mrs. Gwathmey. Unless providentially prevented, I shall attend the Annual Meeting of the Woman's Mission Societies of Virginia at Salem, as perhaps I can be of service,—that is, if Miss Heck is not present.

I am about writing to Dr. Barton, as I want to send him a "revise" of his leaflet on China. I will, in that letter, enclose two, which I will ask that he hand to you, as I think you may like to have the information they contain. Please appreciate that I commenced sending letters in regard to Home Board changes to Dr. Barton rather in the way of a joke, as you had said you did not care to be entrusted with "secrets," and I did not know just at what point to stop. *Of course*, there is nothing that I would say to Dr. Barton, that I would not be more than willing to say to you if you were ready to listen to me.

Very truly,
Annie W. Armstrong

P. S. This morning's mail has brought a letter from Rev. L. G. Jordan, of the National Baptist Convention. Our colored brother shows a good deal of enterprise. In proof of it, I send a map which he forwarded in his letter. I think you will agree with me that he has put his work before the people quite well in this publication.

P. S. No. 2. You will appreciate, of course, that the letters Miss Heck expects Mrs. Stakely to send out are letters that have been written to her and will be so addressed.

[IMB Archives]

Armstrong kept J. M. Frost abreast of her dealings with Heck.

January 24, 1898
Dr. J. M. Frost

Dear Brother:

I had the Stenographer to come to the house this afternoon, as I hoped to be free from interruptions to answer a large number of letters, as this morning had to be given to Miss Heck at the Mission Rooms. Three visitors have claimed my attention, so now I am in a "rush," as I have invited a number of ladies to meet Miss Heck at tea and I must shortly attend to some domestic duties. You will, under these circumstances, I am sure, excuse all want of clearness. Now to business.

1. *Request from Louisiana.* Today's mail has brought a letter from Mrs. P. Lyle, Cor. Sec'y of the Central Committee of Louisiana, 1036 Marengo St., New Orleans. She writes:

> "Miss Annie, does the Sunday School Board send out Testaments in French and German? I want 50 of each to scatter in our slums. Down at St. Roch's the German Protestants are worshipping St. R. A German woman told me the other day that she would not pray to any other saint because she was a Protestant, but she was *bound* to pray to St. R., because she *knew* he had cured her from 'Rheumatiz.'"

I do hope you will send Mrs. Lyle the Testaments for which she has asked, as she is an earnest worker, but not gifted with a great deal of prudence, so I think it would be wise to grant her request. I replied to her as follows:

> Yes, the Sunday School Board does make grants of Testaments and Bibles. By this mail I will write to Dr. J. M. Frost, Cor. Sec., asking that he would send you 50 copies each of German and French Testaments. I am quite sure he will grant this request. There may be a little delay in your receiving same, as I do not know whether he has in Nashville copies of French and German Testaments, so he may have to order them, but I think I can promise that you will receive them.

2. *Louisiana missionaries.* Did you note how very far from clear is the statement made by our Brother Ware? He writes:

> "We have now in the field two (2) men in that character work, Elder J. A. Bond and Elder W. H. Lutrick. I sent the name of the

latter to Sister A. The name of the latter was not sent. Brother Lutrick's Post Office is Aimwell, La."

Mr. Ware did send me Mr. Lutrick's name some time since, but not that of Mr. Bond. I have corresponded with Mr. Lutrick and assigned his name to societies, not knowing that he was a Sunday School missionary. I will, however, enter him under that heading and when he is aided, report boxes to you. Do you judge from Mr. Ware's letter that he wishes us to secure assistance for Mr. Bond, or not? Kindly let me know. If so, please notify the brother that he has not sent Mr. Bond's address.

I am now going to tell you something, but I do want to ask that you will consider it confidential. What the outcome may be, I do not know. You doubtless will remember that when the Sunday School Board Recommendations were presented in Wilmington, Miss Heck (both privately and publicly) opposed the Woman's Mission Societies contributing to the Sunday School Board. I had no reason to think she had changed her opinion, and so during the course of the year I have said nothing to her whatever on the subject. When the Bible cards and leaflets were sent out, I forwarded samples to her, but she made no order for same. I did not think it wise to present to her the name of any Sunday School missionary to be given to a society in North Carolina. I did not know, though, until this morning that she looked at things quite in the way she does. I do not think I have ever been more indignant with any of W.M.U. workers than I was with Miss Heck today, and I must say I consider I had just cause for feeling as I did. I will give you the circumstance.

We were going over last year's Recommendations of the Boards, so that we might consider, before the work was brought to the attention of the Executive Committee at a "called" meeting tomorrow, what the President and Cor. Sec'y thought of the present lines of work. After discussing those of the other two Boards, we came to the Sunday School Board. I cannot give you words that were used, but Miss Heck led me to understand that she thought I had acted contrary to the wishes of the ladies as expressed in Wilmington in carrying out the Recommendations of the Sunday School Board as adopted by them. She had reference to the second Recommendation. I enclose copy of them as they now stand. A change was made in the second one as given by you. You presented it in this wording:

"Our Bible Work has grown immensely this year and we desire to see it still further increase. We earnestly wish that our Bible Fund could be enlarged, and should be glad if Woman's Mission Societies would raise $1,000.00 for it."

It was changed to read as given in the printed form which I send you. The motion to change was made by Mrs. I. C. Brown, of East Lake, Ala., Cor. Sec'y of that State, who has since died. As you probably will remember, there was considerable discussion on this subject, and Miss Heck was asked to give her opinion. She left the "chair" to do so, and it was clear to see that she did not approve of contributions being made to the Sunday School Board. I took the opposite ground and warmly advocated the passing of the resolution. After the amendment was carried, I requested that the "chair" should construe the Recommendation, so that the Cor. Sec'y might understand what was intended by the wording. Miss Heck declined to do so, and on my insisting that I must have some definite instructions, the mover of the resolution, Mrs. Brown, said substantially that her idea in offering the resolution was that no definite sum should be stated, but she hoped that larger sums would be contributed than the thousand dollars. As there was no further explanation offered or questions raised, I of course took this as the decision of the entire body. Later, at a meeting of the Executive Committee in Wilmington, a resolution was offered and carried that hereafter no contributions should be reported that were made by Woman's Mission Societies in the different States at Annual Meetings, but those given to the three Boards, and the name of each Convention Board was mentioned. I think you will agree with me that I had ample authority and definite instructions to prepare the blank which we have been using this year. I enclose copy.

Miss Heck seemed to be under the impression that the ladies at Annual Meeting agreed with her in the position she has taken—that "cooperation" meant that we were to use our influence to get contributions made for the Bible Fund, as we did to secure subscribers for the Sunday School periodicals, but that no moneyed offerings were to be made by the societies to the Bible Fund of the Sunday School Board. I certainly had no such understanding, and I am sure any unprejudiced person would come to the same conclusion I did if the facts were given to them. Miss Heck acknowledged that things occurred as I have stated them, but she seemed to think that the majority of the ladies sided with her, although no public evidence of same was given and the Recommendation as passed was unanimous, with the exception of one vote in the negative, which was cast by Mrs. Hollie Harper Townsend, whose husband has charge of one of the chapel cars. Miss Heck, as Presiding Officer, of course did not vote. When I asked Miss H. what she thought the ladies meant by passing a resolution that the contributions to the Sunday School Board were to be reported, she said that meant boxes of clothing, although no such distinction was made at any time in the course of the discussion, or afterwards at the Executive Committee meeting.

When Miss Heck led me to understand that she thought I had used the power I possessed to present the work of the Sunday School Board in the way I desired, I was truly indignant and did not hesitate to tell her quite plainly that I regarded her as altogether mistaken, and that I had ample authority to do what I had done. Later, she in a measure withdrew the reflection she had cast upon my actions in this particular, but I simply let the matter drop without stating whether I accepted her partial apology or not. We then turned to other subjects.

I have given you the circumstance, for I think it only right that you should know of it. As I told you when in Wilmington, if the Sunday School Board is ever to receive contributions from the Woman's Mission Societies, we must not yield at this time, no matter who opposes it. Miss Heck said this morning she did not think the Sunday School Board ought to ask for contributions. I reminded her that the Convention had passed a resolution on this point, creating a Bible Fund, but she is still of the opinion that the money for this great work of Bible Distribution should be *made* by the Sunday School Board. I told her that the reason the Publication Society was enabled to do the large work they are now doing through their chapel cars and in other ways, was due to the fact that the capital upon which they are working was given to them largely by the denomination. When the time comes for the Sunday School Board to offer their Recommendations to the Woman's Missionary Union—I will shortly send for same—I would (personally) advise that there be no change whatever in the two Recommendations that you offered last year—except in wording, to give a little variety—in regard to the Bible Work and sending boxes to Sunday School missionaries. A commencement has been made in this direction, and I believe next year the ladies will be more ready to adopt parallel Recommendations in regard to these two phases of work than they were last year, with the exception of the North Carolina delegation, which it is probable Miss Heck will influence. After the close of our conversation, when the drawing for the title page of program for Children's Day was brought in, I showed it to Miss Heck. She expressed much admiration for it, and when I told her the program had been prepared, she made no objection whatever to it, so I do not know whether she was in a measure convinced by what I said, or not. As I previously stated, I do not know what will be the outcome of this, but I believe I am in the right and I shall firmly adhere to the position which I have taken.

LATER, TUESDAY. This letter, although dictated, could not be written on Monday, so I now will give you a little further information. After considering the matter very carefully, I concluded that I would take right decided ground with Miss Heck. I saw her before she went into the Executive Committee meeting this morning, and told her I considered she had made a very grave charge and that I wished her to feel perfectly at liberty to present the matter to the Executive Committee in Baltimore, or at a full Executive Committee meeting in Norfolk, or to the ladies assembled in annual meeting, so that I might have the opportunity of publicly refuting the charges which she had made. When I first spoke of the Local Committee in Baltimore, she said she did not expect to say anything to them on the subject; that it was simply a difference of opinion in the way she and I regarded the matter. I told her that was not all she had said; that I had been the one to act, and that certainly if I had done as she thought, I was not fitted to hold the position which I do, for I could not be trusted, and if the ladies so regarded it, I would not be willing to fill the office. Miss Heck seemed to wish to pass it over as simply a personal matter. I insisted upon regarding it in the light in which I put it, and finally Miss Heck said she had no idea of speaking further on the subject. I assured her that the action taken by the ladies was such as to warrant me in taking the ground I did, and her declining to construe the Recommendation prevented any one knowing how she understood it. When we went into the meeting of the Executive Committee, you can imagine neither of us felt very calm, but I was glad to hear Sister Alice say afterwards that there was no evidence that we had been crossing swords. When the Sunday School Board Recommendations were considered, Miss Heck made not the slightest objection to any of them and none were made by any member of the Executive Committee, so you see things are outwardly quiet. I am almost certain, from my knowledge of Miss Heck's character, that she will not after this refer to the subject again to me, nor will there be any public opposition to the Sunday School Board Recommendations by her. As to what her future action may be in regard to her connection with the work, I cannot say. Time must reveal that. I sincerely trust there will be no similar experiences in future in carrying out any Recommendations that may come to us from any one of the Boards, for I certainly can assure you it has not been a pleasant episode.

Very truly,

Annie W. Armstrong

P. S. In reading over this letter, I think it is possible you may misunderstand me when I say: "We must not yield at this time, no matter who opposes it." I of course have reference to individual or minority opposition. If the ladies in annual session voted against any Recommendation and it was not carried, I could not, nor would I, as Cor. Secretary, do otherwise than what I was instructed by them to do. This is just the point where Miss Heck and I differ. She considers that I have not carried out the intention of those who adopted the resolution at last Annual Meeting above referred to, and I insist that I have *strictly* followed instructions. I do not propose to make this matter public. None of the ladies in Baltimore knew of it, except Sister Alice. Sister thinks that Miss Heck's purpose in coming to Baltimore was to speak to me in regard to same. I do not know whether she is correct in her surmise, or not.

P. S. No. 2. I am now going to call your attention to something of a pleasanter nature. I have an advance copy of the February edition of *Our Home Field*. I enclose same. Note the first article on first page. From this you will see that Dr. Tichenor has done as he promised.

By the way, if you are not too busy, I wish you would read the third page and let me know if you think I am utilizing the space that is accorded Woman's Missionary Union in the best way. Do not think I am asking for a compliment. I simply want suggestions.

Another item, and then I really must close. This also I must ask that you regard as confidential. In a letter received from Dr. Tichenor this morning, he writes:

"I confess I am not sorry to see the A.B.P.S. *Teacher* making such mistakes. Their motives are anything but honorable and Christian, and hence the more and bigger their blunders, the better I feel—it may be mean to feel so, but I confess I am just that mean."

One good thing that Dr. Rowland has done is—I am quite sure in this matter the three Secretaries of our Boards stand on the same platform.

P. S. No. 3. As you seem to desire it, I now forward you freight receipt for box of Testaments sent to Miss Buhlmaier. The money has been refunded to Miss Buhlmaier, who paid the bill, and you need not trouble to return same, unless you prefer to do so.

[SBHLA, J. M. Frost Collection]

February 2, 1898
Dr. J. M. Frost
Dear Brother:

Please find enclosed letters to Judge Haralson and Dr. Burrows. I want to ask that you carefully read these, and if you do not think they cover the ground in the right way, please return them to me with any suggestions you may deem wise. If, however, they meet with your approval, kindly mail same. Should you desire to do so, I will be glad to have them accompanied by letters from you.

As I previously mentioned, Miss Heck, greatly to my surprise, again introduced the subject of the Sunday School Board Recommendations to me privately, although she made not the slightest intimation at the Executive Committee meeting which was held while she was in Baltimore that she disapproved of the way I had carried out the Recommendations of this year, or that she thought it would be wise to suggest changes in Recommendations of said Board for next year. When she commenced to speak on the subject, she asked how I would prefer the question being brought forward, whether she or I was right in the way we understood the wishes of the ladies in regard to contributions to the Sunday School Board. I told her I had no preference in the matter, that I was simply acting upon instructions which I had received and was ready at any time to meet any charges that might be made. Before the conversation closed, I think she fully understood that I was not willing to withdraw one particle from the stand which I had taken, viz., that the ladies had decided, as shown by their own actions, that they were willing to make contributions to the Sunday School Board and that I had simply carried out instructions received. I told Miss Heck that I intended to refer the matter to Judge Haralson and would be prepared to give his opinion, if there was need for it. I do not think it wise to speak of this matter, either to the Executive Committee in Baltimore, or to the Central Committees in the different States. If Miss Heck decides, after more mature deliberation, that she will bring the question forward publicly, I shall be prepared to meet it. I think it is probable she will consult Mr. White, Secretary of the North Carolina State Board, and perhaps others as to what ought to be done, looking at things from her standpoint. I shall decline to have any further conversation with her in regard to it. She knows my views and I know hers, and nothing is to be gained by our discussing it further. I await your next letter with no little eagerness, as I do want to know how you regard it.

I enclose letter received from Rev. J. M. Phillips, whose name you will remember you sent me. Kindly read the letter and let me know, under the circumstances, if you desire his name presented to a society.

Hoping you had a pleasant visit to Kentucky, I am,

Very truly,

Annie W. Armstrong

LATER (February 3, 1898). This morning's mail has brought letters from Richmond, giving rather an astonishing piece of news. Miss Heck, when Dr. Willingham wrote Feb. 1st, was in Richmond. When I bade her goodbye last Friday, Jan. 28th, she did not give me the slightest intimation that it was her intention to visit that city before she returned home. I knew while in Baltimore Miss Heck had received a letter from Dr. Willingham, suggesting that she should stop there en route to Raleigh, but Miss Heck then said her ticket was on the other line and it would be more expensive for her to do so, and she did not purpose going. I have not the slightest doubt but that she changed her mind in order that she might see Dr. Willingham, and perhaps others in Richmond, in regard to the Sunday School Board Recommendations. At the time of writing, Dr. Willingham had had no conference with Miss Heck. He says:

"Miss Heck is in the city, but I have not had an opportunity to see her but a few minutes as yet. I have an engagement to see her today."

I do not know whether Dr. Willingham will later let me know how he views the matter, or not. If he does, I will give you the benefit of his opinion. *

P. S. I enclose the letter I received from Dr. Burrows.

[Handwritten insert in margin] * I have decided to send Dr. Willingham a copy of the letter I have written to Judge Haralson.

[SBHLA, J. M. Frost Collection]

EXTRACT OF REPLY RECEIVED FROM DR. FROST WRITTEN
Feb. 2, 1898

I have read with great care what you write as to the issue between you and Miss Heck. You are surely in the right so far as I can discern. I remember very well the conversation which I had with Miss Heck, and to which she refers. I would not want any issue between her word and my word, but my feeling was in making that statement to which she refers that although the ladies had not granted the request so far as specifying the sum of one thousand dollars was concerned, and this was the thing which I wanted that had not been done. But in the action which they did take they granted all that I could wish under the circumstances and going as fast as I could expect; indeed I would have been satisfied or rather temporarily content if even they had done less. I think the way in which the women have responded to your appeal is sufficient evidence as to how they regard the instructions. I can fully appreciate Miss Heck's feelings, and it may be that possibly she is influenced some by local surroundings. Now let me make a suggestion: do not take the matter so much to heart as to let it worry you. I would not make too much of an issue with her, but simply go on and do the thing that is to be done. It's too late in the day now for anybody to oppose our Bible work. The endorsement given to it in the Convention at Wilmington and in the various State Conventions and the practical support given to it put it beyond all peradventure. I full agree with you as to the character of our next Recommendation to the Woman's Missionary Union, and shall earnestly support the request which I shall make of them. Of course if they turn both you and me down, why then we will simply stay not turned down, that's all.

Praying that God may guide us in these things, I remain,

Fraternally yours,

J. M. Frost

[SBHLA, J. M. Frost Collection]

March 4, 1898

Dr. J. M. Frost

Dear Brother:

Owing to extreme pressure of work in making arrangements for Week of Self Denial, etc., etc., it has been impossible for me sooner to write to you in regard to the Recommendations of the Sunday School Board and arrangements for Annual Meeting of the Woman's Missionary Union. The intervening time between this and the meetings in Norfolk seems all too short in which to do what is necessary to close the year's accounts, and to prepare for presenting the work in an impressive manner to the ladies when they will gather in Annual Session, so I am going to ask that you will kindly give this letter your careful attention and that you will let me hear from you on the various points as promptly as possible. As I wrote you, during Miss Heck's visit to Baltimore there was a "called" meeting of the Executive Committee and the Recommendations of the Boards for the present year were considered. While there was a number of suggestions offered in regard to changes in Home and Foreign Board Recommendations, when it came to those of the Sunday School Board, no changes were proposed, so I judge from this that the Executive Committee—I have written you as to Miss Heck's opinion given privately—as a whole are perfectly in sympathy with the Sunday School Board methods of work and do not see need for change in any direction. What I now write is simply the opinion of the Cor. Sec. I have received no instructions from the Committee as to suggested changes in Recommendations.

Owing to the opposition of the President to Woman's Mission Societies being asked to make moneyed contributions to the Sunday School Board, I really think this year it will be unwise for you to make any further requests than you did last year of the Woman's Missionary Union, but I sincerely hope you will firmly adhere to the position you have taken—that the Sunday School Board does expect money to be given by the societies to carry on the work of Bible Distribution. There is another phase of Sunday School work which I hope the Sunday School Board may undertake, and for which I believe we can in the *future* obtain contributions from the Woman's Mission Societies, but I do not think it wise to propose this now. When I see you, I can give you my thought and then you can consider the advisability of bringing it forward at a later date.

Now as to the wording of the Recommendations. Please change same so as to give them some freshness, but I think it will be wise for you to use the same wording that the ladies themselves adopted last year when they passed the resolution in regard to the Bible Fund, viz., "Cooperation."

Another suggestion. You will note the Secretaries of the other Boards so word their Recommendations that they are positive requests. Excuse criticism, but to my mind, in the Recommendations you offered last year, it seemed, while you desired the ladies to do thus and so, you hardly expected that they would. My idea is that a Recommendation should be concise and definite in its terms.

I would suggest that you give the same number of Recommendations this year as last, viz., 5, and that you do not combine in one Recommendation contributions to the Bible Fund and boxes to Sunday

School missionaries. Let these be separate as heretofore, each standing on its own merit.

I now desire to make a number of

R E Q U E S T S.

1. That you let me have Recommendations as soon as possible.

2. That you make an address at Annual Meeting of the Woman's Missionary Union of fifteen (15) minutes. At the meeting in Wilmington the following resolution was offered and passed:

> "That the Executive Committee appoint women to prepare brief papers on the work of the three Boards of the Convention, to be read at Annual Meeting of the Woman's Missionary Union, to be followed by limited discussion."

From this you will appreciate that the work of the Sunday School Board will be presented in a paper which we will invite some lady to write, and it will be followed by a "limited discussion." At the close of this discussion, the Recommendations of the Sunday School Board for next year will be read, and it is the wish of the Executive Committee that these Recommendations will be duly explained and emphasized by the Secretary of the Sunday School Board. Kindly let me know if you will make the desired address.

3. That you will, prior to the Annual Meeting, let me have a letter from you explanatory of Recommendations, which could be read at an Executive Committee session in Norfolk and afterwards printed in State papers, when the Sunday School Board Recommendations are presented.

4. That you let me know if your Board will be willing to invite Mrs. M. J. Nelson, of Texas, or any other of the Bible women employed by the Sunday School Board in Texas, to attend the Annual Meeting of the Woman's Missionary Union and present the Sunday School Board work at the service which will be held Sunday afternoon, when missionaries will speak. It is hardly to be expected that a missionary can make these long trips, unless her travelling expenses are paid. The Woman's Missionary Union has no fund upon which to draw for travelling expenses, so the Home and Foreign Boards at times pay the travelling expenses of their missionaries.

5. If you deem it wise to do so, that you write to Mrs. J. Haralson, whom we propose inviting to prepare the ten minutes' paper on the Sunday School Board work above referred to, and use what influence you may have

with her to get her to accept the invitation. If Mrs. Haralson declines, what lady would you suggest to do this service? I very much want someone of influence to write said paper.

6. That you let me know if Friday (morning), the first day of the Convention, you will be at liberty to make the address asked for before the Woman's Missionary Union. I think it will be wise to have the Sunday School Board Recommendations come up the first day, so if there is any division in sentiment, we will have time to consider what ought to be done, etc., etc.

I will now relieve your patience and draw this long letter to a close.

Very truly,

Annie W. Armstrong

[SBHLA, J. M. Frost Collection]

August 11, 1898

Dr. J. M. Frost

Dear Brother:

Your letter of Aug. 10th just received. In reply, I would say that we will in the near future be sending out from the Mission Rooms the next quarter's supply of Monthly Literature to subscribers, so, if you care to do it, you can forward 1,500 copies of the tract you have published, "The Periodicals of the Southern Baptist Convention, an Appeal to the Churches," and I will make use of them in that way and also provide Central Committees with copies. I think it may be better for me to send this publication to the Central Committees than for it to be forwarded direct from the Sunday School Board office to them. If the order for Missionary Day literature which I forwarded several days since has been filled, let this present order be sent as soon as possible; otherwise, I will not be able to utilize your new publication to the best advantage.

It has always been my habit to speak plainly, so I am not going to deviate from that rule now. It is true you have not had anything but strictly *business* communications from me for some little time, and a letter which I received from you is the cause of my silence. I do not know when I have been more astonished, and rarely in my life more hurt, than I was at the way in which you wrote—I have reference to your treatment of the matter which led the Secretaries of the Boards to call for a Conference to which they have invited the officers of the Woman's Missionary Union. You are entirely mistaken in thinking that at that time the *cause* of this trouble between Miss

Heck and myself will not be brought forward. It certainly will be by the Secretary of the Woman's Missionary Union. It is my purpose then, when called on to speak, to tell the truth, the *whole* truth and nothing but the truth, and that cannot be done without my plainly stating what in my judgment has led Miss Heck to act as she has. I have always been ready and willing to let the Secretaries of the Boards know just how I regarded any matter, as I felt that the S.B.C. work, if it was to assume the highest efficiency, must be regarded as a whole. Therefore, if you think it desirable to see me prior to the Conference, which I suppose is to be in Washington between now and the 1st of September, I would suggest your timing your visit to Baltimore accordingly. If you can let me know previous to your coming to our city when you will make this visit, I will be glad to have the information, so I can have ready some data connected with various phases of work which it may be well for you at that time to consider.

If your son will be with you when you come to Baltimore, if you will notify me to that effect, I will be pleased to carry out my original plan for his seeing various points of interest.

Very truly,

Annie W. Armstrong

P. S. As I note you expect to "leave home next week for a little trip, combining pleasure and business," I will send this letter through by "Special Delivery."

[SBHLA, J. M. Frost Collection]

September 29, 1898

Dr. J. M. Frost

Dear Brother:

I have just received a letter from North Carolina which I think it is as well for you to see, so I forward same. No comments from me are needed in regard to the principal subject upon which Miss Heck has written, as you were present in Norfolk and heard Miss Heck say that she was prepared to aid the Sunday School Board, also that last year, while she did not approve of moneyed contributions being asked for the societies for the Bible Fund, she did approve of the Sunday School missionaries being aided with boxes of clothing. Actions and words do not always correspond. I have just replied to Miss Heck as follows:

Your letter of Sept. 26th received, in which you return four letters previously sent you from Sunday School missionaries. I now forward, as desired, eight (8) letters from Home Board Missionaries. I note you write:

"As I have stated before, we prefer families with three or four small children, but of course if you have not letters from such families, we will take those that come."

Not wishing to create a false impression, I would say that I have in hand probably eight letters or more from missionaries who have families of the size indicated by you. As *all* of the Central Committees, however, prefer to have missionaries assigned to them having families of the size you mentioned, and as it is my aim to as far as possible have perfect equality in the work, I do not feel that I can send to North Carolina eight *additional* letters from missionaries having the popular size families, as that would prevent my furnishing some of the other Central Committees with any families of the size names by you. Unfortunately, a large proportion of the missionaries have either no children, a larger number, or grown children, who for various reasons are dependent upon the missionaries for a support.

Hoping you will be able to interest the societies in North Carolina in the missionaries whose letters I send, I am,

Very truly,

In my long experience in dealing with persons, I do not think I have ever encountered one who was so perfectly disregardless of the rights of other people as is the President of the Woman's Missionary Union.

There are several other matters about which I desire to write, but as there is an important meeting which I must attend today, it may not be possible for me to take time to present these, so forward this letter now.

Very truly,
Annie W. Armstrong
[SBHLA, J. M. Frost Collection]

Jan. 21, 1899
Dr. J. M. Frost
Dear Brother:

Your letters of Jan. 10 & 19 both received. I noted the request in the last that I write "at once," and hoped to do so both yesterday and today, but it has seemed impossible. I can now only send a few lines, but expect to answer both letters on Monday.

Our stenographer, who has been with us for over six years, has had an offer from an Insurance Company of higher salary than we have been paying her—I think it probable that she will leave. I can of course train another—when she came to us it was to put up packages—but it does take so much time and patience to do this that I rather dread having it to do.

Very truly,
Annie W. Armstrong

Sunday night
Personal.

I am doing two things this evening that I rarely do—staying home from church and writing a letter on Sunday. I feel though both are justifiable under the circumstances. I have not been feeling well for some days—I am afraid the physician was more nearly right than I was willing to think, where he told me, as he did, when I had the grip, that for the next six months I would have to take great care not to overtax myself, etc., etc.—and this morning I felt so like fainting that I had to leave church during the service. I am expecting tomorrow a new Stenographer, and we are in the midst of preparing for "Week of Self Denial," preliminary arrangements for An. Meeting, etc., etc. so I will have no time to write this letter tomorrow. I feel unwilling to defer longer taking some notice of your protest to my resigning the position of Cor. Sec. W.M.U. *should Miss Heck not come up to her agreement.*

You may not consider that Miss Heck did agree to resign, or rather to decline re-election another year, at the conference held last August in Norfolk. I so understood it, otherwise it was my purpose, to do as stated in the paper which I enclose, and which you will remember I gave you to read when in Balto. prior to going to Norfolk. I think I was right in the decision I then reached, and nothing said by Miss Heck while in Norfolk or since has caused me to change my views.

I do not think you in the least appreciated how outrageous and unfounded were the charges made by Miss Heck against the Cor. Sec.

W.M.U., and how contemptible the methods adopted by her to get others to think as she did.

If Dr. Folk had first accused you of malfeasance in office, and later when that was so plainly proved to be false that no one could possibly have been found to credit such an accusation, to make another in the despicable way she did, I am sure you would have felt as I do—that there must be a change in either President or Secretary.

I have held the office of Cor. Sec. W.M.U. now for nearly eleven years, and in that time, as my Heavenly Father knows, I have been called to make many sacrifices for this work, but they have been willingly and gladly made. If I know myself, I would not refuse to do anything, which would advance its interests, if I was led to see that it was my duty to do so. In this case though I am convinced—unless there should be a radical change in Miss Heck—that there should be a change in one of the officers of the Woman's Missionary Union, and so unless Miss Heck resigns *I must.*

Miss Heck stated, as you may remember, when in Norfolk that she would, the first of March, make her decision public. (It is necessary when there is to be a change in officers for notice to be given previous to an annual meeting so the delegates may be instructed by our workers in the different States how to vote.) If she keeps the promise made—I so regard it—I will continue if elected in Louisville, doing the work as heretofore, but should Miss Heck not come up to her agreement, I will be obliged to give it up. I would say though—I would ask that you do not mention this—Dr. Willingham, with whom I talked this matter over when he was last in Balto. told me, if I was not officially notified by Miss Heck of her purpose to decline re-election at the time appointed by her, March 1, to allow a few days to elapse, and *he* would write to Miss Heck on the subject.

Regarding you as I do not only as the Secretary of one of the Boards, but in the light of a friend, I have been willing to let you know how I look at this matter, and what my course of action will be, as far as I now see.

Before closing, permit me to say, I hope you appreciate that I am always willing to receive suggestions from any one of the Secretaries of the Boards, and I hope you will never hesitate to tell me plainly when you see things in a different light from the way I do. My idea of friendship is for one to be true under all circumstances—if uncomfortable things should be said to be willing to say them.

Very truly,
Annie W. Armstrong

As I have been writing this Mother has been sitting by the side of me, and it was pitiful to hear her say, "I am tired in my mind and body." While I do not think she realizes her condition, yet she certainly must be "tired." Her days are "days of weariness." I am thankful that, as a usual thing, her nights are not "nights of pain." Doctor, I do not want to grow bitter or uncharitable, but do you know, it seems to me almost fiendish, for Miss Heck to have acted as she has, at a time when she knew how full my heart as well as hands were.

[SBHLA, J. M. Frost Collection]

March 8th, 1899
Dr. J. M. Frost
Dear Brother:
Your letter of recent date received. It finds me with a large amount of mail that I must try and answer this morning, as the afternoon has to be given to attending a Missionary meeting at our own church (Eutaw Place) and trying to secure the active cooperation of the ladies there in the Week of Self Denial. For this reason I am quite hurried, and so will have to ask that you excuse all want of clearness in statements.

1. *Letter from Miss Heck.* Before this reaches you you will have had my letter of March 7th and telegram of March 8th. Miss Heck's want of promptness in giving notice as she promised she would March 1st of her purpose to decline re-election, caused me to feel that if friction was to be avoided in the future I must take some decided step to let her see that I appreciated that there must be some change in W.M.U. officers. I did not feel that either Miss Heck, or I, would be able to stand the strain that we would be under if we both went to Louisville with things in an undecided state. Neither did I feel that it was fair to those, who had charge of our work in the various States, to spring such a matter upon them. The letter received from Miss Heck this morning—copy of which I enclose—puts an entirely different coloring on the whole matter, and although it will be very disagreeable for me to meet Miss Heck again, I shall, of course, now go to Louisville, unless providentially prevented. At the W.M.U. Executive Committee meeting next Tuesday, I shall simply read Miss Heck's communication and say nothing to the ladies about what my purpose had been.

2. *Design for Envelope.* I enclose specimen. I hope it will meet with your approval. I send by express today the 3 electrotypes. I forward bill for

these and some other amounts due by the Sunday School Board to the Mission Rooms.

Hastily, but very truly,
Annie W. Armstrong

DECISION OF SECRETARY W.M.U.

Her resignation will be presented to take effect as soon as possible unless the President W.M.U. resigns. If the President resigns, she must agree not to use her influence to alienate the societies in North Carolina from W.M.U., or to sow seeds of dissension among W.M.U. workers elsewhere. Should evidence arise that this is being done, the Secretaries of the three Boards will be requested to promise to make a statement which may be publicly used to counteract such influence. If Miss Heck does not resign, the Secretary W.M.U. in resigning wishes to put her intentions on record, not as a threat but as a necessity for properly placing herself before W.M.U. workers, that she reserves to herself the right to make a statement that the cause of her resignation is inability to continue work with a President whose methods are entirely at variance with the Secretary's ideas of right and propriety, also a further reservation: to give facts leading to this position should she deem it best to do so either publicly or privately.

The resignation of the Secretary W.M.U. carries with it a total severance from all denominational missionary offices held by her, i.e., the Secretaryship of Mission Rooms, the Presidency of Home Mission Society in Maryland, as well as the General Sec-[Incomplete]

[SBHLA, J. M. Frost Collection]

April 13th, 1899
Dr. J. M. Frost
Dear Brother:

It gives me pleasure to report four additional boxes sent to Sunday School missionaries. We must in the near future close our books, so I will be obliged if you will return receipts for these as promptly as possible. The total value of boxes to date, sent during the present Conventional year, is $2,982.98. I do not know whether you recall the conversation, but sometime ago I told you that I thought the Box Work for the Sunday School Board would this year aggregate $3,000.00. Last year the total value of boxes sent to Sunday School missionaries was $545.16—more than a five fold increase. It is quite probable we may yet have other boxes reported, and if this is the case, we will go over the amount, which I was aiming to secure for the Sunday School Board.

As to moneyed contributions—that I cannot give until the treasurers' reports come to us from the different states. I doubt though, if you have, or will receive from Woman's Mission Societies $3,000.00. I do know though, that you must have had more than that amount from Children's Day and Missionary Day, and I believe you will agree with me, that the Woman's Missionary Union—although, except in very few instances, do we report the money gathered on these days—does have a large share in securing it. Excuse what may seem a little piece of boasting, but I cannot help feeling gratified at the success that has attended our efforts to aid the Sunday School Board.

I trust you are regaining your strength, and are feeling stronger than I do at present. I would not like any member of the family to know how badly I do feel. I have been having almost constant headaches for some days past, and it would not surprise me at any time if I am forced to give up. I do try not to let Miss Heck's peculiar actions weigh upon me, but I dread more than I can tell you having to be thrown with her again as I must if I go to Louisville. None of our workers in the other states have the slightest idea of the cause of Miss Heck's declining re-election, as far as I know, and I have no doubt in Louisville that there will be an effort made by some to cause her to continue in office. I have declined to suggest any one as her successor. What will be the outcome of this, I do not know, and I really am not able, physically to stand anything more than I have already had to go through.

As a family we are now feeling very much disturbed about Eugene Levering's condition. Day before yesterday he had to be brought home from his office, having had an attack, which I do not think rendered him unconscious, but affected his head and caused numbness. This is the second time he has had such an attack, one coming on when he was in New York a few weeks ago. The physician has ordered him to leave home, but he does not seem willing to go until he knows more definitely what has caused this trouble. We all appreciate that it is the result of over-work. One can hardly imagine a person having more important interests committed to him than Eugene Levering has been trying to advance. The first idea was that he should go to Atlantic City. I suppose it will eventuate in his having to take a much longer trip. If Sister Mamie and Eugene have to be away while mother is as feeble as she is, it will be a great grief to all of us. Does it not seem at times that one's cup of sorrow is almost fuller than can be borne? Jonah is not my favorite Biblical character, but indeed I am getting to have much more sympathy with him than I used to.

Thanks for Mite Boxes which have just come to hand.

Very truly,

Annie W. Armstrong

[SBHLA, J. M. Frost Collection]

August 14, 1899

Dr. J. M. Frost

Dear Brother:

Yours of August 10th received, and it is my purpose to write later in the day in regard to several matters that you have referred in that letter, but as I may be prevented from doing so, I feel that I must, without delay, write to you in regard to a certain question.

The box of literature for Missionary Day has just been received and opened. I note the explanation you give as to the omission in crediting the Program to the Woman's Missionary Union. As I previously wrote you, Miss Heck did this work when President of the Woman's Missionary Union, and her undertaking to do this was part of the agreement made in Norfolk. As neither the Woman's Missionary Union nor Miss Heck's name appears on the Program, it is *more than probable* that Miss Heck will consider that said omission is due to some influence which I have exerted. I must, therefore, beg that you will *at once* write to Miss Heck, and let her know that I had nothing whatever to do with this, and that I am surprised and disappointed that this Program is not credited to the Woman's Missionary Union.

I appreciate that your intentions were of the best in doing as you have done, but am genuinely sorry that you did not mention your purpose before acting, as I would have then given you reasons why any change would be most unwise.

I am sorry to have had to write as I have done, but I am sure that it is necessary that I ask you to make this explanation to Miss Heck. I shall today send Miss Heck, as well as all other State Officers, samples of Missionary Day literature, and ask cooperation in getting Missionary Day observed as generally as possible in the Sunday Schools in their respective States, but I shall make no allusion to the omission of name on the Program to Miss Heck, but leave the explanation to be made by you.

Very truly,
Annie W. Armstrong
[SBHLA, J. M. Frost Collection]

The dust from the conflict between Armstrong and Heck had not settled before WMU was embroiled in another controversy.

The Woman's Missionary Union.
A Critic's View.

When any one speaks of criticizing a person or thing at once it is taken for granted that he means to find fault, or, at least, to point out defects. But this is far from being necessarily true, for the critic may employ himself in bringing to light the excellencies as well as the defects of his subject. For what is a critic but a judge who examines into the merits of persons or things under his eye, to distinguish between what is pleasant and what is not, and to bring each out to view?

And sometimes we speak of kindly critics and unkindly ones, according as the criticisms they make are in commendation of their subjects or otherwise. But neither is this a correct designation. For a critic may be full of kindness and yet feel that he must, in kindness, speak of some things in the subject of his criticisms which are not good. Not unseldom is it that the wounds of a friend are given in love, and are evidences not of any enmity or ill will, but altogether of friendship and real affection.

I can say in the outset of my criticisms that I am a sincere friend and admirer of the Woman's Missionary Union, and of its work. I have, in an humble way, sought to advance its work, recommending it at every opportunity. Hence, if anything approaching to an adverse criticism should creep into my mind before I get through, it cannot be attributed to any but the best motives. If, in my study of this excellent organization and its plans and methods, I should find some things I do not approve, why not tell of them, in the hope that they may be corrected? And then, too, I am open to reply, and to be set straight, if at fault, or corrected, if mistaken. I venture to say that the editors of the *Index* will allow replies, and welcome them, for, in my observations of the fraternity, I have come to believe that they rather enjoy having bright, breezy discussions, provided they are kept within proper bounds.

A DEVELOPMENT

The Woman's Missionary Union did not spring into being all at once, the product of one brain or one heart, as Minerva sprang full-armed from the brow of Jupiter. It was a development out of what had gone before. Before its organization in 1888, women had been at work for missions, and woman's missionary societies had existed in many parts of the country. In some States these had been drawn together into State organizations, having at the head what were known as Central Committees. And these, surveying their State fields, and studying the conditions in them, had been seeking to organize local societies in the churches, and provide in such measure as they could, for their development in missionary thought, purpose and effort. What more natural than that these State workers, coming together at the annual meetings of the Southern Baptist Convention, should conceive the idea of wider fellowship in work?

RAPID GROWTH

When it was first organized, as is always the case with new things among Baptists, it did not have the undivided support of the mission workers of the various States. A great many good people, men and women, looked at it askance, doubting as to where it would lead. Rumors of how women occupied platforms in the North and harangued mixed assemblies were circulating through the South, and our people did not approve of such performances. And accounts had come, too, of separate organizations among the women in that territory of doubtful reputation (then and a little so yet), and it seemed to some excellent ones among us that this new organization might lead to disintegration in mission work and even division in the churches—men on one side and women on the other. And though it had long been the custom in our country churches, and even in town ones, for the men to sit on one side of the "middle wall of partition" that extended the length of the house, and the women on the other, yet that was as far as the brethren were at all willing to allow division to go.

But soon it became apparent that this new organization had nothing in it looking at all to any division, or to any putting of women forward in unscriptural service, and so, by degrees, the objections to it were silenced and prejudices against it died out. It was soon felt that, in its auxiliary relation to the Convention and its firm support of *all* the Convention's work, it would be a force for union rather than division. And soon all State conventions were endorsing it and all workers in missions were recognizing its worth. It is now co-extensive with the Southern Baptist Convention.

GOOD WORK

The Union was eleven years old in May last, and in that time it has done a great and far-reaching work. If I were asked to designate the work which commends it to favor, I should reply: that along the line marked out by our fathers when they organized the Southern Baptist Convention in 1845, and declared its great purpose to be to "elicit, combine and direct" the energies of the denomination in the South in the great work of giving the gospel to all classes and conditions of men. This the Union has done for the women of the South, and, incidentally, through them, is doing for the men as well.

It has put before the women of the South, by leaflets, by programs for meetings, by appeals through papers and magazines, and by various other agencies, including multitudes of personal letters, the needs and claims of every object represented by the Convention, and of every field embraced within the sphere of its labor. Not only so, but the children have been considered, and special provision has been made for interesting them and bringing them into co-operation with their fathers and mothers in the good work of the Lord.

And the energies of these workers have been combined, as well as elicited, so that thousands of little springs, in city and town and country churches and Sunday-schools, have sent their small streams to swell the flow of money into the Lord's treasuries in Richmond, Atlanta, Nashville, and into those of the State Boards as well. As one of many of the blessed results of this combination of energy, the weak society in the poorest country church has learned to forget its weakness, and to rejoice with the largest and wealthiest one in city church, in the great work that they are unitedly doing for their common Lord.

And these energies have been well directed towards the most pressing and most important parts of the Lord's work. Instead of the energies of the women being all frittered away on merely local objects and to sometimes selfish ends, they are directed to the great work—in its various departments—of giving the gospel to the whole world. These combined energies have, at times, been directed in such a way that they have greatly strengthened weak places in the work, and I had almost said, rescued it at times from danger of disaster. Not a Board of our Convention but has felt the thrill of encouragement when, in some emergency, the Union has called upon the women all over the country to come to its help. The members of the Boards have learned to know that that call means help, and help effective and prompt.

WISE USE OF AGENCIES

The Union has very wisely made use of existing agencies for carrying on its work, and so, as nearly as was at all possible, avoided that multiplying of these, which is so much objected to by many; and not entirely without reason. For its mediums of communication with the societies, it has used the organs of the Boards, the *Foreign Mission Journal*, the *Home Field*, and the *Kind Words* child's paper. And, in addition to these, it has sought, through the Vice-Presidents in the various States, to get space in the State papers. It has not established an independent organ of its own, and in that has shown special wisdom. In Georgia, the State Union has made the mistake of establishing such a paper, which I have heard has a very small circulation, does not pay expenses, and so is a burden on mission funds.

Not only so, but the Union has gone further in this wise course, and has declined to receive and handle any money from the societies, even for its own expenses, but insists that all contributions from the societies shall go to the treasuries of the boards, and its own expenses are paid by the three Boards of the Convention jointly. I am of the opinion that, in States where State conventions have all their work under one Board, and have in connection with that Board a treasurer, the Central Committees would do well to follow this good example of the general body, and insist on the societies sending all contributions to the State treasurer, and let their own expenses be paid by the State Board. Experience has shown this to be eminently wise.

SUGGESTIONS

But, some one may say, I thought you were going to make some adverse criticisms also, and I have been looking for them. Well, I have two or three things to suggest, but they are rather suggestions of improvement than criticism of defects.

For one thing, I have been thinking that the Union is making its mission card, with suggestions of topics, too much the same year after year. There comes to be something of monotony in studying each year, year after year, the "Home Board" in July, the "Foreign Board" in August, the "Sunday School Board" in September, and now the "Woman's Missionary Union" once each year. And so, in lesser measure, of the other subjects. I am coming to feel that, after so many years of sameness in the study of our own narrow round of mission fields, it would be well if occasionally, say three or four times a year, the societies could have the horizon of their missionary vision enlarged, and be allowed to look upon work being done by other Christians. A lesson on India and Burma would bring the people into touch with a mission work that has had few equals in the intensity of interest it awakens. What do our societies know of any work in China, Japan or Africa, save ours? And how interesting it would be, once in a year, to open to the view of our people the splendid Home Mission work of our Northern Baptist brethren. We would come to see that the great work of the Lord is not confined to the feeble efforts of our own Southern Baptist host. The minds and hearts of our people would be stimulated by reading of the great triumphs which the gospel is making in lands which we do not touch at all, as well as under other laborers in those where we are at work. It will help our people, not a reading people in general, to learn that they are only one division of a great army that is battling for the Lord. It will help us to do our part better if we know how others are doing theirs.

Another suggestion I would venture on which might seem to imply a criticism, is that the Union should be careful not to multiply special "Days" and weeks for special objects. I know these are popular in some quarters, and that they often result in securing much money. But there is danger in their multiplication, not only that they shall lose their charm, but that they shall tend to undo what nearly all our Boards, both State and general, are now striving to impress upon the churches—the duty of steady, regular, systematic giving. Too many specials will derange any regular system in the world, from a railroad to a mission work. I am not referring now so much to what has been as to a tendency towards what may become a serious injury to the work.

And once more, I would suggest that the Union be careful how it multiplies methods of raising money, lest it train the people to forget the one great truth that every Christian should give to the Lord, and give from love. I dread catch-penny methods of inducing people to give to the Lord, by pin stickings in cards, to see who can stick a card full first, and by "Baby Branches," by which mothers are persuaded to organize their babies at two cents a month each, &c., &c. Yes, I find myself putting these things alongside of the now growingly unpopular "pink teas," oyster suppers, and a thousand and one other round-about and questionable methods of raising money for the Lord and his work. I honestly fear the tendency of these things. And I would see the Woman's Missionary Union, which has done so nobly in the past, rise above all such methods of inducing gifts and lead the many women all over our land who look to it for guidance and direction, to the highest plane service for the Lord, both as to work and giving.

[*The Christian Index*, 26 October 1899]

Armstrong was not about to take the Index's criticism lying down. She wrote several letters of inquiry regarding the article's authorship but no one was eager to claim the honor.

October 27, 1899
Rev. I. J. Van Ness
Editor, *The Christian Index*
Dear Brother:
I see in this week's edition of *The Christian Index* there is an article on "The Woman's Missionary Union. A Critic's View." I also notice in said article that there is a call for replies to the criticisms made.

Before considering the question whether I shall personally answer the "kindly" criticism, or request a reply to be made by one of our workers who is thoroughly posted as to the reasons that have led W.M.U. to adopt some lines of policy, which our friend has called in question, I would like to know who is the writer of the article. May I ask that you will furnish me with the name? By so doing, you will much oblige.

Yours truly,
Annie W. Armstrong
[IMB Archives]

October 27, 1899
Dr. J. M. Frost
Dear Brother:
I cannot help realizing that our Heavenly Father is guiding and directing at this time in many ways, and I believe He is keeping us from making mistakes. Although there is an immense amount of mail that I ought to answer, yet before taking these letters up I want to write to you.

This morning I awaked very early, and was considering some matters which I had discussed with you, etc., etc. I then realized as I had not before, that it would not be treating Dr. Willingham right, if I were to do as I suggested yesterday; viz., to see Mr. Barton in regard to the proposed enlargement of the work of the Sunday School Board prior to your talking to Dr. Willingham of it. In the years since I have been engaged in this work, I have tried never to do anything that I would be ashamed of, if it were known, and as I thought of this, I realized that this was something that I would not want Dr. Willingham to know in the future; that while you would not speak to Dr. Barton on this subject, yet I would be really acting as your agent, and therefore, it was one and the same thing. That being the way I was led to regard it, I determined I would write and tell you that I could not ask Dr. Barton to come to Baltimore in order that I might present to him the scope of the work of a "Field Secretary" of the Sunday School Board.

As I told you yesterday, I received a postal from Dr. Willingham stating that neither he nor Dr. Barton would be able to get to Baltimore. You may imagine I was, therefore, somewhat surprised for Dr. Willingham to walk in shortly after my reaching the Mission Rooms this morning. He had been to our house, and finding that I was not there, he had come down to the Mission Rooms. He felt it was only right for him to remain in Baltimore a few hours, as he is needed at home. As I did not feel I could go with him to the Association—mother is no better—our conversation was quite hurried. While talking with him about other matters, I was trying to come to some conclusion as to the wisdom of my referring to the question of Dr. Barton's being asked by the Sunday School Board to accept the position of "Field Secretary." I hope I did not decide wrong, but as you had given me full liberty to use my own judgment in speaking to Dr. Barton, and as you seemed fully persuaded that you *wanted* Dr. Barton, I concluded you would be willing for me to talk to Dr. Willingham. I also decided that if I did, it would do away with all possibility of any misunderstandings arising by you, etc., etc., and of your *thorough* unwillingness to take any steps in this matter, unless it met with his approval. After reaching this conclusion, I tried to find some way of broaching the subject in a tactful manner.

I asked Dr. Willingham if I might be allowed to ask a question of him. He told me, most certainly, I could speak to him on any subject. He did not promise to answer every question, but would be willing to do so if he could. We then had quite a free conversation in regard to the whole matter. I do not think it well for me to report to you just what was said, but I am prepared to advise you to write to Dr. Willingham at once, if you wish to take immediate steps to secure a "Field Secretary." If a delay of a few weeks will not make any material difference, you can see him when you attend the Alabama Convention, as he now expects to go to said convention. If I were in your place, I would most certainly not have any communication with Dr. Barton, either directly or indirectly, on this subject until after consultation with Dr. Willingham. While Dr. Willingham said that he would not have thought it out of the way if Dr. Barton had been approached before he was spoken to, yet I could see it will put the matter on a pleasanter footing, even with Dr. Willingham, should there be a change, for you to consult him first, and it will disarm criticism in other directions.

I expect this is enough on this point for the present. I would be glad, though, to know if I have acted according to your wishes.

I have another confession to make. You will see that the Corresponding Secretary W.M.U. is prepared to think that the Secretary of the Sunday School Board wishes her to use her own judgment and take liberties, when she feels that such liberties may prevent delay and trouble. In other words, you recognize my motive to be good even though my actions may not be exactly suitable. After this preamble, I will state that shortly after you left the Mission Rooms yesterday, the enclosed telegram was brought in. I thought an immediate answer might be necessary, and that I could at least let the sender know that it had not reached Baltimore in time for you to answer it. I therefore opened the telegram. I did not reply to it, as I saw no reply was needed, and you would have the information sooner than I could forward it to you.

I was sorry that it was not possible for us to attend to various items of business, which I desired to present to you while in Baltimore. I will have to submit these in writing, unless you can arrange to pay another visit to Baltimore, when you attend the General Association of Virginia, or the District of Columbia Association. Suppose you make a note of this suggestion.

Mrs. Tyler has just been to the Mission Rooms. Your visit to that home seems to have been mutually enjoyed. As you could not be at #1423 McCulloh St., I was glad to have you stay at Mrs. Tyler's. I consider them, Mr. and Mrs. Tyler, some of the best specimens of Maryland Baptists.

Very truly,

Annie W. Armstrong

P. S. Of course, if you wish me to see Dr. Barton *after* you have conferred with Dr. Willingham on this subject, I will be very glad to do so, if Dr. Barton will come to Baltimore.

P. S. No. 2. I wish you would read an article in this week's *Christian Index*, "The Woman's Missionary Union. A Critic's View" and then let me know if you think Dr. Bell is the writer thereof. I enclose copy of a letter which I have just written to Mr. Van Ness.

[Handwritten at end of letter] It might be supposed that Dr. Chivers had been the author of a part of this article. It voices his sentiments *exactly*.

[SBHLA, J. M. Frost Collection]

October 31, 1899
Dr. R. J. Willingham
Dear Brother:

I find there are several matters of business which I desire to refer to you. Appreciating, though, your kind interest in our home circle, before taking these up I will let you know how things are at #1423 McCulloh Street. Since last Friday I have felt that I ought not to be away from home, so have not been to the Mission Rooms. We have two nurses, one for the day and the other at night. Sister Mamie, Mrs. Levering, is here nearly all the time, and this makes it possible for me to still look after our work. I have first one clerk and then another here, and I am thankful to say I think today I will be able to answer nearly all the letters that accumulated last week, and have things up to date. While it is true the pressure is great, yet to see, as we are plainly seeing in many ways, how our Heavenly Father's loving and protecting arms are around and about us is causing peace even in the midst of trouble.

I sincerely hope that your son is not very sick. Please let me know when you next write, how he is. Present my loving sympathies to Mrs. Willingham.

Now to business.

1. *Contribution of $10.00.* Kindly credit same to Mrs. R. L. Martin, S. C. Send receipt to her at Brandywine, Caroline Co., Va. This is the offering of the dear old lady who made the quilt, and represents the price that she put upon six months' labor. May I ask that you will write to Mrs. Martin, when you send the receipt? I am sure a letter from you would be highly prized by her. You are at perfect liberty to let her know that you are acquainted with the fact that this is a genuine offering of love, but I would prefer you did not tell her that Mrs. Willingham has the quilt.

2. *Contribution of $7.50.* $5.00 of this is an offering to Foreign Missions from Mrs. Mary Choate of Indian Territory, and $2.50 from the Choate Prairie Society of Indian Territory. Kindly send receipts for these two amounts to Mrs. M. F. Coleman, Sulphur, Ind. Ter.

3. *Change of address for Foreign Mission Journal.* The enclosed card gives needed information.

4. *Christmas Appeal for State papers.* Will you kindly read critically the enclosed "Appeal," and let me have your opinion of it? Please appreciate that the main thought of said "Appeal," the joy of service, while it was emphasized very strongly in an article, which I sent to *The Baptist Argus,*

defining the duties of Central Committees, said article did not have a general circulation.

5. *Notice of Christmas Offering in Foreign Mission Journal.* It is your purpose, is it not? to make an appeal for this offering editorially in the December edition of the *Journal*, using in connection with it the plate which we have had prepared for the envelope. I will have an electrotype made of same, and forward it to you in the course of a few days.

You will doubtless remember that when this was done in previous years, there was a second brief appeal made by one of the officers of Woman's Missionary Union—the first year I made it, the second, Miss Heck. When this was in type, a number were struck off and I used them to enclose in letters. While I am both ready and willing to do whatever you think wise, yet I do not care to appear any more frequently in print than is necessary. What think you this year of your using the entire space that you will give to this "Appeal," and let the requests come entirely from you to the Societies and churches—I hope you are going to ask *all* to unite in the offering at Christmas. The "Appeal" which I send to State papers can be printed in W.M.U. Department in the *Journal* in December.

6. *Article in last week's Christian Index.* I have not heard yet from Mr. Van Ness as to the author of same. I rather expect that he will decline to give the name. Whether Dr. Bell did or did not write said article, I am quite sure he is responsible, not only for printing same but for furnishing the information. There is no member of the Central Committee of Georgia, except Mrs. Bell, or brother in Georgia with the exception of Dr. Bell, who probably would not have shown ignorance at some point as to the past history of our organization. I am, therefore, perfectly certain that Dr. and Mrs. Bell are entirely responsible for this article. I consider it a very mischievous publication. It is worthy of the *Western Recorder*.

Now as to a reply. It is contrary to the past policy of the Secretary of W.M.U. to notice newspaper criticisms; but I must acknowledge I would like to have the opportunity to "set straight" the "Critic" in a few directions. I hold in my possession some letters which were written by Dr. Bell in 1892, during the Centennial Campaign, which would furnish "telling shots."

My idea is, if you do not advise to the contrary, to have a reply made to said article by Mrs. A. Tucker, who is the Recording Secretary of the Home Mission Society of Maryland. Mrs. Tucker is one of the clerks at the Mission Rooms. I can furnish Mrs. Tucker with all needed facts, and a few points for her reply. When the manuscript is to be forwarded to Dr. Bell, I will have Mrs. Tucker offer it in a letter written on the official paper of

Woman's Baptist Home Mission Society of Maryland. Dr. Bell, in that way, would know perfectly well that, as President of the Home Mission Society, the article was written not only at my suggestion but under my supervision, and yet he would have no right to credit me with same. Please tell me would you or would you not have such an article sent to the *Christian Index*? Do not hesitate in this, as in any other matter connected with our work, to give me your candid opinion. If the article is written, before it is mailed to Atlanta I will let you see it. Should Dr. Bell decline to allow himself to be used to "illustrate" points in question in his own paper, there would be no difficulty in getting the editor of another paper to accept and print same, if the circumstance was told. Possibly Dr. Pitt would not refuse. I am quite certain Dr. Prestridge would not.

Very truly,
Annie W. Armstrong
P. S. I enclose copy of letter which I received a day or two ago from China. It certainly gives quite a touching incident. I send a copy rather than the original, so you may give it to one of your little girls to read at a Mission Band meeting, if she desires to do so.
[IMB Archives]

Nov. 3, 1899
Dr. R. J. Willingham
Dear Brother:
Enclosed you will find copy of Catechism on China, which we have prepared for use in work among young people. Will you kindly look over it and make any suggestions that you think will be helpful? The answers are brief, but children would probably not memorize longer ones. We have not yet taken up any other country, preferring to consider criticisms or suggestions before proceeding further. We thought of having one division entitled "False Religions" and making answers as brief and clear as possible. For this reason, under "China," Confucianism, Buddhism, etc. have not been defined. Do you think this a good idea?

Another Request. Please send word as early as convenient, *when* you desire to have the Christmas appeal for the *Journal* and also how much space you wish it to occupy.

Having received your advice regarding the article in the *Index*, I will *of course* follow it. However, it is quite a deprivation not to be able to make use of Dr. Bell's strong endorsement and unqualified approval of Chapel Cards, during the Centennial. Mr. Van Ness has been courteous enough not to reply to my communication. Since he refuses to "fess up," I am more convinced than ever that his confrere wrote the objectionable article.

It is now late Saturday afternoon. Mother's condition seems about the same. She rested rather quietly last night, but has not seemed so easy today.

There are other matters about which I will write later.

As Mrs. Willingham is in my opinion an ideal mother, I congratulate you upon the advent of another boy. May I offer the suggestion that it might be well to train this one to succeed his father, as Secretary?

Very truly,

Annie W. Armstrong

Later. Miss Wescott has just been here. No doubt it was cowardly, but I did not feel equal to seeing her disappointment, etc., etc., so I declined to discuss the subject and referred her to Mr. Millard. Mr. M. leaves tomorrow night for Ky. so it is not probable I will know until his return what explanation Miss Wescott gave, etc., etc. When I learn I will let you know.

[IMB Archives]

The Christian Index criticized Armstrong and WMU again in 1901 for overemphasizing missionary work in America, a charge that Armstrong categorically denied.

CHANGES—WHERE?
Annie W. Armstrong

In a recent number of the *Index*, April 11, occurs a criticism of the work of Woman's Missionary Union, by the editor, Dr. T. P. Bell. Its methods are used as "sadly exemplifying" the tendency to press the cultivation of Home Missions as a "basis of supply for foreign missions," to the neglect of the Master's positive command, "Go, disciple all nations." Dr. Bell says "if the *facts* are as he states them, they tell a sad story." We have neither time nor inclination for newspaper controversy, but the "facts" shall speak for themselves. We shall reprint Dr. Bell's late utterance and a different view of Woman's Missionary Union and its leaders, as given by him in February 1897, before the Bap. Theo. Seminary in Louisville.

EXTRACT FROM *THE INDEX*, APRIL 11, 1901.

"Twenty five years ago the women of the South, moved by the holiest impulses, organized societies whose definite purpose was to give the gospel to their heathen sisters. It was 'Woman's Mission to Woman.' And it seems to us that He who waits to 'see of the travail of His soul' must have rejoiced with great joy when it was done. These women were doing noble work. But when it grew large, some people said: This work must not be for the heathen only. We need it in our home land. And other hands took hold on it and other heads directed it, and lo! that which was started for the saving of poor heathen women has been turned aside and aside, until we heard the boast made, some time ago: The women are doing much more for home work now than for foreign. We looked and saw that while $51,757.00 had been given for 'all the world,' $45,203.00 had been given for the 'South,' not counting many more thousands given to other home enterprises. And how is this $45,203.00 expended? $27,089.00 of it in sending boxes of all sorts of things to what are called 'frontier' missionaries, four fifths of whom are not on any frontier, but scattered through some of our best States, many of whom are pastors of churches, giving only part of their time to supplying contiguous weak places, and most of whom are receiving about as good salaries as other men of like ability about them. The women have been diverted from saving their lost heathen sisters, by pathetic stories of life in 'dug-outs,' etc., to giving more that half of all their gifts to the home field, even to men in our strongest Baptist States."

EXTRACTS FROM SEMINARY ADDRESS.

"I pause here to say that this Union is one of the most wisely constructed pieces of denominational mechanism of which I know anything, and that the exceeding wisdom with which its affairs have been managed from its beginning until now is deserving of all praise. There was intense prejudice against the organization in the minds of many men and women, and any false step or unwise notions, especially in the earlier stages of its existence, would have alienated whole States for years, perhaps permanently. But by 1891 every State had joined in the work, and many of its bitterest opponents had been made its sincere friends. And now only a few cranks here and there squeak out occasional discordant notes of opposition to it and its work. If ever Christian workers were guided by the Spirit, these women have been. * * * * * * [10]

You will find in the officers of the Union some of the wisest, most thoughtful mission workers we have; well posted, wide-awake, energetic, helpful leaders. They do an immense amount of work and are full of information about various lines of missionary enterprise. * * * * * *

---

[10] Apparently, Armstrong used ***** to indicate that she was not quoting a portion of text in its entirety.

Not least among the many noble works they have done has been the exciting of an interest in the frontier missionaries, leading to the sending of hundreds of boxes to these hard workers each year."

Now, as to Dr. Bell's *facts* (?) as recorded in *The Index*, April 11, 1901: "*When this work grew large.*" In 1884, Woman's Mission Societies contributed to the Foreign Board, $16,895.00; in 1887, $11,333.00. This is not *growing large* and the fact of this retrograde was one of the forces leading to the formation of Woman's Missionary Union in 1888. Since which organization, in its twelfth year, the contributions from W.M.U. to Foreign Missions—note, *Foreign Missions*—have nearly trebled, being $31,757.00 in 1900. We would ask Dr. Bell if any other agency employed by the Foreign Board, or the Board itself can show a similar growth. We claim to have obeyed "the Commission" at least as well as others. So much for his first *fact*!

(2) "Other hands took hold and other heads directed."—According to Dr. Bell's admission in the address, "Woman's Mission to Woman" started in Baltimore and spread South through the personal influence of Mrs. Graves, the mother of Dr. R. H. Graves. Mrs. J. W. M. Williams, Mrs. Franklin Wilson and Mrs. Mary B. Armstrong were her co-laborers in the formation of Woman's Mission to Woman. Children of these have been continuously members of the Executive Committee of Woman's Missionary Union and their delight has been to carry forward the work so well begun. The change from mothers to daughters is slight.

(3) Dr. Bell says in speaking of W.M.U. contributions to Home Missions: "$45,203.00 were given for the 'South' * * * * $27,089.00 of it expended in sending boxes of all sorts of things to what are called 'frontier' missionaries, *four fifths of whom are not on any frontier*, etc." In answer to this "*fact*," if Dr. Bell had troubled himself to examine the Convention Report, pages CXXV and CXXVI, 1900, he would not have made this gross misstatement and could have learned that boxes to the value of $14,160.00 were sent to Oklahoma and Indian Territory—over *one half* of box gifts and to incontestable "frontiers." Other boxes were sent to destitute sections of Texas, Arkansas, Louisiana and Florida. In the eyes of Dr. Bell, the boxes are not valuable; in the eyes of the missionaries, most so. Yet he will be kind enough to note the relative proportion of *cash* contributions: $18,114.00 to Home Missions versus $31,757.00 to Foreign Missions. The heathen sisters are not entirely neglected.

(4) From Dr. Bell we again quote: "The women have been diverted from saving their lost heathen sisters, by pathetic stories of life in dug-outs,

etc." As to the need and importance of the frontier work, we will call on Dr. I. J. Van Ness, former editor of *The Index*, to reply. In referring to frontier work, he writes:

> "Is there any field, or any special kind of work we have attempted as Southern Baptists that can show for the amount of money spent, such results? Or can even our work in China show more important results, so far as the world's uplifting is concerned? Even Cuba has not, nor can it in the future, be more fruitful. What has been done is but the promise of what is today being done, or, at least, might be done."

In conclusion, we will ask candid readers to decide whether Dr. Bell's judgment has changed, or the methods of Southern Baptist women? Are the "*facts*" upon which his criticism is based, a justifiable foundation?

N. B. Should any readers care for Dr. Bell's entire address before the Seminary and for Dr. Van Ness' leaflet on "Frontier Missions of Today," we will be glad to send them. Address 304 N. Howard Street, Baltimore, Maryland.

[SBHLA, J. M. Frost Collection]

Obviously, Miss Annie was not intimidated by anyone and this letter to I. T. Tichenor demonstrates how forceful she could be.

PERSONAL
May 31, 1899
Dr. I. T. Tichenor
Dear Brother:

I note the suggestion you make, that I write to Mr. Dunson. I am going to beg that you excuse me from doing so, as it is quite evident that the Board does not desire any expression of opinion on that subject from the Corresponding Secretary, W.M.U. In view of the large amount raised by the Woman's Missionary Union last year—$14,129.67 in cash and $22,567.06 in boxes, making a total of $36,696.73, which is more than a third of the entire amount of receipts of the Home Board for the year just closed, (I am certainly not prepared, after hearing the missionaries state that it is owing to the gift of boxes that many of them are enabled to remain on their fields, to consider said boxes as not of service)—and eleven years of unremitting and, I think, successful effort that has been made to aid the Home Board in every possible way, I was surprised when an expression of opinion as to the desirability of proposed changes was being asked, the officers of the Woman's Missionary Union were entirely ignored. *If* a State Secretary, who is certainly not doing one tithe of the work for the Home Board that is done by the Woman's Missionary Union, is asked for his opinion, it seemed to me that it might have been as well to have requested the opinion of those who represent the Woman's Work, but such has not been the case, and it would be altogether out of place for me to proffer an opinion.

Very truly,
Annie W. Armstrong
[SBHLA, J. M. Frost Collection]

CHAPTER 4

"I am standing for two principles"

Annie Armstrong and the
Training School for Women Missionaries

Southern Baptists opened a Training School for female missionaries and Christian workers in the early twentieth century. The earliest correspondence concerning the Training School focused on feasibility and logistics.

Nashville, Tenn.
Feb. 24, 1900
Miss Annie Armstrong
Dear Miss Armstrong:
I want to secure your interest in an undertaking that I think will be of great help in the cause of Missions at home and abroad. We need a Training School for ladies wanting to do Mission work. I have talked with many brethren in Richmond, Louisville and other places. And all agree as to the need of such an institution. And all agree that the place for the school is Louisville in connection with our Seminary. The most of the teaching to be in the Seminary classes such as Old and New Testament in English course on Missions, church history, systematic Theology, & c., enough for a two years' course.

My plans are to get the ladies in Louisville to rent a house near the Seminary that will accommodate 12 or 15 ladies. Then ask some Ladies' Mission Societies to furnish a room each. Put the house in charge of a first class matron. Then find a good Sister who will give some instructions morning and evening in the home and have charge of some practical

Mission work in the city where these ladies can do some work. These matters all to be arranged after the work is started.

It is of great importance that we secure the best possible woman for the teacher and equally important a good matron. Now if you think this is a wise undertaking we want your help (of course the ladies studying pay the actual cost of living). Suggest the best woman you know for teacher and another for matron. I hope arrangements may be made and definite announcement made at the S.B.C. in May. And the first session to begin with the opening of the Seminary next fall. The faculty of the Seminary, except Dr. Mullins, who was not in Louisville when I was there, are heartily in favor of the plan. Dr. Willingham is in favor of it. Please confer with him and others that you think would help in the undertaking. I would be glad to have any suggestions from you on the matter.

And with all of your multiplicity of work I hope you will do what you can for our Chinese Baptist Publication Society. Ask some that can give us help to help us.

With kindest regards to yourself and Miss White, I am,

Yours fraternally,

E. Z. Simmons

Kossuth, Miss.

[SBHLA, J. M. Frost Collection]

February 27, 1900

Dr. R. J. Willingham

Dear Brother:

Your letter of February 26th just received. By the same mail came the one which I enclose from Rev. E. Z. Simmons. You are perfectly right when you say that I do "heartily favor the idea of our having a Training School." It is what I have long desired and felt that it *must come*, but whether Mr. Simmons is adopting the wisest course in trying to arrange for the opening of such a school next fall, without the matter having been very thoroughly considered and information secured from those who have done this kind of work, as to what it involves, etc., etc., I very seriously doubt.

I will write today to Miss Broadus, Dr. Mullins and several others in regard to the plan as outlined by Mr. Simmons. I will also write to Miss Burdette, who is in charge of the Baptist Training School in Chicago, and to Mrs. J. N. Cushing who has charge of the one in Philadelphia. From these two last named ladies, I can get some idea of the expense and what their experience was in the early stages of their work. If you agree with me that it would be well for the matter to be very thoroughly considered before more publicity is given to it, I am going to ask that *you* write to Mr. Simmons and suggest to him that he refrain from presenting the subject to others until some conclusions have been reached by those, who probably would have to be responsible very largely for the success of such an effort. I am going also to request that you will stop in Baltimore, if only for a few hours, on your way to or from Rochester, so that we may be able to consider this question and some others carefully. I will in the meantime obtain all the information I can on this subject, and be ready to submit it to you. Kindly let me hear from you on this point by return mail. I will wait to reply to Mr. Simmons' letter.

Very truly,
Annie W. Armstrong

EXTRACT FROM REV. E. Z. SIMMONS' LETTER
FORWARDED BY DR. R. J. WILLINGHAM

Another matter that I talked to you about. A Missionary Training School for ladies wanting to be missionaries. Everywhere the Brethren are heartily in favor of the enterprise. In Louisville the Seminary Faculty, except Dr. Mullins, who was not in Louisville, are heartily in favor of the undertaking. I talked with the Ladies' Mis. Societies of Walnut St. Ch. and Broadway Ch. They are much interested in the work, and will take hold in a practical way. I suggested that the ladies in Louisville rent a house near the Seminary that will accommodate twelve or fifteen ladies, and then ask some lady missionary societies to furnish these rooms. Secure a first class matron to take charge. And possibly a good practical woman as teacher in the home and a practical mission worker in Louisville. Those studying pay the actual cost of living in the home. The ladies taking such studies as Old and New Testament in English Mission Course, Church History, Systematic Theology, etc., enough for two years. All the members of the Faculty of the Seminary are hearty in their approval of this plan. I hope you will give your encouragement to this work. I believe it will be of great help to us in our mission work at home and abroad.

[SBHLA, J. M. Frost Collection]

March 1, 1900
Dr. J. M. Frost
Dear Brother:

I enclose monthly installment of data for *The Teacher*. I will send that for *Kind Words* probably tomorrow.

I have just had a letter from Dr. Willingham, in which he writes that he will come to Baltimore on Friday, so "we can *talk* over Training School, etc." I would have been very glad if Dr. Willingham could have come a few days later, so that I might have received replies to the letters which I wrote you and others before I saw him. I have had, though, quite a full account of the Training School in Philadelphia from Mrs. J. N. Cushing, who is in charge of same. She gives much valuable information.

My own idea is, if a Training School is established by Southern Baptists, it will be of far more service to the cause of Home Missions (and possibly to the Sunday School Board) than to Foreign Missions, as the Foreign Board can send comparatively few missionaries to the Foreign Field. We may be able in the future to so arrange matters that we will have a number of trained workers to do mission work in our own land. I shall try to prevent anything being done hurriedly. The question should be carefully considered in every light, so I will be glad if you will give the matter some earnest thought, and would ask that you talk over the subject with Dr. Kerfoot when you meet him.

Very truly,
Annie W. Armstrong

P. S. Another thing, and this is *very important*. In outlining some plans for the "Educational Campaign," it seems desirable to Dr. Kerfoot and the Corresponding Secretary W.M.U. that each Board should have a leaflet that would give a comprehensive view of their work to those who are not already interested in Missions, as well as information to those who now know something of the work of the different Boards. Will you give the subject thought, and be prepared, if you approve of the plan, to have ready a leaflet for the Sunday School Board? The two which I enclose have been, as you know, circulated very widely. It might be well to make use of some portions of these, but let it be in a little different shape. I would strongly recommend that the leaflet be not too long. When you see Dr. Kerfoot, you can talk over this matter with him. We have the leaflet for the Home Board. I will ask Dr. Willingham when he comes tomorrow about the leaflet for the Foreign Board.

[SBHLA, J. M. Frost Collection]

March 9, 1900
Dr. R. J. Willingham
Dear Brother:

Yours of March 8th received. I am glad to know that you are again in your office after encountering the heaviest snow storm they have had at the North in 50 years—I am truly delighted that it did not come this way—and in spite of it, speaking seven times in less than a week. You certainly do not allow difficulties to prevent you from carrying out your plans.

I, too, have been very, very busy since I saw you, but my work has been along a different line. I am now going to ask, when you have a little leisure, that you read a number of letters which I have received in regard to the proposed Training School. I feel at liberty to send you Dr. Tichenor's, although it is marked "Confidential," for I wrote to him asking for permission to do so. After reading the letters I will be glad to have your opinion as to what should be done. I have been so busy that I have not as yet written to Mr. Simmons. I think I will now wait to write to him until I hear from you.

There are other matters that I would like to speak of, but I know you are busy so I will simply give you one piece of Baltimore news. Some of us were quite electrified at the report made by the Deacons at a called business meeting at the Eutaw Place Church last Wednesday night. It was to the effect that in view of the work needed to be done in connection with our church in the way of visiting, etc., etc., that our pastor was not able to do if he gave the needed time to study, that the church authorize the employment of an assistant pastor. Said assistant is to be Rev. J. M. Wilbur, who the same night resigned the pastorate of the North Avenue Church. Mr. Wilbur has unusual gifts in the way of visiting. The engagement is only to be for a year, and may work very well, but I must acknowledge it does seem a little queer for Eutaw Place to have *two* pastors, and both of them young men. I would be glad if the ages of the two could be combined, and we have as a pastor a man of sixty years.

Well, well, well, I expect I am getting to be a fossil and do not know what should be done in this "young people's age." Do you not think it would be wise to have at the Second Church, Richmond, *three* young pastors? Perhaps if you had, you might secure your new building—when?

Very truly,
Annie W. Armstrong

P. S. Thanks for forwarding postal. I have filled the order for Self Denial literature.

[IMB Archives]

Macon, Ga.

April 2, 1900

Dear Brethren of the Home Mission Board, Atlanta, Ga. and of the Foreign Mission Board, Richmond, Va.

After consultation with Drs. Frost, Mullins, Kerfoot, and Willingham about the proposed training school for ladies, who are to become missionaries at home and abroad, I present to you the following for action and suggestions as to the following points:

(1) Is such an institution needed? I think it is. Lady missionaries must know the Bible before they can teach it. Feeling this need, many of our ladies have gone to the Chicago Training School for such help, and others are thinking of going. Is it not wise for us to give them this training in the south?

(2) If such a school is desirable, where should it be located? I have talked with a great many brethren about this, and with great unanimity they have agreed upon Louisville, Ky., as the place, in connection with the Seminary. A two years' course of three studies each year could be taken, in Old and New Testament, English, Biblical instruction, Systematic Theology, Church History and Missions. If located at Louisville, the teaching in these studies will not cost anything. The faculty of the Seminary are hearty in their proposal to do this teaching, and it goes without saying that the teaching will be better here than we could get elsewhere. And this will lessen the cost about half. Should it be located somewhere else, we would have to pay for all the teaching. One lady would be needed to teach, and be in charge of the home, and direct in some mission work in Louisville.

(3) A house should be rented, near the Seminary, that will accommodate fifteen to twenty students. A matron should be secured to look after the housekeeping, and ask the lady missionary societies to furnish rooms in the house. The students pay the actual cost of living. In case they could not do this, their churches could help them. This can be arranged for, somewhat as it is arranged for our ministerial students.

(4) The cost of such an institution will not be great, say:

Rent of house one year	$600.00
Matron, with board in home	400.00
Lady teacher, with board in home	600.00
Total, about	$1,600.00

I believe this school is needed, and it will be a great help in extending the Kingdom of our Redeemer. Action should be taken at once, and definite announcements made at our Convention at Hot Springs.

I am,

Yours fraternally,

E. Z. Simmons

Address me at Lexington, Texas.

[SBHLA, J. M. Frost Collection]

Waco, Texas

June 21, 1900

Mr. Joshua Levering

Baltimore, Md.

Dear Brother:

I write to make two inquiries: First, am I the chairman of the committee appointed by the Seminary Board to submit for the consideration of the Board at its next meeting a plan of Bible instruction in the Seminary? Second, who are the members of the committee? Someone has informed me that they are Doctor Mullins, Doctor Taylor of North Carolina, Doctor Landrum of Georgia and Doctor Mallard of Baltimore. Is that correct?

One other matter: I understand that to this same committee was referred the subject of a training school for ladies contemplating mission work at home and abroad. Concerning this last matter a document has been handed me by Brother E. Z. Simmons which he drafted at the request of certain brethren, and after consultation with Frost, Mullins, Kerfoot and Willingham. I enclose you a copy of the paper written by Doctor Simmons. It suggests that if it be desirable to have a training school, that it be located in Louisville, and this paper will have to be considered by this committee. Now it has occurred to me that we ought to have before we decide as a committee on recommendation, the matured view of some of the prominent ladies having in charge the ladies missionary work of the Southern Baptist Convention; among them notably, Miss Annie Armstrong. I will be obliged if you will see Miss Armstrong, show her this paper which I enclose to you and get from her for me a draft of a plan which she would recommend concerning this measure. I can promise nothing as to what the committee as a whole will recommend to the Board, and can promise nothing as to what the Board will do, but I can assure her that her suggestions will receive most respectful consideration.

Fraternally yours,

B. H. Carroll

[SBHLA, J. M. Frost Collection]

Armstrong conferred with Willingham and Frost upon receiving Carroll's letter. Her letters dated June 26, 1900 are almost identical.

June 26, 1900

Dr. R. J. Willingham

Dear Brother:

By this morning's mail I received a letter from Joshua Levering enclosing one from Dr. B. H. Carroll. I send copies of these, and also the paper which has been furnished Dr. Carroll by Dr. Simmons. Kindly read this correspondence.

You will recall while on the train en route from Hot Springs you told me that the question of a Training School had been brought up at a meeting of the Trustees of the Seminary, and that Dr. White, whom you questioned on the subject, stated that it was Mr. Millard who presented the matter. This being the case, I took an early opportunity to ask Mr. Millard for an explanation. I knew he had had no conference with me on the subject, nor with you. Mr. Millard said the matter was brought to his attention by Prof. McGlothlin, and it struck him that it was a good thing, and so he spoke of it. Dr. Landrum advocated it. The matter was referred to a committee to report on a year hence.

I cannot tell you how extremely annoyed I feel at being placed in the position I now am. It is evident from Dr. Carroll's letter that he is under the impression that the establishment of the Training School at Louisville is desired by the ladies in charge of the missionary work of the Southern Baptist Convention. This is, as you know, altogether incorrect. The Executive Committee of Woman's Missionary Union, located in Baltimore, after carefully considering the matter at two sessions, with all the facts which had been carefully gathered as to what it involved to establish a Training School, how the Central Committee in Louisville regarded the matter, etc., etc., decided that they did not consider this an opportune time for the establishment of a Training School, and did not regard Louisville as a desirable place for the location of a Training School when it was established. The Central Committee of Virginia passed similar resolutions, also that of Kentucky. It had been my purpose to refer the matter to the Central Committee in every state prior to the meeting at Hot Springs, so, if the question was brought before the ladies at that time, due consideration might have been given before action was taken. In deference, though, to your expressed wish, I refrained from submitting the question to those who have our work in charge in the different states, as you seemed to think it was unwise to give so much publicity to the matter. As I previously said, I cannot tell you how annoyed I am to be placed in the position of seeming antagonism to any plan which appears to have the endorsement of the Secretaries of the three Boards, the President of the Seminary (see Dr. Simmons' paper, first paragraph), presented to the Trustees of the Seminary by the pastor of Eutaw Place Church, and advocated by the President of the Home Mission Board. I must, though, be true. Dr. Carroll has asked a direct question, and I will have to furnish him with the facts. I will delay writing to Dr. Carroll. Today I will simply acknowledge his letter, and ask that he allow me to take a little time before replying to it in order that I may obtain some information which I desire to furnish; said information will be letters from Mrs. Stakely as President W.M.U., and Miss Broadus, President of Central Committee of Kentucky, Mrs. Gwathmey, Vice-President W.M.U., Virginia. If you are willing to offer any advice at this time, I shall be glad to receive it, and while I cannot promise that I will follow it, it will be carefully considered.

Should you think it wise to let Dr. Carroll know whether the impression is correct that Dr. Simmons has given, that the Secretaries of the Boards are in favor of the proposed Training School in connection with the Seminary, I would be glad to have you write to him.

Very truly,

Annie W. Armstrong

P. S. Your letter of June 25th received, and I will send tracts to Rev. E. Y. Jamison and Rev. R. E. Neighbor, as requested.

[IMB Archives]

June 26, 1900
Dr. J. M. Frost
Dear Brother:

By this morning's mail I received a letter from Joshua Levering, enclosing one from Dr. B. H. Carroll. I send copies of these and also the paper which had been furnished Dr. Carroll by Dr. Simmons. Kindly read this correspondence. It may be well for me also to give you a little additional information.

On the cars in returning from Hot Springs, Dr. Willingham told me that Mr. Simmons had come to him and said that the question of a Training School had been brought up in the Trustees' Meeting of the Seminary. Dr. Willingham said that Dr. Simmons seemed much surprised at this, and did not know how it came about. At Hot Springs I had a very plain talk with Mr. Simmons, and told him that unless he expected to carry on a Training School himself, that it certainly was unwise for him to present the matter until those who had charge of the work had had an opportunity to consider the advisability of same. I went over with Mr. Simmons point by point the ground he had taken, and I think he realized that he had not informed himself as thoroughly as he should have before presenting the subject. Dr. Willingham stated that when Mr. Simmons told he, Dr. Willingham, watched Mr. Simmons very carefully, as he wished to know if Mr. Simmons had had anything to do with it; but he felt sure from Mr. Simmons' manner that it was a surprise to him. Dr. Willingham called two of the Trustees who were in the car with us, Dr. Stakely and Dr. White, of North Carolina, and asked for an explanation. Dr. Stakely did not seem to remember about it, but Dr. White said that it was so, that there had been a proposition of the kind made, and his idea was that it was brought forward by Mr. Millard, our pastor. This being the case, I took an early opportunity to ask Mr. Millard for an explanation. I knew he had had no conference with me on the subject, nor with Dr. Willingham. Mr. Millard said the matter was brought to his attention by Prof. McGlothlin, and it struck him that it was a good thing, and so he spoke of it. The matter was referred to a committee to report on a year hence.

I cannot tell you how extremely annoyed I feel at being placed in the position I am now. It is evident from Dr. Carroll's letter, that he is under the impression that the establishment of the Training School at Louisville is desired by the ladies in charge of the missionary work of the Southern Baptist Convention. This is, as you know, altogether incorrect. The Executive Committee of Woman's Missionary Union, located in Baltimore, after carefully considering the matter at two sessions, with all the facts which had been carefully gathered as to what it involved to establish a Training School, how the Central Committee in Louisville regarded the matter, etc., etc., decided that they did not consider this an opportune time for the establishment of a Training School, and did not regard Louisville as a desirable place for the location of a Training School when it was established. The Central Committee of Virginia passed similar resolutions, also that of Kentucky. It had been my purpose to refer the matter to the Central Committee in every state prior to the meeting at Hot Springs, so, if the question was brought before the ladies at that time, due consideration might have been given before action was taken. In deference, though, to Dr. Willingham's expressed wish, I refrained from submitting the question to those who have our work in charge in the different states, as he seemed to think it was unwise to give so much publicity to the matter. As I previously said, I cannot tell you how annoyed I am to be placed in the position of seeming antagonism to any plan which appears to have the endorsement of the Secretaries of the three Boards, the President of the Seminary (see Dr. Simmons' paper, first paragraph) presented to the Trustees of the Seminary by the pastor of Eutaw Place Church, and advocated by the President of the Home Mission Board. I must, though, be true. Dr. Carroll has asked a direct question, and I will have to furnish him with the facts. I will delay writing to Dr. Carroll. Today I will simply acknowledge his letter, and ask that he allow me to take a little time before replying to it in order that I may obtain some information which I desire to furnish; said information will be letters from Mrs. Stakely as President W.M.U., Miss Broadus, President of Central Committee of Kentucky, Mrs. Gwathmey, Vice-President W.M.U., Virginia. If you are willing to offer any advice at this time, I shall be glad to receive it, and while I cannot promise that I will follow it, it will be carefully considered.

Should you think it wise to let Dr. Carroll know whether the impression is correct that Dr. Simmons has given, that the Secretaries of the Boards are in favor of the proposed Training School in connection with the Seminary, I would be glad to have you write to him.

Very truly,
Annie W. Armstrong
[SBHLA, J. M. Frost Collection]

June 28, 1900
Dr. J. M. Frost
Dear Brother:
Your letter of June 28th received this A.M. I appreciate the kind way in which you have written, and hope with you that the question of the Training School "will work out all right." This morning's mail also brought a letter from Miss Broadus, which I will send to Dr. Carroll. Miss Broadus expresses herself as thoroughly opposed to a Training School for female missionaries being established in Louisville in connection with the Seminary. I would like to write more fully about this and some other matters, but I think you will agree with me that I am hardly in a condition for letter writing when I tell you I have just returned from the dentist's after having two teeth extracted, and the result is an attack of neuralgia, which usually follows in the train of other physical suffering.

I enclose Freight receipt for box of leaflets sent a few days ago. It contains 4,800 copies—I retained 200 for distribution from this point—of Dr. Eager's leaflet, "A 1900 Retrospect of a Century of Religious Liberty" with electrotypes. I hope next week to be able to send Dr. Carroll's leaflet, and possibly Dr. Felix's.

In your letter of June 28 you say,

> "What has become of my eight-page leaflet, the manuscript of which was sent you before the Convention?"

As far as I could see, no plans having been decided upon by the Committee of Nine at the Meeting in Chattanooga, and no one being appointed permanently to take charge of the work, when Dr. Kerfoot was in Baltimore, I declined doing anything in regard to carrying out report made by the Centennial Committee and adopted by the Convention. I therefore return you the manuscript.

I enclose clipping taken from the July *Foreign Mission Journal* which shows the attitude of the officers of Woman's Missionary Union toward this new movement; viz., awaiting instructions. I have not as yet heard from Dr. Kerfoot whether he proposes to accept the offer I made to go to the point where the Committee meets August 1st, so that when plans are adopted in which the Committee desires the cooperation of Woman's Missionary Union, there could be conference with the officers W.M.U.—I am glad to be able to report Mrs. Stakely holds herself in readiness to take this trip, if Dr. Kerfoot, as Chairman of the Committee of Nine, desires it.

Very truly,

Annie W. Armstrong

P. S. The Program for Missionary Day is completed. I expect to receive drawings for title page and mite box on Monday. Will have plates made immediately and possibly send package to Nashville on Thursday.

Foreign Mission Journal clipping:

Committee on Cooperation.—The committee was appointed by a large vote at the Convention to devise means to "elicit, combine, and direct" the energies of the great Baptist hosts at the South, that they might become missionary in deed as well as in name. With a record facing us of 10,000 churches practically anti-missionary, and only one-tenth of the membership giving to missions, there seemed evident need to do something different from what had already been done if there were to be a change. Dr. Kerfoot, as chairman of Centennial Committee, presented the matter to W.M.U., accompanied with a request from the Convention that Women's Societies should aid to secure the needed change. The invitation to help was enthusiastically accepted by W.M.U.

The committee met May 29th, at Chattanooga, composed of the three Secretaries of the Boards, Messrs. Wm. Ellyson and Chas. H. Ryland, of the Foreign Board; Drs. Tichenor and Landrum, of the Home Board; and Drs. Folk and Burrows, of the Sunday School Board. No plan of work was proposed, nor was a Secretary elected. Another meeting of the committee will be held in August. Till then W.M.U. must await instructions.

[SBHLA, J. M. Frost Collection]

In May 1903, Armstrong received word that she had been named chair of the Training School's curriculum committee. As usual, she took her responsibilities seriously.

Atlanta, Ga.

May 19, 1903

Miss Annie Armstrong

Dear Miss Armstrong:

I have divided our committee for the training school into several sub-committees.

I have made you chairman of the committee on curriculum. I will be obliged if you will correspond with the members of the committee telling them of their appointment on the sub-committee and informing them as to service you would like to get from them on the line of the work assigned them.

Truly Your Friend,
(Signed) W. J. Northen
Committee on Curriculum
Miss Armstrong
Dr. Willingham
Dr. McConnell
Mrs. Chipley
A. J. S. Thomas
[IMB Archives]

May 25, 1903
Dr. R. J. Willingham
Dear Brother:
I enclose a copy of a letter which I received from Gov. Northen which I would ask that you read. From it, you will note that Gov. Northen has appointed me Chairman of Committee on Curriculum of the proposed Training School. As you were not present at the meeting of the Joint-Committee appointed by the Convention and the Woman's Missionary Union to present a report at the Annual Meetings to be held in 1904, I would say that Gov. Northen was appointed Chairman of the Committee, and after a free discussion of the subject, it was decided to appoint three Sub-Committees to take the various phases of the subject into consideration. The Committees as follows: Location, Curriculum, and Method of Securing Funds for Support.

Thinking possibly you may like to have wording of the Resolution as adopted by Woman's Missionary Union and which led to the presentation of the subject to the Convention, I append same. It is as follows:

RESOLVED: That the Southern Baptist Convention be requested to appoint a Committee of seven—three of whom shall be the Secretaries of the Foreign, Home and Sunday School Boards—to confer with a Committee of the same size appointed by Woman's Missionary Union to consider the advisability of establishing a Missionary Training School for women; said Committee to report at the meeting of the Convention in 1904, and the Annual Meeting of the Woman's Missionary Union the same year, and if favorable to suggest place of location, nature of operating, method of raising funds etc., etc.

By reference to page 18 of the Minutes, you will see that the Convention appointed the following Committee

"To confer with Woman's Missionary Union (to report in 1904): W. J. Northen, Ga.; J. B. Hawthorne, Va.; A. J. S. Thomas, S. Car.; J. N. Prestridge, Ky.; R. J. Willingham, Va.; F. C. McConnell, Ga.; J. M. Frost, Tenn."

The Committee of Woman's Missionary Union: Miss A. W. Armstrong, Mrs. J. A. Barker, Clifton Forge, Va., Mrs. J. D. Chapman, Anderson, S. Car., Mrs. E. J. Willingham, Atlanta, Ga., Mrs. W. D. Chipley, Pensacola, Fla., Mrs. F. S. Davis, Dallas, Texas, Mrs. W. J. McGlothlin, Louisville, Ky.

May I now ask as member of the Sub-Committee on Curriculum that you will take that phase of the subject under careful consideration? If you have any suggestions as to how I can as Chairman of Committee best present the subject to other members of the Committee, I will be glad to have them. I expect to write to the different Missionary Boards that have Training Schools, and also to the Seminary at Louisville, asking for the Prospectus of said Training Schools and of the Seminary. Would you like to have copies of these? If so, I would be pleased to send them to you.

Praying that our Heavenly Father may give wisdom to each member of the Committee so that we may be able to know how we can best advance His cause in this direction, I am,

Very truly,
Annie W. Armstrong
[IMB Archives]

May 29, 1903
Dr. E. Y. Mullins
Dear Brother:
After considering the matter more carefully, I reached the conclusion that in view of the Convention and Woman's Missionary Union having appointed a joint committee to present a report at the meetings in 1904 in

regard to a Training School, it was better for me not to send you the letters which I offered to forward. I am extremely sorry that any misunderstanding should have arisen, but I am trying to realize that we can leave things in God's hands to be straightened out.

Gov. Northen, who is chairman of the committee on Training School, wrote me a few days ago that he had appointed me as chairman of a sub-committee on "Curriculum." May I now ask that you will kindly let me have fifteen copies of any publication that contains the curriculum of the Seminary?

Asking to be remembered most kindly to Mrs. Mullins, I am,

Very truly,

Annie W. Armstrong

[E. Y. Mullins Collection, Archives, James P. Boyce Library, The Southern Baptist Theological Seminary, Louisville, KY]

December 21, 1903

Dr. R. J. Willingham

Dear Brother:

Please find enclosed a check for $6.00, which is a Christmas Offering from the Missionary and Aid Society of Pittsburg, Texas. Kindly send receipt to Mrs. E. M. Francis, Pittsburg, Texas, and duplicate to me.

There are several important matters that I desire to refer to you this morning, so will take these up seriatum.

(1) *Clerical Permits.* I hold clerical permits on a number of Railroads. Most of these you kindly secured for me. If I remember correctly you told me, when you last obtained same for me, that it would have been easier for you, if I had sent the permits for the previous year so you could have forwarded them when you were making application for renewals of your own. As I do not expect to do any travelling between this and the first of the year, I enclose all the permits which I hold with the exception of the one on the Baltimore and Ohio Road. As that was obtained in Baltimore, I will ask for renewal here. Will you kindly look over these permits, and if there are any of them that you think you cannot secure renewals of, please return same and I will ask Dr. Frost, if he has any influence on those roads, to try and obtain their renewals. I will be much obliged if you will attend to this for me.

(2) *Prospectuses of Different Missionary Training Schools.* As I mentioned to you some time ago, I have secured a large number of these.

You will remember that Gov. W. J. Northen was appointed chairman of the committee on Training School, which is to make a report at the Convention in Nashville and also at the annual meeting of the Woman's Missionary Union. Said committee, if favorable, to suggest place of location, nature of operating, methods of raising funds, etc., etc. At a meeting held in Savannah, which you were not able to attend, it was decided to appoint three sub-committees on location, curriculum, and method of raising funds. Gov. Northen has notified me that I am chairman of committee on curriculum and has appointed you as a member of that committee. I now desire to ask if this is the favorable time for me to send you a number of prospectuses of different Training Schools to which I would ask that you give careful examination and let me have your opinion in regard to the curriculum of proposed Training School.

(3) *Woman's Missionary Union Securing Funds for the Support of Schools in Foreign Lands.* The letters I have received so far from the missionaries in reply to the ones I sent—there has not been sufficient time to hear from the missionaries in China, Brazil or Africa—give most unqualified approval of the plan as outlined. I find though that they are not sufficiently definite in the information they have sent to make me willing to assume the responsibility of dividing the appropriation made by the Board to each school so as to ask for same from W.M.U. workers. I do want to get the matter thoroughly arranged before I present it to Societies and Bands. I am sure that there will be very little difficulty in securing the heartiest cooperation of our workers, and I believe much of the money needed will come from sources that heretofore gave very little. I have already on file several requests from Bands for names of children, etc., etc. I have written to those making application, asking for a little delay in furnishing information in regard to the "desks."

After the letters come I would like to be able to go over these with you and get your views as to how the money can be divided. I realize it will take some hours to do this. After the letters come—how soon can I expect replies to the letters from China, Africa and Brazil?—would it be possible for you to come to Baltimore for a day, or had I better arrange to come to Richmond for this?

(4) *Letter from Miss Nora Norman.* I enclose letter from our sister, which I would ask that you read. Possibly, probably, you will remember that you spoke to me of Miss Norman when at Oklahoma City, so I am sure you met her. Has Miss Norman made application for appointment by the Foreign Board? I was quite favorably impressed with what I saw of her while at

Oklahoma City, and she seemed to be quite valued there. I am under the impression though that she had not been very long at Oklahoma City. As you will note, she is now chairman of committee on Junior work, or as we designate it, Band Superintendent.
Very truly,
Annie W. Armstrong
[IMB Archives]

March 4, 1904
Dr. R. J. Willingham
Dear Brother:
Appreciating that it will be impossible for the sub-committee appointed by Gov. Northen on curriculum for Training School to have a meeting prior to going to Nashville, and realizing after arriving there each member of the committee would have his and her hands full, I thought it better as chairman of the committee to prepare a report and submit same to each member of the committee, asking for it careful consideration. If said report does not meet with the approval of the majority of the committee, we will have to try and have a meeting. If slight changes only are desired by various members it can be arranged through correspondence. I now send report to you.

You probably noted an article entitled "Training School for Missionaries," which appeared in the February issue of the *Missionary Review*, which as stated there was written for the revised "Encyclopedia of Missions" which is soon to be issued by Funk & Wagnalls Co. The report is based largely on this article, but changes made as it seemed to me desirable after examining the curriculums of a large number of Training Schools. Should you approve of the report will you kindly sign same and return it to me as soon as convenient? If it does not meet with your approval, please indicate where you think changes or additions should be made, and I will be pleased to let the other members of the committee know what your views are.
Very truly,
Annie W. Armstrong
[IMB Archives]

April 9, 1904
Dr. R. J. Willingham
Dear Brother:

I have just returned to Baltimore from Philadelphia as there were several matters which required my being there for a day or two. I spent last night at the Baptist Training School. This is the fourth Training School I have visited in charge of different denominations, and I think I now understand right well how the work is being done by others. They are certainly doing a beautiful work in Philadelphia.

As to the school work. In a letter written by you April 8th you say:

> "I enclose to you a letter received today in reference to support of a child. I think it would be best for us to have some understanding how we shall manage these gifts so that there will be no complications. We can arrange this later."

As I wrote you I have been trying to get the facts sent by the missionaries so tabulated that I could give those who are willing to support "desks" or teachers in schools the information required. I am now preparing a book which will have in it all this data. I had thought to write to the different ladies who are asking for this information just as soon as I could get the book prepared. Is it your wish that I do nothing in regard to assigning teachers and desks until I see you again, so that there be some definite understanding? I will take the book with me to Nashville. Let me hear from you on this point as I do want to prevent all misunderstandings.

Kindly let me have the amount that has been designated as Christmas Offering received by you since you sent me the last report.

Very truly,

Annie W. Armstrong

P. S. While in Philadelphia I saw about the printing of the booklet on China which I called your attention to when in Baltimore. We will get out 1,000 copies, making changes so as to present S.B.C. work. I hope to have some copies to take to Nashville. Please do not forget that you promised to try and help us in disposing of the booklets. If we can sell a sufficient number of the publication on China to pay for the edition, we will get out another on Japan and later on Africa. I am much pleased at the orders we are receiving for *Bright Hours*.

[IMB Archives]

April 13, 1904
Dr. J. M. Frost
Dear Brother:
Please find enclosed a list of boxes sent to Sunday School missionaries not previously reported. I would ask that you let me have receipts for these as soon as possible.

This year the Woman's Missionary Union, as it meets a day previous to the Convention, is arranging to have five sessions; two Thursday, two Friday, and a missionary meeting Sunday afternoon. It is our custom to take up a collection at every session. Mrs. J. A. Barker is making arrangements for the annual meeting, but she has left it with me to find out from the Boards what the objects shall be and obtain needed data.

As there are five sessions, I have suggested that the collection at one session be given to the Bible Fund of the Sunday School Board. This is a new departure, but I am sure it will meet with your approval. The other Boards are asking for definite amounts. Do you wish to name one? If so, please let me know what amount we shall call for by return mail; also any data you have in regard to the Bible Fund which you can furnish.

I am more annoyed that I can tell you at something that has occurred, for I am sure it is going to put me in a very false light. You may or may not have heard that there will be a request made for the Training School for female missionaries to be located in Baltimore. That of course is all right. Applications no doubt will come from other cities, but occupying the position I do, as Secretary of the Woman's Missionary Union and as a member of the committee to make the report, it will doubtless be thought that I have had a large part in this, when the truth is I have had nothing whatever to do with it. Our State Secretary desires to do "large things," and he has been pushing this. He has interviewed me a number of times on the subject. He made three visits to the Mission Rooms before he found me in order that he might ask for the names of the members of the committee appointed by the Convention and Woman's Missionary Union on Training School. I positively declined to give him a single name. It did not seem to occur to him that by referring to the Convention Report and the Woman's Missionary Union Report he could have obtained the information without so frequently mounting the three flights of steps at 233 N. Howard St. The Ministers' Conference has endorsed the appeal and at a meeting of the Social Union last Thursday—I was not present but was informed as to what occurred—after an address by Dr. Rufus Weaver on "Maiden Effort," our State Secretary requested that those assembled should resolve themselves into a mass meeting as there was an object of business they wished to present to representative Baptists. The subject of the Training School being located in Baltimore was then brought forward. Dr. Griesemer did not approve on the ground of there being Northern Training Schools, and that Baltimore was not now in a condition to make any moneyed offer which was part of the proposition. I was told that there was very little enthusiasm, but when the vote was taken to appoint a committee looking toward securing a moneyed proposition, there was only one man [who] voted against it. Who the one was who had the courage of his convictions I did not inquire. Mr. George Miller was made chairman of the committee. He, of course, has money and he may be willing to make a generous contribution, as he is very much impressed with the importance of the development of Maryland Baptistically.

Another thing: Mr. Miller is trustee of the Seminary and goes with Dr. Thomas to Louisville April 20th, they being the committee appointed this year by the trustees to visit the Seminary. I can and do recognize that there may misunderstandings arise which I do want to prevent. I have nothing whatever to say and have positively refused when approached on the subject to give an opinion as to the advisability of Baltimore being the place for the Training School, but this will not be known by others and it will be supposed that I have been back of this effort. If so, it is entirely a mistake. I have given you the facts and will be very much obliged if you will positively contradict any statement that may be made that I had anything to do with the proposition to have the Training School established in Baltimore.

Another thing: I have learned that the Baltimore Ministers' Conference on Monday decided to invite the Southern Baptist Convention to meet in Baltimore (I think) year after next at Brantly Church. I certainly for one am not overpowered with the wisdom manifested in this decision. It is, of course, entirely uncertain as to the time when Baltimore will arise from its ashes. Unless we should have another fire in the vicinity of Brantly Church, and on that place hotels be built, the delegates attending the Convention would have to go probably a mile or more to find hotels, as there are none in that section of the city. Well, well, well, I suppose it shows enterprise, but indeed it seems to me it shows precious little common sense with the conditions that surround us to be projecting quite so much. We have got a State Secretary who can *plan* large things.

Very truly,
Annie W. Armstrong
[SBHLA, J. M. Frost Collection]

By 1904, Armstrong began to express her misgivings about the Training School.

June 6, 1904
Dr. J. M. Frost
Dear Brother:

I am more annoyed than words can express at something that I have just learned for I am quite sure it will be misunderstood and place me in a very false light. It is in regard to the Training School.

This morning's mail has brought a letter from Miss Frances Schuyler, Preceptress of the Baptist Training School in Philadelphia. I enclose copy of her letter and also one that she forwarded from Rev. B. P. Robertson, pastor of Fuller Memorial Church, Baltimore. I am going to ask that you kindly read these and then advise me as to what you think best for me to do under the circumstances.

I knew before the meeting in Nashville that the Baltimore pastors had passed a resolution at the Ministers' Conference requesting that the Training School if established should be located in Baltimore and that the matter was also brought up at a meeting of the Social Union and a committee appointed to try and secure moneyed contributions which might be offered as an inducement for locating the school in Baltimore. Dr. Elridge Hatcher, State Secretary, had spoken to me several times on the subject but I declined expressing any opinion whatever as to Baltimore being a desirable place for the Training School, telling him that I was a member of the committee appointed by the Woman's Missionary Union to consider the matter and I, therefore, was unwilling to express an opinion. You, of course, know what was done in Nashville and as a member of the committee I fully and entirely acquiesced in the decision to leave the matter of the Training School with the Seminary "for the present." While in Nashville Dr. Rufus Weaver who appears to be moving in the matter of establishing a Training School in Baltimore met me after the report on Training School had been made to the Convention and made the remark without any solicitation on my part that he thought we had done the right thing.

I knew that Mr. Robertson had said that, if the Training School was not located here, Maryland Baptists ought to have one of their own. It is, of course, perfectly right for any state to do any local work that they may deem wise, but I consider it a very unfortunate circumstance that so soon after the decision at Nashville the Maryland pastors should try and establish a

Training School in Baltimore. You, of course, will recognize that I have nothing whatever to do with this nor will it have my support or help, but W.M.U. workers and those interested in the Seminary Training School will not so understand it. I would like very much to have a little advice. Do you think it would be well for me to come out in a card in the *Foreign Mission Journal* and let it be known that if there is a Training School established in Baltimore that *I have had nothing whatever to do with it nor do I purpose having*?

Hoping to hear from you in the near future, I am,

Hastily, but very truly,

Annie W. Armstrong

[SBHLA, J. M. Frost Collection]

July 2, 1904

Dr. E. Y. Mullins

Dear Brother:

Your letter of June 13th came duly to hand at the Mission Rooms, but absence from Baltimore on a missionary trip and extreme pressure of work since my return has prevented an earlier acknowledgement.

Permit me to reply to your inquiries by sending you two extracts taken from the minutes of the Woman's Missionary Union.

From Report of the Annual Meeting held in Savannah, Ga.,

May, 1903

Discussion of "The Demand for Trained Women Workers; How to Meet It," opened by Mrs. G. W. Truett, Texas.

The following resolution was offered by the Executive Committee and adopted on motion of Mrs. J. A. Barker, Va.

Resolved: That the Southern Baptist Convention be requested to appoint a committee of seven—three of whom shall be the Secretaries of the Foreign, Home and Sunday School Boards—to confer with a committee of the same size, appointed by the Woman's Missionary Union, to consider the advisability of establishing a Missionary Training School for women; said committee to report at the meeting of the Convention in 1904, and the Annual Meeting of the Woman's Missionary Union the same year, and, if favorable, to suggest place of location, nature of operating, method of raising funds, etc., etc.

From Report of the Annual Meeting held in Nashville, Tenn.,

May, 1904

Report of Committee on Training School presented by Miss A. W. Armstrong, Md., and the following Resolution adopted:

Whereas, no notice had been given that there was a Training School for women missionaries in connection with the Southern Baptist Theological Seminary at Louisville, Ky., prior to the appointment of the joint committee by Southern Baptist Convention and Woman's Missionary Union, May, 1903, to consider the advisability of establishing a Missionary Training School for Women, said Committee to report at meeting of the Convention 1904, and the Annual Meeting of Woman's Missionary Union the same year:

And Whereas, Dr. E. Y. Mullins, President of the Theological Seminary, makes public announcement in *Baptist Argus*, April 7, 1904: "We already have such a successful Training School in connection with our work at the Seminary."

With kind regards to Mrs. Mullins, I am,

Very truly,

Annie W. Armstrong

[E. Y. Mullins Collection, Archives, James P. Boyce Library, The Southern Baptist Theological Seminary, Louisville, KY]

March 15, 1905

Dr. J. M. Frost

Dear Brother:

Your letter of March 13th received. As my niece Miss Levering marries today and I leave Baltimore tomorrow on a missionary trip of two or three weeks, my hands are now very, very full, so I cannot write long letters. I feel, though, it is necessary for me to present one or two matters to you before I leave Baltimore. Before I take these up allow me to refer to your letter of March 13th. As to your former letter which mine of March 9th is in reply, I would ask that you kindly re-read your letter to which I replied.

As I understand the matter, I was simply giving reasons why I asked the question that you would furnish me with the name of some one at the office who would reply to letters in your absence. Facts remain facts whether a matter has been referred to in conversation or not and the fact remains that Dr. Van Ness very frequently does not acknowledge letters. I would ask that you request Dr. Van Ness to let you see copy of letter which he wrote me March 11th and the one I sent in reply March 13th. After reading these letters I leave the question for you to answer whether the Secretary of the Woman's Missionary Union has been kindly dealt with in the late correspondence with those in charge of the work at the Sunday School Board office.

Another thing: I do not know whether you have noted an article which has been going the rounds in the papers written by Mrs. George B. Eager in regard to the so-called Woman's Training School at the Seminary and for which a strong effort is being made to have Woman's Missionary Union to furnish the money for its support. You are being quoted as endorsing this at the last Southern Baptist Convention, although you were a member of the Committee that presented the report that declined to take any action. Unless God interposes it is inevitable that there will be much trouble come to Woman's Missionary Union through this action. History will doubtless repeat itself. The same professors are in the Seminary that made Dr. Kerfoot's last years so bitter.

As you must know, the Secretary of the Woman's Missionary Union, Aux. S.B.C. has since the organization of the Sunday School Board done all in her power to aid in making the work you represent strong, and personally to be of assistance to the Secretary of the Sunday School Board, and loyally stood by the Board when a few years ago a vigorous attack was made upon your administration. You will remember that when trouble arose some years ago between the Officers of the Woman's Missionary Union on account of my supporting the Sunday School Board when the President did not wish contributions made to that Board, I did not have your support at that time, and it did seem to me last year when you knew just how I stood in the matter of the Training School you might have refrained from offering the Recommendation which you did in the Convention. If it had to be offered, some one else could have done so and not a member of the Committee. I had not meant to write of this but your letter of March 13th has led me to feel that it is just as well that you should have an insight into something that is at present causing the Secretary of the Woman's Missionary Union much anxiety. Now for two items of business:

(1) You report that the Children's Day Program is nearly ready and ask how many I can use to advantage. You are at perfect liberty to send whatever number you see fit to Baltimore and on my return April 4th I will make as good use of them as possible.

(2) As last year, the Woman's Missionary Union at its Annual Meeting will give the collections at one session to the Bible Fund in charge of the Sunday School Board. I would ask that you write to Mrs. J. A. Barker, Clifton Forge, Virginia, as Mrs. Barker is arranging program, giving her information which can be presented at that time, as to needs of Bible Fund.

It might also be well for me to call your attention to the fact that the so-called Woman's Training School at the Seminary is supposed to be for the training of women missionaries that the Woman's Missionary Union later on is to support. Under these circumstances, it would have seemed that the endorsement should have come from the Woman's Missionary Union, and especially in the light of what now seems to be the purpose of those who are advocating the Seminary Training School, viz: that Woman's Missionary Union *must* support this so-called Training School.

Then again, I enclose clippings taken from the Convention Report of 1904 and from the catalogue of the Southern Baptist Theological Seminary of 1902 and 1903. I have not one of the catalogues for 1903 and 1904 at hand but if my memory does not prove treacherous the wording is the same. You will note it is definitely said: "The following ladies have attended classes regularly but are not counted in the list of students." The name of the one who prepares the catalogue is not given, but certainly it is supposed to have the endorsement of the President of the Seminary. It, therefore, seems very strange that a notice of a Training School by the President of the Seminary should have been "made by himself in the Baptist Papers of the South about a year before the appointment of the joint Committee at Savannah" and the same year no notice whatever made of such a Training School in the annual catalogue.

May I also remind you that at the Committee Meeting in Nashville Dr. A. J. S. Thomas, one of the trustees of the Seminary stated positively that there was no Woman's Training School connected with the Seminary?

Very truly,

Annie W. Armstrong

[SBHLA, J. M. Frost Collection]

April 5, 1905
Dr. J. M. Frost
Dear Brother:

On returning to Baltimore yesterday evening I found several letters from you awaiting me. They have been read with care and as it would cause me to be entirely wanting in truth to say that I feel that the course adopted by Dr. Van Ness in failing to acknowledge letters when sent to him after work done for him as Editorial Secretary of the Sunday School Board is courteous; and that such long delays in Miss Buhlmaier receiving supplies does not militate against the work; and that the course adopted by you in offering a resolution endorsing the so-called Woman's Training School in connection with the Theological Seminary after voting to adopt the report which was presented by Gov. Northen to the Convention when the Committee refused to take any action was right, I simply cannot make any apology whatever but will have to leave these various matters just where they are. It, of course, is perfectly immaterial to you and Dr. Van Ness what the Corresponding Secretary of the Woman's Missionary Union may think. I know it is your desire and also Dr. Van Ness' to please our Heavenly Father, and if that has been done it makes no difference what others may think.

I enclose copy of a letter which I am now sending to various State Officers in regard to program for Children's Day.

I enclose two letters with check for 78¢. Be kind enough to fill order.

I will write to our sister Mrs. J. W. Guy, Dendron, Va.

The check for $100.00 for Woman's Missionary Union expenses has been received. I will hand same to the Treasurer and she will forward receipt.

Very truly,
Annie W. Armstrong
[SBHLA, J. M. Frost Collection]

April 26, 1905
Dr. R. J. Willingham
Dear Brother:

Your letter of April 24th just received in regard to "Home for women at the Training School in Louisville." I am now going to send you copy of a paper which I have prepared at the suggestion of one in whose judgment I have much confidence, giving a history of the Training School movement. What use will be made of this paper I cannot say. I must, though, request that you do not present same at the meeting of the Foreign Board when the subject is brought to their attention. If later, I find it necessary to give the facts to the Board, the paper will be sent, with probable additions. Since it was written I learn the delegates (W.M.U.) in one of the states—probably in all—are being interviewed on this subject. It savors very much of political wire pulling and I would say to you without the shadow of a doubt if the Woman's Missionary Union is prepared to endorse such actions they will at the Annual Meeting in Kansas City have to select another Corresponding Secretary. I would ask that you note specially two headings in the paper "recent action" and "conclusion."

It had not been my purpose to say anything whatever to you on the subject of the so-called Seminary Training School, but as you have written in regard to it, I think it only right that you should have the *facts* before the matter is brought to the attention of the Foreign Mission Board. Dr. Gray has written me that he had received a letter from Mrs. Woody, Chairman of the Committee that has provided the temporary home in Louisville for the ladies attending lectures at the Seminary, and also one from Mrs. T. A. Hamilton requesting that the Home Board would include the Seminary Training School in their Recommendations to the Woman's Missionary Union. Afterwards, Dr. Gray wrote that he had received a letter from Dr. Mullins. I judge you have had similar communications from the parties named. Dr. Frost has not yet let me know what has been done in regard to the Sunday School Board.

I would further say, during the present Conventional year, not one line has ever been written to me by those who are letting no stone remain unturned, in order that they may create public sentiment in favor of passing a resolution at the Annual Meeting of the Woman's Missionary Union, to get the Woman's Missionary Union to support the so-called Training School, which Dr. Mullins claimed was established several years ago at the Seminary, nor to the Executive Committee in Baltimore. I have, though, been notified by ladies in different states as to what was being done, for as they said they thought I should be informed.

I would like to ask how you would regard it, if a similar effort was being made to have the Foreign Mission Board engage in any work, and you as Secretary of that work should not be approached on the subject. I have held the office of Secretary of the Woman's Missionary Union for seventeen years and my Heavenly Father knows that I have never in any way allowed anything to prevent my doing what I felt was for the good of the work; and if after seventeen years of faithful service it is thought that such measures are needed to accomplish anything that can be *proved* to be helpful, certainly persons have not gauged me aright. I say now after making the matter a subject of earnest thought for five years, I thoroughly, entirely and heartily disapprove of the Woman's Missionary Union supporting a Woman's Training School in connection with the Theological Seminary at Louisville. I cannot feel that my judgment is wrong in this matter when I am supported as I am by the expressed opinions of Dr. John A. Broadus, Dr. I. T. Tichenor and Dr. Henry G. Weston.

In a letter which I had from Dr. Tichenor written during the time that Dr. Simmons was agitating this matter Dr. Tichenor wrote, establish a Woman's Missionary Training School anywhere but in Louisville (or words to that effect, I have not his letter which I can refer to).

I leave Baltimore Monday night for Newton Centre, Mass. My object is, primarily to visit the Home for Missionaries' Children, as that was the request of the one who gave the $10,500.00 to purchase the Margaret Home. While there, I shall visit the Hasseltine House which Dr. Mullins speaks of.

I appreciate that you regard all letters sent to you as official, but I make the request (and I think I have a right to ask it of you) that you will refrain from letting it be known by the Foreign Mission Board or any one else what it is probable I shall do if the Woman's Missionary Union in annual session endorse the actions of those who during the past year have been advocating W.M.U. supporting a Woman's Missionary Training School in connection with the Theological Seminary at Louisville.

The envelope is marked personal. I do this in order to insure that no one else reads this communication.

It is only justice for me to say that prior to the Annual Meeting in Nashville (last year) I had a letter from Miss Broadus in which she told me that she hoped I would not consider her inconsistent but that she had in some degree changed her opinion in regard to the Seminary Training School. The only ground she gave for a change was that she found that supplies could be purchased for the "Home" cheaper than she had thought, as they could be bought with those intended for use in the Seminary. Opinions may change, facts do not. Then again, Miss Broadus or no one else is able to say that Dr. Broadus has changed his opinion.

I will write of other matters later in the day.

Very truly,

Annie W. Armstrong

[Handwritten at top of letter] Marked Personal

[IMB Archives]

April 27, 1905
Dr. R. J. Willingham
Dear Brother:
Permit me to give you a little more information in regard to the measures being used to secure votes for the support of the "Home" connected with the so-called Woman's Missionary Training School at the Theological Seminary in Louisville, Kentucky.

This morning's mail has brought a budget of letters sent by a Vice-President of Woman's Missionary Union in one of the states. I quote from one of these letters which she sent to me in the way of information, signed by the following ladies:

Mrs. A. C. Cree
Miss Fannie Moses
Mrs. George B. Eager
Mrs. W. J. McGlothlin
Mrs. S. E. Woody
Executive Committee.

The closing sentences of this circular letter are these:

"Are you in sympathy with this work? How do you think it can best be brought before the W.M.U.? What will be the attitude of your delegation? We urgently ask an immediate reply to these questions."

The letter from which I quote is dated April 19th. Kindly appreciate that a copy of this communication has *not* been sent from Louisville to the Corresponding Secretary of the Woman's Missionary Union to be presented to the Executive Committee W.M.U.

Very sincerely,
Annie W. Armstrong
P. S. I think possibly it is as well that I send you copy of the letter which is being sent out by the Executive Committee of the "Home" in Louisville. Please note that an effort is there made to make Woman's Missionary Union workers think that the Seminary Training School is one thing and the "Home" for young women attending the lectures at the Seminary is another thing. It may be well for these ladies to explain what makes the Seminary Training School that the Seminary claims to have. Is it only, as the catalogue gives, that the women sit in the classes where the men are who are being taught how to preach? Is that a Woman's Missionary

Training School? If so, it is totally different from what is generally conceived to be a Woman's Missionary Training School, and certainly altogether contrary to the curriculum which was prepared by Sub-Committee and was to have been submitted to the Committee on Training School at the meeting in Nashville if Dr. Mullins had not claimed that the Seminary had a "successful" Woman's Missionary Training School.

[IMB Archives]

Official Action of Executive Committee
May 25, 1905
At a session of Executive Committee, W.M.U. held Thursday, May 25, in Baltimore, a very careful review was made of the history of the movement to establish a Woman's Missionary Training School in connection with the Theological Seminary, Louisville, Ky., from its inception, in 1900, by Rev. E. Z. Simmons, returned missionary from China, to its presentation with Home for Students to W.M.U. in Kansas City, Mo. Official records, letters and recent actions preceding and during the meetings in Kansas City were in evidence.

By unanimous vote, the Executive Committee endorsed the attitude of the President and Corresponding Secretary at annual meeting towards the Training School and Home at Louisville, and recognized their devotion to the work by remaining in office till the close of the present Conventional year, May 1906.

The Executive Committee will likewise decline renomination.

[IMB Archives]

May 26, 1905
To Central Committees, or State Executive Committees
Dear Sisters:
At recent Annual Meeting of Woman's Missionary Union, held in Kansas City, I declined re-election as Corresponding Secretary W.M.U. prior to the election for reasons which are not necessary for me to give. The Nominating Committee, however, did not present any other name for the office of Corresponding Secretary. I felt, therefore, that the work to which I have given my life for the last seventeen years, might suffer if time were not given for one to be sought who might be willing and able to do it. I accepted

the re-election, giving notice that at the expiration of this year, I would not serve longer.

Having accepted the office for this year, it is my purpose and desire, as far as God may give me strength, to aid in making this year's work the best in the history of W.M.U. and to leave the charge entrusted to the Cor. Sec. in such condition that it may go on more prosperously in the future.

As, of course, it cannot be known until the Annual Meeting of 1906 who will fill the office next year, I can therefore only proffer help to State bodies. It is my wish to furnish all the information that may be desired as to the relationship between the General Organization and State Organizations, in regard to every line of work now prosecuted by Woman's Missionary Union, the methods adopted in securing information, etc., etc.

Plans as adopted at Annual Meeting in Kansas City call for large increase in contributions this year. It is the duty of the Cor. Secretary to get out the needed literature and present same. The regular correspondence is very heavy, but I now desire to say that if it will be thought more helpful for the Cor. Secretary to visit *some* of the States, so as to furnish the information in person along different lines of work, I will do so as far as possible. The year is too short in which to visit every State, in view of the amount of work that has to be done in Baltimore. I have therefore thought it well to write this letter as soon after my return from Annual Meeting as possible, in order that I may know how to plan the year's work. If you consider that the information needed can be given through letters, I will ask that you do not extend an invitation to the Secretary to visit your State during the year. If, however, you consider a visit desirable, kindly let me hear from you by June 15th, stating when you would like to have a visit, the length of time, etc., etc. It is necessary that I attend the Conventions of Indian Territory and Oklahoma the latter part of September, as steps are now being taken looking to the consolidation of the work in those Territories. I have made no other definite plans, and so hope to arrange the year's work in such a way as to accomplish the best results.

Permit me also to state that it is not my purpose to attend the next Annual Meeting and, after the election of Cor. Secretary, no W.M.U. mail will be answered by me; hence all information desired of the present Corresponding Secretary must be obtained this year.

Kindly appreciate it is my desire that nothing be written or said to me personally in regard to my reasons for declining re-election to the office of Cor. Secretary W.M.U.

Hoping that our Heavenly Father may abundantly bless the work,
Very sincerely,
Annie W. Armstrong
[IMB Archives]

June 19th, 1905
Dr. R. J. Willingham
Dear Brother:
Your letter of June 17th, received. I do appreciate, more than I can tell you, your kind willingness to be of service to the Secretary of the Woman's Missionary Union, at this time. I realize as Secretary of the Foreign Mission Board, it is necessary for you not to appear to take sides in any thing where there is a division of opinion, but right is right, and certain things that have recently been done, are *altogether wrong*. I am coming very much to the opinion, that I am doing wrong in shielding people who are certainly being used by Satan. I have been urged to come out and let the facts be known. Mrs. Peck, of the *Western Recorder*, has urged me to send to that paper a statement, and also urges that it should go to every paper. The *Western Recorder*, under these circumstances, is ready to print syndicate matter. I have declined Mrs. Peck's offer, but think there is more truth than fiction, when she states I am to be "boycotted."

I have nothing to conceal, and I think it only right that some persons should have facts, so I am going to send you a copy of a letter which I sent Miss Broadus, a few days ago, in reply to one she wrote me, marked "personal." It is a new code of Christian ethics, to insult people, and then be relieved of the responsibility of actions, by marking letters "personal." You will note that I have refused to receive any more personal communications from Miss Broadus.

I am going to enclose copy of the letter I wrote Miss Broadus, and ask that you read it. I do not ask that you express any opinion whatever as to Miss Broadus' action, or my letter, but I do feel that I have some rights, and if I refrain from making public the wrong doing of those who are advocating the Woman's Missionary Training School in connection with the Seminary, and the Home for Students, some persons should know the truth. I am likewise going to send you copy of the paper that I read from, in Kansas City, as it differs somewhat from the paper that I previously sent you, some letters having been left out, and others inserted. Kindly read this paper, also.

Now, for several other matters: Last week I wrote you a letter enclosing one from Mrs. McGee, the President of the Local Board of the Margaret Home, also copy of one from Dr. Headdon. In the letter I wrote, I asked your opinion, as to the advisability of offering the position of "Mother," to a Mrs. Gwaltney. I likewise requested, that you would let me have Mrs. Willingham's opinion. No reply has come to that letter, although I have had two others from you since sending the one referred to. You are always so prompt, that I fear, either my letter did not reach you, or your reply has gone astray. Kindly let me know if this is the case. If you wrote, please send me a duplicate of the letter.

I am more sorry than I can tell you, to learn that you, too, are having perplexities. It is not nearly so hard, though, to endure these, when you recognize that the trouble comes from God, but when you know those who are leaders in God's cause, are Satan's emissaries, it takes every particle of religion one has, not to succumb.

Another thing, I failed to say, in a previous letter,—I was so disturbed,—that it will give me pleasure to have you call on me at any time, if Mr. Willingham decides that it will be helpful for Mrs. Willingham, to come to Baltimore. As far as I can now see, it is probable that I will be in Baltimore, until the first of August, only leaving in the interim, for a day or two; after that, I go for a prolonged trip.

Very truly,
Annie W. Armstrong
[IMB Archives]

July 14th, 1905
Dr. R. J. Willingham
Dear Brother:
I enclose letter from Mrs. K. L. Walker with check for $2.50. The letter gives names of club secured for *The Foreign Mission Journal.*

I have been busy today writing letters in regard to the Margaret Home. There are several applicants for positions at the Home. Among other letters written is one to Mrs. Jas. Pollard. I am going to enclose copy of this for possibly Mr. Henry Pollard will make some inquiry of you when he learns that Mrs. James Pollard has not been appointed. I was very glad that Mrs. Pollard in a letter I received from her said some things which I could take hold of without giving the reason which I state in a former letter to you, why I thought it better for us to seek someone else.

Thanks for pictures which came today, but I have not yet had time to examine same. Hope to do so later in the day. I am now having letters written to missionaries in which will be sent application blanks for the Margaret Home. In the list which you kindly forwarded you have marked Rev. Frank Marrs' name. Was that a mistake, or are there any little ones now in that home? They had no children when I was in Mexico so that leads me to ask the question.

I have received a letter this morning from the business manager of *The Baptist Argus*, in which he says: "Will you kindly send us the complete list of the State Secretaries of the Woman's Missionary Unions of the South." The editor of the *Argus* has seemed to think that he is the one to arrange Woman's Missionary Union affairs at the present stage of things. In an issue of several weeks ago, he announced that he knew several women that could take the place of the present Secretary of W.M.U., and suggested where one of them resided. There has been far more wire pulling in regard to the Seminary Training School, by the Louisville people, than should have been tolerated, and certainly they will have to appeal to someone else beside the present Secretary of the Woman's Missionary Union to furnish them with names of W.M.U. workers. A stamped envelope was sent, but I shall consign same to the waste basket.

Very truly,
Annie W. Armstrong
[IMB Archives]

Armstrong may have been aware of "wire pulling" by the "Louisville people," but she blamed J. M. Frost for the Training School debacle.

October 4, 1905
Dr. J. M. Frost
Dear Brother:
Your letter of October 2nd has just been received. I do try to be perfectly honest in the statements which I make and also as courteous as possible, but I believe honesty is more pleasing to our Heavenly Father than courtesy, so while courtesy seems to necessitate my acknowledging the receipt of your letter, honesty compels me to say some things which perhaps you may not think courteous.

I of course knew when you took the seat by Dr. Barton at the church in Oklahoma City, as I was sitting by him on the other side, and while I did not know at that time that you had failed to see me, yet I could have taken the initiative and spoken to you but I did not care to meet you. Before I left Oklahoma City Dr. Barton told me that you had the next day expressed your surprise at my being in Oklahoma City as you had failed to see me the night previous.

I cannot help feeling that you are largely responsible for the state of things which now exists in connection with Woman's Missionary Union work. You were the one who gave the opportunity to those who are advocating the so-called Woman's Missionary Training School at the Seminary to make the statement that in my failing to advocate the training of women to be preachers—it is this and only this—that I am opposing the Convention, for although a member of the committee that declined to make a report when the subject of establishing a Training School and proposing location for same in view of the statement made by Dr. Mullins that he had "A successful Training School at the Seminary," (although Dr. A. J. S. Thomas, a trustee of the Seminary, said at that meeting, "There is no Training School at the Seminary,") you went into the Convention and proposed the endorsement of the claim made by Dr. Mullins. You, of course, knew that the committee did not in any way shape or form endorse the claim made by Dr. Mullins and only yielded the point of discussing the subject because, if it was decided to propose that a Training School should be established and located somewhere else, it would be regarded by Dr. Mullins and the Faculty of the Seminary as a rival. You agreed to take no action and then went into the Convention and proposed endorsing the claim made by Dr. Mullins which was contrary to the spirit of the committee's report. You doubtless consider that you did exactly right, but I feel you did exactly wrong, and your action has caused already a great deal of trouble and will, I fear, result in much harm to the work.

As stated in the previous letter, it would have seemed that after the earnest efforts that I have made for so many years to aid you as Secretary of the Sunday School Board and supported you at every point, you could have allowed someone else at that time to have echoed the wishes of the Faculty of the Seminary and been silent.

I have made an earnest study for five years of the training of women for missionaries and it has led me to the conclusion that it is entirely wrong to have a Woman's Missionary Training School in connection with a Theological Seminary. You may think, and doubtless you do, that I am in a very pitiful minority when announcing this decision, but I think I am in quite good company for I am voicing the opinions of Dr. John A. Broadus, Dr. I. T. Tichenor, and Dr. Henry G. Weston.

On the authority of Miss Eliza Broadus I make the statement that Dr. John A. Broadus would not allow his own daughters to attend the lectures at the Seminary regularly. I know a change has come in the opinions of Dr. Broadus's daughters, but Dr. Broadus is in his grave and can no longer exercise his authority in the matter.

Dr. I. T. Tichenor wrote me when the question of establishing a Training School in connection with the Seminary was mooted by Dr. Simmons in 1900, "Have a Training School anywhere but in Louisville."

Dr. Henry G. Weston said I was at liberty to use his name in quoting him as opposed to a Training School for women in connection with a Theological Seminary. He says that the fifteen miles between Crozer Seminary and the Philadelphia Training School, where he lectures Saturday mornings, is all too short a distance.

Thinking possibly you may not have made as thorough a study of this question as has the Secretary of the Woman's Missionary Union, I enclose copy of a paper which is largely a compilation of official records. The original letters I have in my possession. I would ask for this paper a careful reading.

You may be a little astonished at the statement which I have made and which has led me to oppose a Training School in connection with the Theological Seminary in Louisville, that it is teaching women to be preachers and I see no warrant for same in God's word. I claim, and I think I am right in saying that it has been thought for many years that the classes at the Seminary were for the training of *men* to be preachers. The women have not separate classes but are in the same classes with the men, so if the course of study is suited to make preachers of men, is it not also the same for women?

I would now give a little personal experience. A few years ago I was at a point in Oklahoma where I had gone to meet the ladies on attendance at a District Association. While there I was handed a letter giving me further instructions as to the arrangements that had been made for me. They were on this order. The next Sunday morning I was to take charge of the services at the First Church of Oklahoma City, meet the ladies in the afternoon, and take charge of the services at the Washington Ave. Church of Oklahoma City at night. It is unnecessary for me to say that I declined to meet the appointments made for me Sunday morning and Sunday night, although they had been made by the Secretary of the State Board, Rev. L. L. Smith. The pastors of both of these churches were at that time Southern men. When I declined to keep the appointments I asked Rev. L. L. Smith if he did not know from what section I came. He replied "Miss Annie, do you not know there are women preachers in Kansas?" I had not attended the Seminary Training School so I could reply, "But I am not one of them."

To sum up this whole matter I am standing for two principles; first, the unscripturalness of training women to be preachers, and second, for right methods in Southern Baptist Mission work.

This letter does not require a reply. It is my determination to give the work up at the close of the year. I learn you have suggested the name of Mrs. T. P. Bell as the one to take my place. Doubtless she will have the Seminary endorsement, and with the wire pulling, which some Southern Baptists seem to have become adept in, she may get a sufficient number of votes to be installed in the office, although previous to her marriage Dr. T. P. Bell, who was then Assistant Secretary of the Foreign Mission Board, told me that the next year she would not be elected to the position of President, which she then held and which I was desirous that she should continue to hold. Acting on Dr. Bell's advice I made no effort to try and have Miss McIntosh retain the position as President. Having been so long in Southern Baptist Mission work I have seen some very curious changes. If during the interim between now and the meeting of the Convention in May it is necessary for you to write to me in regard to any lines of work or to see me as to the transfer of the property of the Mission Literature Department, your letters of course will receive prompt attention and I will hold myself in readiness to meet you and Dr. Gray at a time decided upon. I recognize that we hold entirely different views on the subject of the Training School and your actions in regard to same. We must leave the question as to who is viewing the matter in the right light until we appear before God's judgment bar. I am trying as far as I know to do what I feel will meet with His approval and doubtless you are doing the same, but we neither of us think this of the other, so there it must rest.

Very truly,

Annie W. Armstrong

P. S. I send you copy of paper as I have nothing to conceal, and others having seen the paper, I think it only right that you also have a copy. Although urged to do so I have not yet made any statement through the papers. Dr. T. P. Bell has had the entire right of way in this direction. It is a grave question though what I shall do in this particular between now and May.

I have not yet been informed whether in presenting the name of Mrs. T. P. Bell as the next Corresponding Secretary W.M.U. you suggested that a salary be given to her. If that is the case, I would respectfully propose the reprinting of an article written by the editor of the *Christian Index* after the meeting of the Convention in Savannah, entitled "Dimming of the Glory." I can furnish you with a copy of the article if so desired.

[SBHLA, J. M. Frost Collection]

The Christian Index carried several negative articles and editorials regarding Annie Armstrong and WMU in 1905–1906. Even though she was more than capable of defending herself, Armstrong appealed to R. J. Willingham as a "Christian and a gentleman" to set the record straight.

October 6, 1905
Dr. R. J. Willingham
Sec. Foreign Mission Board
Dear Brother:

In conversation with you in Oklahoma City, September 27th, regarding articles in *Christian Index* (1) on visit of Cor. Sec. W.M.U. to Georgia during August and (2) the editorial attack on her by Dr. T. P. Bell of an earlier date, you stated there would be no further articles of such a nature in that paper. My surprise was therefore great on receiving from a friend copy of the *Index*, September 28th, in which appear two articles of similar nature. These articles so thoroughly misrepresent facts and are so detrimental to denominational interests that I am impelled to call your attention to them.

In reply to Mrs. J. D. Easterlin's article, under caption of "Some Serious Charges Against the *Index*," the editor takes grave exception to my visiting a few Societies in Georgia during this time when he considers no other denominational interests but State Missions should be presented—except through the columns of the *Index*. As proof, the issue of August 31st is largely a Foreign Mission number. The editor gives no extended notice of your visit which was subsequent to mine, but cites you as an example of what should be done in the following:

"In this connection we would commend the example of Dr. Willingham. After his address at the Centennial Association the moderator remarked that it was a good time to take a collection. Immediately Dr. Willingham rose and begged the brethren not to do this but to return to their homes and take collections for State Missions in all the churches, and not allow anything to interfere with such between now and the meeting of the Convention in November."

The animus of the Article seems to be that I was interfering with State collections. Allow me to remark that in the ten places visited in Georgia I took no collections, nor was one cent given to me privately or publicly for either the Hospital at Yang Chow or the Tichenor Memorial. On reference to editorial notes in *Foreign Mission Journal*, October, 1905, page 128, I note the following:

> "On a recent trip to Georgia one brother gave us a check for $600.00, the salary of a missionary. A sister said she would take the support of a missionary and send funds soon. Another brother said he and his son would support still another. God is blessing our people and they are blessing others."

In the article in *Index* (Sept. 28) the editor repudiates "the insinuation if not the charge that the *Index* was trying to persecute Miss Armstrong" and goes on to say "We could surely have no object in trying to injure Miss Armstrong and, if we had, there would be no sense in it now that she is about to retire from the work." In this connection I would call attention to previous *Index* article which was a direct attack on me, although he there states I was to give the work up.

Further, the editorial in *Index* (Sept. 28) entitled "Clashing Interests," makes another grave charge. This time it is the regular S. S. Missionary Day for Home Missions. I will quote:

> "And yet, just in the crisis of this campaign for State work, the Executive Committee of the Woman's Missionary Union, in Baltimore, regardless of the conditions in the State—and in several other States, we judge—issues a call to the schools for special services and special collections for an entirely different object. We are sorry to see that the Home Mission Board has endorsed this effort to switch the schools off of the State Mission track and on to another. This is to produce confusion and bring about clashes in the various interests entrusted to the care of the State Board. We fear that the Home Board will lose more than it will gain by aiding and abetting the Missionary Union in this action, which tends to such clash and confusion."

Allow me to give you the history. As stated at 10th anniversary W.M.U., 1898, (see historical leaflet enclosed) in 1894, S. S. Missionary Day, by joint approval of three S.B.C. Boards, was the new work inaugurated, W.M.U. preparing the programs. At that date, 1894, the fall was the season and the last Sunday in September was the date, agreed upon by officers of said Boards. Dr. R. J. Willingham, was Sec. of For. Brd., Dr. I. T. Tichenor of Home Board, and Dr. T. P. Bell of S. S. Board. This order proceeded for ten years till at a conference in Washington, D. C. –November 1903—it was decided by Drs. Willingham, Frost—the Secretary of the Home Board was not present—and Secretary W.M.U. that hereafter each Board would make its own appeal to S. Schools, programs to be prepared for all three Boards by Sec. W.M.U. as heretofore. January was assigned to For. Board; June was retained by S. S. Board for Children's Day—instituted later than 1894. Dr. Gray when coming into office changed time of Home Board appeal to S. Schools from last Sunday in September to second Sunday in October.

As you know it is only within the last three or four years that the Georgia State Convention has been held in the fall; the spring was its time for many years. So the charge made by the *Index* "that the Home Mission Board has made the effort to switch the schools off the State Mission track" at the close of their State year, is not one that should be made in the face of history. State meetings are held at different times during the year. It is not possible to arrange a general plan that shall suit all of these times. In this instance Georgia has made the change and "clashed" with a long established order.

Now, my dear brother, this is in no sense a personal matter. As long as Dr. T. P. Bell saw fit to make personal attacks on me, I did not call on the Boards which I have served faithfully for 17 years without remuneration, to defend me. I did not call on these officers, nor did they come to my help. At this time, the work of W.M.U. and of the Home Board is included in the personal attack by the editors of the *Index* and you are cited as an example of proper conduct in Georgia, according to the *Index's* code of propriety, when the facts are you made collections for Foreign Missions and I did not.

I now call on you as a "Christian and a gentleman" in this crisis to come out and make a public statement and have these false presentations of facts corrected and these attacks to cease. It would seem that I might be left in quiet to do W.M.U. work till the close of Conventional Year, without this miserable newspaper persecution. You called it, June 17th, "a calamity to the work for me to give it up" before the close of the year. I have stayed in it and both the work and I should be protected from these newspaper aspersions.

Having been publicly misrepresented, I will ask that this letter be read at the next meeting of For. Mis. Board.

Very truly,

Annie W. Armstrong

Cor. Sec. W.M.U.

[IMB Archives]

October 9, 1905

Dr. J. M. Frost

Dear Brother:

Your letter of October 7th just received. Permit me to return the paper entitled "History of Movement to Establish Woman's Missionary Training School" and ask that it be placed on file in the office of the Sunday School Board. It is, as you doubtless noted, largely a compilation of official records, and a resolution having been passed at Annual Meeting of Woman's Missionary Union at Kansas City to the effect that investigations should be made as to the work now being done at the Theological Seminary in Louisville and the desirability of sustaining a home for the young women attending the Theological Seminary, it is only right that the records of this movement should be on file in the offices of the Boards so that reference may be made to them and questions answered authoritatively.

I am a Baptist and I thoroughly understand that Baptist claim the right to judge for themselves what God would have them do. I desire to accord this to you and others and would be only too glad if it would be accorded to me and the persecution I am now having to endure would cease. What I call in question is not persons differing from me in regard to the establishing of the so-called Training School at Louisville, but the *methods* adopted by those who are advocating same.

Another thing. You write:

"But I really thought that matters had been altogether adjusted, for you and I were in conversation where I thought every thing was altogether pleasant and knew nothing of the feeling which you had against me, indeed do not think you had at that time."

I judge you have reference to a conversation which I had with you when attending the Florida Convention. If my memory is not treacherous I did refer then to your action in presenting the resolution endorsing the so-called Seminary Training School at the meeting of the Southern Baptist Convention in Nashville, but the matter was not discussed. I sincerely hoped at that time that nothing further would have been done in regard to *forcing* the Woman's Missionary Union to support the Seminary Training School. It is a reflection on the intelligence of W.M.U. workers to try to differentiate the *home* for women students attending the Seminary from the Seminary itself. There would be no home needed if there was no Training School and the Seminary is not supporting the Training School unless they support the home—that is unless they have bought a few more chairs or benches for their class rooms. It has been stated over and over again that the women simply sit in the same class rooms with the men who are being taught to be preachers. When I asked if the professors of the Seminary would be willing to give lectures suited to train women for missionaries, I was immediately told that their hands were too full and this was not the idea. I believe one professor does give some lectures to women alone, but for this he is paid by a lady. Am I not right in thinking that New York Hall, which is the home for the men students, is considered part of the property of the Seminary and arrangement for its maintenance is made by the Seminary?

As to change in action. Much has occurred to bring about friction between the Secretary of the Sunday School Board and the Secretary of the Woman's Missionary Union between January 1905 and October 1905. It is unnecessary for me to state what have been the causes of this, but would simply refer you to a file of letters in your office and also to the action taken at Kansas City, appeals made and newspaper articles that have appeared since then. You may say that you have nothing to do with some of these. My brother, this is true in a certain sense, but you are largely responsible for starting the ball rolling.

I appreciate your candor in letting me have your views as to the future location of the Woman's Missionary Union. You seem to think there is such a thing as Christian courtesy and that Peter enjoins same. If so, it might be well in your presentation of plans for the future of the Woman's Work to regard some of the wishes of those who have had the Woman's Missionary Union work in charge for the past seventeen years. I enclose clipping taken from the July edition of the *Foreign Mission Journal* and would ask that you note carefully the action of the Executive Committee, W.M.U.

Very truly,

Annie W. Armstrong

P. S. On rereading the above I think it wise that I make some explanation, as I neither want to be misunderstood nor misrepresented. In letter written October 4th I made the following statement:

> "To sum up this whole matter I am standing for two principles; first, the unscripturalness of training women to be preachers, and second, for right methods in Southern Baptist work."

I wish it to be thoroughly understood that nothing I have said in this letter should be construed into a change of attitude in the slightest particular. I simply am trying to let it be understood that, while I regard the training of women at the Seminary to be preachers altogether unscriptural, I realize that others may differ from me in this position and I recognize the Baptist principle of individual guidance. The matter of methods though that have been adopted in advocating the Woman's Training School at the Seminary I think only need to be known to be universally condemned.

[SBHLA, J. M. Frost Collection]

HISTORY OF MOVEMENT TO ESTABLISH
WOMAN'S MISSIONARY TRAINING SCHOOL

February 4, 1900, Cor. Sec. W.M.U. received letter from Dr. E. Z. Simmons, missionary from China, in this country on vacation. First intimation of Training School movement. The letter asked Cor. Sec. to suggest name of matron and teacher only. All other arrangements outlined by Dr. Simmons, who purposed that school be established at Louisville in connection with Seminary, to be opened in fall 1900. Dr. Simmons writes:

> "We need a Training School for ladies wanting to do mission work. I have talked with many brethren in Richmond, Louisville and other places. All agree as to the need of such an institution. All agree that the place for the School is Louisville in connection with our Seminary. The most of the teaching to be in the Seminary classes such as Old and New Testament in English, Course on Missions,

Church History, Systematic Theology, etc., enough for a two years course.

My plans are to get the ladies in Louisville to rent a house near the Seminary that will accommodate 12 or 15 ladies. Then ask some Ladies Miss. Socs. to furnish a room each. Put the house in charge of a first class matron, then find a good sister who will give some instructions morning and evening in the home and have charge of some practical mission work in the city where these ladies can do some work. These matters all to be arranged after the work is started.

It is of great importance that we secure the best possible woman for the teacher and equally important a good matron.

Now if you think this is a wise undertaking we want your help. (Of course the ladies studying pay the actual cost of living.) Suggest the best woman you know for teacher and another for matron. I hope arrangements may be made and definite announcements made at the S.B. Con. in May, and the first session to begin with the opening of the Seminary next fall. The faculty of the Seminary, except Dr. Mullins who was not in Louisville when I was there, are heartily in favor of the plan. Dr. Willingham is in favor of it. Please confer with him and others that you think would help in the undertaking, I would be glad to have any suggestions from you on the matter."

As preparations seemed to have gone so far, Cor. Sec. W.M.U. thought it wise to confer with W.M.U. workers in Louisville and elsewhere to learn what was their opinion. *Not one approved.*

March 2, 1900. Letter from Dr. Mullins. He writes:

"There is no objection that I can see to the Seminary's opening its doors to any lady missionaries who desire our instruction. Indeed, it is doing so already for any who may, from time to time, be in the city and wish to attend the classes. They are not enrolled as members of our classes, nor do they take the examinations, but doubtless this point could be arranged satisfactorily to all if the idea of Brother Simmons is carried out. I do not think it would be desirable, nor do I understand that it is proposed, for the Seminary to assume any kind of responsibilities for the enterprise, financially or otherwise, or to have any kind of organic connection with it, except in the way named."

Before official action was taken by the Boards, the Seminary, or W.M.U., Dr. Simmons in the following circular letter to Baptist schools proceeds to canvass for students.

April 7, 1900. Letter from Dr. Simmons:

"After talking with a great number of leading brethren about the need of a Training School for ladies who want to become missionaries at home, and in foreign lands, it is desirable to find out how many would likely avail themselves of the opportunity for such a course of training during the coming season. The plan is to afford this training in connection with the Seminary, the faculty to do the teaching in Old and New Testament, in English, Systematic Theology, Biblical Introduction, Church History and the Mission Course. The ladies to study in the regular classes and take the examinations just as the men do. We want to know about how many are likely to attend, so that arrangements can be made accordingly.

Will you please let me know how many would likely attend from your school, and if you know of others who would be likely to attend, let me know? The making of the proposed arrangements this fall will depend upon the number that will probably attend.

An early answer is desired, so that announcements may be made at the Convention in Hot Springs. Please send answer to me at Kossuth, Miss.

It is proposed to have a separate home for the ladies. Dr. and Mrs. T. P. Bell suggested that I send you this."

April 10, 1900. Miss E. S. Broadus, receiving copy of above circular letter, wrote as follows:

"I cannot tell you the consternation I felt in receiving the enclosed. Would he force the school upon us? I understood that you had asked him not to tell any more that the school would be in Louisville, but to await developments.

It seems he believes in going ahead, regardless of others views and wishes.

The letters you sent were read with deep interest, and I was pleased that three ladies of such good sense, taste and judgment substantially agreed with my views. Of course no one can be so sensible as I that instructions in the Bible can be best obtained at the

Seminary, it is only a question whether the disadvantages do not outweigh even that advantage. I do not see why the ladies cannot go to one or other of the Northern schools, at least until we have more time to consider the question in all its bearing."

May, 1900. Some action referring to women attending lectures in Seminary, having been taken in Trustees' meeting, Dr. B. F. Carroll (B. H. Carroll?) writes to Cor. Sec. W.M.U. to ask her opinion. She again consulted Miss Broadus and others. Miss Broadus writes *June 29, 1900*:

"I appreciate your kindness in giving me an opportunity of stating the views of our Central Committee about the Training School, and I thank Dr. Carroll for his courtesy and consideration in seeking to learn the opinions of those who will be so vitally interested in the school, should it be established.

Our Committee adopted a resolution to the effect that we thought more time should be given to the consideration of the matter before any decisive steps were taken, and that in our opinion Louisville was not a desirable place for the location of such a school.

We suggested that if located in connection with some Female School, already in successful operation, some expenses would be avoided, such as house-rent, salary of housekeeper (or matron) etc. and that the cost of board would probably be less than in Louisville. For less money than these items would amount to, we think competent teachers could be secured from among the professors of said school, or the pastors adjacent thereto, many of whom have been trained in the Seminary.

We think Mr. Simmons makes too low an estimate of expenses, and that he is wrong in supposing there are many ladies here who are able to give largely to such a school. But our main reason for thinking Louisville not a good location, is that we deem it not advisable for the students and the young ladies to be thrown together in this way. And if any of the ladies should attend Medical Schools, the difficulty of the Social question would be greatly enhanced.

Many mothers would hesitate to send their daughters under such circumstances; and Mr. Simmons injured his cause here by intimating that the inevitable matchmaking would be a good thing. We do not feel that it is the business of the Woman's Missionary Union and our Committee to afford such facilities, or to have a

Training School where there would be such temptations to neglect of study. Some of us ladies think it would lower the dignity of the Seminary to have such an adjunct. . . At various times, I have talked with several ladies of good judgment and wide acquaintance with benevolent and missionary matters, and they all concurred in the opinion above stated. I believe there is only one member of the Committee who is in favor of having such a school here, and she was not present when it was discussed. The Committee consists of ten ladies from seven of the Louisville churches."

1902–1903. In Seminary Catalogue no reference made to Training School, but a list of 24 women's names given as having attended lectures, 19 being wives of students; with only 5 unmarried women, all from Kentucky.

1903. As there was no recognized school for the Training of Southern Baptist women; as largely increased gifts to Foreign Missions, made possible the appointment of more women missionaries; and as the Home Board was needing a larger number of women, the Executive Committee W.M.U. offered the following resolution at annual W.M.U. session in Savannah:

"RESOLVED: That the Southern Baptist Convention be requested to appoint a committee of seven—three of whom shall be the Secretaries of the Foreign, Home and Sunday School Boards—to confer with a committee of the same size, appointed by the Woman's Missionary Union, to consider the advisability of establishing a Missionary Training School for women; said committee to report at the meeting of the Convention in 1904, and the Annual Meeting of the Woman's Missionary Union the same year, and, if favorable, to suggest place of location, nature of operating, method of raising funds, etc., etc."

The following Training School Committee W.M.U. was appointed:
Miss A. W. Armstrong, Md.; Mrs. J. A. Barker, Va.; Mrs. J. D. Chapman, S.C.; Mrs. E. G. Willingham, Ga.; Mrs. W. D. Chipley, Fla.; Mrs. F. S. Davis, Texas; and Mrs. W. J. McGlothlin, Ky.
May 8, 1903. Action of the Convention:

A communication from the Woman's Missionary Union was presented by W. J. Northen, Georgia, requesting the appointment of a committee of seven, including the Secretaries of the Boards, to confer with a committee from the Union to consider the advisability of establishing a Missionary Training School for Women, such committee to report at the meeting of the Convention in 1904; if favorably, to suggest place of location and methods of operation, and of raising funds. The Convention ordered the appointment of such a committee.

The following was appointed:

TO CONFER WITH WOMEN'S MISSIONARY UNION (to report in 1904): W. J. Northen, Georgia; J. B. Hawthorne, Virginia; A. J. S. Thomas, South Carolina; J. N. Prestridge, Kentucky; R. J. Willingham, Virginia; F. C. McConnell, Georgia; J. M. Frost, Tennessee.

Governor Northen, a trustee of the Seminary, was made chairman of joint Committee, one session held before leaving Savannah, when it was decided to appoint several sub committees, on Curriculum, Location and Support. Not in Convention, W.M.U. sessions, or Committee meeting was a word said about a Training School existing in the Seminary.

Before annual meeting in Nashville and second meeting of Com. the Cor. Sec. W.M.U., as chairman of Com. on Curriculum, visited a number of Training Schools, Northern Baptist, (Phila.) Methodist (Wash.) Episcopal (N.Y.) Southern Meth. (Kansas City), besides obtaining catalogues of several others. *Not one of them is connected with a theological seminary* except Hasseltine House, Newton Centre, a small institution, where women students are in attendance upon the Seminary classes. At the Baptist Missionary Training School, Chicago, which in twenty years has had 518 women students, professors from the University deliver lectures, but there is no connection with the University. Hasseltine House, Newton Centre has had but 53 students in 14 years.

April 7, 1904, appeared an article in the *Baptist Argus* from Dr. E. Y. Mullins claiming that the Seminary "had a successful Training School," although the catalogue of 1902–1903 had no notice of such a school, only a list of women in attendance upon lectures.

After this claim by Dr. Mullins, Cor. Sec. W.M.U. made further inquiries into the wisdom of connecting Training School with Seminary. Miss Schuyler, Principal of Baptist Training School, Phila., writes after conversation with Dr. H. G. Weston, Pres. Crozier Theological Seminary, and with the students in the school:

> "He said he did not think it advisable to have a school for women in connection with Louisville Theological Seminary. That such a school was for the development of Christian character and true womanliness, and the association of the sexes in a school of this kind, would not, could not, be conducive to the highest good of the young women.

> He said "If it were in my power to move *our* Training School to Upland I would not do it. Nothing could induce me to do it, both for your sakes and ours." Continuing he added: "In a company of a hundred men there are always some *fools* and they would be certain to assert themselves. Nor could you be sure that in the Training School all the young women would be wise and discreet in deportment. It is natural for young people to wish to be together and to be attracted one to the other, and neither men nor women can reach their highest development in any line with mind distracted."

> "Then there would arise a prejudice on the part of those not strongly in sympathy with the School, or with the work of missions, and hints and innuendoes regarding 'Matrimonial bureaus' and 'annexes for sweethearts' would be frequent."

> He said much more than this and spoke with great earnestness and vigor. I asked him if I might repeat his words to you and if you might quote him and he said heartily: "Yes, indeed, I shall not hesitate to let my views be known on this subject." * * *

> I said to our students the other day, at the table, "If you could be associated with the Crozier men in recitation, having our school home near the Seminary, but obliging us to go to their building for lectures would you like it?" A perfect chorus of protest greeted me. Even our married and engaged ones were opposed to the mere suggestion. They discussed it at length, and the verdict was that the freedom of our class-room—the unrestrained, natural conduct and opportunity for frank, earnest discussion upon every theme, was to them of the utmost value. It was amusing too, to note how many of them hit upon the very points of objection you and I had discussed."

Course of Study. After correspondence and personal interviews with those in charge of Training Schools, it was the unanimous opinion that the course of study in the Seminary was not the one needed by a Training School, being a course for preachers; the women are not expected to preach.

April 18, 1904. We again quote from Miss Broadus because she is President of Kentucky Cen. Com. and lives in Louisville. This letter shows her change of view with its reasons:

> "Allow me to call your attention for a moment to a personal matter. You may remember that some years ago I opposed having a Training School for women located in Louisville, and I wish to say that in some respects my opinion has changed. In some important particulars the situation is different now. For one thing the expense will be less than I then anticipated, as supplies could all be bought at the wholesale rates the Seminary has the benefit of. Dr. Mullins wrote for the *Argus* an article that states the situation well, I think. As to the relations between the young men and young women, those problems can be worked out by matrons and directors if there is such a school here. I am not specially advocating it, however, but only want you not to think me inconsistent in I no longer oppose."

May 1904. Committee on Training School met at Nashville, Sub Committees were prepared to report. But before these were called for, Cor. Sec. W.M.U. offered the following resolution, slight amended, which was unanimously adopted:

WHEREAS, no notice had been given that there was a Training School for women missionaries in connection with the Southern Baptist Theological Seminary at Louisville, Ky., prior to the appointment of the joint committee by Southern Baptist Convention and Woman's Missionary Union, May, 1903, to consider the advisability of establishing a Missionary Training School for Women, said Committee to report at meeting of the Convention 1904, and the Annual Meeting of Woman's Missionary Union the same year:

AND WHEREAS, Dr. E. Y. Mullins, President of the Theological Seminary, makes public announcement in *Baptist Argus*, April 7, 1904: "We already have such a successful Training School in connection with our work at the Seminary;"

BE IT RESOLVED: That no action be taken by the Committee but that the whole subject be left with the Seminary for the present.

This resolution was adopted by W.M.U. without discussion and also by the Convention, with the following addition:

Attention having been called to the fact, it was ordered that the statement made by the President of the Seminary that notice of the establishment of the Woman's Training School by the Board of Trustees had been made by himself in the Baptist papers of the South about a year before the appointment of the joint committee at Savannah, should be appended to the report.

On motion of J. M. Frost, Tennessee, it was

RESOLVED, That this Convention hears with pleasure of the training of women missionaries, being furnished by the Southern Baptist Theological Seminary; and while approving and commending the work already done, the Convention respectfully recommends to the Seminary Faculty and Trustees, the further enlargement and better equipment of this department as the needs may demand and as the means in hand may justify, and earnestly hopes that our people shall give this important work their earnest sympathy and support.

This training of women missionaries at the Seminary and yet no mention of it in the Catalogue, save the list of names! The Committee of which Dr. Frost was a member, had not endorsed the Seminary Training School, but only (1) in view of Dr. Mullins claim that the Seminary already had a Training School, and (2) to prevent setting up what might be deemed a rival by some should the decision have been adverse to Louisville, therefore the Committee took no action but left the matter with the Seminary, "for the present." Dr. Frost's endorsement in the Convention was not seemly as a member of the Committee.

June 13, 1904. On receipt of letter from Miss Schuyler, preceptress of Baptist Training School, Philadelphia, relating to the formation of a Training School in Baltimore, Cor. Sec. W.M.U. wrote to Dr. Mullins, enclosing the communications and stating that it was her first information that such a school was to be established. His reply to this letter is as follows:

"Your favor of recent date, with enclosures from Miss Schuyler, Brother B. P. Robertson, and your letter to Mrs. Barker, has been received and their contents noted. I am not surprised at the confusion that seems to exist in the minds of some as to the training school.

Perhaps you can aid me in an embarrassing position which has grown out of the recent action, or rather failure to act, on the part of the Woman's Missionary Societies at Nashville. I have been repeatedly approached by ladies—members of the Missionary Union in most cases—and asked why the Women's Societies dropped the training school after having requested the appointment of the committee to settle the location when the understanding was that they were to give it their support. My only reply has been that I was unable to answer their questions. I have said that my understanding of the matter was the same as theirs when the committees were requested at Savannah, and that I have no means whatever of accounting for the sudden dropping of it when it was determined that it would come to Louisville. I remember very distinctly your own statements to me on the subject.

I note also that in your letter to Mrs. Barker you say "You of course know what was done in Nashville and as a member of the committee I fully and entirely acquiesce in the decision to leave the matter of the training school with the Seminary *for the present*. What are we to understand by this? That the matter of a location is still an open question? Are we to understand that the women are to reopen the question sometime in the future? Are we to be hampered in carrying on our work by the state of suspended judgment in the matter which this expression of yours indicates, and are all the women of the Missionary Union to regard the present arrangement as merely temporary?"

Please note two expressions in above: In first paragraph (1) "The understanding was that they (Woman's Mission Societies) were to give it their support" (2) "When it was determined that it (the Training School) would come to Louisville." Who authorized such an "understanding?" Who "determined that it would come to Louisville?" The Committee appointed by the Convention and W.M.U. declined to take action.

OPINIONS OF NOTED MEN.

Dr. J. A. Broadus. We never allowed our daughters to attend any of the lectures at the Seminary regularly and so stated when written to by a lady inquiring about the attendance of her daughter. He wrote her that "all the young ladies who had done so had married students." He heard nothing further from the lady.

Dr. I. T. Tichenor. When Dr. Simmons was presenting the matter of Training School, the Cor. Sec. W.M.U. inquired of Dr. Tichenor his opinion as to location. He replied: "Have a Training School anywhere else but in Louisville."

Dr. Henry G. Weston. The Woman's Training School is in Philadelphia and the Baptist Theo. School is at Crozier. Dr. Weston considers the fifteen miles between as too short a distance.

RECENT ACTION.

1. Miss Broadus, as Vice President Kentucky, requested President W.M.U. to give space on program for annual meeting 1905, for discussion of Seminary Training School and wrote to other Vice Presidents to unite with her in this request. President declines as contrary to action of last annual meeting, the question having been disposed of by vote of the body.

2. Mrs. Geo. B. Eager, wife of Seminary professor, wrote an article published in many S.B.C. papers advocating the support by Baptist women for the "Home" for students attending the Seminary Training School. Also wrote to State Officers asking their support in this movement.

3. Mrs. S. E. Woody, chairman of Committee of 19 Louisville ladies "who had undertaken the temporary establishment of a home for the young ladies attending the Seminary," appealed to Dr. Gray to include the Training School in Recommendations of Home Board to W.M.U. This request was seconded by Mrs. T. A. Hamilton, Ala., proving conference with State Officers. Dr. Gray declined. The Foreign Board was also requested to take action.

4. Dr. E. Y. Mullins wrote to Home Board on the same subject.

5. Circular letter sent to Vice Presidents from Ex. Com. of Home for women students, asking these officers to commit themselves by answering the following questions. (1) Are you in sympathy with the work? (2) How do you think it can best be brought before W.M.U.? (3) What will be the attitude of your delegation?

6. Request made in Georgia of Vice Pres. to furnish names of delegates W.M.U. "in the interest of the Training School in Louisville."

7. With all these attempts to influence public opinion, no notice of the movement has been sent to Cor. Sec. W.M.U. by those in prosecution of this effort, although it is the universal custom for such officer to be the medium of presentation. As far as known, Maryland has not received any of the communications sent to the other States.

CONCLUSION.
W.M.U. distinctly recognized the right of the Seminary to have a Training School. In Christian courtesy W.M.U. refrained from the consideration to establish another one on well recognized principles for successful work, while the Seminary was demonstrating its ability to meet the requirements. As the President of Seminary has claimed they had a successful Training School, should the Seminary not support it?
[SBHLA, J. M. Frost Collection]

From 1905 minutes of Woman's Missionary Union:

October 16, 1905
To the Foreign Mission Board, S.B.C.
Dear Brethren:—
The Executive Committee Woman's Missionary Union decided to make the enclosed protest at its October session, and intended to send it for presentation to State Central Committees and for publication to the State papers throughout the South. Fearing that those advocating Gospel mission methods might use the facts called to notice, as a weapon against organized work, the Corresponding Secretary, Miss Annie W. Armstrong, urged that it be limited to State Central or Executive Committees, and the officers of the Boards. We will ask that the Statement and Protest be read at the next session of the Board.
Accompanying the copies of newspaper articles, is copy of letter sent by Miss Armstrong to Dr. Willingham which gives historical information regarding Sunday School Missionary Day attacked by editor of *Christian Index*, September 28th, in article entitled "Clashing Interests."
Yours in Christian work,
Rec. Secretary W.M.U.
P. S. The Corresponding Secretary had nothing to do with issuing the Statement and Protest. Its limitation was at her request.

Statement and Protest from the Executive Committee of Woman's Missionary Union, Aux. S.B.C.

After the 17th session of Woman's Missionary Union in Kansas City, May, 1905, the Executive Committee in Baltimore put itself on record as according entirely with the attitude of the President, Mrs. J. A. Barker, and the Secretary, Miss Annie W. Armstrong, in opposing the Training School for Women at the Theological Seminary at Louisville and the Home for Women Students established by the women of Louisville. This attitude represented the support of two principles: The Scriptural position that women are not to preach, involving the corollary of having taught to preach, as the Seminary course for students is intended to do. Also that Christian work must be done by right methods, involving condemnation of the methods by which the support of the Home for Women Students in Louisville has been urged upon Woman's Missionary Union.

It will be remembered that both the officers declined re-election. They consented however to serve for one year that time might be allowed to prepare for needed changes so that harm should not come to the work. It might be supposed that this generous decision to remain in office when both earnestly desired to retire, would have been universally appreciated and respected. But there are those in control of the *Biblical Recorder* N.C. and the *Christian Index*, Ga. (see articles enclosed) who are using this eighteenth year of gratuitous service as an opportunity, and the Secretary, Miss Armstrong, as a target, for criticism, that is unreasonable, ungentlemanly, and unchristian. The aim is to injure the Secretary in the opinion of the public and to discredit Woman's Missionary Union methods of work. The long years of faithful, unremitting service and the very substantial success of W.M.U. efforts will doubtless be a convincing reply to worthy criticism. But the Executive Committee is unwilling to be silent at this juncture and desires to be understood as reprobating newspaper criticism which is misrepresentative of facts, unkind in spirit, and has assumed the character of persecution of an individual.

The Ex. Com. W.M.U.

(Signed) Mrs. A.C. Johnson.

Rec. Sec.

Baltimore, Md.

October 10, 1905

[WMU Archives]

November 8, 1905

Dr. J. M. Frost

Dear Brother:

Your letter of November 6th received. As you seem to feel that it is necessary to watch very carefully the printing of the leaflet lest mistakes be made, I am going to send word to the printer to forward you page proof, as I leave Baltimore tomorrow morning on a missionary trip of ten days, so cannot be responsible for the leaflet being printed in the way you wish. I would ask that you return the page proof to the printer, Pearre E. Crowl Company, 1 E. German St., Baltimore, as soon after you receive it as convenient.

Words cannot express my amazement at your failing to appreciate that in the clipping which I sent the Northern Educational Society is not undertaking to legislate as to matrimony, but simply in the administration of a trust fund after long experience decide who should be aided in order that the greatest good can be accomplished. I did not realize that your sense of the ridiculous was so keen, or I would have called your attention to the fact that the Educational Society is simply seeking to find under what are the best conditions to extend aid. Then again I felt it was only due to those at Newton Center, as it seems to be thought by some that Dr. Mullins, in seeking to establish a Woman's Missionary Training School in connection with the Theological Seminary at Louisville, is patterning after Newton, it should be known how the brethren there regard things. It was a side light which I was giving you.

I have just written to Dr. Willingham in regard to articles in the *Index*—Dr. Willingham declined to make any *public* statement as to his collections in Georgia during the month of September—and wishing you to know some things that I have said to him, I am going to take the liberty of sending you copy of that letter and ask that you read it.

Very truly,
Annie W. Armstrong
[SBHLA, J. M. Frost Collection]

E. E. Bomar served as Assistant Secretary of the Foreign Mission Board and knew Armstrong well. In November 1905, Miss Annie told him how difficult her past few months had been.

November 25, 1905
Dr. E. E. Bomar
Dear Brother:
Your letter of November 24th just received. I am glad to know that the Chinese skirt reached Richmond safely. I, too, received a card from Mrs. Crutchfield, making inquiry in regard to the lost article and wrote her yesterday assuring her that it was all right and had been forwarded to Richmond.

As to list of leaders in Woman's Work in Indian Territory and Oklahoma. I have a list which I use and will furnish same should you so desire, but I cannot assure you that all of these are now officers of Societies. It has been my aim and desire to keep in touch with as many earnest Baptist women in the Territories as possible, in order that I might present S.B.C. interests, believing that the promise will be verified in this case. "In due season ye shall reap if ye faint not." As previously stated I can and will furnish the list if desired.

I am glad to be able to report that Mrs. Calder Willingham passed through the operation more readily than was expected and is suffering less than was anticipated. I was in telephone communication with Mr. Willingham yesterday morning and saw him again last night at Eutaw Place Church, where we are having special services. He seemed quite bright and hopeful. It is his expectation to leave Baltimore one day next week to return to Charlotte and for Mrs. Hardy, Mrs. Willingham's mother, to come to Baltimore when he leaves. We are trying to make both Mr. and Mrs. Willingham feel that they are among friends, and when Mrs. Hardy comes I shall take her under my special care. Owing to my being so thoroughly absorbed in W.M.U. work we have had to give our home in charge of some one else and Sister Alice and I are boarding with the party that has taken our house, so I cannot entertain Mrs. Hardy as I otherwise would be glad to do.

I appreciate what you say as to your desire to be loved. I, too, would rather have love than anything else that this world can offer. I some times think that it takes the dark days to help us to appreciate the sunshine and perhaps trouble may be allowed in order that we may recognize more fully our Heavenly Father's love, and also that there is such a thing as genuine human affection.

When I was a school girl I learned some lines of poetry that struck my fancy at the time, but since sorrow and trouble have come to me I recognize the truth of them as I did not when my experience was more limited. I think I will pass them on to you.

"Nil desperandum! The darkest cloud may have a silver lining,
And round the deadliest plant that grows some blossoms may be
     twining.
The day that dawns mid shadows dark may still be bright at even,
And should our lives a desert seem, there cometh peace in Heaven."

I have allowed myself to write a much longer letter than I ought, but perhaps it is just as well that I have let my thoughts take the turn they have before I take up a perplexing matter in regard to this miserable business of the Seminary Training School. I was thinking this morning how I wished I could be Rip Van Winkle until this time next year when I would be free from all connection with S.B.C. Mission Work. I dread inexpressibly the next six months. I expect though strength will be given to go through with whatever comes.

Very truly,

Annie W. Armstrong

Later: Mr. Willingham has just left the Mission Rooms having spent an hour here. Mrs. Willingham is getting on very well, although today she is suffering from neuralgia. I suppose though it must be expected that various aches and pains will follow an operation. Mr. Willingham is planning to leave Baltimore next Thursday and will probably go to the South Carolina Convention before returning to Charlotte, but that is not decided.

I suppose you know that the church at Charlotte is trying to secure Dr. Curtis Lee Laws of Baltimore as pastor. I certainly hope they will not succeed as Dr. Laws is needed in Baltimore.

[IMB Archives]

November 28, 1905

Dr. E. E. Bomar

Dear Brother:

Your letter of November 27th received and it has given us pleasure to send tracts to the value of fifteen cents to Rev. E. B. English, Louisville, Kentucky.

I also forward a number of catalogues to you by this mail. Thanks for your kind words of appreciation. It is sweet indeed to realize that we can commit not only ourselves but the past as well as the future into God's hands. I cannot tell you how great is the pleasure that I find during this time of misrepresentations and misunderstandings to *know* that the results of the years of service which I have given to God are in His keeping and the records are on High. I find in God's work perfect delight and although I shall completely at the close of this Conventional year sever my connection with S.B.C. Mission Work—I have notified the women of Maryland that in April I will resign the Presidency of the Home Mission Society of the State, which office I have held for over twenty-three years, being the only

President they have every had, and the same month I give up the Presidency of the Society at Eutaw Place Church which I have also held for years—I certainly do not mean to be an idler in the vineyard of the Lord. Already I am being urged to connect myself with undenominational work. I shall today accept a position as manager to take effect in May—at the Aged Men and Women's Homes, two of our largest and oldest institutions in Baltimore. I want no resting time in the sense of idleness, and so I shall as soon as I leave this work turn my attention to other lines of Christian activity. I regret extremely that I cannot give what strength and ability I may have to the advancement of the work as done by Southern Baptists for I am a Baptist out and out, but I now recognize that it will cause friction should I take part in the work at any point, so in all human probability the rest of my life will be given to philanthropic work. Many avenues are opening out before me. I am trying though to listen for God's voice before making final decisions. I believe there is much truth in the expression used by Dr. Chalmers "The expulsive power of a new affection," and I think without doubt I will be able to throw myself as heartily into other lines of Christian activity as I have in Mission Work of Southern Baptists.

I suppose you have heard before this that Mrs. Calder Willingham has the pneumonia. Yesterday morning she was considered critically ill, but last night Mr. Willingham told me she was better and I do not think he seemed to feel apprehensive of danger. Mr. Willingham was planning to leave Baltimore on Thursday, but they told him at the Sanitarium that he must not go, but remain in Baltimore certainly until next week. I saw him twice yesterday, in the morning and again at night, and am glad to be able to say that he seemed quite bright. Of course I know Mr. Willingham has written to his father giving full particulars, but if you think he would care to know the impressions I have received from my conversations with Mr. Willingham, you are at perfect liberty to let him know what I have written.

Very truly,

Annie W. Armstrong

Later: Since writing the above another mail has been brought in and in it I find two letters from South Carolina which I enclose. Many letters of a similar character come to me and you can appreciate how glad they make me, but at the same time it is nearly heart breaking, recognizing as I do that God has and is using the efforts that I have made to develop our women as Christian workers, and then to know that I must give it all up. It is fearful to be so misunderstood. Few of the ladies realize why I declined to serve longer. They do not know that I am standing for what I believe to be principles and I must not make explanations for fear of injuring the work. It is indeed hard. Often, often I have to say over to myself "Vengeance is mine. I will repay saith the Lord."

[IMB Archives]

The Christian Index printed the following editorial on 22 February 1906. It was a snide, petty attack against Armstrong that distorted her sentiments on the Training School.

The Young Woman's Missionary Training School.

During our recent visit to Louisville, Ky., we took particular pains to observe the condition and workings of the Training School for Women, which is operated in connection with the Seminary. We paid a visit to the house in which the young women live, and found it to be a very large and in every way convenient one, and several blocks from the Seminary itself. It is an old mansion owned by a wealthy family, who do not now need it for their own use, and have rented it as a home for the young ladies. The rooms are large, airy and in all respects comfortable. Around the young women are thrown as many home comforts as possible, and the "Mother" of the family takes the best of care of them.

We observed the young women in the class rooms and as they passed back and forth from class to class, or from their home to the recitation rooms, and were greatly pleased with their very modest demeanor, and, as well, with the universal courtesy and respect shown them by the students. There was not the faintest indication of any familiarity, not even as much as is seen between lady visitors to our conventions and the delegates whom they claim as their friends. The utmost propriety of conduct and demeanor, as between ladies and gentlemen, prevailed.

We had heard of its being charged against the Training School that it would prove a sort of match-making institution for the young women of the School and the young men of the Seminary. The great fear that this would be the case has always seemed to us an absurd one. It might well have arisen in the fertile imagination of some maiden lady of uncertain age, who has come to look upon marriage as a dreadful thing, and especially a marriage between two young Christians whose hearts are one in the service of the Master. What if a few of the students and of these young women should marry? Is that reason for opposing so good an institution? Ought the Woman's Missionary Union to be put under the ban because ever and anon one of its workers marries some man whom she has met at conventions, or in the prosecution of her work for the Master? For our part, while we have no fear at all of the Training School becoming a match-making bureau, we should be far from grieving if some of the young ministers at the Seminary should marry some of these consecrated and well-trained young women, in preference to some of the giddy girls who some times catch the fancy even of the young "theolog."

We had also heard the charge made against this school that the young women were being trained to be preachers. Absurd also is this suggestion, evidently diligently sought by some one who was striving to prejudice people against a good institution, against which no real objections could be found. We noticed that the young ladies were present in the classes for the study of the English Bible, Theology and Church History—studies they will need in their work as missionaries at home or abroad; but conspicuously absent from the classes which were studying Homiletics—or the preparation and delivery of sermons, and Pastoral Duties, studies that relate to the duties of the ministry. The young women of the Training School are as far from desiring to be preachers, in the ordinary acceptation of the word, as are the young women who attend teachers' meetings and study the Bible under direction of pastors and other teachers all over our land.

Still another objection that has been urged against this school is that it is the project of a number of ladies in Louisville, Ky. What if it is, if so be that it is a good institution, doing good work? But the facts are against any such charge. The establishment of this school was first agitated by Dr. E. Z. Simmons, of Canton, China, one of our oldest and most faithful missionaries. He felt the need of trained lady workers in China, and on his visit to this country some years ago, earnestly advocated the establishment of the School, clearly outlining its scope and insisting on its location at Louisville, where the young ladies could have the benefit of the superb teaching of the Seminary professors.

The ladies of Louisville, and later of all Kentucky, merely met an emergency. The agitation of the matter had directed the attention of young women to Louisville, and some of these preferred to take courses of study under our own great teachers rather than go to training schools elsewhere, and they began to go to Louisville. It was then that the Louisville ladies nobly and generously took up the work of providing a good home for them, instead of leaving them to find quarters where they might, and be subjected to all the discomforts and inconveniences of common boarding house life. These Kentucky women have done nobly, and their sisters all over the South should gladly and *promptly* render them aid in the good work they are doing. There are many good women in Georgia who, if they knew of the good work this home is doing, and the needs thereof, would gladly help in its maintenance. We would urge such to write to Mrs. George B. Eager, 1410 E. Broadway, Louisville, Ky.

In the home with these young ladies boards a city missionary, a well-trained and accomplished worker, who takes them with her in her ministrations in jails and work-houses, in the homes of darkness and destitution, in mission schools and in the various other places which are the working stations of our city missionaries everywhere. So that these students receive practical training in the great work to which they have consecrated themselves—that of missions, at home or abroad.

[*The Christian Index*, February 22, 1906]

In April 1906, the Executive Committee of WMU responded to requests that "correct" misstatements regarding the Training School.

April 11, 1906
Dr. J. M. Frost
Secretary Sun. Sch. B'd. S.B.C.
Dear Brother:
On account of repeated requests from the President and Faculty of the Theological Seminary that "Statement" by Executive Committee W.M.U. "be corrected" the enclosed action was taken by the Executive Committee April 10, 1906. It is hereby transmitted according to instructions of Executive Committee.
Very truly,
Annie W. Armstrong
Cor. Sec. W.M.U.
[SBHLA, J. M. Frost Collection]

ACTION OF EXECUTIVE COMMITTEE, W.M.U.

April 10, 1906.
By request of Faculty of Southern Baptist Theological Seminary, "the Statement and Protest" sent to State W.M.U. Officers and S.B.C. Boards, Oct. 10, 1905, was reconsidered. The Faculty had asked that the following be corrected: "This attitude represented the support of two principles: The

Scriptural position that women are not to preach, involving the corollary of being taught to preach, as the Seminary course for students is intended to do."

(For a complete understanding of the situation we give the entire paragraph).

"After the 17th session of Woman's Missionary Union in Kansas City, May 1905, the Executive Committee in Baltimore put itself on record as according entirely with the attitude of the President, Mrs. J. A. Barker, and the Secretary, Miss Annie W. Armstrong in opposing the Training School for Women at the Theological Seminary at Louisville and the Home for Women Students established by the Women of Louisville. This attitude represented the Support of two principles: The Scriptural position that women are not to preach, involving the corollary of being taught to preach, as the Seminary course for students is intended to do. Also that Christian work must be done by right methods, involving condemnation of the methods by which the support of the Home for Women Students in Louisville has been urged upon Woman's Missionary Union."

Two reports are hereby forwarded.

MAJORITY REPORT.

Whereas: A Theological Seminary has separate existence from schools and colleges for the single purpose of teaching its students to preach; and, whereas, every study converges toward this point; therefore, all students pursuing this course, in whole or in part, are taught to preach. This is a self-evident proposition.

Whereas: The study of Homiletics, defined in the Seminary's catalogue as "Homiletics, or preparation and delivery of sermons" is "not recommended for the women's course;" yet Mrs. H. H. Steinmetz is entered in the class of Homiletics, in the * catalogue of 1902--3, as having attended this class regularly.

Therefore, be it resolved: That the injury to the Seminary does not lie in the statement of the self-evident proposition that the Seminary course of study is intended to teach its students to preach; nor does the remedy for the injury lie in withdrawing the language of the self-evident proposition. The remedy lies in withdrawing the women students from the Seminary.

Resolved: That the undersigned reaffirm the declarations contained in the original "Statement."

* NOTE:—This catalogue is cited because it is the one furnished by the Seminary's President to the joint Committee from W.M.U. and the Convention, when the question was pending concerning the need for a Training School, its location, curriculum, etc. Prior to the Committee's report, the President of the Seminary made announcement through the *Argus*, April 7, 1904, that "we already have such a successful Training School in connection with our work at the Seminary."

(Signed) Mrs. J. A. Barker Pres.

Mrs. Jas. E. Tyler, (Md.) Vice-Pres.

Annie W. Armstrong Cor. Sec.

Ella V. Ricker Treas.

Alice Armstrong

Mrs. M. B. Brown

Mrs. R. B. Kelley

MINORITY REPORT.

We, the undersigned, constituting a minority of the Ex. Com. Woman's Missionary Union, who voted at the meeting March 20-06, to correct the statement in Circular letter sent out by Ex. Com. Oct. 10-05 regarding the Training School for Young Women Students at Louisville Seminary do hereby state that when said letter was written we believed that young women attending said Training School were being taught to preach.

Since then however information has come to our knowledge which leads us to believe that said action was taken without having all the facts necessary to a full understanding of the matter, and as the statement is now positively denied by the President and Faculty of the Seminary and by the President of the Board of Trustees, we regret having made such statement and desire now to correct it, by withdrawing same.

(Signed) Clara M. Woolford, Chr.

Mrs. A. C. Johnson

Mrs. W. R. Nimmo

Mrs. Wm. C. Lowndes

Mrs. A. J. Clark

Mrs. Helen M. Grady

NOTE:—The Minority Report was not presented until Ex. Com. Meeting April 10th, 1906.

Resolved: That a copy of this majority and minority report of W.M.U. Executive Committee be sent to the President of Board of Trustees of the Seminary, to the President of the Faculty, to State Executive or Central Committees, W.M.U. and Secretaries of Boards, S.B.C.

[WMU Archives]

Once she decided to step down from her role as Corresponding Secretary of WMU, Armstrong wanted to make her final year the best ever.

June 16, 1905
Dr. R. J. Willingham
Dear Brother:
I have just sent the following telegram to you:

"Telegram and letters received obviate necessity of requesting your coming to Baltimore. Will write."

Doubtless you were surprised at my asking by telephone that you would come to Baltimore, and allow me to express my warm appreciation of your willingness to accede to my request without giving reason. While I do not want to go into the matter, a little explanation is certainly due you. You may or may not know that those who have been instrumental in bringing about the present condition of affairs in W.M.U. work, do not seem satisfied at the public announcement which I made in Kansas City and re-affirmed since, that at the close of the present Conventional Year, my connection with W.M.U. work will cease, but are continuing their misrepresentations. In some directions it appeared that things had gone so far that I would be forced to close the Mission Rooms in the near future. Recognizing as I do that to give the work up at this time with no one prepared to take it might cause serious loss to the mission work as done by Southern Baptists, I thought it well to see you and ask your advice as to how best to arrange for a transfer of the work.

Kindly recognize that it was not my purpose to ask from you any expression of opinion as to what has been done, or even to give you additional facts, simply to ask of you as Secretary of the Foreign Mission Board to whom Southern Baptists have committed that branch of work, how

I could best guard the interests of both Home and Foreign Missions in laying the work down which I had agreed to keep during the present Conventional Year. I should not have given you any additional facts unless you had asked for them, so please do not for one instant think that in my asking you to come to Baltimore it was with any idea of requesting you to act the part of mediator or of enlisting your sympathies.

As stated in telegram, on reaching the Mission Rooms this morning I received a telegram and several letters which make it possible for me to keep on with the work until the close of the year unless there are some new developments. Before ceasing to refer to this, to me intensely disagreeable matter, allow me to say if you can do anything to cause those who seem so anxious to prevent my doing effective work, to refrain during this year from efforts to increase friction, I will appreciate you doing so. You have full permission to assure those who desire changes that it is not only my unalterable determination (unless God should work a miracle) to sever my connection with the Woman's Missionary Union in May, but also to resign the Presidency of the Woman's Baptist Home Mission Society of Maryland which I have held for nearly twenty-four years, and that of the Society of Eutaw Place Church which office I have also held for years. After the meeting of the Convention in May 1906, I do not propose in any way, shape or form to have anything whatever to do in Mission Work as conducted by Southern Baptists, so even in Maryland none need fear my opposition to whatever plans they may desire to present. This being the case, I do not feel that I am asking too much to be allowed to continue in the work without further molestation during the present year and give what time and ability our Heavenly Father vouchsafes me to the cause which is so dear to my heart.

I am sorry to have to send you such a letter, and I hope this is the last time I shall be forced to refer to unpleasant matters in connection with this year's work. I do want your help in doing the best year's work Woman's Missionary Union has ever done, and in leaving the work in such shape as that it can go on without loss to the cause when it passes into other hands.

I think it is only right as a Christian to say, that in totally severing my connection with mission work as done by Southern Baptists, it is not my purpose to become an idler. I recognize the Master's field is wide and there are many places where laborers are needed so I shall endeavor to work elsewhere as heartily as I ever have in the past.

Very truly,
Annie W. Armstrong
[IMB Archives]

May 4, 1906
Dr. J. M. Frost
Secretary Sunday School Board
Dear Brother:

It gives me pleasure to send you advance copies of the Annual Reports of the Woman's Missionary Union.

The Woman's Missionary Union has just closed its most successful year. By reference to page nine of the Secretary's Report you will see that during the past year the Woman's Missionary Union has contributed $152,733.39 to Home and Foreign Missions and Margaret Home for Missionaries' Children. This is a gain of $14,374.74. It is peculiarly gratifying that the increase this year is so large for the Woman's Missionary Union has received no large contributions during the present Conventional Year, while last year the amount reported, $138,398.65, included the gift of $10,500.00 from "A Christian Mother" for the purchase of the Margaret Home for Missionaries' Children in charge of the Woman's Missionary Union at Greenville, South Carolina.

I would also call attention to the amount contributed by the Woman's Missionary Union in eighteen years. It is $1,286,370.49. Another interesting item will be found on page ten of the Secretary's Report. During eighteen years Woman's Missionary Union has placed in the hands of its workers 4,234,573 leaflets and pamphlets.

I also send Digest of State Reports which will be presented at the Annual Meeting of the Woman's Missionary Union at Chattanooga.

Very truly,
Annie W. Armstrong
Cor. Sec. W.M.U.

P. S. It might be well also for me to call attention to the fact that while the contributions increased this year $14,374.74, the expenses only increased $495.98—total expenses for the year, not including the expenses of Christmas Offering and Week of Special Effort for Home Missions which are paid by the Foreign and Home Boards, were $4,158.65. The small per cent of expense to receipts is due to no salaries being paid officers.

[SBHLA, J. M. Frost Collection]

CHAPTER 5

"It is not my purpose to become an idler."

Annie Armstrong's Life Beyond Southern Baptist Missions

Despite her passionate commitment to WMU, no one could ever accuse Annie Armstrong of being a one-dimensional person. She promised herself that she would not be an "idler" once she stepped down as Corresponding Secretary for WMU and the following letters suggest that Miss Annie had many things to occupy her time, beginning with her love for Baltimore and sundry local interests.

October 16, 1900
Dr. E. E. Bomar
Dear Brother:
I hold in my hand a letter which I have just received from Mrs. J. D. Easterlin, Corresponding Secretary of Woman's Missionary Union of Georgia. She writes:

> "I am so very anxious that the Foreign Board prepare new leaflets on China for distribution at this time, when the people are saying, 'it is no longer necessary for them to contribute to missionary work in China.' I am afraid there will be a great falling off in that direction if something is not done. Every time I send out a package of literature, this thought comes to me, and I wish I had something new and stirring on this subject. I have little or nothing in the way of leaflets on China."

What think you of this? I agree with Mrs. Easterlin that it would be helpful if we could at this time put into circulation one or two strong leaflets on China. Please think of this, and see if anything can be done. I enclose samples of Christmas literature.

I did not know that you had never been to Baltimore. As that is the case, I would like to have the pleasure of showing you a little of our city. I was amused several years ago when some ladies from Texas and Missouri came to Baltimore after attending the Southern Baptist Convention in Washington, to have them say after I had been showing them a few of Baltimore's sights: "Why, Miss Annie, they told us in Washington that there was nothing to see in Baltimore, and we think Baltimore much prettier than Washington." I thought perhaps the difference was, they had a guide in Baltimore, and in Washington they had attempted to go around by themselves. If you will accept me as guide, I will try and see if you cannot find something in Baltimore that will excite your admiration.

During the Association I shall be right busy, so will be obliged, should you accept my offer, if you will let me know when you expect to arrive, and how long you can stay, for then I can propose a time for sightseeing which will not prevent our being at the Association when you are needed to speak and I want to be part of the audience, or at the Ladies' Meetings, when I may not always be perfectly silent.

Very truly,
Annie W. Armstrong
P. S. Will you kindly send to Mrs. W. P. Anderson, 23 Bailey Street, Atlanta, Ga., Mrs. Pruitt's present address? I was indeed sorry to hear of Mrs. Crocker's death.
[IMB Archives]

October 19, 1900
Dr. E. E. Bomar
Dear Brother:
Your letter of October 17th received. May I ask that you will kindly have sent to the ladies whose names I will give on a separate sheet of paper, the numbers of copies which I will indicate of each of the leaflets which you enclosed? These ladies are officers of Central Committees, and they will distribute the leaflets to the Societies in their respective states.

I would also ask that you give your clerk instructions that she *promptly* fill all orders for these leaflets which I will forward in the near future. It is probable that I will ask that you send to different Central Committees six or eight thousand of each of the leaflets (Total number to all). If you have not that number on hand, will you kindly have reprints made? I ask that the orders be filled promptly so that the leaflets can be forwarded to Societies with other literature which will be sent to the Central Committees from Baltimore.

It has occurred to me at this stage of things that it might be well to print in leaflet form some telling paragraphs from letters received recently from different Chinese missionaries, with an introduction by you, or some other member of the Foreign Board. I wish you would think of this.

As I have by no means gotten things straight at the Mission Rooms, I can and do realize that you dread to allow the office work to accumulate, but during your stay in Baltimore, I think you will be able to sandwich in a little sightseeing, if you have any fondness for that sort of past-time. One day this week business required my going to the new Court House, which has been lately erected in Baltimore—I believe it is considered the finest building of its nature in the world. It cost $2,000,000.00 and is really worth a visit. Then again, while we have nothing to equal the Congressional Library in Washington, we have several libraries in Baltimore of which we are quite proud. I would like you to see these.

Very truly,
Annie W. Armstrong

ORDERS

Mrs. W. C. Golden, 709 Monroe Street, Nashville, Tennessee.
"China And Our Missions There"   600
"Something Of The Situation In China"   600

Mrs. L. F. Stratton, 1705 Twelfth Ave., S., Birmingham, Alabama.
"China And Our Missions There"   600
"Something Of The Situation In China"   600

Miss M. L. Coker, Society Hill, South Carolina.
"Something Of The Situation In China"   400
"China And Our Missions There"   400

Miss F. E. S. Heck, Raleigh, North Carolina.
"Something Of The Situation In China"   500
"China And Our Missions There"   500

Mrs. J. D. Easterlin, Marietta, Georgia.
"Something Of The Situation In China"   600
"China And Our Missions There"   600

[IMB Archives]

Annie Armstrong's association with Marie Buhlmaier sparked her interest in helping immigrants.

February 17, 1894
Dr. R. J. Willingham
Dear Brother:
Your letter of February 16th, enclosing MS. on "Giving" by Dr. T. P. Bell received. Before returning MS. to Dr. Bell and asking that he re-write same, I would like to know if the Foreign Board desires to order a number of copies of this leaflet for free distribution, should Dr. Bell accede to the request made to re-write MS. and place same at the disposal of the Mission Rooms.
Very truly,
Annie W. Armstrong
[Handwritten at end of letter] I will forward the information desired by Mrs. Brooks about the work being done for the immigrants in Balto.
[IMB Archives]

Baltimore, Md.
Oct. 31, 1897
My dear Miss Armstrong,
Having been especially impressed by the work at the Immigrant Landing last week, I thought of telling you of my experience.
On passing through the Pier to go upstairs, I noticed a number of people who were evidently ready to leave for Europe. The incoming steamer being delayed several hours, I at once determined to improve the time of waiting by going among the people mentioned above, so I took an armful of papers and several Testaments and started downstairs.

Immediately upon reaching the foot of the stairs, I saw a young girl trying to get upstairs, while one of the officers was trying to keep her back. On seeing me, he asked me to tell the girl that she could not be permitted to go upstairs unless she presented a card of admittance. As I turned to do as he requested, the girl met me by saying: "Oh you are the missionary!" I wondered how she knew, but could not stop to ponder long before she said: "I don't want to go upstairs now, don't you remember me? Don't you remember I landed here two years ago on my way to Pittsburgh? I have not forgotten you, often I have spoken about you and when I decided to go back to Germany, I wondered and wished to meet you again. I knew you straightway as you passed through before, and was anxious to see you. You were kind to me, you helped me." I now asked her if I had not given her a Testament at the time. She said: "yes." I inquired if it had not been a comfort in her times of disappointment? Whereupon she answered: "Yes indeed, a comfort and a joy." She further told me that she had attended the German Baptist Church in Pittsburgh, that her brother was a member there and that she herself is seriously considering her own soul's salvation. I now took occasion to urge upon her the necessity of accepting Christ at once, speaking words of cheer and comfort as well as warning. Although she tried to keep them back, the tears came again and again, while in the meantime a number of the passengers gathered around, listening intently. We parted with the firm hope of meeting again in heaven.

It is needless to tell you, I was glad to hear of the good, which is being done by meeting these strangers at our gate. Oh, what will the harvest be!

Turning from this girl, I approached a family, giving them papers, and, upon learning they had not the Word of God, also a Testament. Leaving them, I was followed by a woman who had noticed the Testaments in my hand. She asked would I not please give her a copy, she was so anxious to have one. Of course, I gave it to her. Beginning conversation, I was startled when she told me her story. How she came to America a number of years ago, having earned every cent of her expenses by hard work, and how after reaching Milwaukee without a relative or friend in all the land, after vain attempts to secure a situation, she became so despondent and fully determined to take her own life. She was prevented, however, by a voice calling her: "Don't do it!" She recognized "God's voice" and followed Him. "There and then I have found my God," she said. Furthermore, she told me that as she is hard of hearing, she never got any good from going to church, but right here lately a minister held open air meetings in a park, and learning of these she availed herself of the opportunity, and getting very close up to him under the tree where he stood, she could hear and understand every word. "And then the beautiful singing! Oh the beautiful hymns! I tried so hard to get me a copy of those hymns, the day before I started away from Milwaukee. I walked the length of the city, but didn't succeed in getting them." I asked her the name of the hymns, but she did not know; then I asked her to repeat some of them, when she began "The Great Physician Now Is Near," whereupon I joined in and we repeated together the first verse; she was astonished. "Why do you know that too?" "Yes," said I, "we have the hymns in our church hymn book, but come tell me one or two more." She now told me, that she had only attended seven Sundays and didn't know much of any of them, only sentences or chorus, but another is "Oh Beulah Land," and another "Beautiful Words of Life." I was now fully convinced that it is the translation of the "Gospel Hymns," in German which we use in our Baptist Churches, and I promised that after hearing of her safe arrival, I would certainly send her a copy of the "Gospel Hymns." The woman's heart was so full, she didn't find words to express her feelings till finally she exclaimed, "Oh, but that will be a terrible joy!"

My heart was full too; as I stood in the midst of these people looking into their faces, speaking to this one and that one, giving out the tracts and papers in so many different tongues. The thought came to me: if only I were able to meet not only the immigrants coming to our shores, but also those leaving them, surely it would pay! And then the thought of those leaving sick at heart, poorer than ever, all their hopes blighted, filled me with a great pity and a desire to be helpful to them.

A number of times it has so happened that the steamer came in on the same day one sailed, and whenever possible, I try to reach both parties. But never before did the opportunity present itself in like manner. Surely God has given us a wonderful work to do. Not only can we thus do "Home Mission Work," but also "Foreign Mission Work!" Not only is the Word of Light and Truth sent into all parts of our Home Land by these foreigners who come to us, but it is carried back with the foreigner into foreign lands.

What a grand and noble work our Home and Sunday School Boards are doing! "Praise God from Whom all Blessings Flow."

When I left the Pier, after 10 P. M., I was indeed very tired, but also very happy; thanking God who has permitted me to work in this, His vineyard.

May God's richest blessing rest upon all the labor and the laborers of our Boards.

Yours in the work,
Marie Buhlmaier
[SBHLA, J. M. Frost Collection]

November 4, 1897
Dr. R. J. Willingham
Dear Brother:

I have been wanting to write to you for several days, but last week, owing to the State Association, a number of letters had to remain unanswered and I have not yet been able to quite get things straight. I cannot understand how the Secretaries of the Boards manage when they are away for weeks at a time from their offices, for if I let even one day's mail remain unanswered, it seems to require a week or more to catch up.

Before referring to several matters of business, I want to say that I am truly sorry your little boy has Scarlet Fever. I hope before this the doctor has pronounced all danger past. As we have had this sickness several times in our own family, I know how necessary care and caution are to prevent the spread of the disease. Please present my kindest sympathies to Mrs. Willingham. Which one of the children is it that is sick? I hope none of the others have contracted the fever.

I know you will be pleased to hear that Mr. Barton made a very pleasant impression during his recent visit to Baltimore. I am sure he won not only friends for himself, but for the cause. He is a strong speaker. I will now present several items of business seriatim.

1. *Circular in regard to the Christmas Offering, to be sent out in December Foreign Mission Journal.* In a letter written by you Oct. 11th, you say:

> "I will take pleasure in writing an appeal to be put on your circular letter issued from the *Journal*, but I do not think my appeal ought to occupy all the circular. Let that be only a part and let there be also connected with it an appeal from you as Secretary of the Woman's Missionary Union. The plate which you have would answer excellently to put at the head of the circular."

I will comply with your request and send you in the course of a few days a short appeal from the Secretary of the Woman's Missionary Union, to be printed on circular; I will also forward electrotype above referred to. When Mr. Barton was in Baltimore, I suggested to him that it might be possible to make the Christmas Offering more general than heretofore, so what think you of calling on the churches to unite with the Woman's Mission Societies in the Christmas Offering? If you approve of this idea, would it not be well to make editorial notice of same in the *Journal* and let your appeal on the circular be a two-fold one? Certainly large sums are expended by our people at Christmas times, and if we could get them to grasp the thought embodied in the Christmas Offering, I am sure the treasury of our Foreign Board would be largely increased.

2. *Subscription to Foreign Mission Journal.* I enclose 35 cents as annual subscription for the *Journal* from Mrs. W. S. Eastwood, West Point, Virginia. She desires the subscription to begin with the November number.

3. *Set of maps for the Mission Rooms.* At the last meeting of the Mission Rooms Committee, I reported to the Committee what you had said in regard to furnishing maps to the Rooms. They seemed quite gratified at the kind offer you had made and a vote of thanks was passed.

4. *Baptist Mission Rooms.* Appreciating that having the Maryland prefix to the "Baptist Mission Rooms" limited in some directions the distribution of literature, which we are trying to make as general as possible, permission was asked at the last session of the Maryland Union Association to allow a change in name. This was granted, and hereafter the Rooms will simply be called "Baptist Mission Rooms." Will you kindly make the needed change in the standing advertisement in *Foreign Mission Journal*?

5. *Misses Wilcox and Stenger.* I am glad the Board is considering the advisability of having these ladies connect the work they are doing with that done by the Board. For many reasons, it seems to me it would be a good thing to accept them as our missionaries.

6. *New openings.* I suppose you know something of the work that has been done by Miss Buhlmaier, missionary of the Home Board, in Baltimore not only among the resident population of Germans, but in meeting the immigrants as they land. For several years past the Sunday School Board has been supplying Miss Buhlmaier with Testaments and Bibles, and we believe that God has in a marked degree blessed this effort to place in the hands of the incoming foreigner the Word of Life. I received a day or two since a letter from Miss Buhlmaier, telling of a new phase of work, viz., among immigrants who have failed to find their expectations realized in the

United States and are now about returning to Germany. I enclose copy of the letter, as I think it will be of interest to you. The question now is: Shall we at the port in Baltimore use the opportunity to place in the hands of disappointed and disheartened Germans the Word of Life to read on their long voyage back to their native land? I consider this is a God-given opportunity to do Foreign Mission Work. I am going to write to Dr. Tichenor and ask that the Home Board authorize Miss Buhlmaier to meet the outgoing steamers, as well as the incoming ones, and if they are willing to have this done, I will then see if the Sunday School Board will supply the needed Testaments and Bibles. How closely the work of the three Boards of the Southern Baptist Convention is interwoven. When you next write, I will be glad to have your opinion in regard to this matter. If you have not met Miss Buhlmaier, you can hardly appreciate how fitted she is to speak comforting and cheering words, and then lead those to whom she is talking to realize that there is One to whom we can go in all times of sorrow and trouble.

I do trust Mr. Barton will not run any risks of contracting the fever en route to Texas. In a letter I received from Dr. Frost this morning, he says:

> "Tonight I leave for Texas. My family is almost up-in-arms against my going, out it seems very important that I should be present. I shall go through St. Louis and Indian Territory, and so run completely around the infected district."

Very truly,
Annie W. Armstrong

P. S. I am very glad to know that you are to have Dr. W. R. L. Smith at the Second Church. I hope we will see something of him in Baltimore. When he first entered the ministry, he acted as supply for one or two summers for Dr. Fuller and was quite a favorite with us.

P. S. No. 2. I have no doubt you have heard something of the Italian Mission which has lately been started in Baltimore. Mr. Galassi, on the recommendation of Dr. Eager, has been employed for several months jointly by the Young People's Unions in Maryland and the Home Board. He felt quite encouraged in regard to his work, but no public effort was made to gather the Italians for service until last Sunday. The priests had warned the Italians under their influence that they must not attend said service, or take any part in same, else dire calamity would befall them. About 20 came to the service, which was attended by a large number of our Baptist people. The Italian woman with whom Mr. Galassi has been boarding, had been specially warned that misfortune would follow her if she harbored this Protestant missionary. Humanly speaking, it did seem a most unfortunate thing that during the time of the service, while this woman was present, her little child fell on the sidewalk and broke her arm. Of course this will militate against our work.

[IMB Archives]

December 30, 1899
Dr. J. M. Frost
Dear Brother:
I would very much enjoy having a chat with you about various matters, but there is quite an important letter which I must send to Dr. Kerfoot before he leaves for Cuba. Said letter will require a good deal of earnest thought, so I must give the afternoon to it. I will now briefly call your attention to two items.

1. *Request for a grant of Testaments to be distributed among sailors.* Kindly read the letters which I enclose from Mrs. J. E. L. Holmes and Mr. Jenkins in the order marked. Mrs. Holmes is, as you probably know, the widow of Dr. Holmes, who for years was pastor of the church in Savannah, and a sister of Joshua Levering. Annie, as well as Joshua and a younger brother, Leonard, are very much interested in the Port Mission, and The Anchorage which is connected with it. I think a great work is being done there. The object is to bring good influences to bear upon the seamen as they come to our port, and to keep them out of the hands of "sharpers." In connection with the Port Mission is a flourishing Sunday School. You will probably remember that about a year ago the Sunday School Board made a grant of Testaments to the Port Mission. The Testaments, as a general thing, are put in what are called "Comfort Bags," said bags containing a few necessaries, such as buttons, needles, thread, etc., and given to the sailors as they leave on their voyages. If you can grant the request, which I most heartily endorse, kindly send Testaments to Mrs. J. E. L. Holmes, Port Mission, 815 S. Broadway, Baltimore, Md.

2. *Application for aid from Rev. H. H. George.* Kindly read the letter from this brother which I enclose. To me he is a stranger. I do not find his name on the list of missionaries which you have forwarded from time to time. You will see from this letter that Mr. George states that Mrs.

Kuykendall gave his name to a lady in Louisville, and also says that as a barrel which he received did not contain all the clothing he desires, he now asks for further assistance. Possibly, probably, Mrs. Kuykendall did give his name, but if so, I really think it would be well for you to write to her husband in regard to it, for, if either Mr. or Mrs. Kuykendall undertake to give to individuals or Societies the names of missionaries, it will cause trouble. Mr. Kuykendall, as Secretary of the Sunday School Board of Oklahoma, is authorized, is he not? to refer names of missionaries needing help to you. We certainly ought to have system in our work, and I consider it only right to try and secure same. I will make no reply to Mr. George until I hear from you.

I note what you say in your letter of December 26th, about dropping Dr. Miller's name. I most heartily endorse that decision but I do think it is only courteous to him, as he sent one week's notes, although altogether unsuitable, to acknowledge same. Will you do so, offering what explanation you deem wise, or if you will return his letter to me, I will write.

Very truly,

Annie W. Armstrong

P. S. Did you note in the January edition of the *Foreign Mission Journal* the article in regard to Dr. Barton's resignation, and his acceptance of the position of Field Secretary of the Sunday School Board? Should Dr. Barton decide to become Secretary of the Arkansas State Board after this announcement, I think it will put him before the public in not a very desirable light—it would seem that he did not know his own mind.

[SBHLA, J. M. Frost Collection]

February 8, 1902

Dr. E. E. Bomar

Dear Brother:

It gives me pleasure to enclose a check for $8.25, which is a Christmas Offering from the W.M.U. of the First Baptist Church, Bonham, Texas. Will you kindly return receipt for same to Mrs. Fannie Myers, Bonham, Texas, and let me have duplicate?

I would also be obliged if you will let me have an itemized statement of the amount received from the different states for the Christmas Offering. This is the first report that will have been made in the *Foreign Mission Journal*, and so I would ask for the full amount. Dr. Willingham sent me an itemized statement of the amount last month but so little had come to hand at that time that I did not think it wise to make a report.

No one could doubt that the "foreigner" is in our midst, if he or she had spent the afternoon as I did yesterday at the Immigrant Pier. I rarely go there—this is only my third visit in the ten years we have been doing this work—as I cannot speak the different languages and feel that I can do more to aid the cause by remaining at the Mission Rooms, and seeking to inform our women as to needs, etc; but as I had never seen a steamer unload, I thought it might be well for me to see that phase of the work, so I went with Miss Buhlmaier yesterday. There were 1400 immigrants that landed from that one vessel. Healthy, hearty looking specimens of humanity, but it was a revelation to me to find that there are so many people who have so little of this world's goods. Most of the men carried in their hands a box or valise of some description; the women, on their backs, bundles of clothing. As I watched the registration, when they have to show to the inspector what amount of money they have, there was only one that I noted who had over $10.00—they must have some money beyond their ticket, or they cannot remain in this country. When I went to the part of the building where the baggage had been put, there were probably not over twenty-five trunks or hampers and about the same number of sacks of clothing. These included the baggage of the cabin passengers, of whom there were very few. It was to me pitiful, indeed, to think of those hundreds and hundreds of people coming to a strange land, and having so little to start life with.

Miss Buhlmaier, our own beloved missionary, is the only woman missionary to meet these forlorn creatures, and give them a welcoming hand and after ministering as she does to their comfort in various ways, give them copies of God's Word. There are two Lutheran male missionaries, but one of them said the other day, he had to try to get the people to take his tracts while they gathered around Miss Buhlmaier eager for what she had to give them. He explained the difference by saying it was because she was a woman. Rather a high tribute to pay our sex, but I think it is due to their appreciation of her loving ministry which wins their hearts and then makes them willing to receive her message.

I think I will ask you to read the enclosed leaflet on this subject, which we are now distributing.

I had not intended writing so long a letter but I have not yet quite gotten over the feeling which was excited by my visit of yesterday.

Very truly,
Annie W. Armstrong
[IMB Archives]

My dear Miss Armstrong:

Looking forward into the new Conventional year & also looking back upon the year just closed & the work done, several thoughts suggest themselves which I would like to tell you of.

1. Would it be possible to have a better system of supplying the necessaries at the Landing? Time & again we ran short in the supplies & could not at all times give the Literature we desire to give to the Immigrants. These unavoidable delays of the past could perhaps be avoided in the future if the supplies could be sent regularly & systematically. To this end I have tried to think of:

2. the possible need for the present year.

a. As was stated in my report, over 8,000 copies of Scripture have been distributed among the newcomers last year. Yet, if the shelves had never been empty about 2,000 copies additional could have been used advantageously. Now we all desire to give the precious Truth to any & all who have it not, although we are well aware that it means an outlay of money. Yet can money compare with the worth of even one soul who may be brought from darkness to light?

Should Immigration continue as it now appears we will likely need *Gospels & Testaments* as follows: of Testaments *200 Polish, 300 Bohemian, 500 German*; of Gospels: 2,000 Bohemian, 2,000 German, 5,000 Polish; a total of 10,000 copies of Testaments & Gospels.

b. *Literature*: Beside the German, Bohemian, Croatian, Hungarian, Lithuanian, Hebrew & Polish we ought also to have Slovenian, Romanian & Servian; Publications in these languages can all be had from the American Tract Society.

I have tried to make a careful selection of the tracts in the various languages needed & as they are not numbered the titles must be given; in not one instance do the Tracts come higher than 1 cent a piece, & many only 1/2 or 1/4 cent.

Slovenian—3,000 tracts are needed from the following:

The Lord's Day	A Sleepless Night
John Fauler's Conversion	The Disobedient Annie
Two Deathbeds	The Voice of Warning
The Swearer's Prayer	Peter Lohbeck
Christ Knocking	Little Lydia

Servian —1,000 Tracts:
How William Came to the Knowledge of the Truth
The Dairyman's Daughter
The Jailer of Philippi
The Good Shepherd
The Way of Salvation

Romanian—1,000 Tracts:
Springs in the Desert
Good News
New Birth
Lost Road
The Two Old Men
The Sparrows Saw It

Croatian—3,000 Tracts of No. 1 & 2,000 additional as follows:
Fear Not It is I
Come and Welcome
The Good Shepherd
How Wm. Came to the Knowledge of the Truth
This would make a selection of five Croatian tracts instead of only the one as heretofore.
Total of Croatian tracts needed *are 5,000.*

Lithuanian—400 Tracts
Polish Handbills—10 packets
Bohemian Handbills—10 packets
German Hebrew—250 Tracts: No. 3, 4, 6, 7, 10 to select from.
Hungarian—600 Tracts including as many as are available of the numbers mentioned in the last column of Hungarian Tracts entitled: "Imported Hungarian Tracts" on page 26 & 27 of catalogue.

As an emergency reservation I would be pleased also to have the following *German* Tracts 2,000 *pages* called "Pocket Tracts" if possible all the numbers given, also those called "Glad Tidings" 200 copies on page 11 of catalogue.

Let me enumerate:

Croatian	5,000 Tracts
Slovenian	3,000 Tracts
Servian	1,000 Tracts
Romanian	1,000 Tracts
Lithuanian	400 Tracts
German Hebrew	250 Tracts
Hungarian	600 Tracts
Polish Handbills	10 packets
Bohemian Handbills	10 packets
German Tracts	200 copies of Glad Tidings
German Tracts	2,000 pages of Pocket Tracts

According to the catalogue the cost of these publications would be about 80 or 85 dollars. Do you think it possible to get so much? Of course we do not need it all at once, but it would certainly mean a great deal if right at the beginning of the year the Boards could find a way to furnish us the above mentioned in regular intervals. I am entirely out of German, & the Bohemian is low, & that in the face of three ships near & two to sail within a few days. I shall feel greatly obliged if you can help me get this work in such shape that will tell for most good. Will you be kind enough even if you do not approve of the entire request, to notify Dr. Frost just as quickly as possible about the pressing need for German Gospels & Testaments at once, & the Bohem. will not last the entire week.

I would have saved you this & would have written Dr. Frost direct as usual, but I thought for this once it might be better to refer it to you.

I am so glad the letter is so far ended; it did seem I should never succeed that far, so many interruptions & hindrances came up. But here it is, & may the Lord bless this & every effort to the Salvation of souls for His Name sake.

Very gratefully yours,
Marie Buhlmaier
2201 E. Madison St.

Baltimore, Md.
May 23rd, 1903
[SBHLA, J. M. Frost Collection]

May 23, 1904
Dr. J. M. Frost
Dear Brother:

It now gives me pleasure to send you the pledges taken at Nashville for the Bible Fund. As you will see from the list they aggregate $190.00. There are pledge cards for all excepting one pledge made by Mrs. A. J. Wheeler of Nashville for the Woman's Missionary Union of Tennessee for $75.00. Please make entry of that. Miss M. E. Wright either turned over to you or some officer of the Sunday School Board the cash contributed. Will you kindly let me have a receipt for $5.00 which was contributed by a Maryland woman, crediting that $5.00 to Maryland, and the balance of the cash, credit to Tennessee and let me have receipt for that amount?

Miss Buhlmaier was at the Mission Rooms on Saturday and seemed much disappointed that she had not up to that time received the tracts which she asked should be sent to her in the letters which I handed to you when in Nashville. It seemed to be a positive grief to her that she had to allow a number of the immigrants to go without tracts that came on the previous steamer, her supply in some directions having been completely exhausted. I, of course, recognize how full your hands were during the Convention, but hope that you did not forget to mail the letters without delay. I now send you the letter which Miss Buhlmaier wrote to me enclosing the letters which I handed to you. Please give it a careful reading.

As I mentioned to you when in Nashville I do hope that you will make more generous appropriations of Bibles, Testaments and tracts to the Immigrant Work. We now have three missionaries at this work—two in Baltimore and one at Galveston—and I am sure we ought not to miss a single opportunity of reaching the immigrants as they land on our shores and putting in their hands gospel truths. Do you not think having as large a balance as you had to carry over last year in the Bible Fund will make Southern Baptists think that our facilities for distributing copies of God's Word are small and hence the contributions will dwindle instead of increase unless we can prove to them that this is not the case? I think you will agree with me that the amount promised by Woman's Missionary Union at annual meeting shows an interest in the Bible Fund and we will be glad to cultivate same if the money is used.

You will note that Miss Buhlmaier asks that you devise some plan by which delay can be prevented in her receiving the tracts and Testaments. Would it not be helpful for you to give a standing order that a certain amount of literature be sent to Miss Buhlmaier quarterly? She has had such a large experience in the work that she can no doubt tell you about how much literature she would need each quarter.

Hoping that you have recovered from your fatigue and are feeling quite well, I am,

Very truly,
Annie W. Armstrong
[SBHLA, J. M. Frost Collection]

Armstrong developed a close relationship with Bayview, Baltimore's "poor house."

June 19, 1893
Dr. H. H. Harris
Dear Brother:
Your letter of June 15th received and I am glad to know that it will be possible for you to visit Baltimore next week, as there is a number of matters that I would be very glad to have a little conference with you about. I have noted the two points to which you have called attention with regard to "Missionary Day" and will consider both of these carefully, but will wait until I see you before any definite action is taken.

May I ask that you will let me know what day it will be convenient for you to be in Baltimore? Wednesday June 28th I expect to spend the day at our city Poor House as I have charge of the work conducted by the ladies in connection with that institution. I could get some one to take my place but if another day will suit you as well, I would prefer not to break the engagement. Any other day during the week that you will appoint I will arrange to be disengaged and will be pleased to see you for any length of time you may be able to give me.

Very truly,
Annie W. Armstrong
[IMB Archives]

December 22, 1894
Dr. R. J. Willingham
Dear Brother:
While this is a business letter, yet I think I have such a pleasant piece of news to give you, that it may be regarded as seasonable. When I read the enclosed letter from Mrs. Barnes, Dr. Tichenor's daughter, this A.M., I felt that there was no Christmas present which I would probably receive this year that would give me nearly the pleasure this letter gave, so I am going to be generous and share it with you. I have been so anxious for Mrs. Wilson to resign and so feared that she could not be gotten out of the position without much difficulty, that it seems I can hardly realize that she no longer is the Secretary of the Georgia Central Committee. I have no doubt that she and her sister will try and organize a Woman's Auxiliary to the Gospel Mission, but it will not be nearly so difficult to cope with her under those circumstances as it was when apparently she was a friend to our work, but really undermining it.

I have had a number of letters in regard to these troubles in Ga. since I last sent you an installment of same, but I thought I would defer troubling you with these until you were more rested after your round to conventions. Unless you wish to see them, I will not now forward them, as this letter of Mrs. Barnes shows that what Miss Wright and others in Ga. have been trying to accomplish is now done. If, after reading Mrs. Barnes' letter, you desire to offer any suggestions in answer to the questions she has asked of me, I will be glad to have them. I think, though, I can now give the ladies of the Central Committee in Ga. what help they need without troubling you further, as I am right familiar with the ground which has to be gone over. I have replied to Mrs. Barnes' letter, sending her the information she wished and also offering her any assistance in my power. Should the Central Committee need any outside help, I will try to go to Ga. either for their annual meeting or prior to it. My duties at home seem to make it very necessary for me to remain in Baltimore, but I am getting to appreciate that if the work requires me to leave, in some way or other the way opens.

By the way, it seemed a few days since that, in all human probability, the Cor. Sec. W.M.U.'s place was to be vacant, but God ordered it otherwise. I was one of a party who met with an accident which came very near being fatal. The circumstances were these.

I was returning from Bayview, our city poor-house, where I had spent the day with four other ladies, doing what was in our power to cheer the inmates, and we were driving in a phaeton from the institution to take the electric car at the terminus of one of the city lines. The Philadelphia cars cross the road over which we were driving. The driver of the phaeton misunderstood a signal of the flagman and instead of stopping, went right on and the gates were shut down with our vehicle inside. There was a double track, but if it had not have been that the horse stumbled and fell, we would undoubtedly have been on the second track when the train passed, which it did almost immediately. The flagman seeing the condition of things, signaled to the train, but it was too close upon us to do anything except slow up. Some men, when they saw what was occurring, rushed to our rescue and held the horse down, he being within a very few inches of the track that the car was on. Without waiting for the door of the phaeton to be opened, the five ladies, one and all, in some remarkable manner, got through an opening and no one was injured. The accident might have been a very serious matter with two of the committee, as one of the ladies had only 10 weeks ago had a stroke of paralysis, and the day previous, her physician had said she must avoid all excitement. Another one had for years been unable to engage in the work on account of heart trouble, but the promise was verified, "Thou wilt keep him in perfect peace whose mind is stayed on Thee because he trusteth in Thee," for, astonishing as it may seem, there was not one of the committee who made the slightest outcry or seemed very much disturbed. While one would not choose to go through such experiences frequently, yet it does prove how safe we are in God's keeping.

Wishing you and all your loved ones a happy Christmas, I am

Very truly,

Annie W. Armstrong

[IMB Archives]

January 27, 1897

Dr. R. J. Willingham

Dear Brother:

I write to ask if you will let me have a number of copies of the leaflet, "Light on the Workings of the Foreign Mission Board," to distribute among the Woman's Mission Societies. I think the facts it contains would be of help in presenting the work of Foreign Missions. If you can let me have 3,000 copies, I think I can use them to advantage. Our stock of leaflets (I of course have reference to W.M.U. supply) has gotten very low. You will remember that while you were in Baltimore during our State Association, you told me I could select 4,000 leaflets and distribute these among the Societies. We have had no later grant from the Foreign Board. You will appreciate that we have thousands of Societies, and of course that number of leaflets goes a very small way toward providing information for our workers. Please consider the matter and let me know what can be done. I am sure money expended in furnishing missionary literature is returned to the Board tenfold.

I have just received a very kind communication from Miss F. B. Hawley, of New York—one of those who arranged for the late Woman's Conference. She writes:

"We are very sorry not to be able to send you detailed report of the Conference of Jan. 15th, but our Stenographer proved a failure. I mail you a paper, containing an account of the meeting," etc., etc.

Let me know if you care to see this paper and if so I will forward it.

I know your time is precious, and I am now hurrying to get through a number of letters, as I must attend a missionary meeting this afternoon and prepare to give a talk at same, but I have had recently such a strong proof that God does, if we are willing "to labor and to wait," give a bountiful harvest "in due season," that I must take time to tell you the circumstance.

I think I have mentioned to you in times past a work in which I have been engaged for twenty years at our city poor-house. It has been to me a blessed work, and although I have been urged frequently to give it up since my time has been so occupied with our mission interests, yet I never have felt willing to do so. Our efforts have been directed to bringing religious influences to bear upon the poor unfortunates in that institution—the number varies from twelve to nineteen hundred. I am sure much good has been accomplished and the whole tone of the institution in these years has largely changed, but we have never been able to secure any permanent help from the officers, so Christian influences were entirely from the outside and of course could not be constant, as the Committee only visits the institution one day in each week. Last Wednesday, however, I was interviewed by an officer, a lovely Christian woman who has been there for several months, and she told me of her earnest desire to reach a class of men—those that are employed—who were not able to come to any service which we held. Having influence with the other officers, she had obtained permission to use a dining room in the building in the evening to gather these men together. Her time is of course limited, also her strength, but her idea was, if she was provided with books, papers, etc., she would make arrangements for a Reading Room. I immediately saw what a large opening this was and told her to "go forward," and I would see that she had the needed material; to give notice that Sunday evening there would be this gathering. No doubt many persons would have thought it was the height of audacity my making such a promise. The next day (Thursday) was held the Quarterly Meeting of the Woman's Baptist Home Mission Society of Maryland, which required my being away from the Mission Rooms that day, and having been at the poor-house on Wednesday, it seemed that I could do nothing more that week, but I felt it was an opening which God had made and it would all be right. Before I left Bayview, it had commenced to snow and riding in the phaeton brought on an attack of Neuralgia, which I feared would prevent my going to the meeting the next day, but how wonderfully God does smooth the way before us. When I reached home, I found in the Library three large bundles of literature, and when I opened these I saw just what was needed to start this work at Bayview, a year's file of the *Christian Herald* (Dr. Talmage's paper), probably 100 copies of *Harper's Weekly* and a number of magazines. The one who sent them of course knew nothing of this opening. The time of sending was certainly directed by our Heavenly Father. If they had come the day before, I should have taken them to the Institution and simply scattered them. Oh, how true it is: "Before they call, I will answer, and while they are yet speaking, I will hear."

This is not all. I felt it might be helpful to give this circumstance to the ladies at the Quarterly Meeting, which I did. At the close of the morning session, some lady, without my having intimated that money was desired, came and handed me a contribution that will be used to purchase hymn books which are needed. The next day I saw in the paper that the father-in-law of my nephew, Eugene Levering, had been made President of the Board of our Circulating (Pratt) Library. I have since then asked for an appropriation of books from the Pratt Library for Bayview. I have not the slightest doubt but that it will be granted. This could not have been done years ago. "In due season," though, it came about.

Very truly,
Annie W. Armstrong
[IMB Archives]

May 18, 1898
Dr. J. M. Frost
Dear Brother:

I have just returned from Bayview, our city poorhouse, where I have been spending the day. I find the proof of your leaflet has been sent in by the printer, so I forward it. Will you kindly return same as soon as possible? When sending proof, let me know if you desire additional copies of the leaflet sent to Nashville. As you will remember, we are to use this leaflet, with two others—one for each Board, Home and Foreign—to send in packages to pastors, the Boards paying for same. The number of ministers, I believe, is about 11,000. In addition to this, we will send the leaflet to the regular subscribers to the Monthly Literature and keep it in stock at the Mission Rooms. I thought, though, you might want to have some for distribution from the office at Nashville, hence my inquiry. It will be cheaper if the entire number that will probably be used can be printed at once, rather than to have a second edition. You of course appreciate that those sent to pastors, as well as what may be ordered by you, will be furnished at cost. No advance is asked by the Mission Rooms on literature furnished the Boards.

Another thing. The Home and Foreign Boards both furnish the Woman's Missionary Union with leaflets to distribute to societies free in the interest of their work. If you wish copies of this leaflet sent to Central Committees and by them distributed to societies, let me know how many to print for that purpose. It requires from three to five thousand of any publication we issue to reach W.M.U. workers in the different States.

I am correct in thinking, am I not, that the Convention Annual is to contain a list of the pastors in the Southern States. From what Dr. Burrows told me, I judge the Year Book is very, very faulty in this particular. I am waiting to receive the list of ministers which I suppose is to appear in the Convention Annual, before having envelopes addressed for packages of literature. It will be a great convenience if I can have at once three copies of that portion of the Annual which contains the ministers' names and addresses. If you can secure these for me, please send them without delay.

I am not at all certain that I have expressed myself clearly, for a day at the poorhouse uses up all the wits I possess and leaves me in quite an exhausted state, so please excuse all incoherency.

Yours worn-outedly,
Annie W. Armstrong

P. S. I enclose sample of paper for leaflet. Let me know if you like this color.

[SBHLA, J. M. Frost Collection]

October 4, 1899
Dr. R. J. Willingham
Dear Brother:

I judge you have returned from your trip to Kentucky, and, as there are several matters I want to speak of, I will now present them to you. I will have to do so, though, briefly, as I must in a few moments leave the Mission Rooms.

1. *Change in President of Virginia Central Committee.* You have no idea how much I appreciated your kindness, when you were so pressed in making arrangements for leaving home, to take time to see Miss Hutson. I judge, though, from a letter which I received since from Mrs. Gwathmey, that it is not probable that Miss Hutson will continue in office. I have decided, under these circumstances, that it is my duty to go to Salem, and so I am making my arrangements to do so. Mother seems a little stronger than she was, and so it is probable I can go.

2. *The Maryland Union Association.* I have just written to Mrs. Willingham, asking her if she would not come to Baltimore with you to the Association, and for both of you to be our guests while here. If you will let us treat you as members of the family, your visit will simply give pleasure. Mother is not able to come down stairs; perhaps, once or twice during the day she will walk from one room to another, but, unless she should grow worse, (if that be the case I would not hesitate to tell you) there is really no reason why you should not accept the invitation which I now extend.

If Mrs. Willingham does not think she can leave home—I hope you can persuade her to the contrary—we would be glad to have you stop with us. I want, though, that you should feel perfectly at liberty to decline, if you think it would be better for you, during the Association, to be where you could see more persons. It will depend upon how mother is, whether I could invite any of the ministers to meet you at our home. The Association will be held at Grace Church, which is in the eastern part of the city. The cars, though, will enable us to reach the church in probably thirty minutes.

Later. Since writing the above I have been home to dinner and found there Miss Rebecca Norris, Dr. Hartwell's sister-in-law. She said that Mrs.

Hartwell wrote that Dr. Hartwell was growing stronger all the time and able to do more and more each day. His recovery seemed almost a miracle.

3. *Miss Wescott.* Last night after Prayer Meeting Miss Wescott, who has been away, came to me and said that she expected to leave Baltimore today—as trained nurse she at times takes positions away from Baltimore—and probably would not be back until about Thanksgiving Day. She then went on to say that on her return she would ask that I would write the letter for her. I, of course, knew that she had reference to a letter of endorsement to her application for appointment as Foreign Missionary. I did not reply fully to this remark, but afterwards I told Mr. Millard that either he or I probably had quite an uncomfortable duty to perform; that Miss Wescott would not be appointed by the Foreign Board. He wished to know the reasons and I told him that before discussing the subject with him, I preferred that he would write and ask you to let him see the letter which you forwarded to me during the summer. You will remember at that time you told me to show it to Mr. Millard, but he was out of the city. Mr. Millard seemed to want me to give him the facts, but I declined as I preferred that he should see the letter before we had any conversation on the subject. If Mr. Millard has not written to you in regard to this, I suppose he will in the course of a day or two.

4. *Annuities or Legacies.* I think you will enjoy reading two letters which I have received recently from Mrs. W. W. Ashburn of Atlanta. After receiving the first, I wrote to Mrs. Ashburn asking permission to have portions of it printed in W.M.U. department in *Foreign Mission Journal*, as I hoped it might incite some one else to assume the support of a "representative" on a foreign field. Since reading the second letter, it has occurred to me that possibly Mrs. Ashburn might be willing to make over some property to the Foreign Board, so that for all time she could be represented in China. Do you know enough of her financial ability to judge whether this is possible, and would you approve of my making the suggestion to her?

5. *Letters from missionaries under appointment.* As I wrote you, I sent letters to several of the missionaries that the Board has recently appointed. I enclose replies that have come from two. Mr. and Mrs. Hamilton were among the frontier missionaries for whom we secured aid. Last year, a box was sent to them from North Avenue Church, Baltimore. This will cause those missionaries to become objects of peculiar interest to the membership of that church.

I must draw this letter to a close, as I am due at the Primary Union.

Very truly,

Annie W. Armstrong

Still later. This letter has been written in stages. I have just returned from the Primary Union—an undenominational organization—where I went to make an appeal for workers for our Bayview Mission—the city poorhouse. As President of the Bayview Mission, I felt peculiarly responsible to secure additional workers, as my hands are now so full I cannot give to it the attention I used to. Then again, if I attend the Annual Meeting in Virginia, I have to be away the day which I give to that work this month; so you can appreciate, under these circumstances, how truly glad and thankful I was to be able to secure promises from six ladies who will go this month, and who may go regularly. It does seem that when our Heavenly Father shuts one door, He opens another.

[IMB Archives]

October 17, 1901

Dr. R. J. Willingham

Dear Brother:

Please find enclosed copy of a letter which I have received from Miss Duncan, who made a pledge of $5.00 for the building of the house in Canton for our unmarried, female missionaries. I also send copy of the receipt which she forwarded—the original I will send to Miss Broadus. I would now ask that you erase from the list of pledges Miss Duncan's name.

There are several quite important matters which I desire to refer to you—one or two new plans which have completely taken hold of me—but as I hope to see you in the near future, I will not take time to write of them.

I enclose a leaflet which we have just gotten out, giving the plan of the "Home Department" in full. This leaflet we will distribute quite widely. I want very much that the ladies should make their canvass for "Home Department" members, holding the booklets in reserve, as they are expensive, until they have obtained promises from those they seek to interest. I know there is such a thing as "A penny wise and a pound foolish" policy, but I do want that we should exercise all possible economy. The "Home Department" supplies with other plans which I desire to inaugurate, necessarily cause a larger outlay; so it will not be possible for me to keep W.M.U. "Expense Account" within the limit of last year, but I think I can promise the Boards without the shadow of a doubt that whatever expenses we ask them to meet for Woman's Missionary Union will be returned to their treasuries increased ten-fold. May I ask that you will give the leaflet which I now enclose a careful reading, as questions, no doubt, will be asked you in regard to the "Home Department" plan.

I am feeling a little used up today and when I tell you what occurred yesterday, I do not think you will be surprised. I spent the day at our city poorhouse, and during a meeting of which I had charge, one of the inmates had to be taken out of the room in a fit. A little later, during the singing of a solo, one idiot attempted to stop a second idiot who had joined in the hymn, thinking a duet more desirable, and as the first idiot used rather forcible arguments to restrain the singer, several rounds of fisticuffs ensued. Our meeting, though, proceeded, and when I was about to close, happening to look through a door which opened in the passage, and which faced another door of a room directly opposite, I saw sitting there a Catholic priest. He was near enough to have heard the talk which I had been making. It was my purpose when I noticed him, at the close of the service to take an opportunity of saying something to said priest, but one of the other ladies spoke to him at some length. She was new to the work, and I was a little curious to know what had been the subject of her conversation. She informed me that she had invited the priest to attend our meetings, and said that the inmates had seemed very much interested. He replied that he had noticed they were. When we left the institution, just ahead of us were five priests. I am told that they make a *daily* visit to Bayview. Of course under these circumstances, it is very hard for Protestants to make much headway when the Catholics are willing to expend so much time and labor in looking after even such poor forlornities as we find in the Baltimore almshouse. I have charge of the ladies' mission at Bayview, and I have no idea of giving the work up. It is though, quite wearing on the nerves, and requires a good deal of physical strength. I suppose, though, what I saw yesterday is only a sample of what the missionaries have to undergo frequently.

Very truly,
Annie W. Armstrong
[IMB Archives]

December 7, 1904
Dr. R. J. Willingham
Dear Brother:

I have just returned from the City Poor House where I have spent the day. It is the largest opportunity, I expect, in the City of Baltimore that one can have to reach the unsaved in one day, outside of the Jail or Penitentiary. I started the Ladies' Bayview Mission nearly thirty years ago, and it was a positive pleasure to me to go back there today, after a year's absence. The demands made upon my time by our Mission work there so exacting that I felt I must give the Bayview work up, and did so for a year; but felt forced to resume same, as no one could be gotten to take my place as President and the work was simply going to pieces. I really have not time for it, but I do not feel that it would be right for me to let the work be discontinued, when it seems to mean so much for the poor unfortunates that are at Bayview in such large numbers.

I return the letter which you forwarded. It seems to me all right; but, would it not be better to let it be addressed to "Superintendent," instead of "Superintendents?"

The size of the picture, unmounted, is 10 1/2 X 8 1/2 ins.

Hastily, but very truly,
Annie W. Armstrong
P. S. Circulars received; thanks for same.
[IMB Archives]

Annie Armstrong loved children, and she maintained a keen interest in Baltimore's orphanages.

June 2, 1898
Dr. R. J. Willingham
Dear Brother:

Your letter of June 1st received, enclosing check for three hundred dollars ($300.00) for Woman's Missionary Union expenses. I return receipt for same with thanks.

I appreciate very thoroughly your taking time to write to Miss Heck, letting her know that I did not ask for your opinion when I gave you the facts in regard to the questions upon which she and I differ. I so thoroughly despise (excuse so strong a word, but I know of no other that expresses my feeling) anything that tends to getting persons to take sides in a matter, unless it is presented publicly when both parties that differ are present, that I did not want Miss Heck to think that I was asking the officers of the Boards for their opinions. (I of course make an exception of Dr. Frost in this particular, as the question at issue between Miss Heck and myself is in regard to the work of the Sunday School Board, and therefore that Secretary is more interested in the matter than even the Secretary of the Woman's Missionary Union). I wrote Dr. Frost, under date of Feb. 2nd, the following:

As I previously mentioned, Miss Heck, greatly to my surprise, again introduced the subject of the Sunday School Board Recommendations to me privately, although she made not the slightest intimation at the Executive Committee meeting, which was held while she was in Baltimore, that she disapproved the way I had carried out the Recommendations this year, or that she thought it would be wise to suggest changes in the Recommendations of the Sunday School Board for next year. When she commenced to speak on the subject, she asked how I would prefer the question being brought forward—whether she or I was right in the way we understood the wishes of the ladies in regard to contributions to the Sunday School Board. I told her I had no preference in the matter; that I was simply acting upon instructions which I had received and was ready at any time to meet any charges that might be made. Before the conversation closed, I think she fully understood that I was not willing to withdraw one particle from the stand which I had taken, viz., that the ladies had decided, as shown by their own action, that they were willing to make contributions to the Sunday School Board and that I had simply carried out instructions received. I told Miss Heck that I intended referring the matter to Judge Haralson and would be prepared to give his opinion, if there was need for it. I do not think it wise to speak of this matter either to the Executive Committee in Baltimore, or to the Central Committees in the different States. If Miss Heck decides, after more mature deliberation, that she will bring the question forward publicly, I shall be prepared to meet it. I think it is probable she will consult Mr. White, Secretary of the North Carolina State Board, and perhaps others as to what ought to be done, looking at things from her standpoint. I shall decline to have any further conversation with her in regard to it. She knows my views and I know hers, and nothing is to be gained by our discussing it further.

I find this gives my views, not only at that time, but in regard to later developments, and I propose to adopt the course of conduct which I have therein outline.

Would you not be glad and thankful if the work could go forward without misunderstandings? It does seem, with the many perplexities which you have to meet, that I ought not to bother you with those that fall to my share. I have often thought of a remark which Dr. H. H. Harris made to me some years ago. I was telling him I did not mind the work connected with the prosecution of mission affairs, but the "worries" seemed to use me up completely and leave no strength to work. Dr. Harris replied to this remark: "Miss Annie, do you not know that 'worry' is part of the work?" Possibly (probably) he was right and our Heavenly Father permits the perplexities to arise, in order that we may be kept humble. When we see, as sometimes we do, that God has blessed efforts that we have made to advance His cause, if there was not the dark side to our work, we might become unduly exalted. Yesterday I did have a great pleasure. It has been some time since I was able to visit the Colored Orphanage in Baltimore, which a few years ago I was instrumental in getting established and which is now entirely in charge of the colored people. This orphanage has in it 36 children, and to see their bright faces yesterday and to note how well they were being taken care of—clean and neatly dressed—made me feel that the time and effort expended in this direction had brought forth a hundredfold. The house is being bought in which the orphanage is through a Building Association, and things are getting upon quite a firm foundation.

Again expressing my warm sympathy in the trouble which you are having in the management of Mexican affairs, and hoping that light will soon be given, so that you may know just what course to adopt, I am,

Very truly,

Annie W. Armstrong

P. S. I enclose letter which I have just received from Northfield. I suppose you also have had one, but thinking, as the envelope was addressed: "Baptist Board of Foreign Missions," you might not have, I pass it on. I know it is not necessary to ask that you give the needed information as to the address of our missionaries.

[IMB Archives]

July 6, 1899
Dr. R. J. Willingham
Dear Brother:
I have been trying to write Miss Wescott as comforting a letter as I knew how, for I do realize that she feels that after making every sacrifice that any human being can make—since the age of fourteen banished from her father's house, struggling all these years to obtain the education that would fit her for usefulness on a foreign field, and then to give up the hope of spending her life with the one who had won her affections—it is hard that she cannot accomplish the purpose which caused her to make these sacrifices. I trust there need only be a little temporary delay in her appointment, but the outlook to her seems very dark. I am glad now—I expect you will also—to be able to turn my thoughts to something of an entirely different nature.

I have a pleasant piece of news to give, but I must ask that you will not mention it. I had a visit from Mrs. Schimp today. She tells me that she has had her will drawn up by a lawyer—it is yet unsigned—and she has left the house in which she lives and what money she has in banks to the Home & Foreign Boards. It had been her purpose to leave the house to the Md. State Board, to be used as a shelter for Baptist women, whose earnings were not sufficient to enable them to pay rent, but the Board was not willing to accept it on those conditions. The Orphanage started by Dr. Wharton and which he had turned over to the Baptists of Md. had proved to be any thing but a blessing—it has been given up and a number of unpaid bills is all that remains of it—and the Board I consider wisely declined to have property left which would necessitate the starting of another Institution. They would of course be pleased to receive the property and convert it into money for the carrying on of State missions, but Mrs. Schimp is not willing to do this, and as her desire cannot be carried out in the matter of providing a "Home" she prefers to leave it to the Home & Foreign Boards.

There is another phase of this question which I would now ask that you consider, and then let me know what you think wise for me to do. As I previously wrote you, I have very little doubt but that any will Mrs. Schimp may make will be contested. She has some very mean relatives. One time when she was confined to her bed, they came to her house and made a search for her papers. Mrs. Schimp thinks she has had her will prepared so carefully that it will not be possible for it to be upset. Much more intelligent people have been under the same impression, and their relatives have been able after death to have their wills set aside—recently an eccentric old man died in Balto. leaving $50,000.00 to an Institution of which Sister Alice is Secretary, and relatives are contesting that will. Do you think it would be well for me to try and get Mrs. Schimp to transfer the deed of her house to the Boards now, and let a contract be signed by which she would be at liberty to occupy it during her life time? I see how this could readily be done if the property was to be given to either Board, but as her idea is that it shall eventually be divided I do not know whether it would meet the wishes of the Boards for there to be this joint-proprietorship. I will be glad to have your *personal* opinion. I will of course appreciate that it is not officially given, and therefore not binding. I do want to know though how the subject strikes you before I speak of it again to Mrs. Schimp, for if it is probable that it would not meet with the sanction of the Boards it is useless for me to try and get our friend to change her present plans—the Boards will have to take the chances of losing the property.

I really do not know what amount of money Mrs. Schimp still has in the banks and which it is her purpose to leave to the Boards, but I was glad to hear her say, if she lived until next year she thought she would then turn over more money to the Boards. I shall try and get her to do this, for of course money as well as property will be grasped if possible by relatives at her death, regardless of her wishes.

It really is astonishing how large a sum this ignorant woman and her husband accumulated during the years when they could work, and how willing she now is to part with what represents so much toil and sacrifice. She is making provision for the education of an orphan boy, whose mother she knew.

I would be glad to hear from you in regard to this as soon as convenient for it would be easier for her to make any transfer before her will is signed than afterwards, as I am sure she would not want to have a second one prepared.

Very truly,
Annie W. Armstrong
[IMB Archives]

Armstrong was interested in promoting racial harmony. She worked closely with leaders from the National Baptist Convention on numerous issues, particularly "woman's work" and literature distribution.

January 6, 1897
Dr. R. J. Willingham
Dear Brother:
I hold your letter of Jan. 4th in my hands, in which you kindly say: "I hope you have gotten settled in your new rooms and will soon feel at home." Settled? No indeed. I have no idea that we will be able to get things straight for two weeks to come. The carpenters have not yet left and then we have to have painting done before we can even begin to have carpets repaired and laid. I am succeeding, though, amid the confusion, in keeping the work from getting into arrears.

We are having a variety of experiences. All the morning we have been having water works. The building is heated by steam and is a new experience to the janitor. I am glad to say, though, the absurd side is to me so apparent, that I am not taking things very much to heart, but to business.

1. *Expenses for Christmas Offering.* Please find enclosed bill from the Mission Rooms for the literature, etc., for the Christmas Offering. When convenient, we will be glad to have check in payment of same.

2. *Advice.* I am afraid you will think it is hardly worth while to offer advice to the Secretary W.M.U. when she—as in the case of securing Advocate for W.M.U. at the Seminary—does not accept same after it is given. While in this last instance, I did not feel it was wise to act as you suggested, yet you have no idea how grateful to you I am for giving me your opinion when difficulties arise. There is a question which I will in the near future have to confront, and I would be very, very much obliged if you would let me know how it appears to you.

Yesterday I received word that Rev. L. G. Jordan (colored), Secretary of the National Baptist Convention, will shortly come to Baltimore and will arrange to have the colored woman from Washington, whom he expects to take a prominent part in inaugurating mission work among the colored women, to meet him here so they can have some conference with me in regard to the organization which is about to be formed for the colored women. One important phase of the subject is the location of their Executive Committee. I want to ask if you think it desirable to have same in Baltimore. As you probably know, there are more colored people in Baltimore than in any city in the world. I do not know whether the Baptists here are as strong as in some other cities, but some of the ministers are men of ability, and if their aid can be secured, it will be very helpful. Then again, there is a woman here who I think would make an efficient President, if not Cor. Sec'y. I have worked with her for fourteen years and consider her not only a very devoted Christian, but gifted with a great deal of good, common sense. She was formerly a teacher, but I do not think she is a very well educated person. Should the general organization for colored women be located in Baltimore, we could quite materially aid those who have the work in charge without its appearing publicly that we were doing so. I of course appreciate that it will take a good deal of time and strength to help those who will have this work in hand before their officers will know how to grasp it. As I have been led to regard the matter, however, an immense amount of good can be done—not only in developing the colored women here at home, but in doing work in Africa—if we can get the colored women organized as missionary workers.

If you are not too busy, please take a few minutes to consider this question and then let me have your opinion.

Very truly,

Annie W. Armstrong

[IMB Archives]

January 26, 1897

Dr. J. M. Frost

Dear Brother:

I enclose a letter which I have just received from Texas, asking for tracts for distribution among the colored people. We have none suitable at the Mission Rooms. Will you make a grant to the Society, which proposes to do this work? I am not acquainted with Mrs. Owen, but have no doubt the ladies at that point will do good work.

As you kindly gave me your opinion in regard to the proposed organization of the colored women, I think you may be interested to know in what shape that matter now is. Last Tuesday morning we had quite a prolonged conference, lasting about four hours, with Rev. L. G. Jordan, Secretary of the National Baptist Convention (colored). He had arranged to have meet him here a colored woman from Washington, Nannie H. Burroughs. I had invited Rev. G. R. Waller (missionary of the Home Board and pastor of one of the Baltimore colored churches), Mrs. W. J. Brown and Mrs. W. J. E. Cox to be present at the interview, these ladies being members of the Standing Committee on Work among the Colored People. The ground was very carefully gone over and I believe we were guided in the decisions reached. I will not trouble you with details, but simply state what was decided.

1. That the general organization should not be at once effected; that at the next Annual Meeting of the National Baptist Convention, which occurs in Boston in September, on Recommendations of the Boards, the Convention would call on the women to organize.

2. That preliminary work would be done in the interim and that the Secretaries of the Boards would try, as they went from point to point, to interest the women in missions and get the pastors in sympathy with this movement; also to get articles in State papers to the same purport.

3. That the women were to be asked to contribute for Home, Foreign and State Missions, or (where the pastors preferred) the amount raised for State Missions to be used for Church Aid.

4. That a Constitution and By-laws for Woman's Mission Societies should be printed in the February edition of the *Afro-American Mission Herald*, with other articles calculated to interest the women in the work; that hereafter there would be a Woman's Department in that paper—the Constitution was prepared last Tuesday morning (it is to a great extent the one now used by our own Societies)—and I will for the present largely furnish the data for said department.

5. That mite boxes will be furnished by the Boards and this material will be sent out, at the request of the Boards, by a colored woman in Baltimore and to her will be referred letters of inquiry in regard to organization of Societies, etc., etc. This woman is a Mrs. Martha Clark whom I have known, and with whom I have worked for 14 years. She is, I consider, not only a very earnest Christian, but a person of remarkably good sense and of some executive ability.

6. That during Inauguration Week in March a Mass Meeting will be held in Washington to interest the colored women who may be there in missions, but not at that time to effect a general organization. The woman, Nannie H. Burroughs, whose letter I forwarded you, will between this and September try to interest the women of the churches in the District of Columbia, getting them to organize Missionary Societies and be prepared to unite with the general organization when formed.

You will appreciate that in carrying out the plan as outlined, while the officers of the Woman's Missionary Union will not appear to have any part in this movement, we will be helping those who have this work in charge in every way in our power. I am sure, for many reasons, it is better for us to be working out of sight and trying to fit the colored people to do their own work. When the time comes, I shall of course try and get the ladies in the different States to show the colored women in the various communities how to organize Woman's Mission Societies.

I have been quite pleased with what I have seen of Mr. Jordan, and I think it will be very easy to aid him in getting things in shape. He will be in Baltimore again shortly. You have no idea how glad and thankful I am that God is allowing us this opportunity to help to elevate the colored women as well as to assist the work in Africa. I am sure the truest elevation comes through working for others. As this is a formative period in this work, I will be very glad to have your opinion of the plan as outlined, and any suggestions which may occur to you.

Some weeks since Dr. Whitsitt wrote, saying that he desired to have the February Missionary Day at the Seminary given to the presentation of the Woman's Missionary Union Work, and asked that I would invite a speaker. He (Dr. Whitsitt) suggested the names of several gentlemen in Kentucky in order that travelling expenses, which he expected W.M.U. to pay, would not be heavy. I did not consider that the *Western Recorder* had educated the Kentucky pastors to regard W.M.U. methods in a very favorable light, so preferred not to accept Dr. Whitsitt's suggestion. I was also quite anxious that it should be thoroughly understood that Woman's Missionary Union was auxiliary to *all* of the Boards, S.B.C., so invited Dr. Bell to be our champion, at the same time telling him that W.M.U. allowed those who advocated their cause the honor of paying their own travelling expenses. Dr. Bell has very kindly acceded to the request, secured passes and will make the asked for address in Louisville February 3rd. In a letter I had from him several days since, he said: "I have succeeded in getting passes all the way both for myself and wife, whom I want to meet some special friends in Louisville." etc., etc.

By the way, I had a letter a short time ago from Rev. J. D. Jordan, Secretary of the Southern B.Y.P.U., in which he said:

"What we will do for an organ in the future, I cannot say. Some want to adopt the *Union* of Chicago, others want to adopt the A.B.P. Society's papers, others want us to start a paper, and others think the newspapers can do the work. I have no idea what we shall do. Have written Dr. Frost about enlarging weekly *Kind Words* to eight pages and giving us four. Have no idea how it will strike him."

Is it probable that you will do as Mr. Jordan has requested, enlarge the weekly edition of *Kind Words* to eight pages?

Here is a pleasant item. Eutaw Place Sunday School has now a Home Department numbering over one hundred, and the school has noticeably increased since the canvass has been made for persons to join the Home Department. I am sure this method of work is calculated to do an immense amount of good.

I expect I will have to close and let other matters wait until my next.

Very truly,

Annie W. Armstrong

[SBHLA, J. M. Frost Collection]

July 2, 1897

Dr. J. M. Frost

Dear Brother:

This letter I purpose making rather a "news bulletin," but before giving these items, I have one matter of business to refer to, viz., grant of Bibles to Miss Buhlmaier. After receiving your letter in regard to this, I sent for Miss Buhlmaier, as I thought she could better judge which sized Bible was most suited for the work. When I explained to her that it required quite a large outlay to purchase the Bibles, her German frugality immediately showed itself and she suggested that for the present we would dispense with the Bibles altogether, as the Sunday School Lessons for the next quarter would be in the New Testament. That being her decision and she now has on hand a supply of Testaments, I will not make the order which you authorized for Bibles.

You have no idea how many subjects there are that I really want to talk over with you. I do hope you will find it possible to make a little visit to Baltimore—not a flying one—some time in the near future. If Mother continues as well as she is at present, I am going to insist that when you do come you make our home your headquarters. You will remember we have the first claim, as you did not stay with us last fall. Next week Mrs. Gwathmey of Virginia will be here—I shall try and see if I cannot cause her to become reconstructed in regard to the Sunday School Board. It is probable she may remain until I have to attend a District Association the 20th of July. After my return from that trip, I shall be glad to see you at any time. Now for some news.

1. *Work among the colored people.* I am glad and thankful to say I can report material progress in this direction.

(a) *Miss Burdette's visit.* While Miss Burdette was here, we tried as clearly and forcibly as we could to put before her the Southern side of this question. I endeavored to get her to appreciate that Southern Baptists were doing a *large* work among the colored people—not through employed missionaries, but directly themselves. I told her that my earnest desire was to lay this work so upon the hearts of our Southern women, that they would, in the same degree as they did before the war, feel the responsibility of the religious advancement of the Negro. I told her that I considered the Negroes being in our midst was a God-given opportunity to reach the Africans, and the work in the past showed that our people had not been wholly derelict in their duty. We further tried to get Miss Burdette to realize that the reason why the Northern missionaries had not been able to secure the active cooperation that would have made their work more effective, was due to their disregard of the customs of the people among whom they went—in foreign lands, it is necessary for the missionaries to know the habits of the people if they would be helpful to the natives; also that friction would continue as long as the missionaries of the Northern Boards were encouraged before Northern audiences to so misrepresent the Southern people by giving exceptional cases of injustice, wrong doing, etc., etc., and leading persons to believe that these were the custom. I insisted that they had no more right to hold the Christian people of the South accountable for lynchings than we had to reflect on New York Baptists for what occurred in the slums of that city. There is a mob element everywhere and we must make distinctions. Another question which was discussed was the advisability of both Northern and Southern white Baptists using what influence they might have with the colored people to get them to do missionary work among their own people, and our helping them to devise plans and means to make their work effective. At present the Woman's Baptist Home Mission Society, headquarters Chicago, of which Miss Burdette is Cor. Secretary, receives some small contributions from colored Woman's Organizations. I urged Miss Burdette to consider if it would not be more helpful to get these women to send their offerings to the Boards of their own Convention. The amount contributed was so small, that it did not very materially help the work of the organization which she represented, and it would give vastly more hold on the colored people—the leaders—if we all were to throw our influence in this direction. Our object is to help the colored people, and certainly the best help is to train them to do their own work.

Miss Burdette gave her side of the question, which was that at times the Southern people had treated the Northern missionaries, not only discourteously, but in an altogether unchristian-like way. She evidently felt that we could aid their Society very materially by endorsing their work. I tried to get her to appreciate that said endorsement could only be secured by the objectionable features which I have previously stated being eliminated. My impression is that Miss Burdette regards the Cor. Sec'y W.M.U. as an idealist, not a practical worker. She acknowledged that the plans which I suggested were good, but I do not think she considers them feasible. Since her return home, I have heard from Miss Burdette and will give you a quotation from her communication. She wrote: "I have not forgotten the matter we discussed in Baltimore and we are *thinking*. May God Himself direct our thoughts—ours in Chicago, yours in Baltimore—so that we may be of one mind in the Lord."

What will be the result of the Conference, I of course cannot predict, but I do believe some good was accomplished.

(b) *Rev. L. G. Jordan.* Mr. Jordan has recently made several visits to Baltimore. During these, plans have been devised for getting the Woman's Work in shape. I will not take your time or mine to give said plans in detail, but will say a temporary President and Cor. Sec'y have been appointed, both of them living in Baltimore, and I am trying to do what I can to help these officers grasp the work. Sufficient will have been done prior to the Annual Meeting of the National Convention, which occurs in Boston in September, to enable the leaders of the colored people who will there gather to understand what is desired, and at that time to have the Woman's Work put on a permanent basis. While Mr. Jordan was in Baltimore, I saw him several times—he spent two mornings at the Mission Rooms, beside my attending two meetings that he addressed—and I really feel that he is an earnest, good man, and has the work of Africa thoroughly on his heart. He of course has had little experience as yet, and probably is not working as wisely as he will later on.

While here he told me of something which I think will interest you in connection with the publishing of Sunday School literature by the colored people. About ten days ago was held the New England Convention of colored Baptists. It met at Hartford, Conn. Those interested in the publication of the Sunday School literature had thought that it might be wise to try and have the National Convention meet at another point instead of Boston, as it was supposed the New England colored people would fully sympathize with the Publication Society and so might cause trouble at the approaching Annual Meeting. It was proved, however, at the Hartford Convention, that this was not the case. Dr. Simmons (white man) is District Secretary in New England. He presented the claims of the Publication Society at Hartford. Mr. Vass, whose territory it is not, was there to help create public sentiment in favor of the Publication Society, but a grandson of Frederick Douglas, Charles H. Morris, of Boston, to Mr. Jordan's extreme surprise, very eloquently advocated the Negro publications, and there was an overwhelming majority vote in favor of same, so you see on Northern territory the Publication Society has met with a defeat. Rather a queer experience, was it not?

I judge from what you have said, that you are acquainted with Dr. Boyd and have aided him at times with advice. If so, it might be well for you to suggest that he attend more State Conventions and scatter the literature at that time. Mr. Jordan says he has been to a number where the question would be raised as to which of the publications it would be well for the Sunday Schools in that State to take,—those issued by the American Baptist Publication Society, or the colored people—and Dr. Boyd would not be there, nor would there be any of the periodicals. Mr. Jordan said he would be willing to have same distributed if packages were committed to his care. I think he attends a large number of the Conventions. You of course appreciate, as I do, that the Society will at that time be very free with their literature.

My time is up, so I cannot send you the additional information I wanted to forward.

Very truly,

Annie W. Armstrong

P. S. I have just had a very pleasant visit from Dr. Malcolm McGregor, who will preach tomorrow for Dr. H. M. Wharton. I was amused, as I was showing him around the Mission Rooms and calling his attention to some charts,—one for the Home Board—that he should say: "Miss Armstrong, I want to ask your advice about preaching tomorrow a sermon applicable to the day (July 4th) and speaking of the needs of the country." I told him I thought it would be helpful and that there was a sermon in the diagram before him. After reading the lettering, he agreed with me that this was the case. Right strange, was it not, for Dr. McGregor to put aside the sermon that he had prepared and preach one of an entirely different nature, because he was impressed with one of the charts we had suspended on the wall?

[SBHLA, J. M. Frost Collection]

547 Third Street
Louisville, Ky.
Jan. 14, 1898
Miss Annie W. Armstrong
My dear Sister:
The enclosed is a letter from the Publication Society.

My dear Brother Jordan:
Your favor of the 6th, to Dr. Rowland, has been referred to me for reply as this matter comes under my direction.

I am very sorry that you did not drop in and see me when you were here, as I should have answered your question very promptly in the affirmative. We shall take pleasure in giving you any reasonable space in the *Baptist Teacher* such as is accorded to other missionary organizations. It will have to be subject, of course, to editorial approval, and possibly to editorial revision, as we do not accept anything from any writer whomsoever without that condition. I think that your organization deserves that kind of recognition, and if you will give us the items in good shape, so that they will not require much working over, and will simply deal with facts and not arguments, you shall have it with very great pleasure.

Wishing you much success in your work, in which I feel a very hearty interest, I remain,
　　Sincerely yours,
　　　　C. R. Blackall

I have written Sister M. C. Kenney and asked her to assist me in the Woman's Department and Bro. E. C. Morris and asked him to furnish me matter referring to the general work of the denomination.

Will you help me arrange a short program for missionary conferences? (Or some name suitable) to be held by the District men.

These will be held three or more in a state. I hope to put every man to work in dead earnest in Feb. Please suggest eight or ten subjects by women and men. What do you think of Dr. Brooks' speech?

We are straining every nerve to overcome the opposition and to do what we can for the poor down trodden ones in dark Africa and with aid of God and such noble women as yourself and some others, we will come out more than conquer. I suppose ere this that Brother and Sister Tule and Bro.

Jackson are on the field and we are now busy trying to raise a quarter's salary. Since the organization of our friends at Washington, D. C., we have not heard a word from them. It does seem that their plans to economize were disclosed at their selection of a man at $1,200.00 a year.

Pray for the work and the workers. Let me hear from you soon. I am,

Yours I. H. N.,

L. G. Jordan

[IMB Archives]

June 2, 1902

Dr. R. J. Willingham

Dear Brother:

There are several matters connected with the work about which I desire your opinion, so will proceed to state the subjects as briefly as possible.

1. *Sunday School Missionary Day.* Kindly read a letter which this morning's mail has brought from Dr. Frost. You will note Dr. Frost is very unwilling that I should not furnish as hitherto, Programs for Sunday School Missionary Day and Children's Day. I do not wonder at this, for Dr. Frost had not the slightest trouble whatever in regard to preparation of same. I have not only furnished him with manuscripts, but had electrotypes made of title pages for Programs, and cuts for Mite Boxes. As I told you, I felt that as the Convention had created the Sunday School Board, it was only right that all appeals to Sunday Schools should come through the Sunday School Board, and we handed over to Dr. Frost the Missionary Day, after Woman's Missionary Union had inaugurated it, and it was quite well established. I had thought that Dr. Frost, having such large opportunities for advertising, the collections would be far better. Instead of that, they have steadily decreased, and last year, as you will note from Sunday School Board report, the Foreign Board only received from Missionary Day, $575.94. The receipts from Children's Day, which are for the Bible Fund, have been steadily increasing. Dr. Frost explains this by saying that the money from Missionary Day is not sent to him, but to the Home and Foreign Boards. The Publication Society receives from Bible Day and Children's Day about $30,000.00. I cannot think that Dr. Frost is doing all that could be done in the way of advertising Missionary Day and Children's Day, and I have urged him repeatedly to make more of these occasions. I have so frequently spoken to him on the subject, that at last he seemed to be quite annoyed when I referred to it, so I simply dropped the matter.

A year ago I told Dr. Frost that I would not prepare the Programs, but he then seemed to think that I had given him too short notice for him to secure any one else. As that was probably the case, I went on with the work, and have now not only furnished him with the Program for Children's Day, which is to be next Sunday, but Missionary Day, which will be the fifth Sunday in September; so you see he has had ample notice of my giving up this work, as manuscripts were furnished for the Conventional Year, 1902–1903, before I told Dr. Frost that I would not be responsible for the Programs next year.

As I mentioned to you, W.M.U. will now arrange to interest the children specially in Foreign Missions in connection with the Christmas Offering, and for that a Program will have to be prepared, and for Home Missions, in connection with the Week of Self-Denial, when we also must have a Program. If I do as Dr. Frost now requests, it would require me to be responsible for four children's Programs and I really do not think it is necessary. Please let me have your opinion on this subject.

My idea is, if Dr. Frost has more trouble in getting the Programs or has to prepare them himself, he will then be impressed with this phase of his work, and push it.

I really cannot keep adding to the work which I am trying to do unless I am relieved in some directions. Dr. Frost has now Dr. Van Ness and Mr. Spilman to aid him, beside having the money to employ as many assistants as he needs; so I think the time has gone by when it is necessary for the Secretary of Woman's Missionary Union to do quite as much as she has done for the Sunday School Board in the way of providing manuscripts. Then again, the Mission Literature Department is the property of the Sunday School Board, and Dr. Frost does not do anything to help this forward, except to provide one manuscript a year for Sunday School Board leaflet, and he did give the study topics for the Sunday School Board this year. There are great possibilities in the Mission Literature Department, and I do want to have some time to avail ourselves of these.

2. *Legacies and Annuities.* I enclose a letter received today from Dr. McConnell, and would ask that you read what he says in regard to the publication which we are about to get out.

3. *Missionary Libraries.* I would also refer you to Dr. McConnell's letter for his opinion on this subject.

4. *Work among the Colored Women.* I have for years been trying to aid the colored people, and we have reached a point where I am sure the efforts made in the past are bearing fruit. More and more am I persuaded that it is

not a wise thing for Southern Baptists to unite with Northern Baptists in work. I do believe there can be and there should be the kindest feeling between the two divisions of Baptists in the United States, but let us work separate and apart the same as we do from Methodists, Presbyterians and other evangelical denominations. In the Northern States, "Trusts" are born, and it seems to me that even in religious work, the Northern people feel that they must dominate. I know this is Dr. Tichenor's feeling after long years of experience, Dr. Frost's likewise, and the Cor. Sec. W.M.U. agrees with them.

I am looking and hoping for a great work to be done by the colored people themselves, and I believe they are our best agents. It is unquestionably true that we now have the opportunity to influence and help colored women in a remarkable degree in the work they are doing. I enclose two letters which I would ask that you read from the Recording Secretary and the President of the Woman's Auxiliary of the National Baptist Convention. I met Mrs. Layten as she requested, and spent nearly two hours at the depot last Saturday, helping her to formulate plans. I am trying to get the Colored women to recognize that it is much better for them not to do independent work, but be in reality, Auxiliary to the Boards of the National Baptist Convention, and let all funds contributed by the women be expended by the Boards, and the Woman's Work be directed by the Secretaries of the General Boards. I have suggested that they ask the Secretaries of the Boards to furnish them with Recommendations as do the Boards of the Southern Baptist Convention—the Woman's Missionary Union—these to form the basis upon which they work. This policy is entirely different from that adopted by Northern women, but in the fourteen years in which it has been tried by Southern Baptists, it has proved successful, and I believe the colored women will find that their work will increase, and friction will be prevented, if they will adopt this method.

5. *Home for Missionaries' Children.* I have written to all of the missionaries whose names you sent that have children. I think you will agree with me that there will be no difficulty in our securing homes for those for whom they are needed after reading an extract from a letter which came this morning. It is from Miss Shankland, of Nashville, Tenn., who is "the mainspring" of W.M.U. work in that state. She writes:

"Your letter was the first intimation I had of the proposal to furnish homes for missionaries' children. One of our ladies seems to want such a child as soon as possible. It will be a popular plan, and a good one, I believe."

Here is a piece of news. Mr. Wilbur told me last night that he had telegraphed to Atlanta, declining to allow his name to be presented to the Jackson Hill Church as pastor. His reasons for this I cannot give, as they were told me in confidence, but suffice it to say that Mr. Wilbur * considers that the one who has been of late so busy in trying to thwart all measures proposed by the Secretary W.M.U., has been paying his attention to the present assistant pastor of Eutaw Place Church, and necessitated Mr. Wilbur's taking this action. I do not mean that he is totally responsible for it, but is one of the factors. I suppose Mr. Wilbur will now accept a call which he has had to Philadelphia. I am extremely sorry that we are to lose him, in the Southern Work.

Very truly,

Annie W. Armstrong

P. S. By the way, If you have not as yet arranged for Mr. Rawlinson for the summer, possibly, as Dr. Eager leaves this month for Europe, the Seventh Church pulpit will be vacant. Mr. Charles Bagby, 1407 McCulloh St., is one of the deacons of that church, and a letter from you in regard to Mr. Rawlinson would no doubt receive a favorable consideration.

[Handwritten insert] * This is conjecture on Mr. Wilbur's part.

[IMB Archives]

APPENDIX 1

CONSTITUTION.

Preamble.

We, the Women of the churches connected with the Southern Baptist Convention, desirous of stimulating the missionary spirit and the grace of giving, among the women and children of the churches, and aiding in collecting funds for missionary purposes, to be disbursed by the Boards of the Southern Baptist Convention, and disclaiming all intention of independent action, organize and adopt the following:

CONSTITUTION.

ARTICLE I.—*Name.*

This organization shall be known as the Executive Committee of the WOMAN'S MISSION SOCIETIES—(auxiliary to the Southern Baptist Convention.)

ARTICLE II.—*Object.*

The two-fold object of this Executive Committee shall be:

1st. To distribute missionary information and stimulate effort, through the State Central Committees, where they exist; and where they do not, to encourage the organization of new societies.

2nd. To secure the earnest systematic co-operation of women and children in collecting and raising money for missions.

ARTICLE III.—*Officers.*

The officers shall be a President, a Vice-President from each State, a Corresponding Secretary, a Recording Secretary, and a Treasurer, with a local committee of nine managers, who shall reside in or not remote from the place appointed at the annual meeting. These shall constitute the Executive Committee, five of whom shall be a quorum for the transaction of business.

ARTICLE IV.—*Annual Meeting.*

The annual meeting for the election of officers and transaction of business shall be held each year at such time and place as may be determined at previous annual meeting or by the Executive Committee.

ARTICLE V.—*Representation at the Annual Meeting.*

The officers of the committee and three delegates from each State shall be entitled to vote. Only such delegates as are personally present and duly accredited by the Central Committee or State societies they represent shall be entitled to vote.

ARTICLE VI.—*Conduct of Meetings.*

Every session of the Executive Committee shall be opened and closed with religious exercises.

ARTICLE VII.—*Amendments.*

The Constitution may be altered or amended by a two-thirds majority vote, at any annual meeting, three months previous notice having been sent through the State secretary to the Executive Committee. The corresponding secretary shall notify each vice-president of proposed amendment.

BY-LAWS.

ARTICLE I.—*Duties of Officers.*

SECTION 1.—President.—The President shall preside at the annual meeting and at all meetings of the Executive Committee; shall appoint all committees not otherwise provided for; shall organize new societies; and shall be, ex-officio, a member of all standing committees. She may, through the Recording Secretary, call special meetings of the Executive Committee, when in her judgment needful, or at the request of five members of the Executive Committee. In her absence, the Vice-President from the State where the committee may be located shall take her place.

SEC. II.—Vice-Presidents.—The Vice-Presidents shall be considered an advisory board of the Executive Committee, who are entitled, when present, to a vote at its sessions.

SEC. III.—The Corresponding Secretary.—It shall be the duty of the Corresponding Secretary to send to the Corresponding Secretary of each State, and to societies where there is no State organization, three months before the annual meetings, a blank for the report of such organizations, and from these reports the Corresponding Secretary shall collate the annual report. She shall conduct the correspondence of the Executive Committee, and shall be authorized to organize societies, and to transact all necessary business connected therewith.

SEC. IV.—Recording Secretary.—The recording secretary shall keep accurate records of the annual and special meetings of the Executive Committee. She shall also give due notice of the meeting of the Executive Committee designating the special topics for consideration, if there be any; shall notify officers of their election and committees of their appointment; and shall perform the other duties usual to her office.

SEC. V.—Treasurer.—The treasurer shall keep an accurate account of all receipts and disbursements of money, as reported to her by central committees and shall present a detailed account thereof to each annual meeting. The fiscal year shall terminate two weeks before the annual meeting, and the books shall then be closed. She shall also perform all other duties usually pertaining to her office.

ARTICLE II.—*Election.*

SECTION I.—Officers.—The officers, with the exception of vice-presidents, shall be elected by ballot, on the morning of the last day of the annual meeting. Each Vice-president shall be nominated by the delegation from her own State, and shall be elected by acclamation, unless otherwise ordered. An assistant corresponding secretary may be appointed by the Executive Committee.

SEC. II.—Tellers.—Tellers having been appointed by the meeting, an informal ballot shall be cast for each officer and the delegates shall then proceed to vote by ballot for the two highest nominees for each office.

SEC. III.—Local Committee.—The local committee of nine members shall be nominated by a committee appointed for that purpose, and shall be voted for at the annual meeting.

APPENDIX 2

Brief Chronology Of Woman's Missionary Union Auxiliary To Southern Baptist Convention During Annie W. Armstrong's Tenure As Corresponding Secretary[11]

1884 Women who met together during SBC in Baltimore resolved to meet annually during the SBC. Women covenanted to pray on the first Sunday morning of each month for the success of woman's missions work.

1885 SBC refused women delegates their seats and amended its constitution, changing *members* to *brethren*.

The women, at second annual meeting, sent their resolutions to be printed in the SBC minutes: (1) Women do not want a separate and independent organization; (2) Women want to work through the churches and to have representation in the SBC, through state conventions, as heretofore.

SBC recommended that state conventions, not mission boards, foster central committees.

1887 Maryland Baptist women opened the Mission Rooms, from which missions literature was published and distributed.

---

[11] This chronology is an abridgement of Eljee Bentley's more comprehensive work in Catherine Allen's, *A Century to Celebrate: History of Woman's Missionary Union* (Birmingham: Woman's Missionary Union, Auxiliary to Southern Baptist Convention, 1987) 427–41. Reprinted and edited by permission of Woman's Missionary Union, SBC.

Woman's Mission Societies at their informal annual meeting requested each state central committee to appoint three delegates to the 1888 meeting.

1888 Women delegates from 12 central committees met at Broad Street Methodist Church in Richmond. Delegates from ten states adopted a constitution, forming the Executive Committee of the Woman's Mission Societies (Auxiliary to Southern Baptist Convention). Baltimore was chosen as headquarters and officers were elected.

Organization agreed to aid HMB in building a church and enlarging a cemetery in Cuba.

Woman's Executive Committee in consultation with the FMB initiated a special offering to send a missionary to China to relieve Lottie Moon.

FMB and HMB agreed to pay expenses of the Executive Committee, as all contributions were to go to the boards.

1889 State central committees were encouraged to push young people's work and to organize associational or district committees.

Women planned next year's work based on recommendations by FMB and HMB.

1890 Women changed organization name to Woman's Missionary Union, Auxiliary to Southern Baptist Convention (WMU).

Sending boxes of clothes and other necessary items to frontier and other needy home missionaries became part of WMU's plan of work.

WMU agreed to raise enough money to support all women foreign missionaries.

WMU's Executive Committee employed a clerk and purchased a typewriter.

1892 First week in January was observed as a week of prayer in connection with the Christmas offering. In 1926 the week was changed to the first week in December.

WMU's plan of work included work with foreigners and black women.

WMU participated in SBC's centennial of missions, raising money for a chapel fund and furnishing materials for Sunbeam Bands and for an August Children's Day in the Sunday Schools.

1893 WMU sent the Sunday School Board leaflets and mite boxes for Missionary Day in Sunday School. Beginning in 1904–1905, FMB and HMB each had its own day in SS, and WMU supplied literature for both.

1894 SSB presented recommendations to WMU and began contributing toward the expenses of WMU, continuing to contribute through 1947.

WMU voted at Annual Meeting to raise an additional $5,000 before August 1 to pay off the FMB debt. The women raised $5,397.

1895 Week of Self-Denial was observed the third week of March to relieve the HMB of debt. Until 1922 Self-Denial was the name of the offering, despite many efforts to change it to Thank Offering. By 1911 the first week in March was customary.

1896 WMU adopted Sunbeam work at the request of the FMB. George Braxton Taylor, with Anna Elsom, had begun Sunbeams in 1886.

Each state was assigned a specified amount toward the goals of $30,000 each for the two mission boards. This system of apportionment became standard practice, lasting until 1943. Apportionments for the Training School continued as long as WMU owned the school.

Southern Baptist Theological Seminary began using one of its missionary days to promote WMU work. In 1900 space was offered in its magazine.

1897 WMU began contributing toward the SSB's Bible Fund to furnish Bibles for missionaries. Contributions continued until 1932. WMU also sent boxes of clothing to Sunday School missionaries.

1898 WMU recommended that states have associational vice-presidents, each one in charge of the work in her association.

1899 Money was given through WMU to all three boards to be invested and to pay an annuity, thus establishing for all three an annuity plan.

WMU recommended that the churches adopt a graded system of missionary education with organizations for all age levels, beginning with Baby Bands.

1900 WMU established HMB's Church Building Loan Fund. In 1903 WMU undertook to raise $20,000, a memorial to I. T. Tichenor, to put the fund on a secure basis.

WMU, at the request of the SBC helped lead the New Century Movement, an effort to induce every church and every member to make regular contributions.

WMU encouraged women to begin schools in mountain regions.

WMU corresponding secretary began traveling the states to promote the work and to visit home missionaries. The boards paid her travel expenses.

1901 Ownership of the Maryland Baptist Mission Rooms, founded in 1886 with Annie Armstrong as secretary, passed to the HMB and the SSB. It was later called the Mission Literature Department of the SBC. The operation, publication, and distribution of literature remained with the women.

Delegates to the WMU Annual Meeting were given badges entitling them to seats on the floor of the SBC.

WMU recommended a home department for every church to reach those who could not attend meetings. In 1904 WMU recommended that missionary home departments be merged with Sunday School home departments.

Annie Armstrong addressed the Woman's Auxiliary of the National Baptist Convention, which had organized with her advice in 1900. In 1902 WMU approved her work with the black organization.

WMU recommended that societies collect missions libraries and place missions literature in Sunday School libraries.

1903 Salary was approved for the corresponding secretary. Annie Armstrong declined to accept.

Emphasis on enlistment of young women was launched.

1904 WMU called attention to the mission society as an opportunity for Bible study.

WMU encouraged members to a careful study of proportionate and systematic giving. The practice but not study of giving had been recommended earlier.

1905 Using a gift of $10,000, WMU opened Margaret Home, a home for children of missionaries who were overseas, in Greenville, South Carolina.

1906 WMU recommended that each state organization observe a week of prayer for state missions. As early as 1895 WMU had recommended that state central committees cooperate with their state boards or conventions, making all departments of state work their work.

HMB and SSB returned ownership of the Literature Department to the Maryland Baptist Union, who transferred it to WMU.

WMU issued its first periodical, the quarterly *Our Mission Fields*, to provide complete programs for the monthly meetings of societies.

BIBLIOGRAPHY

Allen, Catherine B. *A Century to Celebrate: History of Woman's Missionary Union*. Birmingham: Woman's Missionary Union, Auxiliary to Southern Baptist Convention, 1987.

Baker, Robert A. *The Southern Baptist Convention and its People, 1607–1972*. Nashville: Broadman Press, 1974.

Estep, William R. *Whole Gospel, Whole World: The Foreign Mission Board of the Southern Baptist Convention, 1845–1995*. Nashville: Broadman & Holman Publishers, 1994.

Evans, Elizabeth Marshall. *Annie Armstrong*. Edited by Nan F. Weeks. Birmingham: Woman's Missionary Union, Auxiliary to Southern Baptist Convention, 1963.

Hunt, Alma. *History of Woman's Missionary Union*. Nashville: Convention Press, 1964.

James, W. C. *Fannie E. S. Heck: A Study of the Hidden Springs in a Rarely Useful and Victorious Life*. Nashville: Broadman Press, 1939.

Lawrence, J. B. *History of the Home Mission Board*. Nashville: Broadman Press, 1958.

Littlejohn, Carrie U. *History of Carver School of Missions and Social Work*. Nashville: Broadman Press, 1958.

Morgan, David T. *Southern Baptist Sisters: In Search of Status, 1845–2000*. Macon: Mercer University Press, 2003.

Scales, T. Laine. *All that Fits a Woman: Training Southern Baptist Women for Charity and Mission, 1907-1926*. Macon GA: Mercer University Press, 2000.

Sorrill, Bobbie. *Annie Armstrong: Dreamer in Action*. Nashville: Broadman Press, 1984.

INDEX

Allen, Catherine B., 1
American Baptist Publication Society,
    10, 17-18, 31, 33-34, 41, 85, 87, 89-
    90, 99, 103, 118, 151-152, 156-157,
    159, 161-164, 166-168, 170-172, 197,
    207, 241, 345-348
Armstrong, Alice, 13, 21, 26-27, 29, 34-
    35, 44, 47, 50, 55, 60, 65, 71, 85-86,
    92-93, 100, 103, 116, 135, 156, 181,
    189, 199, 208-209, 297, 304, 338

Baptist and Reflector, 52, 72
Baptist Argus, 58, 232, 263, 274, 288,
    290, 304
Baptist Courier, 55, 57
Barton, A. J., 6-8, 11, 23, 35, 48-49, 57,
    60, 106, 161, 171, 175, 203, 229-231,
    274-275, 314-316, 318
Bayview, 7, 324-325, 328-329, 332-334
Bell, T. P., 16, 18, 21-22, 30, 34, 63, 70,
    72, 79, 84, 88, 95, 100-101, 114, 171,
    231, 233-235, 237-238, 277-278, 280,
    285, 311, 342
Biblical Recorder, 49, 295
Bomar, E. E., 12, 19-20, 64, 83, 111, 118,
    121, 133, 135, 296, 298, 308-309, 318
Box work, 2, 28, 47, 62, 77-81, 118-120,
    123-128, 132-134, 162, 178, 184, 205,
    207, 214, 217, 221-222, 236-239, 259,
    331
Boyd, R. H., 96-97, 346
Broadus, Dr. John A., 91, 268, 275-276,
    292
Broadus, Eliza, 39, 58-59, 241, 248, 250-
    251, 268, 272, 276, 285-286, 290,
    293, 332
Buhlmaier, Marie, 23, 31-32, 40-41, 104-
    105, 109, 116-117, 158, 210, 266,
    311, 314-316, 319, 322-324, 343
Burroughs, Nannie H., 340-341
Burrows, Lansing, 75, 107, 151

Carroll, B. H., 28, 247-251, 286
Christian Index, 3, 21, 34, 84, 145-146,
    153, 161, 163, 166-171, 224, 228-229,
    231, 233-235, 237-238, 278-280, 294-
    296, 300, 302
Compere, E. L., 123, 125-126

Dixon, A. C., 65

Eager, George B., 28, 116, 251, 264, 269,
    302, 316, 351
Eager, Mrs. George B., 103, 264, 269,
    293, 302
Easterlin, Mrs. J. D., 11, 79, 149, 171,
    278, 308-309, 311
Ellis, Rev. F. M., 71, 84
Eutaw Place Baptist Church, 4, 10, 26,
    34, 45, 84, 86-87, 138, 155, 220, 244,
    248, 250, 297, 299, 306, 343, 351

Flippo, O. F., 21, 99, 156-157, 159, 161-
    163, 169-172, 174
Foreign Mission Journal, 11-12, 25, 34-
    36, 40-41, 48, 51, 57, 66, 68-70, 113-
    114, 119, 135, 150, 153, 162-163,
    184, 227, 232-234, 251-252, 262, 273,
    279, 282, 314-315, 318, 331
Frost, J. M., 6-8, 11, 17-18, 21-26, 28,
    30, 32, 35-36, 38-40, 43-44, 46-47,
    54, 56-57, 60-64, 73, 75, 79, 81-83,
    85, 90, 92, 96-97, 101, 104-107, 112,
    115, 118, 127-128, 131, 134, 136-137,
    153-155, 157-158, 161, 178, 180, 182,
    184, 189, 191, 194, 199-200, 204,
    210-212, 215-218, 220-221, 223-224,
    229, 231, 238-239, 241-243, 246-247,
    249-252, 254-255, 259-263, 265-267,
    274, 278, 281, 283, 288, 291, 294-
    296, 302, 307, 314, 316-318, 322-324,
    329-330, 335, 340, 342-343, 346,
    348- 350

Gambrell, J. B., 27
Gambrell, Mrs. J. B., 24, 127
Gordon, A. J., 17
Gospel Missionism, 3, 48, 89, 138-140,
    142-144, 146-152, 163-165, 167-168,
    170-172, 294, 325
Gregory, O. F., 41, 51-52, 90, 101
Gwathmey, Mrs. A. M., 12, 23, 104, 140,
    144, 203, 248, 250, 330, 343

Hailey, Mrs. O. L., 72-73
Haralson, Jonathan, 3, 75, 77-78, 189,
    194-195, 198-199, 210-211, 335
Harris, H. H., 12, 21, 98, 100, 324, 336
Heck, Fannie E. S., 3-4, 29, 31, 34, 72,
    107, 139, 162, 170, 179-181, 184,
    188, 190-191, 194-197, 199-200, 202-
    213, 216-223, 233, 334-335
Home Mission Journal, 150

Jordan, L. G., 96, 203, 339-340, 342,
    345-348

Kerfoot, F. H., 15, 25-26, 52, 61, 68, 91-
    92, 107, 136-137, 243-246, 251-252,
    264, 317
Kind Words, 7, 31, 56, 85, 92-93, 106,
    109, 121, 128, 136, 158, 227, 243,
    342
Kuykendall, Mrs. W. H., 56, 63, 69, 104-
    105, 318
Kuykendall, W. H., 41, 104, 318

Levering, Eugene, 13, 50, 86, 106, 175,
    197, 222, 328
Levering, Joshua, 85, 246-247, 249, 317
Levering, Mary Elizabeth (Mamie), 47-
    48, 175, 222, 232
Livermore, Mary H., 7
Lowndes, Mrs. W. C., 28, 83, 181-183,
    304

Millard, Junius, 10, 51, 55, 86-87, 131,
    155, 235, 247, 249, 331
Mission Rooms, 6-8, 10, 18, 21-22, 25,
    27, 29, 32, 35-36, 39-45, 47-51, 55,
    65, 69, 71, 94, 99, 103, 107, 113-115,
    122, 133, 135, 137-138, 150, 155,

158, 164, 197, 201, 204, 215, 221,
    230-233, 259, 262, 298, 305-306,
    310-311, 315, 319, 323, 328-330,
    339-340, 345-346
Mite box, 2, 26, 73, 87-88, 90, 93, 117,
    154, 223, 252, 341, 348
Moon, Lottie, 3, 102, 113, 138, 150
Morris, E. C., 347
Mullins, E. Y., 18, 27, 71, 241-242, 245-
    246, 254-255, 262-263, 267-268, 270,
    275, 284, 288, 290-291, 293, 296

National Baptist Convention, 166, 203,
    338-341, 350
Northen, W. J., 253-257, 266, 288

Our Home Field, 14, 119, 153, 162, 209,
    227
Our Missionary Helper, 142, 144-147,
    149, 172
    Ray, Jeff, ix

Religious Herald, 22, 45, 172-173
Rowland, Dr. A. J., 21, 31, 87, 89-90,
    103, 151-153, 156-157, 159, 161,
    167- 170, 172-174, 209, 347
Rowland, Mrs. A. J., 103, 151

Schimp, Mrs. Anna, 65-66, 97, 337-338
Simmons, E. Z., 3-4, 19, 241-242, 244,
    246-250, 268, 270, 276, 283-286, 293,
    301, 346
Sorrill, Bobbie, 1
Star Card, 2, 104-106, 108-110

Teacher, The, 17-18, 39, 54, 84, 87, 89,
    95, 99-100, 107, 115, 151, 158, 163-
    168, 171-173, 209, 243, 347
Tichenor, I. T., 2-3, 17-18, 27, 55, 101,
    104, 143-144, 146, 194-195, 197,
    199-200, 209, 238, 244, 252, 268,
    275-276, 279-280, 293, 316, 325, 350

Van Ness, I. J., 26, 28, 47, 61-62, 64,
    229, 231, 233, 235, 238, 263-264,
    266, 349

Weaver, Rufus, 259, 261
Western Recorder, 167, 233, 272, 342
Wharton, H. M., 49, 90, 142, 337, 346
Whitsitt, William Heth, 36, 49, 58, 91-92, 342
Willingham, R. J., 2, 9-15, 19, 24, 32, 39, 41, 43-44, 47, 50-52, 58, 65, 66, 82, 90-91, 102, 104, 110, 112, 119-120, 123, 131, 137-138, 140, 149, 151-152, 154, 161-162, 170, 174, 182, 185, 188, 194, 196, 198, 200-202, 211, 219, 229-232, 234, 241, 243-244, 247, 249-250, 253-255, 257-258, 266, 269, 272-273, 278, 280, 284, 288, 294, 296, 305, 311, 314, 318, 325-326, 330, 332, 334, 337, 339, 348
Wilson, Mrs. Stainback, 138-140, 142-145, 148-150, 171, 325
Woman's Christian Temperance Union, 7